THE UPPER ROOM

Disciplines

2025

UPPER
ROOM BOOKS®
NASHVILLE

THE UPPER ROOM DISCIPLINES 2025

© 2024 by Upper Room Books®. All rights reserved.

Upper Room Books® website: upperroombooks.com
Cover design: Left Coast Design, Portland, Oregon
Cover photo: Shutterstock.com

At the time of publication all websites referenced in this book were valid. However, due to the fluid nature of the internet some addresses may have changed, or the content may no longer be relevant.

Writers of various books of the Bible may be disputed in certain circles; this volume uses the names of the biblically attributed authors.

ISBN: 978-0-8358-2041-7 (print)
978-0-8358-2042-4 (enlarged-print edition)
978-0-8358-2043-1 (epub)
Printed in the United States of America

An Outline for Small-Group Use of *Disciplines*

The Upper Room Disciplines intentionally invites a diverse community of theologians and writers to meditate and offer reflections on scriptures that will nurture your soul and call you more fully to engage with the world that we are co-creating with God.

Christ is among us in fresh ways when we gather together, listening to God and to one another. We suggest gathering each week with a small group to discuss your reflections on the lectionary readings and *The Upper Room Disciplines*. Follow the simple liturgy below for a one-hour meeting. One person in the group may act as convener every week, or the role can rotate among group members.

Liturgy for Discussion

GATHERING

Light a candle to signal the beginning of your time together. Enter into one minute of silence with these words:

> **Loving God, we rest, still and quiet in your embrace.**
> **With childlike trust and simple confidence,**
> **we find peace in your arms.**[1]

Close the silence with a prayer or simply, "Amen."

OPENING

One: God is revealed with each reading of scripture.

All: **Jesus, Emmanuel, be present with us. Holy Spirit, open our ears in our conversation together and inspire us to live faithfully in the world.**

SCRIPTURE

The convener reads the scripture suggested for that day in the Disciplines.

One: The word of God for the people of God.

All: **Thanks be to God.**

Allow for a minute or two of silence.

Convener asks: What word or phrase stood out to you in the reading? What is God's invitation to you in this reading?

Group members respond in turn or as led.

REFLECTION

The convener reads the scripture overview for the week and then uses the following questions to guide discussion. After giving each prompt, the convener may give participants time to reflect silently or journal before inviting group members to respond aloud.

- How does the theme for the week touch your life personally? What wisdom, comfort, or challenge do you hear for the context you are living in and for the wider world?

- What relationships or situations came to mind as you read the *Disciplines* meditations this week? How were you called to act or make a response in your life this week?

- What new insight to scripture did you hear? What from the meditations has challenged your theology or discipleship this week? How might you respond to the challenge?

PRAYING TOGETHER

The convener invites everyone to name joys and concerns that the group can pray for now and in the coming week. The convener or another volunteer then prays for the group, closing with this prayer:

In your compassion, gracious God,
> you hear the cry of the poor, the needy, and the lonely ones.
May we also hear the cries of our brothers and sisters,
> responding in love as you have shown us in your Son,
> our Savior, Jesus Christ. Amen.[2]

BENEDICTION

End your time with this collective benediction:

**Indeed, faithful God, you have shown us the path of life and given us a heritage of unspeakable richness.
You call us now into joyful trust of the future you bring.
We abide in you. Amen.[3]**

---

[1] *Upper Room Worshipbook,* 331.
[2] *Upper Room Worshipbook,* 260.
[3] *Upper Room Worshipbook,* 236.

Contents

An Outline for Small-Group Use of *Disciplines* 3

Foreword 11
Rachel B. Hagewood

January 1–5 13
Songs for All Seasons
Whitney R. Simpson

January 6–12 19
Transformed By Faith and Fire
Jackson Droney

January 13–19 27
God With Us
Stephanie B. Dunn

January 20–26 35
Joy Amidst Grief
Ande I. Emmanuel

January 27–February 2 43
Love Never Ends
Libby Baxter

February 3–9 51
Called to Follow
Jorge Acevedo

February 10–16 59
Adages of Blessings and Troubles
Earlie Pasion-Bautista

February 17–23 67
Renewing Our Faith
Andrew Wilkes

February 24–March 2 75
The Revealed Divine Presence of God
R. Sidwell Mokgothu

March 3–9 83
Our Failures and God's Faithfulness
Candice Marie Benbow

March 10–16 91
Recognizing God
Daniel Wolpert

March 17–23 99
Seek the Lord
Osheta Moore

March 24–30 107
Abundant Grace
Herb Mather

March 31–April 6 115
Contradictions
Keegan Osinski

April 7–13 123
Obedience to God
Robert Schnase

April 14–20 131
For Us and for Our Salvation
Edgardo Colón-Emeric

April 21–27 139
Unbelievable Truth
Mary Charlotte Johnson

April 28–May 4 147
Deepening Devotion
J. Dana Trent

May 5–11 155
The Righteous Shepherd
Brian R. Bodt

May 12–18 163
Letting Love Guide You
Angela D. Schaffner

May 19–25 171
Not as the World Gives
Benjamin J. Dueholm

May 26–June 1 179
Transformation as Salvation
Julie O'Neal

June 2–8 187
The Promised Holy Spirit
Rhoda Manzo

June 9–15 195
The Gift of Divine Connection
Sara Cowley

June 16–22 203
Navigating Life with God
Erin Beasley

June 23–29 211
Determined Discipleship
Kira Austin-Young

June 30–July 6 219
Doing It God's Way
Rachel Gilmore

July 7–13 227
Measuring Life in Mercy and Love
Jes Kast

July 14–20 235
The Justice of Reconciliation
Nicolas Iglesias Schneider

July 21–27 243
God's Extravagant Generosity
Rolf Nolasco, Jr.

July 28–August 3 251
Redeemed Community
Elizabeth Mae Magill

August 4–10 259
Aligning Faith and Action
Charlie Baber

August 11–17 267
God Makes a Way
Stanley R. Copeland

August 18–24 275
Unshakable Essentials
Leslee Wray

August 25–31 283
Called to a New Way of Life
Bonface Ghero Wanyama

September 1–7 291
The Difficult Words of God
Derrick Scott III

September 8–14 299
There Is More Than This
Felicia Howell LaBoy

September 15–21 307
All-Consuming
Michelle Stiffler

September 22–28 315
With God and with One Another
Cedrick Bridgeforth

September 29–October 5 325
God Who Lives in Us
Nadiyka Gerbish

October 6–12 333
A Practice for Spiritual Growth
Mark W. Wethington

October 13–19 341
Thankfulness in All Things
Shonda Nicole Gladden

October 20–26 349
Experiencing God's Accompaniment
Cristian De La Rosa

October 27–November 2 357
The Faith of the Saints
Erin Racine

November 3–9 365
Focus
Heather Neal Bennett

November 10–16 373
For the Transformation of the World
Mara Richards Bim

November 17–23 381
A New Kind of Power
Garrett Jacob

November 24–30 389
Giving to God the First
Nathalie Nelson Parker

December 1–7.. 397
Liberation and New Life in Christ
Gift K. & Mazvita Machinga

December 8–14.. 405
Already but Not Yet
Danielle Buwon Kim

December 15–21.. 413
Practicing Depth
Mindy McGarrah Sharp

December 22–28.. 421
Justice Comes
Dottie Escobedo-Frank

December 29–31.. 429
Beginnings
Greg Pimlott

The Revised Common Lectionary for 2025............................... 433

A Guide to Daily Prayer.. 439

Foreword

The Upper Room Disciplines has been a source of strength and comfort to readers for decades. Taking on the task of ushering its annual birth into the world is a role I don't take lightly, yet it is one I am honored to claim as the newest editor at Upper Room Books. I have focused my life's work on training and educating people to be deeply faithful followers of Christ. Any educational experience contains two important components: consistency and a solid curriculum. *Disciplines* provides both.

Consistent, daily practice is essential to educational aspirations. Doing something over and over provides multiple opportunities for engagement, connection, and growth. Education experts say a person must encounter an idea seven different times before it becomes knowledge. The routine practice of reading and prayer provided through the *Disciplines* offers the consistency needed to grow in God's grace. I pray the practice will draw you closer to God.

The other foundational component, a solid curriculum, is a path that provides a starting point from which to grow. The use of the Revised Common Lectionary provides such a solid curriculum. Each time you return to these scriptures, your faith is strengthened and developed in new ways. As we journey through the life of faith, we encounter scripture along a spiral path, returning to familiar words. Yet each time we come to a scripture we have studied before, we engage that scripture in a new way. The scripture itself is unchanged; it is we who are different, with a different experience, location, perspective, and understanding of God's work in our lives.

This year, we return to the same scriptures we most recently encountered in 2022. The scriptures are the same, yet we are different. Our world is different, our understanding of God's work in the world is different, and our understanding of our call to be God's agents in the world is different. As you encounter anew the scriptures of this lectionary cycle, I pray this firm foundation of scripture gives you the opportunity to grow in new directions.

Each annual edition of *Disciplines* brings together a variety of voices that lead our collective conversation with scripture. I pray that you find both the familiar and the wholly different in these pages. You will hear from authors who look different than you and who live differently than you. But each person who has written—like each person who reads—is a recipient of God's redemptive love and grace. Together, we make up a beautiful body, called by God to share God's love with a hurting world. May the routine and the depth of *The Upper Room Disciplines* call us to our collaborative work to make real the kingdom of God.

RACHEL B. HAGEWOOD
Senior Developmental Editor
Upper Room Books

Songs for All Seasons

JANUARY 1–5, 2025 • WHITNEY R. SIMPSON

SCRIPTURE OVERVIEW: Jeremiah delivers happy news, a promise from the Lord of a brighter future day. God will bring back the scattered peoples from everywhere to their homeland, and their mourning will turn into joy. The psalmist encourages those in Jerusalem to praise God for all that God has done. God gives protection, peace, and the law to the children of Israel. The author of Ephesians encourages his readers with confidence in God's eternal plan. God's will was to send Christ and adopt us into God's family. We have been sealed with the Holy Spirit. The opening to John helps us understand the eternal scope of God's plan. From the beginning, the Word has been with God but then became flesh and lives among us to reveal divine glory.

QUESTIONS AND SUGGESTIONS FOR REFLECTION

- Read Jeremiah 31:7-14. Consider those who live in exile from their home or from their family relationships. How can you share Jeremiah's words of God's comfort?
- Read Ecclesiastes 3:1-13. In what season of life do you find yourself? What are you praying for in this season?
- Read John 1:1-18. What does it mean for you that the true light enlightens everyone?
- Read Ephesians 1:3-14. How can you live your daily life from the perspective of God's cosmic time? How will you praise God?

Whitney R. Simpson is a deaconess in The United Methodist Church who is passionate about embodied spirituality at the intersection of spiritual direction and yoga. Whitney is the author of *Holy Listening with Breath, Body, and the Spirit* (Upper Room Books, 2016) and *Fully Human, Fully Divine: An Advent Devotional for the Whole Self* (Upper Room Books, 2022).

NEW YEAR'S DAY

There is something extraordinary about the start of a new year. No matter the season of your life, a fresh year offers a new perspective. And while I do not make resolutions, I am inspired to refresh my personal and soul-care habits each January.

One way I tend to my soul at the start of the year is to ask God for a word that brings clarity or focus to the year. I first learned about claiming a word for my year from author Christine Valters Paintner many years ago. At the new year, in contemplation, I ponder what God may be inviting me into and how I may be most present in that season. I ask God for words to arise, and they often do—in books, songs, billboards, or anywhere God draws my attention. I compile those words, ponder and pray over them, and one eventually rises to the top.

Each season of the year, I am amazed at how God meets me with my word. I am in awe of how what I thought my word meant shifts and provides new learnings along the way.

Pause today and ask God for a word or words to bring you into the new year. It may be a word that has already grabbed your attention as the previous year has ended, or it may be one that stands out to you from scripture, a song, or a poem. Once you have a few words in mind, sit down with God and ask for clarity regarding the word God wants to speak to you through this year.

God, I am here, and I am listening. Guide me in this new season. Amen.

My mom taught me always to send thank-you notes upon receiving a gift. When I send a thank-you note, often the recipient of my note tells me it was not expected but appreciated. Sending and receiving thank-you notes is a fading trend, and I completely understand how easy it is not to prioritize this activity. Though the habit has long since been instilled in me, sometimes my notes are delayed or fall off my task list completely. There are too many other things vying for our attention, and faster and easier ways to communicate.

In the same way handwritten thank-you notes have faded, I think we often forget to thank God for the gifts in our lives. We may practice gratitude and focus on the gift for which we are grateful, but do we genuinely thank the giver? Do we acknowledge that what we have received comes from the one who created us?

I sense our humanness is why scripture invites us repeatedly to give thanks and praise to God. We need the reminder; we need the nudge. We need this action item continually added to our task list.

Earlier in verse 7 the psalmist invites us to show our gratitude with a song of praise to God. Our praise can take many forms—a song of gratitude; a simple, audible thank you; a shout of thanks to the one who has made us.

Consider pausing now to offer praise to your Creator. Imagine your praise being a thank-you note God gets to open today. It's not required or expected, but it sure is a nice touch. What does your praise sound like? For what gifts does God hear appreciation from your heart?

Dear Lord, thank you, thank you, thank you! Amen.

This week's scripture passages repeatedly invite all of us into singing with thanksgiving and praise. And while there are many ways to give thanks and praise, there is something powerful about using our voice—and not only in song.

While I enjoy singing, I cannot really carry a tune. Yet I have found numerous ways to use my voice. As a deaconess in The United Methodist Church, I have made a lifetime commitment to love, justice, and service. I use my voice to speak up for the marginalized and the oppressed, to alleviate suffering, to work to eradicate causes of injustice that rob others of dignity and worth, to help others reach their fullest human potential, and to serve the global community of the church. I use my voice when I speak up, when I serve, when I teach, when I give, when I preach, when I share, or when I write. My voice can be heard whether or not I can carry a tune.

Expressing ourselves with our voice is good for the soul. God longs for us to use our voice—whether through singing or in other ways.

Scripture tells us that God has blessed us, so we should bless our God. And this "us" is not limited to any particular group. Paul wrote to both the Jews and the Gentiles. He reminds his readers that all of us have been blessed by God. Who do we include in our "us"? Do we consider everyone blessed, or do we exclude some from our understanding of who God blesses?

How might you use your voice to speak up for those not included in the "us" today? How might you use your voice to remind yourself and others that God is inclusive and loving and wants to bless all of "us" today?

God, help me speak truth with compassion. Empower me to include someone who would otherwise be excluded and to use my voice today to speak your love. Amen.

I love to worship. I grew up in the church and have experienced many different kinds of worship over time. Yet admittedly, I sometimes watch other Christians worship and realize we (myself included) are missing an important aspect of worship: We forget to use our whole bodies.

Did you know that singing is good for our bodies and spirits, whether we can carry a tune or not? Singing stimulates our vagus nerve, which signals our bodies that it is time to de-stress. Even simple humming can make our brain feel more at peace. Likewise, embodied worship helps our bodies connect with God; it is good for us.

My friend David grew up in Uganda. He's now a pastor in America and has started a school in Uganda to offer education and hope to his rural village. The impact of the Raise the Roof Academy in this tiny village astounds me. Many of these children are orphans. They have so little, and yet they are overflowing with hope! I can listen to the students sing and feel God's presence with them and me. I sense their hope overflowing.

David tells captivating stories about God's work amidst the extreme poverty in his Ugandan community. He once told me that the only thing his people have is hope.

Ephesians says, "We are called to be an honor to God's glory because we were the first to hope in Christ" (CEB). How are you living out hope today? How are you embodying hope? We may not dance and sing like my friends in Uganda, but we can live our lives with hope, praise, and thanksgiving, connected to the One who created us.

Holy God, show me how to embody your hope. Amen.

SECOND SUNDAY AFTER CHRISTMAS

John 1 tells us God's word is life, and that life is light, and the light shines in the darkness.

As a writer, I especially love words. An app I use that helps me check my grammar and evaluate my writing recently told me I used sixty-one percent more unique words than the average user. I love words, probably too much.

Whether or not you are a word person, God tells us that just one Word leads to everything we need in this life. One Word gives us life and light.

Jesus is our Word.

In Jesus, God became human. Jesus knows what it is like to live on this earth. He shows us how to live a life of faith and offers us hope. He includes those who get excluded and always shines light where there is darkness.

Do you have a word for this year yet? Take a moment to compile any words that have risen up. Consider your past year and what you long for in this new year. Make a list of every word that surfaces in your contemplation with God. Now ask God to help you pick just one word.

Ponder how your word will offer praise and thanksgiving to God and how it reflects the life of Jesus. How will your word help you use your voice to be true to God's word in 2025?

It takes discipline, strength, and courage to be in the light with God—to use your voice. Will you give yourself permission to praise God and seek the light of Christ in this new year? Hum it out of tune; sing it out loud, on or off key; dance to it, with or without a beat. God longs for you to embody praise and thanksgiving and to find hope in the coming days with Jesus. Let him light the way.

Jesus, light the path of my life with your words. Amen.

Transformed By Faith and Fire

JANUARY 6–12, 2025 • JACKSON DRONEY

SCRIPTURE OVERVIEW: This week's readings illuminate key touchstones in our faith journey, all of which are drawn together in baptism. The prophet Isaiah invites us to consider living with divine hope, and the psalmist reminds us to use our power for the sake of the poor. Then, Paul challenges us with a call to radical inclusion. And the three wise men show us how to be present, open, and hold expectations lightly. These readings invite us into a deeper relationship with God. Things are not what they seem at first glance or consideration. We're invited to keep growing in our walk of faith. With water, John baptizes Jesus who will in turn baptize us with fiery, life-changing love. Living in response to that love makes our faith journey not a chore or obligation but a source of deep joy and inspiration.

QUESTIONS AND SUGGESTIONS FOR REFLECTION

- Read Isaiah 60:1-6. How do you define divine hope?
- Read Psalm 72:1-7, 10-14. In what ways do you have power to effect change? How does championing the poor fit into your walk of faith?
- Read Ephesians 3:1-12. How has your understanding of what it means to include everyone changed over time? What was hardest to change?
- Read Luke 3:15-17, 21-22. What difference does being a baptized child of God make in your life?

Jackson Droney is the Director of Operations and a pilgrimage leader at the Shalem Institute for Spiritual Formation. Jackson is the co-editor of *Soul Food: Nourishing Essays on Contemplative Living and Leadership* (Church Publishing, 2023).

EPIPHANY

During election season, political candidates often say, "Our best days are still to come!" It's a rallying cry, a rhetorical flourish aimed to lift the audience. And yet in recent years it hasn't landed so well, at least in the United States. Polls consistently show that a significant majority of Americans think the country is headed in the wrong direction. This overriding pessimism seems to be one of the few things our disparate country can agree on. And it's understandable that we would feel this way.

My generation, the millennials, are expected to be less materially well-off than previous generations. Wars are waged for unclear reasons with staggering loss of life as a result. Our politics have careened out of control to the point that four years ago today a mob stormed the U.S. Capitol under the false pretense of a stolen election. The global pandemic whose death toll and social consequences are unlike that of any illness we've seen in over one hundred years has wreaked havoc on our relationships and mental health. Moreover, racial injustice, most visible in instances of police brutality such as the murder of George Floyd, continues to divide and marginalize our siblings.

But also on this day, we remember the journey of the magi to find the Christ child. While the promises of political candidates may not rouse much hope in me these days, I hear these words of Isaiah—"Arise, shine, for your light has come"—as a prayer beckoning me to a deeper, divine hope. They remind me that our triune God is still at work in "thick darkness." Engaging the world as it is, strife and all, is necessary to follow and contribute to God's longing for wholeness. God is at work in the world. Divine hope allows us to join in, even when things seem bleak.

O Holy One, help us see the ways you are at work in bringing wholeness to the world. Give us the courage to discern what is ours to do to support your longing for wholeness. Amen.

In this reading the psalmist prays for God to instill justice in the king. In the psalmist's social and political context the king has exclusive power to make history-altering decisions, so praying for the king to judge with justice is essential. Indeed, we look to our leaders today to be fair and just in their actions and decisions. But how can we embody this prayer for ourselves?

Each of us has some power to effect change in our day-to-day lives. We have agency in our households, workplaces, schools, faith communities, and other organizations we belong to. We all have power in how we relate to our natural environment and one another. How do we use this power for just ends?

When conflict emerges in our households, do we fall back on our learned or innate solutions, or do we pause to reflect on what is just in this particular circumstance? When a colleague under performs in the workplace, do we ignore it because we don't want conflict, or do we get curious about what could be going on and ask questions openly without judgment? When some parents object to books about LGBTQ+ persons and racial diversity being included in school curricula, do we bow to the loud voices, or do we consider whose voices aren't being heard? When the church budget comes before us and we see how little church staff are paid, do we simply accept fiscal constraints, or do we ask whether this community should expect staff support for less than a fair living wage? When a friend is struggling, do we keep our distance, or do we show up and offer a ministry of presence?

We may not be royalty, but we are empowered in big and small ways in the various spheres of our lives. How can we use this power to bring about God's justice here on earth?

O Holy One, your justice is great. Help us identify the power we have, and empower us to use it for just ends. Amen.

The psalm describes how this just king is respected by other rulers because he cares about "the needy." He is revered because he champions those who are poor. Many Christians may read this passage and nod their heads. Yes, God cares for the vulnerable. Jesus blessed those in poverty. And so it's not a surprise to see a psalm that touts a king who champions the "needy."

But what about us today? Do we revere champions of persons underprivileged in our own times? Many of us and our churches support charitable causes such as soup kitchens, food banks, homeless shelters, and clothing drives. These acts of charity help real people with their immediate basic needs. They make a meaningful difference. And yet such acts do not change the social and systemic causes of poverty.

When leaders attempt to address those underlying causes, they are too often vilified. Dr. Martin Luther King Jr. was assassinated not when he spoke about racial integration early in his ministry but later when he began to focus more on economic justice.

Rather than discerning how to ameliorate—let alone eliminate—poverty, we often seem intent on blaming and shaming those experiencing it and their champions. Scarcity-minded thinking, jealousy, resentment, racism, and violence drive our negative responses to those in poverty and their champions and prevent progress from being made toward systemic changes that would transform the lives of many.

The king in the psalm redeems the "poor" from oppression and violence. If we are not called specifically to that holy work ourselves, then at least we can honor those who are doing it with our active support and reliable presence.

O Holy One, we give you thanks for the champions of the poor who go against the grain of society in the name of your justice. Help us find the courage to join their ranks and honor their work. Amen.

Paul has a purpose, and he makes it clear in this passage. He has been sent by God through Jesus Christ to let the world know that non-Jews—the Gentiles—are included in God's plans for humankind. Jesus didn't come just for Jews, Paul declares. He came, died, and rose for all. Everyone is included. This is a message Paul conveys over and over again in his letters. He is eager to share this message so that "rulers and authorities in the heavenly places" will change their behavior and act accordingly.

Churches are traditional places with a lot of traditional people. And that's fine. Traditions and liturgical rhythms remind us of important truths and can foster a deeper sense of connection and belonging. Problems arise, however, when tradition succumbs to nostalgia. Traditions give us grounding as we move forward; nostalgia turns our focus from moving forward to the past.

What it means to include everyone has changed over time and will continue to do so. Race, gender, and sexuality have different meanings today than they did in Paul's time. A little more than fifty years ago people with same-sex attraction were considered mentally ill. A little more than thirty years ago buildings didn't have to be accessible to those with physical disabilities. And while we have made progress to eliminate explicit race-based discrimination in our laws, we still have a long way to go to end racism and white supremacy and the more subtle ways they distort our churches, relationships, and social structures.

Our traditions and behaviors toward one another should adapt and evolve as our understandings of one another and humanity evolve. Paul was an early leader in this regard, widening the circle of Christians to include the Gentiles and calling on church leaders to change how they led in light of this truth.

O Holy One, we give thanks to those who have helped us see how to live out the reality of your radical inclusiveness. Help us do the same. Amen.

There's always more to say about the complexity and urgency to live out the gospel in ways that are truly inclusive of everyone. I could spend more words on race, gender, class, and sexuality and how we fall short of including everyone with respect to those parts of human identity. Often, though, it's the decisions we make that don't appear to have a direct connection to inclusivity that can have the biggest impact on whether we're being truly inclusive.

A publicly affirming and inclusive church I'm familiar with has shifted its worship service three times over the past five years, each time moving the start time earlier and earlier. At the same time, they wonder why younger folks and persons who identify as LGBTQ+ don't attend. Might they consider that younger people or people with children do not get up as early on a Sunday as they do on a work day? Might they consider that many LGBTQ+ people find community at queer establishments on Saturday evenings and would prefer a later service time on Sunday morning? When presented with the possibility of a later service, though, they don't budge. The earlier time works for them, and they like it that way.

I don't know if this church would attract more younger or queer people if they had a later service. There are many other variables that go into attracting newcomers. But an unwillingness to consider the needs and wants of those who are in a different life stage or a different demographic than ourselves prevents many relationships from having the opportunity to begin. Our intentions don't mean much if we're not willing to change our behavior, cede some ground, and let go of something.

O Holy One, help us see what blocks our ability to share your love with others. Give us courage to let go of our attachments so that we can more deeply welcome our neighbors. Amen.

I find the magi mysterious. They come to King Herod from the east—far from Israel—in search of the newborn king of the Jews. Do they assume that King Herod has recently had a baby, an heir to his throne? They initially go to Jerusalem and then to Bethlehem by following a star, which means they made their journey at night. What did this allow them to see and experience differently? When they find Jesus and Mary they are overcome with joy. They kneel and pay him homage. What helped them know they had found the child they sought? Not finding Jesus in a royal palace, they could have determined they got the wrong address and left. Instead, it seems like they had a gut reaction, a moment of realization, a connecting of all the dots of their journey. We don't know for certain, but we can sense the awe and reverence they felt. Then they disappear shortly after leaving their famous gifts of gold, frankincense, and myrrh, and they know not to return to Herod and tell him where Jesus is.

The magi were not Jews, but it appears they were guided by the Spirit and their faith. They didn't know exactly where they were going. They had a guide (the star) but also stopped to ask for directions. They put one foot in front of the other and were open to what they found. They were able to receive the unusual situation of a teenage mother and her baby and trust that this was who they had come searching for. And they were able to discern that Herod's request was not well-intentioned.

Much of our lives are mysterious. We aren't in control of everything, and we can't know how everything will work out. As we make our pilgrimage through life, how open are we to having our expectations turned on their heads? As we put one foot in front of the other, do we notice how our journey takes shape and what mysteries are revealed to us?

O Holy One, help us receive signs of your presence and leading even when they defy our expectations. Amen.

BAPTISM OF THE LORD

Today's passage opens with John naming three elements associated with baptism: water, Holy Spirit, and fire. While John baptizes with water, Jesus will baptize with the Holy Spirit and fire. While John calls on his followers to change their lives and prepare for the coming of the Lord, Jesus calls on his followers— then and now—to radically love God and neighbor in ways that change everything about what it means to be alive. The passage ends with all three parts of the Trinity in the scene. God speaks, Jesus prays, and the Holy Spirit descends.

Fire and water can be cleansing agents, removing what doesn't belong and leaving the object that was cleansed ready for another use. We clean utensils with water so they can be used again. Fields are sometimes burned after the harvest so they're ready for the next planting season. Water, however, is a bit more appropriate for us humans to use as a cleansing agent and symbolic element at baptism. If you've been baptized, it's not too likely that you were baptized with real fire. There may have been some candles lit nearby, but I hope the pastor or priest didn't try to put fire on your forehead.

In baptism, we are brought into new life with the Triune God. We are sent from baptism to live in relationship with God and neighbor by the example of Jesus, the power of the Resurrection, and the work of the Holy Spirit. Baptism is fiery because it ignites our passion for life in Christ and the potential transformation of the world.

God, thank you for the inspiration you bring to us in baptism. Help us to be bearers of your restorative flame of love. Amen.

God with Us

JANUARY 13–19, 2025 • STEPHANIE B. DUNN

SCRIPTURE OVERVIEW: The Epiphany theme of God-with-us in the chaos of the world is present throughout the texts this week. In Isaiah, the postexilic Judean community returns to its home and cries out to a faithful God for full restoration of Jerusalem. Psalm 36 looks to God's steadfast love that surrounds all that is, even in the face of oppression. The apostle Paul writes to a community whose chaos is internal, reminding them of God's abundant love expressed in a beautiful diversity. This diversity ought to inspire celebration rather than division. In John's Gospel, we see a miracle that points to the inbreaking of God's joyful kingdom on earth.

QUESTIONS AND SUGGESTIONS FOR REFLECTION

- Read Isaiah 62:1-5. Where are you experiencing the call not to remain silent in the face of injustice?
- Read Psalm 36:5-10. How are you experiencing God's steadfast love in your life?
- Read 1 Corinthians 12:1-11. What spiritual gifts have you identified in yourself? How might you celebrate the gifts of others around you?
- Read John 2:1-11. How can you bear witness to God's excessive love?

The Rev. Stephanie B. Dunn is a United Methodist minister who has served local churches for over fifteen years and is now a coach who walks alongside clergy and nonprofit leaders as they align their inner and outer lives, making space for the authentic self to flourish. An avid lover of the outdoors, Stephanie can often be found on camping adventures with her family. She loves engaging with creative outlets such as writing poetry and painting with watercolor as a way to connect with God. She is the author of *Draw Close: A Creative Companion for Lent* (Upper Room Books, 2024).

These verses from Isaiah were written in the context of a postexilic Judean community that had returned to Jerusalem. Those who returned home arrived at a place marked by desolation and abandonment. The disaster that they came home to was one more blow to a people who had experienced unrelenting oppression. As a leader in the community, the prophet had a decision to make. He could call for the people to return to Babylon, a place where they would always be outsiders, but a place that nonetheless could offer them some semblance of livelihood. Or he could direct them to look forward with hope for Jerusalem's restoration.

The prophet chose the latter. "For Zion's sake I won't keep silent, and for Jerusalem's sake I won't sit still" (CEB). Isaiah commits to an unwavering pursuit for the complete restoration of Jerusalem, despite standing in a place where it seems that restoration is impossible.

Hope in the face of impossibility is a hallmark of our Judeo-Christian faith. In these verses, we see Isaiah standing firmly in hope despite all signs indicating that restoration is impossible. The people were standing between despair and hope. They chose hope. We too face such choices today. Next week, we will celebrate the life and legacy of Dr. Martin Luther King Jr. Despite living in a world marked by racism and injustice, Dr. King pursued his dream with unwavering belief in God's faithfulness. While we have come some way since Dr. King's assassination in 1968, we still have a long way to go. We can easily succumb to cynicism. But these words from Isaiah offer us an invitation and a challenge to choose hope. Because we know that God is faithful, we can choose hope with confidence that a more just world is possible.

O God, I lift up my voice and will not keep silent. May I look to your light of love, choose hope, and chase after your justice. Amen.

We enter the Epiphany season riding on waves of Christmas joy. The image of an infant King bringing salvation into the world invites us to experience deep and abiding hope. Many continue to reflect this hope in the Christmas trees that have yet to be taken down and the twinkling lights that still glow in windows. Alongside this hope, we carry the world's uncertainty, fear, and pain into this season as well. The Epiphany texts invite us to hold our hope alongside our very human experiences in this chaotic world.

In Psalm 36, the psalmist holds the tension between experiencing overwhelming oppression and the promise and hope found in God. The love of God is steadfast, the psalmist rejoices. The Lord's steadfast love is found in every place and in every time. God's love is, indeed, the very life-source of all that is. "Within you is the spring of life. In your light, we see light" (CEB), the psalmist sings.

In some homes, the residual Christmas joy is still carrying us along. In others, all that is left are brown tree needles that remind us of what has been left behind. Still elsewhere, the joy of Christmas has been a stranger all along. Regardless of where we find ourselves in this season, may we find hope that God's steadfast love is dependable, drawing us and the world to take refuge in the shadow of God's wings.

Gracious God, your love is steadfast. In the breadth of our experiences, we rest in the hope that is found in your presence. Amen.

In the Christian tradition, we lean heavily into the symbol of light throughout Epiphany. In this season we consider what is illuminated. Who do we understand the Christ child to be? What does it mean that God is with us? Or—even more fundamentally—who do we understand God to be?

Today's verses from Psalm 36 shed light on who God is. The psalmist offers a profession of faith as an act of worship. Who is God? God is love. God is faithful. God is righteous. God is just.

The activist, poet, and writer Maya Angelou followed this rule of life: "When someone shows you who they are, believe them." The psalmist has experienced God as completely dependable. God has shown God's character, and the psalmist believes, writing about God's steadfast love using the Hebrew word *chesed*. English translations fall short of capturing the essence of this word that is central to the Hebrew Bible's understanding of faithfulness. To express *chesed* is to give oneself completely in love and compassion. It is often expressed as steadfast love toward God. But here the psalmist uses *chesed* to describe the heart of God's character. The psalmist writes of God's steadfast love because they have experienced God's love and compassion in every aspect of their lives.

These verses from Psalm 36 are placed in the context of a psalm that is crying out to God for help. What is the character of this God who will come to our aid and to the aid of all of creation? God is *chesed*: steadfast love, faithful, righteous, and just.

God, your love is steadfast. Come to the aid of the world. Shine your light of love in my life that I may go into the world embodying your profound love for others. Amen.

ALWAYS READ

We don't have to get too creative to imagine the community Paul was writing to in his Corinthian letters. It was a community in distress, chaos, and conflict. These seem to be regular marks of modern American Christian communities across all spectra. Our current emphasis on status and stark individualism sounds eerily familiar as we read this week's text from First Corinthians.

What kind of future does a church like this have? Will it ever experience unity, or is it doomed to schism? Is healing possible, or will it always be known by its woundedness? Paul has hope. His hope is deeply rooted in the presence and work of the Holy Spirit. For Paul, the Holy Spirit's work of bringing a diverse body of people together in unity is a hallmark of the church. When God's people give themselves over to the work of the Holy Spirit, a community will be marked by a diverse body of people coming together to offer a variety of gifts to share the goodness of God's work with the world.

The fractures within Christianity today run deep. "What will become of us?" is a question that churches of all types wrestle with. In this week's text from First Corinthians, Paul offers both hope and a challenge. Oftentimes even in spite of us, the Holy Spirit is at work, bringing life and gifts for the good of God's world. The challenge is for us to open ourselves up and trust in the Spirit's work.

Holy Spirit, open my heart to the gifts that you have given me. Help me to see and celebrate the gifts of others so that your world will come more alive in you. Amen.

I have a bad habit of storing up special gifts never to use them. I have had to throw out more expired special food items than I care to admit. When someone I care about shares something special, I hold on to it hoping to use it at an important or meaningful time. These items often accumulate in the dark corners of my pantry only to be thrown out when they are discovered months later and have overstayed their shelf life. I noticed this unfortunate practice of mine a few years ago and have tried to correct it as much as I can. I attempt to put gifts given to me to use, even in ordinary circumstances, celebrating the goodness of the friendships represented in each gift.

In today's text, we can easily understand Paul's instruction on what to do with gifts: use them. But don't just use them; share your gifts as an act of service for the good of the community. He wrote, "A demonstration of the Spirit is given to each person for the common good" (CEB). The Holy Spirit is at work in each of us. Let that sink in. God has uniquely gifted you. But for what purpose? To stash it away for what you determine to be the "right" time? No—the gifts of the Spirit are not for one's own edification or ego. Nor are the various gifts a status symbol or a mark of religious superiority. Plainly and powerfully put, our gifts are to be used in service to one another and God's world. Imagine a world where each of us is connected enough with ourselves and the Holy Spirit to know what our gifts are and to put them to use for the "common good." Such a world would surely be a glimpse of God's kingdom on earth.

Come, Holy Spirit, and empower each of us to use the gifts we have been given in service to one another and to the world. Amen.

One of my favorite parts of serving in the local church was joining young children in Godly Play circles. In our circles, we talked about Epiphany as the time in the church's calendar when we come to know who Jesus is. Placing the story of Jesus' wedding miracle at the beginning of the season of Epiphany is appropriate. This story reveals God's extravagant grace and glory made known in Jesus.

Our modern quests for understanding can lead us to approach this story by poking and prodding at the miracle of turning water into wine. Our curiosity and scientific musings can lead us to want to explain exactly how the miracle happened. But in this story there is an invitation to simply and powerfully trust. Mary's trust in Jesus gives us a foundational model for what trust looks like. "Do whatever [Jesus] tells you," Mary says to the servants. While she understands that Jesus' time might not have been in that particular moment, she maintains her confidence in Jesus' ability to act.

Our world is filled with opportunities to doubt. When we consider the chaos around us, we can easily fall into despair, understandably becoming deeply cynical and without hope. The story of the wedding at Cana offers us so much more than a party scene. It places Jesus' abundant grace and glory at the center of a scene of scarcity and concern. This story is often seen as a playful introduction to Jesus' ministry. While it's certainly a story of joy, we should be careful not to miss the profound message of this miracle. In this story, we see the promise of God's abundance, grace, and glory that is more than we can imagine.

O God, open my heart to trust in your grace and glory poured out on the world. Amen.

The texts this week highlight the liminal nature of Christian faith. Our world is broken, and the temptation is always there to believe that restoration is beyond reach. The world is not as it should be. And yet our faith compels us to maintain a posture and perspective of hope.

In this week's Gospel story of the miracle at the wedding at Cana, there is what Jesus did and then there is what Jesus' actions pointed to. Miraculously, Jesus changed an excessive amount of water into wine so that the wedding guests had an abundant amount of good wine to drink. Within the Hebrew tradition, an abundant amount of good wine is a sign of God's joyous kingdom. The first act of Jesus' ministry in John's Gospel is a sign that he is the one ushering in God's joyous kingdom. John closes this story by saying, "[Jesus] revealed his glory, and his disciples believed in him" (CEB). In this act, Jesus' followers begin to have an understanding of who Jesus is. We too are invited to respond to this story in faith.

Through this miracle, we get a glimpse of the fullness of God's joyful kingdom, of where our hope lies. What is possible in the here and now, where racism, misogyny, and injustices seem to close in on all sides? *Not much,* our cynical nature replies. But in this story, we see what is possible in Jesus. Our hope is rooted in Jesus Christ, the one through whom we come to know God's abundance. Such abundance has the audacity to show up in the most ordinary places.

Gracious God, your abundant grace and love are found everywhere. Open my heart to see your plentiful glory so that your light will shine in my heart and in the world. Amen.

Joy Amidst Grief

JANUARY 20–26, 2025 • ANDE I. EMMANUEL

SCRIPTURE OVERVIEW: Our scripture readings this week express a mixture of joy and grief. In Nehemiah we read about the restoration of hope in Israel juxtaposed with the grief of what they have lost. The psalmist provides a descriptive way the firmament reveals to us the mighty acts of God amidst our human errors and brokenness. Paul uses the analogy of human anatomy to reveal the kind of life that is joyous, hopeful, and fulfilling in Christ Jesus. Luke portrays Jesus as the one who fulfilled the scriptures by taking human form—Incarnation—to free us from captivity.

QUESTIONS AND SUGGESTIONS FOR REFLECTION

- Read Nehemiah 8:1-3, 5-6, 8-10. How do you find joy, hope, and peace in God's word, most especially in hard times?
- Read Psalm 19. What areas of nature reveal to you the mighty acts of God?
- Read 1 Corinthians 12:12-31a. How do you take on more to support the body of Christ when others struggle? How do you allow others to take weight from you when you struggle?
- Read Luke 4:14-21. How do you respond to God's call to stand and speak for the liberation of people who are captives of the systems and barriers created by our modern society?

The Rev. Ande I. Emmanuel is senior pastor of The United Methodist Church Antakiya Mayodassa Jalingo. Ande is a graduate of Wesley Theological Seminary in Washington, D.C. and an elder of the Southern Nigeria Annual Conference of The United Methodist Church.

Growing up in Nigeria, I recall several events such as a fishing festival, an annual harvest festival, and other celebrations that brought the whole community together. Amidst such celebrations were those who were grieving the loss of their loved ones, particularly those who had died since the last time the event had been celebrated. Yet even in their grief they still celebrated.

The Israelites' journey as a community was a journey of joy and grief. The Israelites had a special covenant with God to be God's people. But the Israelites constantly broke this covenant, rejecting God's decrees, worshiping other gods, and acting against God's commandments. Their disobedience had led to the destruction of their homeland and their temple. Their grief must have been overwhelming. Seventy years later, God allowed them to return, first to rebuild the temple with Ezra the priest and later with Nehemiah who, as governor, helped rebuild the city walls of Jerusalem. In today's reading, we see how they celebrated the rebuilding of the temple and the walls by reading the law aloud. Yet as Ezra read, the people became overwhelmed by their grief for the ways they had dishonored God. Mixed in with their joyous praise for God's redemption was grief over their disobedience.

We who follow God today find ourselves disobedient to the law of God as revealed in Jesus Christ. We resent people and exclude those who are different from us. We judge people by our own standards and expect them to conform to our opinions before we will love them or welcome them. But Christ's sacrificial love reminds us that even as we grieve the ways we fail, we can celebrate the unending grace of God.

Dear God, give me the grace to follow you that I may find joy in every grieving situation, through Jesus Christ my Lord. Amen.

In the beginning of chapter 8 of the book of Nehemiah, Ezra read the law of Moses to all those who could listen, and the leaders of the rebuilt community helped the people understand what was being read. The reading and understanding of the law caused much grief amongst the people, and they began to cry. They had strayed so far from what God wanted them to do that their past disobedience grieved them to the point of public tears.

For Christians almost three thousand years later, we believe God has claimed us as God's children through the baptismal covenant made in Christ Jesus. As contemporary Christians we are faced with challenges that are clear indications of our departures from the law and commandment set forth before us by Jesus Christ. When we take a look at what is happening around us socially, politically and economically, we realize that we have so much to grieve in our world. War in Ukraine and Russia, in Israel and Palestine, political upheaval in Sudan, military junta in parts of Africa, many people dying as a result of hunger and diseases—these are only a few examples of our broken world.

Today's text reminds us to go back and listen to the laws of our God. Returning to God's word can give us joy amidst the grief we see in our world today. Ezra told the people not to be sad, but to go back home to eat and drink and share what they had with others. Ezra gives a clear response for our grief: Don't let it freeze us into inaction, but let it prompt us to celebrate the goodness of God and share that goodness with others. We cannot ignore the grief experienced by many—even by us. But we can find joy in community and be encouraged for the work of bringing God's joy to those who so desperately need it.

Dear God, when my grief for the world overwhelms me, push me to action. Bring joy into my life, and guide me to be an instrument of joy to others. Amen.

Governments around the world, especially in the region of Africa where I live, fail to support and protect the people they are intended to serve. Many individuals are hurt by the systematic hardships experienced in our world today. This has left a lot of people asking, *Where can we go to experience peace and thrive?*

Psalm 19 offers a greater hope in finding a place of joy, happiness, and peace amidst the world's brokenness. The psalmist extols all of creation as the place where we can hear the powerful voice of God revealed—the heavens and the firmament, the sun, the day and the night. The heavens proclaim daily in all languages of the world the acts of God. Everyone hears it in their own tongue. The psalmist further declares the heavens as the tent of the sun. Imagine the beauty of that image: We are under God's big tent as we go about our daily activities. What a joyful image of safety to behold!

Nature is a declaration of the existence of God and a demonstration of God's eternal power and divine nature. Every day as we go outside and see or feel the effects of the sun, it is a reminder to us of God's eternal power and divine nature. Our response is to glorify God.

I know life has given us many reasons to grieve. We cause pain and suffering to others, intentionally and unintentionally. But God has revealed God's self in a special way. We can find joy amidst the pain and suffering we both encounter and cause, and we can be reminded of our call to share God's peace in the world. Whenever you feel overwhelmed by the grief of the world, go into nature, take a deep breath, and behold the beauty of the creation. Let it remind you of God's eternal presence.

God of creation, thank you for revealing yourself in nature for us to be reminded of your eternal presence. Amen.

Joy Amidst Grief

I remember my first trip as a pastor to a village in Nigeria where I baptized fifty-two people. At the end of the baptismal ritual, the people I had baptized, who were mostly older people, asked me for a favor. I thought they were going to ask for money, but to my greatest amazement they asked me to give them Bibles. I asked why they needed Bibles because most could not read or write. Their answer was more amazing: "We've never owned Bibles. We need them because they are the living word of God."

The word of God gives wisdom, enables discernment, and transforms our lives. Through God's word, we know where we come from. We recognize our failures to keep God's commandments and our need for redemption through Jesus Christ.

Psalm 19 describes two major qualities of God's word. The first is that God's word has value. Verse 10 states that God's words are of greater value than a great amount of pure gold or the sweetest honey from the honeycomb. In the ancient world, gold and honey were valuable assets. God's word is more valuable than the most valued possessions in our world.

The second quality of God's word is that it has the power to change lives. God's word directs us on how to live our lives and rewards us for keeping such directives. These directives and rewards for obeying shape the way we live each day.

We don't just hear the word of God, however, and instantly receive the benefits of these qualities. We must respond to what we learn from God's word. The psalmist models this as well, praying for forgiveness and surrendering to God. The word of God is powerful, but only if we allow it to be.

Dear God, clear from me hidden faults. Let the words of my mouth and the meditation of my heart be pleasing to you, my rock and my redeemer. Amen.

Nigeria is a country of about 210 million people who speak over 500 different languages. This diversity has not been as much of an asset as it could have been. In several instances it has brought tribal and interreligious conflicts that have caused much harm to many people. The government has been engaging traditional and religious leaders to work on unity and to see our diversity as an asset, not a liability. We are still learning how to be united as Nigerians despite our tribal and religious differences.

Paul's first letter to the Corinthians was written to address the problem of division in the church. Corinth was a center of commercial activities in Asia Minor, making it a diverse metropolitan city. The Corinthian church was not left out in this diversity. Paul wrote purposely to address Christians on the problem of division in the church and to advise how the church should handle such divisions.

Paul talks about the unity of the church over and over again because he sees the church as one body. He presents the unity of the church in the manner Jesus presents it in John 15:5—"I am the vine; you are the branches. Those who abide in me and I in them bear much fruit, because apart from me you can do nothing." Our unity in Jesus Christ empowers us to be fruitful. As we go about our work, let us keep in mind that Jesus Christ values the unity of the church over the arguments that divide us. In unity, we work toward the common good of the whole body in order to bear the fruit Christ calls the church to bear.

Unifying God, thank you for reminding us how we can be united in our diversity. Give us the grace to be united as your children, and forgive us for the division we have created among ourselves. Amen.

Paul's message to the Corinthians has two parts. As we explored yesterday, unity is an essential principle of working together in the church community. But unity isn't uniformity. We don't need to be identical to one another to be unified in our work for Christ. Hand-in-hand with the principle of unity is the principle of diversity. The church needs everyone's unique gifts to be effective and to love beautifully.

My father has served as an usher in the church for most of his life. People often ask him why he loves this particular role, or if there isn't a "better" job he could do for the church. His response is always, "I am called into the ministry of ushering and given the gift to usher." Through my father's conviction, I have grown up understanding that everyone in the church has a special gift given by God to use in building a united church.

God gave us different gifts so that we can combine our gifts and work together. One way we can grow in the church is by appreciating the diversity of gifts God has blessed us with. We need to make the church an open place for everyone to exercise their God-given talent. When I was assigned as pastor at The United Methodist Church Antakiya Mayodassa Jalingo, where I now serve as the lead pastor, the first youth I met with asked me what my mission was for their church. I responded that I am here to make one big happy family by making this sanctuary a welcoming space where everyone can exercise their God-given talent. Three years later, the congregation lives into this, calling themselves "one big happy family." If we look at the church as a family, we avoid having an inflated view of our own importance, and we are better able to thank God for all the other people who contribute to the church in diverse ways.

Mighty and everlasting God, thank you for the gift of your church. Thank you for blessing us with diverse gifts that work together to build your church. Amen.

The Hebrew Bible has quite a number of prophecies that point to the coming of Jesus. Some of these notable prophecies are in Isaiah 7:14, Isaiah 9:6-7, and Micah 5:2. In today's passage, Jesus reads from Isaiah 61 as the foundation for his teaching and preaching. These words, found at the beginning of Isaiah 61, can be seen as a mission statement of the ministry of Jesus Christ. In it we see the good intentions God has for humanity amidst our disobedience to the law. Jesus came to give us hope and set us free from our captivity.

As a Christian preacher living in Northern Nigeria, I have experienced much of the grief Jesus sought to relieve in his ministry. I have seen the ugliest levels of poverty, such as in the life of a mother of nine children who sold one of them in order to feed the others. I have seen situations of severe captivity, such as in the deadly Islamic extremist group Boko Haram's kidnapping of over three hundred school girls in Chibok and Dapchi. I have seen places in Northern Nigeria where tribal and religious conflicts have displaced millions of people. When Jesus talks about freedom, for me this freedom is concrete release from anguish. It is joy amidst tangible grief.

There is no doubt that we live in a broken world with many reasons to grieve: Our national and international news channels are full of stories that often break our heart. Our joy is shattered by what we see around us. But in the midst of this grief, there remains a message of hope. We have been richly blessed to go into the world around us to share this good news of joy with others in Christ's name.

Dear God, thank you for your words of hope and joy in the midst of our grief. Help us receive your call to act in faith on your word and share your joy and love with others. Amen.

Love Never Ends

JANUARY 27–FEBRUARY 2, 2025 • LIBBY BAXTER

SCRIPTURE OVERVIEW: Throughout scripture, God's covenant love for humankind is consistently affirmed. In First Corinthians, Paul proclaims that love never ends. The additional readings this week provide assurances of God's eternal love. In love, God calls and sends Jeremiah to bring God's word to God's people. The psalmist assures us of God's care for us from birth, a constant rock and refuge, our hope and our trust. Luke records the words of Jesus in the Nazareth synagogue that proclaim the wideness of God's mercy and love for all people. God continues to call us to remember that love never ends.

QUESTIONS AND SUGGESTIONS FOR REFLECTION

- Read Jeremiah 1:4-10. How is God calling you to be a part of God's work in the world?
- Read Psalm 71:1-6. In what ways have you experienced God as a refuge?
- Read 1 Corinthians 13:1-13. How do you use the gifts God gives you in the service of love?
- Read Luke 4:21-30. How do you keep your heart and mind open to hear and act on new revelations of God's love for the world?

The Rev. Libby Baxter is a retired ordained deacon in the Tennessee-Western Kentucky Conference of The United Methodist Church, who served twenty years on the ministry staff at Calvary UMC in Nashville, TN.

Though I knew a few psalms in my youth, I really began to love the psalms in middle age. While attending the Upper Room's Two-Year Academy for Spiritual Formation, I began a practice of reading five psalms a day, resulting in reading the book of Psalms in its entirety each month. It's a practice I've continued on and off through the years. In the psalms, I have found expression of every human emotion I've experienced—fear, anger, and lament but also hope, trust, and praise. The human condition is so honestly laid out that it rings true even now. The psalms look at the world with unflinching reality while affirming that ultimately God rules the world. I often need the reminder that the persistence of suffering and evil in the world should not deter me from joining with God to bring light into the darkness.

Which of us has not felt the despair of the psalmist in the opening lines? We pray to be heard, to know that God hears our cries and answers with love. We pray for a strong fortress to shield us from the many storms we face in life—literally and figuratively. We pray for a rock to anchor us when our faith wavers and we are tempted to despair. We pray for justice in a world that often seems to be in "the grasp of the unjust and cruel." The psalmist pleads for these things and affirms that God will provide them.

This faith is affirmed in Hebrews 11:1: "Now faith is the assurance of things hoped for, the conviction of things not seen." The psalmist acknowledges that suffering and injustice exist, and the psalmist prays, as we do, for deliverance. We do so in hope and with conviction of God's love for the world.

Dear God, thank you that we can come to you with all our emotions, sure of your eternal love and presence. Amen.

TUESDAY, JANUARY 28 ～ *Read Jeremiah 1:4-10*

God's call to Jeremiah follows a familiar biblical storyline: God calls, the person resists, God reaffirms the call, and God empowers the person to fulfill the call. Jeremiah objects that he is not worthy, and we are reminded of similar objections from other biblical heroes: Moses questions (Exod. 3:11); Isaiah is afraid (Isa. 6:5); Sarah laughs (Gen. 18:12); Jonah even tries to physically flee from God's call (Jon. 1:3).

We may put ourselves in their situations and wonder what we would do, but we don't have to consider this hypothetically. The truth is we are also called by God to be God's people in the world. Our calls may not be as dramatic as Jeremiah's, but they are just as valid. Sometimes we don't feel up to the task, sometimes we laugh, and sometimes we are afraid.

The biblical call stories show us we are not alone. God says to Jeremiah—and to us—"Do not be afraid." Fear is a part of our human experience, but in God's eternal love for us, God addresses our fear and reassures us that we are not alone. First John 4:18 says, "There is no fear in love, but perfect love casts out fear." God's perfect love seeks us, calling us to allow that love to cast out any fear and join with God to work in the world.

Our call to specific ministries may change throughout our lives. I was called to be an active layperson for many years before I was called to ordained ministry, and in retirement, my call has again changed. Each call was accompanied by fear, but each call was also accompanied by God's eternal love and empowerment. Thanks be to God.

Loving God, thank you for the many ways you call us to partner with you in love for the world. Amen.

Paul's words to the Corinthian church in chapter 13 may be one of the most recognized passages in all of scripture. Even those with no religious background will likely have heard them at wedding ceremonies. We innately understand the truth of these words—love is patient and kind; love is not rude or resentful but gracious and forgiving. We pray that couples who are ready to commit their lives to each other already have considerable practice in living out the attributes of love. They will certainly have many opportunities to do so in the future.

Paul's words are appropriate for weddings, but they call us to a wider application of love. They describe God's love which we find embodied in Christ, a love we pray will be mirrored in all our relationships. It is a love that never ends. This love begins with God's eternal love for us, empowering us to grow in love for God and neighbor throughout our lives.

Weddings generally focus on the romantic type of love, one accompanied by intense feelings and emotions that may wane in the normalcy of everyday life. But Paul calls us to a more thorough understanding of a love that doesn't depend on the situation. It is a love grounded in our will, in our decision and commitment—with God's help—to love in the way of Christ. It is a love that looks outward, affirming that love is meant to be shared with others through acts of compassion and justice. This is a love worth celebrating in marriage and in all of our relationships.

God of love, thank you for first loving us and showing us your love through the life, death, and resurrection of Jesus. Empower us to share Christ's love with others in all we do. Amen.

Our Gospel passage continues where we left off last week, with Jesus teaching in the synagogue of his hometown. In verses 16-20, he reads the scripture from Isaiah. Then, as the crowd waits with almost bated breath, he finally speaks his own words: "Today this scripture has been fulfilled in your hearing." He announces that this long-awaited promise of God—to provide deliverance—has now been fulfilled in his very existence.

Jesus clearly proclaims the purpose of his mission to the Nazareth synagogue. His earthly actions will embody Isaiah's words—releasing those in captivity; bringing sight to the blind, both literally and figuratively; and freeing the oppressed with the good news of God's all-encompassing love. The stories of Bartimaeus, Zacchaeus, Mary Magdalene, and others remind us how the prophet's words were fulfilled in Jesus.

Just as Jesus was filled with the Spirit, the church today is called to be filled with the Spirit to continue the work of Jesus. All Christians are called to listen to Jesus, watch his actions, and discern in Christian community the paths toward carrying out Christ's mission. As the body of Christ, we are called to bring light and healing for mind, body, and spirit. In Jesus, the prophet's words were embodied and fulfilled; as disciples of Jesus, may we follow him in mission.

God of power, thank you for the freedom and power to continue the mission of Jesus through our acts of love. Amen.

My praise is continually of you." The psalmist, speaking from the vantage point of older age (vv. 17-18) affirms that praise is our proper response to God's eternal love and faithfulness. One of the blessings of aging is the ability to look back and see where and how God has been present through the joys and sorrows of one's life. Remembering God's eternal love is the catalyst for the psalmist's praise, and it becomes the foundation for assurance in God's future faithfulness.

One of my professors in divinity school regularly reminded us that doxology precedes theology. It is a reminder that even before we begin to consider the mysteries of God, we acknowledge God as our creator, our redeemer, and our sustainer, and we give thanks. The psalms are a gift, a continual reminder to us that no matter our present life circumstances, praise for God's covenant love must come first.

In First Thessalonians, Paul advises his readers to "rejoice always, pray without ceasing, give thanks in all circumstances, for this is the will of God in Christ Jesus for you" (5:16-18). Paul echoes the psalmist in declaring that praise for God is foundational to our spiritual lives even, perhaps especially, when life is difficult. This practice of praise fortifies our relationship with God and helps us to readily turn to God, whom we trust as a rock and a fortress in time of need. We may not give thanks *for* all circumstances, but *in* all circumstances God's love surrounds us—and for that we praise God.

Steadfast God, we praise you for your constant faithfulness. May our praise for you continually be in our mouths and on our hearts. Amen.

Amidst conflict over the use of spiritual gifts, Paul gives the Corinthian church instructions on how each gift is important to the body of Christ. In chapter 12, Paul writes about the variety of spiritual gifts and how each one is important in the body of Christ. In chapter 13, he asserts that it matters not what gifts they have but how their gifts are used. They must be used in the service of love. Paul reminds them that the spiritual gifts they possess, as individuals and collectively as the body of Christ, mean nothing if the use of those gifts does not further the love found in Jesus Christ.

Love never ends. At the end of our lives, even at the end of all time, it will be love that remains. When we finally see God face to face, we will understand love as "the greatest of these." Our ability to live that truth in community today is a foretaste of heaven.

For over twenty years I have met weekly with a Covenant Discipleship group where we hold one another accountable in learning to love. In this group, I have learned the truth of today's passage from First Corinthians. Various spiritual gifts are spread among us, and we encourage one another to use our gifts in acts of worship, compassion, devotion, and justice. We rejoice in one another's growth, and we encourage each other in failure. Sometimes love comforts, and sometimes love confronts, but love in the way of Jesus always rejoices in the truth and does no harm. I give thanks for the community of disciples that continues to teach me that love is the more excellent way.

God of grace, help us to use the gifts you have given us with love. Amen.

How quickly things can change! In this passage we go from "All spoke well of him and were amazed at the gracious words that came from his mouth," to they "led him to the brow of the hill . . . so that they might hurl him off the cliff." At both the beginning and the end of Jesus' earthly ministry, Jesus is greeted with praise followed closely by rejection and violence.

Why this sudden change? Jesus is challenging their assumptions about how God is going to work out the plan for salvation, and it is not what they expect. Using stories from their own scriptures, Jesus reminds them that God's grace has been poured out in unexpected ways in the past, and the same will be true for Jesus' ministry. Christ's gifts would not be offered exclusively to the people in his hometown, but given to all.

We should not be surprised that it was difficult for those present to accept Jesus' message. There are those who embrace the good news of God's inclusive love and mercy for all and those who don't. It is still so today. The message is still true, as well: When we do not accept that God's love is for everyone, we give up our ability to participate in that love.

For years I was reminded daily of how a prophet can be rejected in his hometown. A plaque outside my office door told the story of a former minister of our congregation, a courageous prophet who had been a leader in the civil rights movement. The congregation was deeply divided over his actions, and some left to start a new church. Like many others who cast their lot with those who are oppressed, he paid a price personally and professionally. Thanks be to God that there are those among us who continue to challenge our assumptions, proclaim God's love for all, and work for justice.

God of all, thank you for calling and empowering prophets who follow Jesus and call us to deepen our understanding of your expansive love and justice. Amen.

Called to Follow

FEBRUARY 3–9, 2025 • JORGE ACEVEDO

SCRIPTURE OVERVIEW: One of the most profound and puzzling themes in sacred scripture is the call of God on ordinary and often under-qualified women and men to join God's mission in the world. The old preacher's mantra, "God does not call the qualified. He qualifies the called," seems accurate when you peruse the Bible. In our texts this week, God taps multiple persons who seem unqualified at first glance: Isaiah in a time of mourning and grief, who is also profoundly self-aware of his sinfulness; a killer of the church turned pillar of the church in Paul; Simon Peter and his fishing partners James and John, whom other rabbis had overlooked; and David, the unconsidered son of Jesse who rose to the monarchy, fell to his own lusts, and became the author of beautiful sacred poetry that Christ followers across the centuries and miles still read for inspiration. All of these and a host of other biblical characters serve as witnesses to those whom God calls to follow.

QUESTIONS AND SUGGESTIONS FOR REFLECTION

- Read Isaiah 6:1-13. Have you ever had a transcendent encounter with God like Isaiah did? Describe it.
- Read Psalm 138. How have you seen God uplift the lowly and the humble? How have these experiences changed the way you live out your faith?
- Read 1 Corinthians 15:1-11. How do you pass along the message of good news?
- Read Luke 5:1-11. What is God asking you to leave behind so that you can more powerfully join Jesus in his mission in the world?

The Rev. Dr. Jorge Acevedo is a leadership coach, author, and speaker. His titles include *A Grace-Full Life* (Abingdon Press, 2017), *Holy Living: Neighboring* (Abingdon Press, 2019), and *Everybody Needs Some Cave Time: Meeting God in Dark Places* (Invite Press, 2023). Jorge is the retired Lead Pastor of Grace Church in Cape Coral/Fort Myers, FL.

My call to ministry came while sitting in a physics class at my local community college in Orlando, Florida. Not having been raised in the church and having recently given my life to Christ, I did not have a reference point for a "call to ministry." Sitting on the top row of the auditorium studying to be an architect and listening to a totally forgettable lecture, I pondered whether I wanted to do "this" for the rest of my life. My soul screamed, "No!" Then I heard a voice. "What brings you joy?" I responded in my head to the voice, "Teaching eighth-grade Sunday school." And with that, I got up from my seat, gathered my books, and walked out of the auditorium.

From the community college, I drove to my church to see if I could talk to my pastor. He was in his office and graciously gave me his full attention as I shared what had happened in that classroom. "What's going on in me?" I asked Pastor Yates. "Jorge, I think God is calling you into the ministry." Just as the priest Eli helped young Samuel learn to hear the voice of God, my kind shepherd was helping me.

I believe that every follower of Jesus is called to ministry. Our baptism is our common ordination into a life of service in the church and the world. Some, like myself, are called into vocational ministry. Many more are called to follow in the context of living and working fully in and with the world. We must listen for the voice of God amidst our daily lives, paying attention to where God is calling us to go. Often, God's call comes in a season of death. Like Isaiah hearing God's call to a prophetic ministry "in the year that King Uzziah died," we often have to experience a death of our plans to surrender to God's plans.

O God, you are the one who calls us to follow you. Help me to die to whatever keeps me from full surrender to your question, "Whom shall I send?" Amen.

In over forty years of ministry, I have preached or heard others preach on the call of Isaiah from Isaiah 6:1-8 many times. A holy vision of a majestic God and worshiping heavenly hosts, Isaiah's keen self-awareness of not only his sinfulness but the sinfulness of his people, the clarion call of God for someone to go, Isaiah's faithful "Yes" to that call—this story preaches well.

What I have never heard preached on, even from my lips, are the next verses from Isaiah 6:9-13. After this spectacular audio-visual display, God tells Isaiah that when he preaches, the people will not listen. When Isaiah asks, "How long?" the Lord responds, *Until the place is devastated and ten percent of the people remain.* God does not call Isaiah with a promise of a vital or vibrant ministry as we understand it. There is no promise for people to respond to Isaiah's preaching positively; in fact, God promises that Isaiah's call will continue until the land is devastated and homes and cities are empty.

Most of us don't get an early prediction of the results of our ministry from God like Isaiah did. We sense a nudge to join Jesus in ministry by joining the food bank team or serving on the Sunday hospitality team at our church, and we obey, often hoping to bring growth and life to the ministry. If we knew for sure our work would not be met with our earthly understanding of growth, would we begin the work at all?

The most beautiful and meaningful part of Isaiah's calling may be that he accepted the call and remained obedient to God in spite of the promised hardship. Sometimes, joining God in God's mission will be very hard. We will serve, and no one will notice or respond. Still, we are called to serve.

You are the God who calls your children to join you in serving people. More than anyone, you know how fickle humans can be. Help me to stay faithful to your calling in my life regardless of the results. Amen.

In my coaching of pastors, I primarily focus on two areas. First, I tend to a leader's walk with God. Are they abiding in Christ? (see John 15:4). Second, I concentrate on a leader's work for God. Are they abounding in the work of the Lord? (see 1 Cor. 15:58). One of the tricky parts of this kind of work is that the order matters. My faithfulness to God goes before my fruitfulness for God. My walk with God precedes my work for God. It's so easy to emphasize the mission and forget the spiritual formation required for the mission. When we get it right, our "being" is a priority from which our "doing" flows. Or, as I learned in recovery, "You cannot give what you do not have."

Psalm 138 is a beautiful poetic song of worship written by David, the shepherd boy turned warrior king. He understands that intimacy with God goes before the laundry list of tasks he does for God. In the dozens of psalms written by David, we discover that his praise was wholehearted. It came from a deep place in his soul. David was not afraid of unbridled adoration and unrestrained lament. But his worship was also full-bodied. He engaged all the senses of sight, sound, touch, and smell. He shouted, bowed, raised his hands, and got quiet before the Almighty. This is what made David a man after God's own heart (see 1 Sam. 13:14).

As you consider God's calling on your life this week, do a spiritual examen or self-inventory. Is your walk with God a priority in your life? Does your ministry flow from a deep well of abiding in Christ? Are the wellness containers of your life sufficient for the opportunities and challenges of your life?

Lord, teach me the way of heartfelt and whole-body worship.
Help me to prioritize my walk with you so that my work for
you flows from a place of deep intimacy. Amen.

In the late seventies, as a new follower of Jesus, I learned the camp song "Pass It On." I am so grateful that the women and men who mentored me as a young apprentice of Jesus taught me that following Jesus also meant learning to give away what had been so kindly given to me. I was one voice joining the chorus of countless others throughout the centuries and in different lands among distinct people, echoing the words "pass it on" to a broken, needy world.

Later, in the rooms of recovery from my addictions, afflictions, and compulsive behaviors, I learned that "having had a spiritual awakening as the result of these steps, we try to carry this message to alcoholics, and to practice these principles in all our affairs" (the twelfth step of Alcoholics Anonymous). Part of my recovery journey was to learn to "pass it on."

Similarly, Paul wrote to the first-century followers of Jesus in Corinth that he too had passed it on. He wrote, "For what I received I passed on to you" (NIV). Paul was not the message, but he was the messenger. The good news of Jesus' death, burial, resurrection, and appearance to many, including Paul himself, was the story that he received and then passed on to others.

My good news "pass-it-on" story is that I was an empty, wandering teenage addict who was introduced to Jesus by John, a man working for a campus ministry at my high school in Orlando, Florida. John stood in a long line of faithful people who passed on what they had experienced of the resurrected Jesus. He passed it on to me, and now I pass it on to others.

Lord, our world is in desperate need of the good news of Jesus. Keep me aware of any opportunity this day to "pass it on." Amen.

For years, I sang the first line of the hymn about amazing grace without thinking much about the second line, "a wretch like me." This was until I heard a pastor preach on these two lines. The brilliant orator said, "I only know my wretchedness in light of God's amazing grace." This single statement transformed my understanding of God's grace and my sinfulness. Clarity about my real spiritual condition comes only when I bear in mind God's relentless love for me. The order matters.

The order matters for many of our faith stories. In 1 Corinthians 15:3-7, Paul recounts the gospel story. Then, with this clarity about God's grace expressed in Christ, he writes, "I am the least of the apostles and do not even deserve to be called an apostle, because I persecuted the church of God" (NIV). Paul and hymn writer John Newton agree. Paul only understood his desperate need for a savior when looking at himself through the lens of grace. The order matters.

Reading the Creation story in the order it is presented matters. In Genesis 1 humanity is made in the image of God. In Genesis 2 humankind is "God-breathed." Both Creation stories recount the splendid generosity of God toward us. Then, in Genesis 3 comes the tragic rebellion. The grace story comes before the sin story. The order matters.

When we understand that God's grace is the initiator of all things, it changes our understanding and experience of it. All our acts of mercy and justice are not done in an effort to gain God's favor and forgiveness. They are our response to the amazing grace we have already received. The order matters.

God, you made me in your grace with potential and possibility. I also know that I am broken and desperately need your amazing grace. Help me to live this order well today. Amen.

Jewish boys in the first century studied the Torah in synagogue schools. Around the age of 12 or 13, some of the more gifted students would continue studying with a local rabbi in a "house of study." A famous rabbi would tap the most gifted young men, and they would travel with the rabbi as a *talmid*, the Hebrew word for "disciple" or "apprentice." The aim of this teaching relationship was for the disciple to become like their rabbi. For the boys not chosen by a rabbi, they would return home and learn their father's trade.

Knowing this context heightens the intensity of Jesus calling his disciples. In Matthew's Gospel, he records Jesus as telling the disciples, "Follow me, and I will make you fishers of people" (4:19). Luke tells a fuller story, describing Jesus teaching to the crowds from the boat and conveying weariness in Simon Peter, James, and John as they wash nets at the end of the day only to have Jesus tell them to go fishing again. Hesitantly, they do and catch a windfall of fish. An astonished Simon Peter confesses his sinfulness, and Jesus responds by calling Simon to join him in fishing for people. Apparently, Simon Peter had already been passed over by other rabbis and had already taken up his father's trade of fishing. His opportunity to be a rabbi's *talmid* was resurrected by Jesus.

One of the patterns we see in the Bible is that God often calls the least, the last, and the left out to do God's work. Persons whom society has rejected were often tapped by God for missional assignments. From Rahab to Ruth to Mary, from David to Peter to Paul, God loves to resurrect untapped purpose and long-dead dreams in us all so that we may join God's work of bringing restoration and peace to the world around us.

Thank you, God, that you are the one who restores deep longings in your children who want to follow as apprentices of Jesus. Amen.

Saying yes to God's calling on our lives requires saying no to many other things. When I sensed my call to vocational ministry, one of the first things I did was tell my parents. At the time, neither of my parents were Christ-followers. My mother was stunned, and my father was mad. His vision for my life was that I would be an Air Force pilot. He told me that if I went off to college to pursue ministry, I would have to leave behind my 1976 Chevy Camaro. I loved this car dearly. In a moment of youthful zeal and obedience to the voice I heard in the last row of the community college auditorium, I slid the keys across the table to my father. My "yes" to God meant saying "no" to my car.

In today's reading, after Jesus' charge to Peter to join him in fishing for people, Luke comments that Simon Peter, James, and John "left everything and followed him." Their "yes" to Jesus required saying "no" to their fishing enterprise. Their "yes" to their heavenly Father likely meant saying "no" to their earthly fathers.

In Mark 3, Jesus' family is concerned that Jesus is "out of his mind." The crowd tells Jesus his brothers and mothers are nearby looking for him, to which Jesus responds, "Who are my mother and my brothers?" Then he looks at those seated in a circle around him and says, "Here are my mother and my brothers! Whoever does God's will is my brother and sister and mother" (3:33-35). The redemptive beauty of this story is that after Pentecost, Mary, his mother, and James, his brother, are named among those who followed Jesus. In my own story, years later in their fifties, Mom and Dad would join me in following Jesus too.

Jesus, I want to follow you no matter the cost. Help me to say "yes" to you and "no" to anything that keeps me from obeying your call. Amen.

Adages of Blessings and Troubles

FEBRUARY 10–16, 2025 • EARLIE PASION-BAUTISTA

SCRIPTURE OVERVIEW: Adages are short sayings intended to express some sort of truth, often shared as advice or encouragement. Overused adages carry some element of truth, but they warrant deeper reflection than they're often given to discover what is actually true about them. This week we will consider adages that relate to our scripture readings, exploring what our scriptural heritage has to say about trust, growth, and healing. Jeremiah contrasts those who put their trust in themselves with those who trust in God. The psalmist encourages us to consider what feeds us as we grow. Paul's letter to the Corinthian church calls into question the ways in which we live differently in light of the truth of the Resurrection. In Luke's version of the Beatitudes, worldly success is not necessarily an indication of God's blessing.

QUESTIONS AND SUGGESTIONS FOR REFLECTION

- Read Jeremiah 17:5-10. Examine your heart. In what ways do you place your trust in "mere mortals" instead of in the Lord?
- Read Psalm 1. How do you seek to meditate on God's law day and night?
- Read 1 Corinthians 15:12-20. How has your understanding of the resurrection of the dead changed your living?
- Read Luke 6:17-26. How do you understand the paradoxes of Jesus' blessings and woes?

Earlie Pasion-Bautista is a United Methodist layperson who has worked with church leadership in various capacities, including leading Discipleship Resources-Philippines, who publishes *The Upper Room Disciplines* in the Philippines. Earlie is an entrepreneur and the mother of two boys.

*T*rust *in the Lord.* This charge is often issued from one well-meaning person to another without much thought as to what trust really looks like. We find it easy to trust in things that we can see, hold, or otherwise concretely experience. But trust requires faith, and faith is unnecessary when proof is present.

The scripture for today presents a comparison between those who trust in humans and those who trust in the Lord. Relying on our own strength and trusting humans alone can stagnate our growth—like a shrub in the desert—and leave us wanting when dry seasons come. While we can trust in our own and others' strength, it's prone to failure. But the blessing of trusting the Lord brings confidence that even in the midst of challenges, our roots will remain connected to the source of water, and we won't be dried up. In this scripture, we see the outcome of trusting. But what does it look like to trust in and depend on God?

Oftentimes, I tell myself to trust in God whenever I am faced with uncertainties and challenging decisions. Sometimes I find it difficult to trust God because I am impatient; I can't just wait for circumstances to unfold. When I feel this impatience, I pray. I try to calm down instead of rushing into things and deciding quickly.

Trusting the Lord involves accepting that there are life circumstances beyond our control, and trusting God means we don't work to grab hold of that which we cannot control. When we can step back, pause, breathe, and remember that God is in control, it is as if our roots dig a little more deeply and closer to the living stream of water that is God, grounding us in trust and allowing us to bear fruit.

Dear Lord, our source of sustenance, help us keep our roots connected to you. May we learn to make every day an opportunity to trust your ways. Amen.

Follow your heart. Today we associate the heart with passion, emotion, and love. For Jeremiah's audience, the heart was in charge of the mind and the will. In both understandings, the heart is that which guides our actions. No human can understand the heart, but God does. God searches it; God knows our hidden motives.

When it's difficult to logically decide something, we say, "Follow your heart." We often rely on "feeling right" about something or someone when deciding to move forward. It's not encouraging to hear scripture say that the heart is perverse.

The COVID-19 pandemic led to the rise of the personality development industry. Many of us coped through this challenging time in history by attempting to improve ourselves, adapting and trying to be resilient. Many were forced to shift careers because of massive layoffs; many have chosen to adapt to working at home and are finding new ways to thrive. Personality development coaches and trainers, be it in fitness, business, relationships, or life in general, have taught us to look into the self—self-awareness, self-care, self-love, self-confidence—focusing on what we can do. They would say, "Follow your heart."

However, being a disciple of Christ calls us not only to follow our heart, which could deceive us, but also to trust in the leading of God. Truly knowing ourselves and having a strong relationship with God through scripture reading and prayer can help us rethink our actions and understand times in our lives when we have trusted our own feeling or strength instead of God's. A "change of heart" could be God's leading for us to trust God's will rather than rely on the self.

O God, examine our minds and search our hearts. Realign them to your heartbeat and to your plans. Amen.

*B*loom where you are planted. God calls us to different places according to the gifts and graces we have. God sends us where God needs us.

I graduated from college with a degree in journalism during the time when extra-judicial killing of journalists was prevalent in the Philippines. Instead of pursuing journalism as a career, I entered the book and magazine publishing industry, in part to assure my mother that even though I lived far from her, I was safe.

Concurrently, I served as national church youth leader. My publishing experience paved a way for me to work full-time as the publishing coordinator for Discipleship Resources-Philippines. I held that position for twelve years. During that time I obtained two seminary degrees but have not entered the ministerial work of the ordained. Many have asked me, "Why won't you become a pastor?"

I know why I did not practice my journalism degree. But as to why I have chosen to work as a layperson and not become clergy, I struggle to articulate a valid reason to those who see ordination as a fulfillment of my potential. But I feel that God calls me to various lay ministries and then enables me to serve in these roles to the best of my ability. I feel rooted in my role as a layperson and intend to bloom there to produce fruit for God.

When we obey and remain faithful to our calling, we will be like trees planted near the water source. Each of us is called to where God needs our hands and feet. When the time comes that I start to think I am like chaff tossed by the wind or I am no longer bearing fruit, I will be ready for God to plant me somewhere else.

Dear God, thank you for calling us and planting us where we can reach you as a source of strength and where you can lead us to bear fruit. Amen.

*F*ake it until you make it. Here's another piece of advice from some personality development coaches. They mean that for you to be able to gain confidence and competence in reaching your goals and dreams, live as if you are already there; act as if you have already accomplished them.

When he was about nine years old, my eldest son started praying about his hope in heaven: "Lord, thank you for giving Jesus Christ to die for our sins, for saving us. I pray that when we die, we will be with him in heaven." Surprised, I asked him why he was praying about death and heaven. He said that he believes that Jesus is his Savior and that because Jesus died and was raised from the dead, we will be together again after we die.

Are we sure about our faith and salvation in Christ? Do we live differently in light of our belief? When we believe that Christ was raised from the dead, then our lives should be a testament to that belief. Otherwise our faith is meaningless. Doing what is good, leaving our fears behind, having confidence in what we preach, and avoiding the temptation to harm others are manifestations of our faith.

In a world where we are told to fake it, perhaps we could rather say "Faith it until you make it," living transformed lives as a result of Christ's resurrection. Our life is worth living because of our belief that Jesus lives.

Dear Jesus, may our faith in your resurrection empower us live truthfully in the present as we show what the future holds because you live. Amen.

*T*ouch heals. Not a lot of churches that I know of have a healing ministry. Many do hospital visitations and pray for the sick, but the sense of touch is often left out of the picture. And after what we have been through in the pandemic, touching and embracing have become even more rare.

When I was a child, I remember my mom laying her hands on my back before I went to bed. I could hear her whisper prayers for God to keep me safe and healthy. For her, it was so important that she touched my brother and me as she prayed.

Now that I am a mother, I practice the same with my children. But I don't do it only after they are already in bed. We encourage one another to give and receive a hug to end the day. We call it "recharging." It feels good to give and receive energy and a healing touch with those you love.

Many people followed Jesus because they believed that he could heal their diseases. Jesus was capable of healing simply through his words, but he often used his hands to touch the ones he healed, making the experience much more intimate and powerful. Many sought Jesus' healing touch, believing that when they touched him, they would be healed. Many of us follow Jesus to this day because we are also in need of healing.

Jesus is no longer physically with us, yet as disciples we can extend his healing touch to others. Our hands can do powerful things to channel healing. Laying hands on those we pray for, touching the sick, making a prayer shawl or a get-well card— these and many other works of our hands can bring healing power to those in need.

God, our healer, give us the courage to lend our hands to provide a healing touch for someone in need. May our sense of touch be used as a channel of your healing mercy. Amen.

Sana all. This Filipino expression means "I wish everyone could have the same thing or experience." It is often said to express desire or envy of other people's circumstances. With our world becoming more consumer driven than ever before, we sometimes equate being blessed with an abundance of material possessions or finances. So with an underlying feeling that we have been cheated of something, we say, *"sana all."*

Those Jesus calls blessed in Luke are not those we usually envy—those who are poor, hungry, weeping, hated, rejected, insulted, and excluded. On the contrary, those who are rich, who have plenty, and whom others speak well of—these are the folks we envy. But they are also the ones Jesus warns. Does this mean disciples of Jesus cannot be rich, happy, or spoken well of?

Jesus spoke seemingly contrasting statements, saying those who are poor will be heirs of the kingdom, those who are hungry will be filled, those who weep will laugh. The blessings and the woes can open our eyes to look at the disparity of the socio-economic status of those in our community. They give hope to those who feel disadvantaged, allowing them to see the promise that God will lift them up. On the other hand, these warnings open the opportunity for those on the advantaged side to see how they could share their privileges to uplift others.

What we can all hope for is the ability to become channels of blessing to other people, especially those who are in need. Blessings do not come from material things only. Some people may simply need someone to spend time listening to them. Others find comfort in physical touch, and some may desperately need us to be present with them in their grief. Jesus has set the example for us. Our work is to follow.

God, teach us to recognize our privileges and learn how to share them with those who are at a disadvantage. Prepare us to be channels of your blessings every day. Amen.

What you focus on grows. Our final adage for the week teaches us that the more we think about something, the more it will become part of us and our reality.

Whenever I lead retreats, I sometimes ask the participants to raise their hands if they have daily personal devotion time or are consistent in their daily Bible reading and meditation. Not a lot do. Sometimes, even the church leaders cannot confidently raise their hands. Honestly, I sometimes fall short.

My mother is one of the few people I know who is consistent in her daily Bible reading and meditation. She reads *Siled ti Kararag, The Upper Room* daily devotional in Ilokano in the morning, and *The Upper Room Disciplines* in the evening. Whether she is in her home or elsewhere attending conferences and events, she doesn't end a day without her Bible and devotion. My mom is a very optimistic person, someone who can always see the bright side in every situation and who discerns answers through prayer.

Psalm 1 captures the two ways people live their lives—in righteousness or in wickedness. One trait of truly happy people is "these persons love the LORD's Instruction, and they recite God's Instruction day and night" (CEB).

What we focus on grows. We don't strive to read the Bible and pray daily in order to gain some big status symbol of success. When we focus on God's instruction, the habitual interaction makes God's word part of who we are—in our thoughts, words, and actions. The Lord is wise and knows our ways; God rewards us for our righteousness and destroys us for our wickedness. Let us focus on what is good so it will grow in our lives.

Lord, may your word live in us day and night. May we always choose the way of the righteous. Teach us to follow your ways. Amen.

Renewing Our Faith

FEBRUARY 17–23, 2025 • ANDREW WILKES

SCRIPTURE OVERVIEW: The passage from Genesis and the psalm challenge us to resist the understandable yet self-destructive road of fretting and choosing revenge in our relationships. They also comfort us with the assurance that once-wounded relationships can be healed and stitched back together. The New Testament passages, interpreted together, call us to consider two topics in relation to one another: the nature and feel of the Resurrection and the identity of our enemies. Both passages suggest that embodiment matters, that our earthen vessels are neither opponents nor enemies of spiritual development. Nor are they automatic allies in spiritual growth. Instead, our embodied lives are always potential vistas for experiencing resurrection, for self-identifying our bodies as blessed, not cursed; beloved, not burdensome, through the presence of the lynched yet living Christ.

QUESTIONS AND SUGGESTIONS FOR REFLECTION

- Read Genesis 45:3-11, 15. What does repair and reconciliation look like in your current family context?
- Read Psalm 37:1-11, 39-40. What kind of faith practices—and what kind of God—could help you and your loved ones to pivot from fretting to trusting and relying on the Divine?
- Read 1 Corinthians 15:35-38, 42-50. Where do you envision resurrection occurring? What difference might it make to consider where and when resurrection happens among human beings?
- Read Luke 6:27-38. How might you love the "enemy" with renewed determination—including those portions of yourself that you may have been socialized to curse and despise?

The Rev. Dr. Andrew Wilkes is the co-lead pastor of Double Love Experience Church in Brooklyn, NY. Andrew is the author of *Freedom Notes: Reflections on Faith, Justice, and the Possibility of Democracy* (Calalous Publications, 2018) and the co-author of *Psalms for Black Lives: Reflections for the Work of Liberation* (Upper Room Books, 2022).

Joseph's kissing of his siblings symbolizes the possibility of tender masculinity in a world ripped to pieces—like Joseph's coat of many colors—by toxic, predatory masculinity. From chapter 42 where he speaks "harshly" to his brothers (v. 7) to chapter 50 where he speaks "kindly" to them (v. 21), Genesis records Joseph demonstrating a developmental process worth noting.

The story of Joseph exhibits a social-emotional process of growth that demonstrates both his introspection and his interpersonal confronting of his brothers with a blend of gentleness and directness. He is neither a pushover nor does he seek to steamroll over his kindred for what most readers would acknowledge as Joseph's just, legitimate grievances of betrayal, abandonment, and abuse.

Instead of adopting a tit-for-tat ethic, Joseph adopts an ethic of courageous truth-telling and self-disclosure in community. His story affirms the biblical promise of reconciliation and lays a foundation for the potential moral implications of God's kingdom. This restorative ethic positions Joseph to reveal his identity to his siblings as well as to unearth his confidence in a God who still turns to good those purposes which some human beings—indeed, sometimes an intimate partner, a family member, or a close friend—mean for evil.

Reconciling God, guide us in deciding when, if, and how to pursue the art of restoration in our relationships. Inspire us to affirm that our lives are formed by the biblical promise of reconciliation. Hear our prayer and help us to embody our prayer in our loving and living, through the power of Christ. Amen.

Managing the ancestral legacies of parents and forebears can impact the lived experiences and lived theologies of descendants, sometimes for the good and sometimes for the bad. In the case of Joseph, stewarding family relationships with his brothers following the death of their father, Jacob, occasioned a litany of emotions. Those emotions, as displayed in the Genesis narrative, include fear, mourning, and grief but also a hunger to face the bracing possibilities of renewed relationships.

Chief among those bracing possibilities are Joseph and his siblings' decision to practice a courageous and candid relationship that reversed their inherited family pattern of duplicity and deception, as shown through much of the interactions of their father, Jacob, with their uncle, Esau. Their remarkable scene of fraternal healing illustrates that the past need not always be prologue; instead, our families may be a few difficult conversations, prayer vigils, and therapy sessions away from authoring an unprecedented future of solidarity, kinship, and communion.

Near the beginning of Genesis, Cain and Abel fail to be one another's keeper. By the conclusion of Genesis, Joseph and his brothers, through trial and error, eventually keep faith with one another. Where Cain and Abel choose the lethal reality of sibling rivalry, Joseph and his brothers, with God's recurring help and accompanying presence, choose life and the repaired interdependence of sibling restoration.

Holy One, prepare our hearts to inherit and interrogate our family histories with grace. Prepare our family members to act with courage in choosing a future of forgiveness. Help us bear nonviolent witness to better family relations that we never dared think possible. Let our aspirations become reality, to your glory and the reconciliation of our families. Amen.

Fear is not the existential opposite of trusting in God—fretting is. Fretting grows anxiety in ways that make us focus on ourselves. Trusting grows faith and assurance that help us focus on God. Fretting sets the stage for an endless succession of tomorrows trapped in low expectations. Such expectations may not be unwarranted, but they are almost always exacerbated by the eroding, stress-inducing power of worry. By contrast, the psalmist's trust in God as our refuge—a theme echoed throughout the entire psalm—can release inner resources for leading a grounded and courageous life.

Trusting God can help replace the embodied patterns that fretting has normalized and crystallized into our nervous systems. Pacing the floor in anguish, sloshing down another cup of coffee, thoughtlessly beginning yet another task without completing the preceding one—the list of behaviors that form an open container into which our worry pours can be extended further, and often feels like a running, never-to-be-completed to-do list. Trusting God, however, affords us the opportunity to undertake activities such as interlocking our fingers in prayer to "wait patiently" for God; singing at the top of our lungs as we "take delight in the Lord"; and, in a month dedicated to Black histories and futures, reading and reviewing the complex stories testifying to a God who makes the vindication of oppressed people shine, who makes, in the fullness of time, the justice of long-frustrated causes advance in undeniable power like the noonday sun.

Trustworthy Presence, persuade our world-weary selves to once again make the ancient swap, trading in the seductive, unproductive practice of fretting for the meaningfully, subtle ways of entrusting our entire selves to your capable care. In the name of the Christ, we offer these words. Amen.

Black church traditions have long argued that trouble doesn't last (Rev. Timothy Write wrote a song about it). Some Buddhist traditions teach a similar truth, contending that our embodied reflections on the impermanence of evil are potential sources of peace and avenues toward being at ease with life and at home within our bodies. The psalmist too makes an analogous case for the expiration date of wrongdoing and all manner of evil.

Consider the claim of the psalmist in verse 10: "Yet a little while, and the wicked will be no more; though you look diligently for their place, they will not be there." What a breathtaking assertion! It is also a potentially embodied claim, meaning that our bones, brains, and yes, the very air we breathe can be blessed—or buoyed—by this belief: God's grace outlasts the long-tenured work of injustice, inequality, and inauthentic spirituality. Hear the words once more: The wicked will, one day, be no more. The words of God, cutting their path like water over the most entrenched evil, will one day wash away evil's presence altogether. On such an occasion, may we each in our own way enter into the knowledge of the psalmist who claims that God is our "refuge in the time of trouble."

Ancient of Days, ready our hearts and steady our minds in the mood and spirit of prayer. With fatigued imagination that yet holds inner determination, may we believe that you are hard at work, employing the good that we cannot see, using the beauty that has escaped our notice, and instilling the truths we have not yet come to affirm to defeat all manner of interpersonal, social, and ecological evil. In the name of Christ. Amen.

The late Rev. Peter Gomes, chaplain to Harvard University's Memorial Chapel, once preached that Christians are "resurrection people." In making that claim, he sought to contend that resurrection is more than an individual experience of faith. Instead, resurrection is a reality belonging to an entire people, to all those who trust that the God of life can raise us upward and forward in the arc of a time beyond this time. Resurrection people act with enough faith to look forward to our destiny with God, yet with enough humility to admit our fuzzy knowledge about the details that are leading toward that destiny. We affirm with Paul that our perishable bodies will somehow be exchanged for an embodied, yet imperishable form of existence.

With hopes for God's good future remaining intact, we can venture a word about the value of God's goodness in the present moment as well. Paul's principal image in this passage is a seed that eventually bears fruit. The claim is most clear in verse 44, where Paul contends that each of us is sown as a "physical body," yet raised as a "spiritual body." The structure of Paul's argument evokes both hope and responsibility, implying that what we do in history, before the trumpet of verse 52 sounds, will make a difference in heaven, in the life to come. Infused with that hope, sense of responsibility, and the memory of Paul's letter to the Galatians, "let us not grow weary in doing what is right, for we will reap at harvest time, if we do not give up" (6:9).

God of seedtime and harvest, of life's routines and resurrection, be with us in our coming and going, in our reaping and sowing. Endow us once more with the courage to walk in our identity as resurrection people, as those who are both familiar with the jagged edges of history, and captivated by the claims of a once-crucified, now-glorified Christ. Amen.

Enemies, sometimes, can be redefined as neighbors, as Jesus will teach in Luke 10. Here, in chapter 6, Luke describes what the difficult yet doable tradition of loving your enemy entails: blessing those who curse us, praying for those who abuse us, doing good without necessarily expecting the return of that good. With great appreciation, the nonviolent Christian witnesses of Septima Poinsette Clark and Martin Luther King Jr. come to mind as persons who deeply embodied the beauty and efficacy of Jesus' tradition of loving your enemy as being compatible with deep self-respect.

It is a sobering, well-documented fact that individuals of privilege and social power often mislabel persons of marginal status and comparatively little power as opponents, as the other. The compliment is often paid in return as well. In splendid contrast to such understandable reciprocal yet harmful practices, Jesus calls his disciples to the path of what we can call nonviolent direct action, grounding that work in God, whose mercy covers all human flesh.

Enemies as well as neighbors often share the same history, the same lands, and in some cases, the same God. It is the genius of the Christ—and our joyous obligation as disciples of this miracle worker—to love our enemies with the prayerful hope that every enemy is a potential neighbor, that every strained relationship is awaiting conversion to the more excellent way of love.

God of mercy, love, and justice, equip and empower us to embody mercy in our dealings with those whom society has trained us to see as enemies, trusting that our neighbors, siblings, fellow disciples, perhaps even ourselves, lie beneath the encrusted contempt that we have picked up along the way. Remind us that we are never more fully your children than when we embody and exhibit mercy in every direction. Amen.

Luke's version of the Golden Rule appears in verse 31, reading: "Do to others as you would have them do to you." The Golden Rule is not a call for enlightened self-interest, but a divine challenge to curate anti-transactional, covenant relationships. In an age dominated by financial concern, Jesus through the Golden Rule interrupts the coldness of cost-benefit thinking in relationships with his urgent summons in verse 35 to love the enemy, do good, and lend to those experiencing need, all the while expecting nothing in return.

The authority of the summons flows from the moral integrity and unique anointing of Jesus' life and Spirit-filled ministry. The Golden Rule calls us to put effort into relationships because of the inherent value of human beings, not because pouring into relationships is an investment strategy to accumulate social capital. In this passage, Jesus implies that disciples should differentiate themselves among humanity by their practice of doing good with neither the motive of an immediate reward nor the delayed incentive of accessing a reward further down the line. Disciples of the Christ, filled with the same Spirit as Jesus, are called to and capable of modeling God's loving-kindness in relationships. Let us do likewise as we have opportunity and occasion to do so.

Liberating and love-inspiring Christ, encourage us to trust the still, small voice within, calling us to minister to people and their environments for their own sake. Motivate and deepen our practice of mercy so that our very lives will mirror and reflect divine benevolence in the world. In the name of the Christ we pray. Amen.

The Revealed Divine Presence of God

FEBRUARY 24–MARCH 2, 2025 • R. SIDWELL MOKGOTHU

SCRIPTURE OVERVIEW: God's glory is always revealed, even if incompletely. Moses' time with God on the mountain and his deepened relationship with God leads to his skin radiating, a reflection of God's glory. The psalmist recalls God's glory, recognizing God as the holy king who is worshiped by all and who answers our calls. God is also the lover of justice, equity, and righteousness. Paul writes to the Corinthians of the new covenant, in which God's glory is now more openly revealed in Christ, removing the need for a veil like Moses wore. Luke reports on Jesus' transfiguration, when his face began to shine like that of Moses. God's voice reinforces the revelation of the Transfiguration, declaring Jesus to be God's Son and the revelation of God's glory.

QUESTIONS AND SUGGESTIONS FOR REFLECTION

- Read Exodus 34:29-35. Consider the ways you provide evidence of your faith. Do you display it for your glory or for God's?

- Read Psalm 99. How do you seek a healthy balance of awe and intimacy in your relationship with God?

- Read 2 Corinthians 3:12–4:2. In what areas have you seen preachers compromise the gospel with populism? Who are the people of faith that you have experienced as consistent in truth-telling?

- Read Luke 9:28-43a. Is there any particular moment or experience that is a transfiguration moment for you? What need do you beg Christ to address?

The Rev. R. Sidwell Mokgothu is the resident bishop of The Methodist Church of Southern Africa in Pretoria, South Africa.

Moses has taken a pause from the Exodus journey and has spent forty days and nights in the presence of God, consulting on the covenant and receiving the remade tablets of the Commandments. He has, in the previous chapter, been promised this accompanying glory as a guarantee of God's presence.

As Moses is spending time up close and personal with God, he is building an intimate relationship with God. The evidence of this time spent closely with God is the shining skin on his face. The change in his appearance is so dramatic that Aaron and the other Israelites are afraid of him. Moses calms their fears and shares God's message with them, and from that point on he wears a veil to cover his face when sharing God's message with the people.

Moses asked for God's presence and support. God offers presence to those who are ready to spend time with God. Like Moses, we are provided with the opportunity to come closer and build our own relationship with God. Unlike in the case of Moses, who was the only one of his time who had the opportunity to meet with God, today any believer who is ready to connect with God has the opportunity to do so without any mediator. Christ has removed the veil once and for all.

The text testifies to the impact of time and a nurtured relationship with God through worship and prayer. Those who spend time with God have the blessing of God's glory manifesting in them. Like Moses, they radiate with the glory of God. They do not return with nothing.

Those who spend time in a deepened relationship with God are empowered with the life-giving gospel that serves as commandments to direct them in this life. They are imbued with God's glory, a glory that shines for all to see.

May we shine and radiate your glory, O God. Amen.

The psalm presents the Lord as the God who is holy, available, and present to all. God is the king who is exalted and worthy of humans' worship. God is also enthroned for the heavenly creatures to praise. Heavenly creatures have always responded to the enthroned God with full-time worship, as the prophet Isaiah witnessed in the temple (see Isa. 6:3). Not only human and heavenly beings but even the whole earth is expected to quake and tremble at God's presence. God is exalted, revealed, and made accessible to all. Like the heavenly beings and creation, the people are required to respond through worship as they praise the "great and awesome name" of the Lord.

God's holiness is the attribute that has made the Lord God special and different from the other gods. Christian believers pray as Jesus taught them for God's name to be "hallowed"—to be made holy. We recognize God as one who is unique and whose character is perfect. As a result of this uniqueness, God is set apart from idols.

It is this holy God who calls on those who follow Jesus to be holy, perfect, and set apart just as God, in Jesus Christ, is perfect. On our own, we human beings do not have the capacity to be holy and perfect. Our holiness is derived from our imitating Christ. Holiness is about followers of Christ leading lives that are different from the dominant cultures of power, abuse, and corruption. The Christian act of consecration is about praying for ordinary human beings and dedicating them to live according to God's will and to serve God faithfully as they serve all of God's creation.

Lord, consecrate us for your service. Amen.

The writer of the psalm points out attributes of God beyond the main attribute of holiness. Whereas the world is exposed to powerful kings who oppress the powerless and vulnerable people when they govern, God is lifted as the lover of justice, equity, and righteousness.

God's justice is not the same as worldly justice. Worldly justice is based on legal systems that seek to punish the wrong-doers and balance the scales for the victims by avenging against their perpetrators. Worldly judicial systems are vulnerable to the powerful who are able to manipulate them. The rich buy justice. The poor and disenfranchised suffer disproportionately. God's justice, on the other hand, is focused on defending the oppressed and seeking the well-being of the poor and the exploited who are always the victims of power and systems.

Alongside God's justice is equity. This flows from the biblical teaching that all human beings are created in the image of God (see Gen. 1:27). Equity is an intentional endeavor to break human-created barriers such as race, gender, age, tribe, disability, and sexual orientation. Equity is about formulating fair laws and policies that give equal opportunities, particularly to those who have been denied before.

Linked to God's justice is the righteousness of God, the standards of what is right and good. God's sense of righteousness is what allows God to be able to evaluate and judge what is happening in the world with justice, mercy, and grace.

These three attributes were manifest in many priests as exemplified by Moses, Aaron, and Samuel. These servants called on God and God responded. Like them, Christians the world over are called to be living embodiments of justice, equity, and righteousness.

God, we pray that we may be embodiments of holiness and lovers of justice, equity, and righteousness. Amen.

Paul writes to the Corinthians as those who have the hope and the ability to act with great boldness. The experience of Christians today is different from that of Moses, who covered his face with a veil to protect Israel from seeing his transfigured face.

Unlike the old covenant that was based on laws as demonstrated in Exodus, the new covenant is based on the freedom granted by the Holy Spirit. The veil that Moses put on kept "the people of Israel from gazing at the end of the glory that was being set aside." This veil is now removed, and God's people can look at the radiant glory of God. God's people are able, like Moses in the old covenant, to access God and establish long-lasting relationships with God.

It is only Christ—holy and set aside—who has the power to remove the veil. All that the people need to do is to turn to the Lord for the veil that is covering their minds to be removed. This message is still important today. There are many who practice a theology that says access to God is only granted to priests, as if they are a class privileged above laity. According to Paul, all believers have access to God and are given opportunities to build close and unmediated intimate relationships with God.

Those who are committed to this relationship with God through Christ are those who are being transformed into the image of Christ, as they have this wonderful experience of looking at the glory of God. The image of this glory is reflected in them and provides the future privilege of "being transformed into the same image from one degree of glory to another."

God, may your Spirit unveil our faces to be transformed from glory to glory. Amen.

Paul presents what could serve as his credentials to this community of faith. He is very aware that he, humanly speaking, should be without any right to offer anything on behalf of God because of his history. However, he writes as one who is convicted by the gospel of salvation found in God: "Therefore, since it is by God's mercy that we are engaged in this ministry, we do not lose heart."

He states upfront with boldness that he is a beneficiary of God's mercy. It is this mercy and grace that accords him and his co-workers the privilege to be in the ministry of Christ. Those who know this undeserved mercy of God do not allow themselves to be held ransom by their history of sin. Paul refuses to lose heart and to let his past be used to manipulate his guilt. Paul and his co-workers are committed to the calling to preach God's gospel without fail. There is nothing that is going to discourage them.

Paul resisted the temptation to preach a dishonest and falsified message. He was, however, very open and committed to preaching and manifesting the truth that can be put to scrutiny. There are many false teachers today who manipulate and take advantage of those they serve. But those who are in the ministry of Jesus must refuse populism that leads to the compromising and twisting of the gospel. They cannot afford to dilute, distort, or adulterate the word and preach what the people want to hear. We live in a world that needs Christian workers and preachers of God's gospel who display righteous integrity, who speak the truth even when it is uncomfortable or unpopular.

God, empower all those who have the privilege to share in the ministry of Christ to be honest and committed to their calling of telling the truth. Amen.

The Transfiguration is one tradition that is shared by all the Synoptic Gospels—Matthew, Mark, and Luke. The narrative tells of Jesus' encounter alongside three disciples of his inner circle: Peter, James, and John. This is the same trio that he will take to the garden of Gethsemane before his crucifixion. Jesus brings them closer not so they can rise and shine above the others but as trusted confidants, especially in his most difficult moments.

As they will do in the garden, his trio of supporters struggles to stay awake in prayer. Instead of Jesus waking them as he will do in the garden, it is the appearance of Moses and Elijah that rouses Peter, James, and John from their sleep. They see Jesus transfigured and begin to overhear Moses and Elijah conversing with Jesus. Peter misunderstands the importance of the event. He seeks to capture the moment in time by building altars to the presence of the three prophets—an action often taken in the Hebrew scriptures to mark a significant encounter with God.

Before Jesus can correct Peter, God intervenes in a cloud that overshadows those on the mountain. God speaks to reveal and affirm Christ as the chosen Son of God who must be listened to. The living Christ is on the move, and the disciples are called to listen and to follow, not stay stagnant in place.

The Transfiguration is a phenomenon that exposes the disciples to the majesty and glory of Jesus Christ. The close encounter with God has changed Jesus' physical appearance, just as it did Moses' appearance. Christ extends this transfiguration experience to those who are with him in the moment of prayer. It connects those who follow Christ with past faith traditions and the hope that lies in the future.

We pray for the life-transforming experiences of those who encounter you, O God. Amen.

TRANSFIGURATION SUNDAY

Luke reports that following the Transfiguration, Jesus and the disciples descend the mountain. Christian disciples who have experienced intimate relationship with Christ do not bask in that glory to feed the egoistic self. A church that has experienced the Transfiguration is a church that has the imperative to go down the mountain and return in mission to those waiting and living at the foot of the mountain.

When Jesus and the disciples go down the mountain, they are immediately met with a great crowd. It is out of this crowd that a man emerges who shouts out of desperation, begging Jesus to heal his son. The child is a victim of an unclean spirit that has seized and abused him. It is not clear which disciples the man had begged for help—perhaps those who stayed at the foot of the mountain while Jesus and the three went up. Whoever it is, Jesus is disappointed and angry at their failure, so angry that he labels them a "faithless and perverse generation." He has tried hard to invest in them for so long but is not seeing the impact he wants.

Christians who have the opportunity to be close to Christ and yet do not allow Christ to impact them are missing the point. The Transfiguration and ensuing return down the mountain and healing of the boy show that we are invited to be transformed by Christ so that we can then do God's work in the world. Yet Christ does not write off the disciples, nor us, for failing. He continues to give more opportunities to grow and serve in ministry.

Christ, increase our faith to be able to heal and transform others in your name. Amen.

Our Failures and God's Faithfulness

MARCH 3–9, 2025 • CANDICE MARIE BENBOW

SCRIPTURE OVERVIEW: As we begin the Lenten season, the practice of fasting and denying ourselves for forty days can seem harrowing. All the texts for this week remind us that we do not embark on this journey alone. God goes with us. We start the week with the texts for Ash Wednesday, with Isaiah admonishing us to ensure that we are on this journey for the sole reason of drawing closer to God. As we step deeper into Lent, the remaining passages emphasize the humanity that we bring to this season of fasting. Luke reminds us that we are not walking a new path. Jesus has already gone before us.

QUESTIONS AND SUGGESTIONS FOR REFLECTION

- Read Psalm 51:1-7. How do you work to free yourself of any guilt you may have from past mistakes? How do you help to foster that same feeling in others?

- Read 2 Corinthians 5:20b–6:10. What kinds of problems have you endured because of your faith? How have those struggles influenced your understanding of what salvation is and how it is received?

- Read Luke 4:1-13. Are you aware of times when distractions derailed previous fasts? What did you learn from those experiences? How can those lessons help you on this fast and in the future?

- Read Deuteronomy 26:1-11. Remember a time when God answered a prayer and a deep longing of your heart. How did it make you feel? How did you mark the experience?

Candice Marie Benbow is an author, national columnist, and public theologian. Candice is the creator of The ThirtyOne, a women's faith and lifestyle media company. She is a member of Zion Hill Baptist Church in Atlanta, GA.

In our world, "quid pro quo" is the name of the game. We seldom do a good deed for another person without expecting something in return. Even if we have no immediate request, we definitely remember what we did for them when we need something from them. In many ways, it's natural for us to develop this habit. After all, an important part of being in community is the give and take of relationship. But our intention when helping others and the specificity with which we keep score can harm our relationships rather than help them.

What about when we behave this way with God? When our prayer and fasting aren't rooted in a desire to grow deeper in intimacy with our Creator, they become efforts to get God to do what we want. Sometimes this effort is intentional: We pray and fast with the expectation that God will give us exactly what we want as a result. Other times we don't set out to hold expectations of God, but old ways of thinking start to creep in. We think we are turning over our wants and needs to God in prayer, but we also hit God with a righteous side eye when our petitions are over and we still do not have the outcome we want.

In the face of our transactional mindset, God is gracious with us. God helps us reorient to what truly matters: relationship *with* God. Getting closer to God will never be about what it can tangibly yield for us. Instead, it is about living in a close, committed relationship with the God of all creation.

Gracious God, teach me to set and sustain honorable intentions as I draw closer to you. Help me to remember that the outcome I seek should always and only be to grow deeper in the knowledge of your love and compassion. Amen.

Psalm 51 is regarded as David's plea for God's mercy after he has raped Bathsheba and murdered her husband, Uriah (see 2 Sam. 11). In David, we see the depth and breadth of the human condition, from the best to the worst. After the prophet Nathan confronts him, even David can't believe that he has stooped so low. He knows better. God has been amazingly gracious with him and has walked closer to David than nearly anyone else in the course of history. That should be enough to keep David from temptation. But it isn't. He finds himself in a mess of his own making.

Like David, we all have been confronted with the messiness of our humanity and been disappointed in ourselves because we should have known better. Choosing to consecrate ourselves through fasting can bring those disappointing memories to the forefront of our minds—though, if we're honest, they're never that far away. When you really have a heart for God, it hurts you when your actions hurt God's heart.

When we have committed sins against God and against one another, we must make it right. Psalm 51 shows us how. David's brutal honesty in his own time of fasting and prayer is a powerful example of confession. He names what is wrong within himself and then asks for a new heart. Naming our own failures and putting them out there for God to see is challenging and uncomfortable, but ultimately necessary and healing. When we confess our shortcomings, we can move beyond them and become everything God calls us to be.

Understanding and compassionate God, forgive me when I walk in contradiction to your ways. Forgive me for every time my actions break someone's heart—including my own. Guide me as I learn to forgive myself. Amen.

ASH WEDNESDAY

Time often feels like a very abstract and elusive thing. In the same moment you believe you have your entire life ahead of you and all the time in the world is at your disposal, you can also become deeply aware of how fleeting time actually is. Ash Wednesday has a way of bringing time into focus. As we gather and hear the words "you are dust, and to dust you shall return," we are reminded that time for us is finite. We feel time's precious nature more acutely when we acknowledge how much time we've spent doing unimportant or harmful things.

When we are on a journey to get closer to God, it's easy to look at the time we've spent operating contrary to God's goals and become frustrated. The time we've spent in fear, sin, and inauthenticity can breed shame and guilt. How could it not? God has been so faithful to us that it seems nonsensical to respond with anything less than perfect faithfulness in return.

God is already intimately acquainted with every foolish mistake we've made. We can learn so much when we take the time to reconcile with God. We confess our sins not because God needs to hear how we have missed the mark but because confession is a process by which we acknowledge our failures and let go of their weight. As we begin the Lenten journey to the Cross and ultimately to the Resurrection, we remember that while we may have missed opportunities in the past, the road ahead is full of new opportunities to respond faithfully to God.

Gracious God, thank you for the countless opportunities to be made right in you. Renew my spirit at the beginning of this Lenten journey. Let these next forty days be a time to draw closer to you and closer to the fullness of who you created me to be. Amen.

We live in a world where every experience has to be posted online. If you don't show proof to your followers on social media, then it didn't happen. People can become so intent on capturing a moment that they miss being present in it. Everything must be manufactured for public consumption, carefully designed for the approval of others.

The contrast between a life of fasting and prayer and a life that focuses on what's trending is remarkable. Intentionally pursuing spiritual disciplines isn't at all like pursuing the likes and comments of strangers. Instead of being outwardly focused, spiritual disciplines teach us to turn inward toward our own, true self and toward the Spirit of God. Fasting and prayer are genuine attempts at knowing the God who works in us and through us. In a world of fast-paced consumption, the Spirit is a constant in our lives—present with us in times of abundance and in times when a loving word cannot be found anywhere else.

Churches go on corporate fasts. Families and close friends take time away to bond with one another. Even Jesus spent forty days in the wilderness, separate from his ordinary life. It is in this model that we shape the forty days preceding Easter as Lent. During this time, we may forego something or take on a new spiritual practice, all in an effort to shake up our routines. We step away from the rush of life and into the presence of God for the sole purpose of drawing closer to God.

Loving God, help me be honest about my motivations and intentions. I never want to stray from what I truly want—more of you. Help me to draw closer to you and to your love. Amen.

We owe everything to God. Everything we have is because God loves us deeply and has placed good things in our lives. This isn't some kind of plot twist; it's obvious. Yet once we have what we've been seeking, praying, and fasting for, it's easy to forget how much God has worked in our lives.

Today's passage from the book of Deuteronomy brings the instructions to the Israelites following their entrance into the Promised Land. God knows how quickly the Israelites can and will forget that their land was given to them by God. To ensure they remember, they are to dedicate the first and best parts of their harvest to God. With every harvest they pull from the land, this practice will remind them where the land came from and to whom they should give thanks. It is both a symbolic act of gratitude and a reminder of God's faithfulness.

Can you remember the last time you asked God for something incredibly life-changing and received it? What did you do? Did you mark that moment in your life and make an offering for it? We may not celebrate the moment by sharing fresh fruits, vegetables, and grains with God—or maybe we do. We all have gifts we can use to thank God for the way our prayers have been answered. In the days and years ahead, our action also reminds us of what God has done. We will need those reminders when we are faced with challenging circumstances. How glorious it is to have the proof that God heard us before and will hear us again!

Gracious God, thank you for all the times you heard my prayers and answered them. You have been consistent in hearing me and caring for me. As I share the petitions of my heart, know that I offer up my life in sincere gratitude. Amen.

I love my cold-and-stormy-weather gear. How did humans make it through much of history without umbrellas, gloves, and scarves? Since the beginning, we have made clothing to cover our bodies, to protect us from the elements. I love the cozy feeling of being wrapped up in my winter coat with a warm hat on my head. Though I am out in the rain, sleet, or snow, I am covered. Because I have the necessary measures in place, the storm's impact on me will be minimal.

How much more valuable is the cover that God provides for us when we are facing the challenges of living a life for Christ? Psalm 91 outlines the ways God will protect and conceal those who take refuge in God from the harsh conditions of life. This does not mean that Christians won't face obstacles or insurmountable challenges. None of us will escape experiencing pain and sorrow. What it does mean is that because we have found a hiding place in God, we are never alone as we traverse life's difficulties. God's care and compassion will remain constant.

The more comfortable we become seeking peace and refuge in God, the less likely we are to run from our storms—even when we are afraid. In moments of intentional prayer and fasting, we recognize just how blessed we are to have this kind of safety and security. Even more so than a coat and gloves protect us from winter weather, God's protection will see us through any challenge.

God our refuge, thank you for the safety and security that I find in you. When I must face the insurmountable, grant me the peace to remember I do not face it alone. Amen.

First Sunday in Lent

Paul has gone down in history as Christianity's greatest hype-man. There is no denying his ability to rouse even the saddest of spirits. With just a few words, he will have you believing that you *can* do all things through Christ. And there is no person who needs that message more than a Christian who has committed to forty days of fasting, because when you are in the thick of it, you need somebody to remind you that food isn't everything. God is. And closeness to God is attainable when we give up worldly necessities.

Paul knows that there will come a moment in the journey when his readers will become frustrated and overwhelmed by what we did—or didn't do. We will need to be reminded that there is no need for shame or guilt when we call upon God to help us through our trying times. According to the scripture, everyone who calls upon God will be dealt with generously. What a blessing God's generosity is, especially in a season of trading in the physical things we rely on for the One we rely on.

We may think our past mistakes, especially the ones that haunt us, can never be forgiven. But the graciousness and generosity of God invites us into safety as we travel through the wilderness of Lent. We are secure—even from the self-sabotage of overthinking our past.

Powerful God, I am indebted to you for the ways you continue to cover my heart and my mind. Thank you for being generous when I call. As I journey closer with you this Lenten season, I ask that you offer beautiful reminders that my past is just the past and that I walk anew in you. Amen.

Recognizing God

MARCH 10–16, 2025 • DANIEL WOLPERT

SCRIPTURE OVERVIEW: In seminary no one ever spoke about God's one annoying quality: invisibility. Although many would assert that you can "see God" in different aspects of our world, the honest truth is that God is invisible, in every normal sense of that term. Understanding this truth, our passages this week explore how we can recognize the Divine Presence. Abram seeks to recognize God in his life; the psalmist seeks God's instruction; Paul encourages his readers to live lives that show Christ to others; and Jesus proclaims that nothing earthly will stop God from moving. To see God is one of our great desires. As we read and meditate on these passages, may we know God's presence.

QUESTIONS AND SUGGESTIONS FOR REFLECTION

• Read Genesis 15:1-12, 17-18. When confronted with the seemingly impossible, what is your normal response? What helps you to be open to God's infinite providence?

• Read Psalm 27. How does fear affect you? How does your spiritual life help prevent fear from ruling your life?

• Read Philippians 3:17–4:1. Perhaps this passage is challenging for you with its hints of religious conflict and the contrast of heavenly and earthly things. How do we engage parts of the Bible that are hard or foreign to us? How do we relate to Jesus directly through our life of prayer?

• Read Luke 13:31-35. How is God present in your work in the world for justice? What is your prophetic witness?

The Rev. Daniel Wolpert is a spiritual director and Presbyterian pastor. A healer and student of the spiritual life, Dan teaches and leads retreats in the fields of psychology, integrative medicine, and spiritual formation. He is the co-founder and former Executive Director of the Minnesota Institute of Contemplation and Healing (MICAH) and the author of *Creating a Life with God* (Upper Room Books, 2023) and *Looking Inward, Living Outward* (Upper Room Books, 2024).

Although Abram was trying to live a faithful life and follow God's will for him, it seemed he had reached a dead end. He and Sarai were old, far beyond child bearing years, and without offspring there was no legacy to leave, no continuation of this promise. So Abram is confused: What is God doing with him? Is God even paying attention?

This is a familiar situation to many of us today. Life is confusing and complex; things don't go the way we plan or the way we wish. Recognizing how the Spirit might be moving within our confusion or our suffering is hard.

In the Hebrew Bible, coming to God with questions or concerns and bringing God our confusion isn't a bad thing. Sadly, many churches today teach just the opposite: We shouldn't question; we should have faith! How dare we lowly humans ask what God is up to? Yet the figures in the Hebrew Bible do this all the time. Abram is conversing with God much like he might argue with a friend or a colleague: "Hey God, you gave me no kids! What gives?"

Of course many years later Jesus does tell us that we are his friends, and our incarnational faith touts a God who is with us. So Abram isn't concerned about questioning but about seeking a way to recognize what God is doing in his life. And God responds. Although God doesn't yet reveal the mechanics of how the promise will come to pass, the experience of God's reply is powerful enough for Abram to believe in God's action. He has recognized God's presence.

Gracious God, give us a heart that is unafraid to question you, to ask for understanding. And may your replies help us to see you more clearly. Amen.

TUESDAY, MARCH 11 ~ *Read Genesis 15:7-12, 17-18*

What follows Abram's questioning of God is a description of ritual action which strains our modern sensibilities. The sacrificing of animals and Abram's ensuing trance state is certainly not something common to our culture. Yet this scene was not uncommon in ancient faith practice. There is hardly a single book in the Bible in which dreams, trances, and other extreme states of mind brought on by hunger or thirst do not play a role in helping people recognize the Divine.

The history of Christian spiritual practice understands that communication with God happens through both sensory and non-sensory experiences. God's characteristic of invisibility means our regular sensory experience is often inadequate in our search for God. Spiritual practices of all kinds tune our mind and awareness to those aspects of the world that often go unnoticed or are out of sight altogether. And while the modern world frequently derides such unusual experiences, I've heard many people describe unusual events they keep secret for fear of being called crazy. They are far more common than we admit and are indeed means for recognizing God.

As Abram is drawn into his trance state, he hears God in the vision of a flaming torch and smoking pot. And while we might never have such a vivid experience, this story can encourage us to attend deeply to our life of prayer and all the thoughts, feelings, dreams, and insights which come to us as we seek to recognize God.

God, help us to be open to the many ways you speak to us. In silence, in vision, in the midst of our busy lives help us to recognize your presence and your promises. Amen.

One subtitle for this psalm is "Triumphant Song of Confidence," which is fitting. The psalmist is quite confident. Yet part of me wonders if perhaps the psalmist protests too much. Is the writer really unafraid? Or is the psalmist actually terrified, singing aspirationally to gain confidence and bravery? Fear is a common human emotion. Safety can be hard to find. And so it isn't surprising that "fear not" is a frequent biblical instruction; as we encounter God in our spiritual life, we do conquer fear.

Whether for the fear God has assuaged or the fear they still face, the psalmist clearly desires to recognize the work of God in their life. And in the psalm we encounter spiritual teachings detailing what we can do to aid our recognition. The "house of the LORD" is an idea central to the biblical understanding of our relationship with God. The notion of placing ourselves in a space where God lives provides an image of hospitality, of safety, of homecoming. And of course when we come to someone's home, we encounter them! So if we desire to recognize God, what better way than to go to God's house?

But where is this place? Well, as God is everywhere, we can say that the whole of creation is God's house. Yet that isn't necessarily what we experience day to day. Many talk about special or sacred spaces that have a holy feel to them. Sometimes these are church spaces or beautiful spaces in nature. We can also create such spaces. On my office desk I have created a very small altar with an icon, a candle, and a few pictures. Every time I look at this arrangement I pause and turn my attention to the sacred: I recognize my presence in God's house. Doing so helps drive out fear and helps my spiritual confidence to flourish.

God who drives out fear, help us dwell with you. In doing so, may we know that you shelter us and protect us. Amen.

The desire of our heart is to recognize and see God. As in the first few verses of the psalm, here in the last section we find another instruction regarding our spiritual life: Recognizing God requires that we listen to God's teaching. We hear the psalmist's plea to be taught and led.

For decades, literally, I struggled to find a good answer to the great American question, "What do you do for work?" Although I've had many jobs and am part of several professions, the standard answer to this question—naming your job—never sat well with me. Finally it came to me that my vocation is being a "student of the spiritual life." I am always listening for God's teaching, and I recognize how much I have to learn and how far down that path I still can go.

While the term "life-long learner" has gained in usage, far too many of us cease active learning once we are done with formal school. Yet humility—the first step of the spiritual life—calls us to recognize how little we know when faced with the vast nature of God's mind. The desire to be taught is central to the biblical wisdom tradition. The wise person isn't one who has learned everything, but rather is one who is still God's student.

Recognizing God in our lives arises out of our walk down the spiritual path, our walk with Jesus our teacher. As we commit to the spiritual life, we enter the land of the living, and we indeed see the face of God.

Gracious God, give me the heart of a student, of one ready to be taught. As I learn from you, may I see your face and recognize your presence. Amen.

Dualism, the creation of pairs of opposites, is common not only in the Bible but also in our daily experience of reality: good/bad, right/wrong, best/worst. Dualisms are an extension of the basic dualism that our mind creates when it develops the experience of the separate self: our experience of "I" and "other." This ego process is always dividing reality into things that we like and things we dislike. And this process disrupts the basic unity of the universe.

We need dualisms to engage in the world. The separation of self is an essential developmental milestone. If I didn't know the difference between my hands and my keyboard, I couldn't type these meditations. The problem with these divisions is that they can cause immense suffering as we relegate people and nature, into categories of "good" and "bad," "saved" and "unsaved," and on and on. What starts as a helpful tool soon becomes the vehicle for oppression.

In the letter to the Philippians we see Paul using the dualism of "earth" and "heaven" to try to teach the new followers of Christ how to live in the world. Because these dualisms aren't fundamentally real but rather are a product of the human experience, we should be able to let go of them when they are no longer helpful. In our modern era, with a cosmology that is far different than Paul's, distinctions such as heaven being good and earth being bad have lost value for many. However, the basic teaching to follow a life-giving path remains central to our faith and to the spiritual life. Rather than worrying too much about what others are doing, our life of prayer calls us to focus on our life and experience: Are we living the way Jesus calls us to live?

God, lead us beyond dualisms to your unifying vision for reality. Help us to follow the example Jesus sets for us, to live in the world with love and care. Amen.

This short passage, coming as Jesus slowly wends his way toward Jerusalem, begins with the ominous warning: "Herod wants to kill you." It's scary when the local ruler wants you dead, and the person in this position has been trying to kill Jesus since he was born. The Herod we read about in today's passage is the son of Herod the Great, the Herod who recruited the wise men as spies attempting to find the location of the baby Jesus.

This Herod is out to get Jesus not because Herod is an atheist, or a pagan, or somehow anti-God. Rather he is out to get Jesus because God is a threat to the unjust rulers of the world. In this passage we see clearly a theme that is part of the biblical tradition since First Samuel: God is very concerned about the injustice that rulers will enact upon the people in their bid for power. In the biblical world, the only just ruler is God, and of course, earthly rulers don't like anyone above them.

Sadly, the spiritual life is often portrayed as a single, individual affair: me and my spiritual life. Yet nothing could be further from the truth. God is interested in the redemption of the entire world. God is interested in the kingdom of God on earth—the beloved community where there is no more war and where the lion and the lamb lie down together.

The individualistic view has led to the variety of prosperity gospels that populate our faith communities: God is present if we are rich. I've never heard a proponent of these distortions of Christianity say that a sign of God's presence is that the local ruler wishes to kill you! Yet indeed, that is a sign of God's presence; that one is on fire for justice such that the powers of the world feel threatened.

God of light and wisdom, help us to recognize you in the struggles for justice. Amen.

SECOND SUNDAY IN LENT

Jesus now invokes the prophetic tradition and identifies himself and his work with this lineage. Yet what is a prophet? This word has often come to mean someone who tells the future, yet this understanding is not at the heart of biblical prophecy. The prophet is someone who reads the present with great clarity and insight and is able to speak the truth regarding how society is no longer following God. The prophet is seeking to correct the king's behavior—always a very risky job.

If the prophet discusses the future, it is always in reference to the failings of the present. The future is simply an unfolding of the present. This is the basic cause and effect of our life as creatures. We exist within God's creation and when we ignore God's desires for love and justice, we will suffer the consequences. Looking at history we can see this cause and effect playing out again and again.

Waking up to the reality of the present moment is therefore the core component of the spiritual life. We must awaken to our individual and collective roles in turning toward or away from God. Yet prophets are regularly killed because we don't want to hear what they have to say. We wish to stay asleep.

Prophets can also be a voice in our own head. How many times have we said, "I knew the right thing to do, but I didn't do it." Ignoring our inner wisdom kills our own prophetic voice. Groups and social systems do this all the time. "We don't do it that way" is perhaps the most prophet-killing phrase in history. And Jesus laments. Throughout this Lenten journey, may we dedicate our lives to hearing and following God's prophets into the kingdom.

God, show yourself to us. Help us to see you in all that we do and all that we are. Amen.

Seek the Lord

MARCH 17–23, 2025 • OSHETA MOORE

SCRIPTURE OVERVIEW: The passages this week are invitations to know God in our most vulnerable moments. In Isaiah we're invited to come to God with all our needs—thirst and hunger. In the psalm the psalmist makes room for our wondering and our wandering and invites us to seek God, the source of our confidence and care. Paul's message reminds us to practice humility, lest our boldness lead to self-righteousness. And Jesus' parable in the Gospel of Luke calls us not to give up on doing the work of living a life of faith. These invitations honor the questions many of us have around our faith—how does God respond to our real life experiences of need, confusion, and being overwhelmed? The invitations from the scriptures give us an embodied hope in our spiritual formation: God desires for us to tend to our bodies, to pay attention when we are overwhelmed. An embodied faith is a flourishing faith.

QUESTIONS AND SUGGESTIONS FOR REFLECTION

• Read Isaiah 55:1-9. How is your soul thirsting for God this season? How can you create time and space to seek God?

• Read Psalm 63:1-8. What is your first memory of experiencing God's love? How can you pay special attention to God's presence as you fall asleep tonight?

• Read 1 Corinthians 10:1-13. How can you embrace the good work of humility in your relationships today?

• Read Luke 13:1-9. For what do you need to repent?

The Rev. Osheta Moore is a spiritual director and Moravian pastor in Saint Paul, MN. Osheta is the author of *Shalom Sistas: Living Wholeheartedly in a Brokenhearted World* (Herald Press, 2017) and *Dear White Peacemakers: Dismantling Racism with Grit and Grace* (Herald Press, 2021).

When I was a camp counselor, we were told three things. One: Day three is when homesickness is at its worst, so plan fun things for your campers accordingly. Two: The cabins that don't clean up their tables at mealtime will be punished by the kitchen staff withholding the good desserts. And three: Whenever campers say they don't feel well, ask them first, "Have you had water today"? Seven times out of ten, it's thirst: They are dehydrated and need water. My job as a counselor was to remind them and lead them to the abundant water fountains on campus.

Isaiah 55:1-5 is a passage that invites us to partake in the abundant and satisfying grace of God. The prophet Isaiah calls out with urgency, imploring all who are thirsty and in need to come to the waters. This invitation extends beyond mere physical thirst; it addresses the deep spiritual yearning within each soul. Isaiah is much like the wise camp counselor asking, "Have you had water today? Do you know that you are thirsty?"

The metaphor of water is powerful and resonant throughout the Bible, symbolizing life, cleansing, and renewal. In this context, it represents the free and unmerited grace that God offers to all. The prophet emphasizes that one can come and drink without money and without cost. God's grace is not transactional; it is a gift freely given to those who recognize their need.

Sometimes, like my campers with sugary drinks, we try to satisfy our thirst with things that contribute to our dehydration: praise from others, leaning into our own wisdom, and controlling situations around us. But what if we instead choose to be satisfied by scripture, Christian community, and times of quiet in the presence of God? This is the water that really quenches our thirst. These are means of grace that satisfy our souls.

God, I will heed the invitation to come and drink from the wells of your grace. Amen.

M y friend has a gift that I sometimes envy. She can walk into an antique shop, slowly peruse the aisles, patiently consider piece after piece and always leave with a treasure. She has a gift for seeking beauty in ancient things and creating a purpose for those things in her life right now.

Isaiah 55:6-9 provides an invitation of hope and encouragement to seek ancient beauty for our lives right now. The prophet urges us to "seek the LORD while he may be found; call upon him while he is near." This requires intention, patience, and vision. Oftentimes we feel disconnected from God not because we don't want to know God, but because we're not paying attention. We're not looking for God in the midst of our day-to-day lives. However, God shows up in surprising ways, ways we would have overlooked like a lamp pushed to the back of the shelf. But this light is exactly what we need to have clarity and peace in moments of hardship.

Our instinctive human response may be to rely on our own understanding or to seek solutions that make sense to us. But God desires for us to know God's care-giving love, to trust and believe that God's ways are for our good.

When faced with adversity, seeking God becomes an intentional choice to align our hearts with God's. It is also an act of humility, recognizing that our understanding is limited, that we need the guidance of the One who holds the bigger picture. The promise that God is near resonates with the assurance that even in the darkest moments, God's presence is a source of comfort and strength.

God, help us navigate the uncertainties of life by seeking you persistently. May we find solace, direction, and refuge in your unwavering love. Amen.

In my work as a spiritual director, I offer a loving space for people to process their faith. For some who have been Christians for a while, there sometimes is an admission that God is no longer an active presence in their lives. It's in these moments that I ask them to take me back to when they first fell in love with Jesus and to tap into those memories of God's presence. Where did they first behold the power of God's love and glorious care for them?

Psalm 63 is an honest expression of deep longing for God's presence and a recognition of the soul's need for communion with God. The psalmist, believed to be David, declares, "O God, you are my God; I seek you; my soul thirsts for you." These words resonate with a heartfelt yearning for a tangible experience of God's nearness, a yearning many of us feel.

Amidst this yearning, the psalmist recalls moments of encountering God. He remembers sweet moments in God's presence and the awe he felt when he was younger. This is my hope when I ask a directee to remember, for this act of remembrance is more than nostalgic reflection. It is a deliberate choice to draw strength from past encounters with the Almighty.

In times of spiritual dryness, we can cling to the memory of God's steadfast love and deliverance. Remembrance is a powerful spiritual discipline, reminding us that our God is not distant or indifferent but actively involved in our lives. The God who showed up for us in the past is the same God who sustains us in the present and will continue to do so in the future.

Lord, help us cultivate a habit of remembrance in our spiritual journey. May it be a wellspring of hope, a testament to your faithfulness, and an anchor for our souls in the midst of life's challenges. Amen.

Psalm 63 captures the essence of a soul anchored in God. The psalmist declares, "My soul is satisfied . . . when I think of you on my bed and meditate on you in the watches of the night, for you have been my help, and in the shadow of your wings I sing for joy." These verses are a deliberate and reflective engagement with God's presence.

Every evening when I lay my head down, I try to go back through the day remembering how I experienced God's presence, looking for missed opportunities to reflect God's love, and praying for the upcoming day. In these quiet moments of the night, I turn my thoughts toward God, initiating a profound form of spiritual reflection. Dedicating the last five to ten minutes of my day, when I am falling asleep to rest in God's presence, helps me keep up with a rhythm of reflection. This spiritual practice is called the Daily Examen, from Ignatius of Loyola in his book *Spiritual Exercises*.

Psalm 63 invites us to consider our actions and responses in the light of God's truth. The Daily Examen encourages a similar reflective posture, inviting us to discern moments of gratitude, moments of struggle, and areas where growth and transformation are needed. When this is a regular practice, God seems closer and more mindful of me. Love grows in this intimacy.

The assurance of being under the shadow of God's wings inspires a sense of security and trust. This imagery reinforces the idea that our daily reflection is not a solitary journey but a partnership with God. As we engage in this practice, we find solace and joy in the shelter of God's presence, fostering a deepened awareness of God's abiding love.

Tonight, consider practicing the Examen under the shadow of God's wings.

My husband and I pastor alongside one another. After twenty years of marriage and ministry together I trust his commitment to the Lord, but I have moments where I am so full of self-righteousness and a desire to be right that I can speak and act toward him in unloving, unchristlike ways.

The apostle Paul reflects on the Israelites' journey through the wilderness. As I read this passage, a crucial lesson emerged for me. Amidst the recounting of God's provision and guidance Paul offers: "If you think you are standing, watch out that you do not fall." Despite witnessing miraculous events and partaking in divine provisions, the Israelites trusted in their own strength and righteousness. They sought life and worth apart from God. Paul uses their example to emphasize the dangers of spiritual pride. The backdrop of the Israelites' experiences serves as a sobering reminder to Paul's readers against self-righteousness.

Paul urges believers not to become overconfident in their own abilities or spiritual standing since we too are susceptible to the same pitfalls that ensnared the Israelites. We need humility—to recognize our dependence on God and acknowledge our vulnerability to temptation. The subtle trap of self-righteousness can cause us to ignore our need for God's grace. Humility is a protective shield in our relationships with God and others.

As a practice of humility, I go back to my husband, ask for forgiveness, and commit to repair. And with grace, we commit to living in humility and hope with one another. With whom is God calling you to live in a righteous relationship today? With whom do you need to choose humility and ask for forgiveness for any self-righteousness?

O Lord, may we cultivate a spirit of humility in our walk with you and others. Examine our hearts, show us any self-righteousness, and remind us of our need for grace. Amen.

As followers of Jesus, we want our lives to reflect his sacrificial love and draw people in to know him. However, we are human. We sin. We cause rifts in relationships. Take care, beloved. All is not lost.

In 1 Corinthians 10:13, the apostle Paul provides a reassuring promise: "No testing has overtaken you that is not common to everyone. God is faithful, and he will not let you be tested beyond your strength, but with the testing he will also provide the way out so that you may be able to endure it." This verse unfolds like a beacon of hope for those of us trying to live holy lives that please God. God's faithfulness endures, and as God's children we have God's unwavering support. The assurance that no temptation is beyond our ability to withstand is a testament to the empowering grace of God.

God is not a distant observer but a loving parent intimately involved in our lives. In times of temptation or adversity, God doesn't merely watch from afar; rather, God actively provides a path for us to navigate through the challenges. The imagery here is that of a loving coach, ensuring that we are not overwhelmed but equipped to endure.

As I walk this path of faithfulness, I take comfort in the realization that God is not a distant deity but a companion along the path of life. God cheers us on in the face of trials, offering us grace that is sufficient. This truth transforms our perspective on challenges, turning them into opportunities for God to showcase faithfulness in our lives.

God, in moments of struggle, help me remember that you are with me and for me. Remind me of the depth of your reconciling love. Empower me to overcome not in my strength alone but through your presence. Amen.

THIRD SUNDAY IN LENT

Jesus tells the story of a man who planted a fig tree in his vineyard but found it without fruit for three years. Frustrated, he decides to cut it down, but the gardener pleads for one more year, promising to cultivate and fertilize it.

We all experience times of feeling unsure about our spiritual formation. We experience a disconnection, a deep sense of loss, or, one might even say, the death of our spiritual connection with God. This parable comes alongside us with this guidance: Don't give up. Repent and change. Remember God's faithfulness.

When I have sessions with directees, I find that we often circle around these cautions. I invite them to consider using the time we have to tend to their root systems so that they can bear good fruit. I remind them that we have a good gardener who tends to us and cares for us.

As the gardener intercedes on behalf of the fig tree, Christ is our compassionate mediator. His plea for one more year should give us hope—we're not alone in this work of growing and bearing fruit. The added promise to cultivate and fertilize signifies God's continuous work in our lives, providing opportunities for growth and transformation.

If you're feeling cut off from God, not seeing any fruitfulness in your spiritual life, consider the guidance from this passage. Devote time to praying for wisdom and energy to continue, praying for forgiveness and strength to make changes, or praying for the Spirit to remind you of God's love for you. Then offer a prayer of praise. Tend to the root system of your spiritual life so that you can in due time bear fruit.

Loving God, we respond to your relentless, loving, patient call. Show us where our root systems need care and give us the path toward healing. May we bear fruit that draws others to you. Amen.

Abundant Grace

MARCH 24–30, 2025 • HERB MATHER

SCRIPTURE OVERVIEW: Lent is a time for focusing on our need for God and remembering God's abundant resources for filling that need. When the Israelites finally pass into Canaan, they observe the Passover as a reminder of God's deliverance of them from Egypt. The psalmist, traditionally David, rejoices in the fact that God does not count his sins against him. Paul declares that through Christ, God has made everything new. God no longer holds our sins against us, and we in turn appeal to others to accept this free gift. Jesus eats with sinners and tells the story of the prodigal son to demonstrate that no matter how far we stray, God will always welcome us home with open arms. God never stops pursuing us, even if we feel unloved or unworthy.

QUESTIONS AND SUGGESTIONS FOR REFLECTION

- Read Joshua 5:9-12. What stories do you tell about your faith? What do these stories help you remember?
- Read Psalm 32. When have you hidden from God? When has God been your hiding place?
- Read 2 Corinthians 5:16-21. How does your life display for others that life in Christ eliminates worldly identity labels?
- Read Luke 15:1-3, 11b-32. Do you identify with the prodigal son, the elder son, or the father in the parable? Are you ready to rejoin God's household on God's terms? Are you ready to welcome everyone home?

The Rev. Herb Mather is a pastor, denominational staff person, farm kid from Minnesota, and, in retirement, a volunteer with The Malawi United Methodist Church.

The youth traveled overnight to begin a weeklong trek in the Appalachian Mountains. Their first day on a trail was short, but the afternoon temperatures were warm for that two-mile slog up the mountainside. The burden of wearing forty-pound backpacks made their muscles complain. The youth groaned.

The psalmist uses similar language describing the weight on a sinner's conscience. Heaviness and shame make us groan when we have hurt someone or broken a promise. Greed or envy often slyly override our sense of decency and justice. Simply put, we've done stuff we should not have done and neglected to do what we should have done. When we ignore these transgressions, we feel the weight in our bodies.

This psalm doesn't focus on the pain of those who are sinned against but on the misery of the sinner. Sin and guilt are heavy burdens to carry around. Guilt can't be rationalized away. Excuses or weak alibis don't stand up in a heavenly court. Nor does it help to shrug our shoulders and say, "Oh, well, I am only human." Burdens are not eased by evasions. Our bones groan.

It is not our Christian duty to grovel before God or to revel in our misery, as boasting about our sins can be a way to resist making changes. Instead, acknowledging and owning our sinfulness frees us to accept God's gift of forgiveness. It is the first step in being reconciled with God. Healing a relationship with the sinned-against lifts the burden. God forgives us, lifts the burden, and provides guidance. The groaning is replaced by an invitation to God's joy.

Hiding from God weighs heavy on us. Walking with God is freeing. God invites us sinners to join with one another to sing out in joy!

Merciful God, we confess that we have messed up in the past. Forgive us. Guide us. Thank you for lifting the weight from us and inviting us to sing in joy. Amen.

Verses 8-9 of this psalm are written as a direct address from God to the reader or hearer. The phrase "with my eye upon you" evokes in me images of a Santa-like god who sees all and expects obedience to the rules. With what tone of voice do we hear these words? Verse 9, however, undercuts this connotation in its advice: Don't be like a horse or a mule who does not understand the rules but only obeys because they are forced to. These verses are not a threat. They are an invitation not just to follow God's law but to understand the reasons for the law and live in the law with love.

As a boy my first job away from home was cultivating corn with a horse-drawn cultivator in the days before herbicides. The corn had to be plowed three times each season until it was tall enough to shade the weeds and grasses that wanted to take water and nutrients from the young plants. Most of the day the horses dutifully plodded along. But when we turned around at the far end of the field to head back toward the barn at about 11:45 each morning, their calm demeanor changed. They sensed it was lunch time and strained to rush for a rest. No more plodding. I would tug on the reins as hard as I could to keep them from racing. They rebelled against the reins and bits. They did not want to obey my rules.

Rules and laws govern much of life. We naturally want to rebel. The psalmist proclaims an alternative. God wants us to be guided by an inner spirit that frees instead of rules. Jesus echoed this psalm when he proclaimed, "You have heard it said . . . but I say to you . . ." (Matt. 5:21-48). The root rather than the reins give freedom. Yes, there are rules, but God's love within us energizes and frees. We are invited to trade the reins for the peace of Christ flowing within us.

Enter our hearts, O God, that we may find the freedom to sing for joy. Amen.

Years ago while hiking above the tree line in the Rocky Mountains of Colorado I faced an unanticipated challenge. I had hiked on the Appalachian Trail where tree blazes mark the route. Now the trail indicators were cairns, stacked piles of stones. But stones appeared everywhere. Were those rocks accidentally in that pile or were they placed to show the trail? No other cairns were in sight. I was unsure of which direction to go.

By the fifth chapter of Joshua, the children and grandchildren of the Israelites who had fled Egypt have arrived in the Promised Land. They have crossed the Jordan and set up camp. There are no more pillars of fire by night or clouds by day. Now what? Before plunging ahead, they pause and reflect on their history—of their ancestors' escape from slavery in Egypt and wandering in the wilderness. They do not deny shameful times—creating a golden calf or complaining about their food and the weariness of their journey. They also remember the guidance and providence of God that came in the pillars and the manna. They feel the assurance that God will be with them in their new circumstances.

We find ourselves facing new quandaries on our life journeys. Some changes are those we have longed for, but even wonderful opportunities bring both excitement and fear. What do we do when faced with new situations? The Israelites remembered. On that Colorado mountain, I remembered that a topographical map and a compass were in my backpack. As I plunged ahead on the trail, a hummingbird came to drink water from the sloshing canteen on my backpack. It was as if the Holy Spirit were saying, "I will be with you." It was a wonderful hike.

Loving and forgiving God, may we remember and celebrate your faithfulness during our life's journey. In confidence, we move ahead. Amen.

The manna stopped! The Israelites saw no more of the mysterious white substance that fed them during their wilderness trek. After crossing the Jordan, they produced food from the land God had promised. This must have been a big change from the ways of the past forty years—those entering the promised land had never eaten anything but manna. Imagine growing up eating only mid-western food with little spiciness and suddenly finding only very hot five-star Thai cuisine available. The end of the manna means an entirely new diet, but it is symbolic of much more. No more manna symbolized the life-altering shift into the Promised Land.

The Israelites didn't give up manna for forty days, but forever. Many enter Lent with a commitment to give up something or to engage in a new discipline. These are six-week commitments to change from the regular routine. Such disciplines are helpful as training for when we face unknown and difficult changes ahead. But do we take on these practices during Lent only as a temporary shift, or do we use the forty days of Lent to reshape our existence, to start permanent transformational changes that will allow our lives to be better shaped into the image of God?

We will always face change. Indeed, the story of scripture is the story of change, from Adam and Eve leaving the garden to the "new heaven and new earth" described in Revelation. God keeps doing new things. We rarely notice incremental changes in life. But radical changes are both difficult and inspiring. The Israelites likely anticipated the end of the manna as they planted, plowed, and cultivated the seeds that would grow into crops. They took on new practices that shaped them for the new things God was doing in their lives. Our spiritual practices can do the same for us today.

We thank you, O God, for practices that bring us closer to you as we meet the challenges we face in life. Amen.

Juanita had just returned from a department store and was obviously steaming when she stormed into my office. "How can a woman six feet tall be invisible?" she asked. Clerks had assisted other customers but seemed unable to see her. Other customers were White. Juanita was Black.

A planning committee met to select workshop leaders for a denominational training event. Each presenter recommended by the committee was a white male until one participant called this to the group's attention. Even (perhaps especially) in church we fail to include folks who are not just like us.

Paul has a history of urging the Corinthian church to stop looking at others through the cultural norms, the human standards. In a previous letter (see 1 Cor. 11:17-34) he scolded them for leaving out those in their congregation who were poor. Their celebration of the Lord's Supper included a full meal, not only bread and wine. Those who worked longer days got leftovers. It was likely not intentional. They probably never thought about it. The church leaders didn't consider an alternative to human standards.

In Paul's time, Jews were often overlooked by Greeks, those enslaved were overlooked by the free, females overlooked by males. Who are overlooked in our communities today, and why? Is it because of their economic worth, their color of skin, sexual identity, nation of birth? We are called to acknowledge what the world overlooks, to regard others as God does.

Let us perceive those the world ignores. Listening to others, especially those different from us, is a step toward reconciliation. It takes a conscious effort to live by God's standards instead of the world's standards. All are invited. No exceptions!

Reconciling God, open our eyes and hearts to those who are invisible from a worldly point of view so all may join in the foretaste of your heavenly banquet. Amen.

People grumble. They grumble about political decisions. Pastors often hear grumbling about hymns chosen for the church service. Some pastors even grumble about their congregation.

Our daughter, Linda, came in from the yard one winter day. "My snow fort fell down," she grumbled, visibly upset. My wife's immediate temptation was to tell Linda that she could go back out and build another one. Then she remembered advice that it is more helpful to respond to feelings than to give rational advice. Lillian paused and said, "That really makes you mad, doesn't it?" Linda took a deep breath, shrugged her shoulders and said, "I guess I will have to go out and build it again." With that, she headed back out to the yard and rebuilt her fort.

Jesus heard a lot of grumbling, much of it directed at him. He did not respond to grumbling with arguments. He told stories. We call them parables. In the beginning of the fifteenth chapter of Luke, Jesus hears the grumbling of the Pharisees about whom he spends time with. Instead of arguing, he tells a story.

The story of the prodigal son could be called the story of the grumbling son. The younger son is unsatisfied with his life at home. But after leaving, he is unsatisfied with his life away. Fortunately, he understands how his own actions and discontent have led him to his current situation. He seeks to remedy it through contrition and a shift to an attitude of gratitude instead of grumbling.

We wander and grumble. God looks for us, not to condemn us but to welcome us back into the fold. God's welcome mat is always out. We are invited to put the welcome mat out for others who may have wandered, to remind them of God's unending love and open arms.

Loving God, thank you for those times you have sought us when we wandered. Open us to invite others to experience your love. Amen.

Fourth Sunday in Lent

Often when exploring this parable, emphasis is placed on the lesson(s) learned by the younger son about the unending love of the father. Some interpretations focus on the actions of the father. Few, however, emphasize the perspective of the older son. If we were not to learn something from his experience, why would he have been included in the story? At different times in our lives, one emphasis may seem more relevant than another.

Today let's look at the parable from the viewpoint of the older brother. He didn't know his younger brother had come home until he came in from the field and heard a party going on. Why hadn't he learned about the party from his father? Many of us can resonate with the older son. It is no fun to be overlooked, and when we are, it's easy to grumble and refuse to participate in the celebration.

In high school I was the starting tackle on the football team until three practice sessions before the first game. A new guy showed up, and I was relegated to second string. I was not pleased.

When we are overlooked it's natural to feel upset, especially when someone else seems to get a benefit we feel we deserve. We remember our efforts and ignore our blessings. Our hurt at being overlooked presents us with a choice: We can turn away and grumble about what we have lost, or we can celebrate what we still have. Lent is a good time to take stock and remember God's grace in our joys as well as in our disappointments. Fortunately our team went undefeated that year and I played in the second half of most games. It was a lot of fun to be part of a team that celebrated victory. It was wonderful to attend the party.

God, sit with us in our hurt over what we have lost, and encourage us not to miss out on the celebration that remains. Amen.

Contradictions

MARCH 31–APRIL 6, 2025 • KEEGAN OSINSKI

SCRIPTURE OVERVIEW: All four of this week's scripture readings invite us to consider the holy practice of acceptance. Both the psalm and the passage from the prophet Isaiah express in verse the reality of trials and pain as well as the deliverance that comes from the Lord. The abundance of pain and the abundance of joy require equal measures of courage to face. Likewise, the Gospel passage from John has us take seriously the needs of those actually in front of us and give of our precious attention and care. Finally, in the epistle to the Philippians, the apostle Paul encourages us to give up, saying that letting go will often bring us closer to God than our desperate grasping for rightness or status. The life of Christ is one that faces pain and hardship seriously, receives blessing openly, and cares for others generously.

QUESTIONS AND SUGGESTIONS FOR REFLECTION

- Read Isaiah 43:16-21. How do you respond to this God who insists on doing new things for the sake of the people?
- Read Psalm 126. Pray this psalm three times: (1) pray all the verbs in the past tense in thanksgiving; (2) pray all the verbs in the future tense as a prayer for help; (3) pray verses 1-3 in the past tense, verses 5-6 in the future tense. Which was hardest to pray?
- Read Philippians 3:4b-14. What props or credentials do you need to let go of?
- Read John 12:1-8. What motivations does your discipleship reflect?

Keegan is the librarian for theology and ethics at Vanderbilt University in Nashville, TN. Keegan is a member of the Church of the Nazarene.

Not all pain is meaningful, but all pain is redeemable. The pain we experience eventually appears hand-in-hand with joy. They are not strangers. They are not enemies. They are twins, born from the same womb of the universe in which God is making all things new. Great and lovely things are going to happen, just as the weeping and the tears have happened (and, of course, will happen again).

We might think of our joys, our restoration of fortunes, as a reprieve or a reward for weathering our storms, but in truth we are always tossed between them, always holding both our seeds of tears and our sheaves of joy in either hand. They are not dependent on one another or meted out in even balance. They simply are. Our work is to see them for what they are, to carry them lightly, to consider them with curiosity and gratitude, and to pray for the peace of our own hearts through it all.

Theologian Frederick Buechner once described the impartiality and wonder of grace as God saying to us, "Here is the world. Beautiful and terrible things will happen. Don't be afraid." The acknowledgment of fear and the exhortation not to be afraid should not be overlooked. Abiding in both pain and joy requires a certain measure of bravery. We must persist with the difficulties of life, but we must also be faithful to receive and enjoy the beauty that comes our way. Allowing ourselves to lean into bliss can be a challenge that is just as demanding as withstanding our sorrows. Lucky for us, our lives afford us all plenty of practice doing both.

Identify something you've sown in tears and something you've reaped with shouts of joy.

A path in the sea does not calm the waters. A way in the wilderness does not tame the beasts. Rivers appear in the desert, but the desert does not end. You may still be burnt, if not parched. You may still continue to trudge through the sand, though you've been gifted a full canteen. The promise is not, and never has been, a removal from or a removal of suffering. Suffering in its many unjust and excruciating forms continues always and ever. Instead, there is promise of a new thing.

The prophet Isaiah heralds the new ways of care and succor God provides to God's people. This is the difference between restoration and transformation, between reanimation and resurrection: the mangled and broken things are not stitched back together, functional but wonky, damaged goods now passable. They are completely supplanted by God's new thing, which refreshes and renews from the roots. An entirely new river, powerful and alive, appears where there was nothing but dry weeds and earth.

Yet all these new things occur in the same place. Your life is always happening *in* your life, and difficulties may take the shape of the vessel in which they are borne. Likewise, then, the way that God makes is *in* the sea, *in* the wilderness. The path is in the mighty waters, and the river is in the desert. Your deliverance may not be a removal from a troubling context or a change in a challenging circumstance. The new thing, the redemption, may find you in the midst. It may even be within your own heart.

What might it mean for you to see a way when you're still in the wilderness or find a river when you're in the desert?

Theories are well and good and deserve our attention, but they should never obscure the flesh and blood of human beings in front of us. The "other" stands before us and demands a real response. And as Christians pursuing holiness, we endeavor for that response always to be love. Interpersonal encounters can be fleeting, yet every person we come into contact with deserves the outpouring of our care and attention, perhaps even to the point of excess. Unlike money or perfume, love is an unlimited renewable resource.

Jesus tells Judas, "You always have the poor with you," framing "the poor" as this broad generalization, this abstracted category. "But," he says, "you do not always have me." Jesus is here and now. Mary's gift, prodigal though it may be, is concrete, material, just like Jesus. And she is praised for this appropriately sensuous offering. Care and attention to the reality of things, as they currently and actually are, is always preferable to considerations of potentialities or ethereal utopian dreams.

The trick is that real life demands nuance, problem solving, and energy. A close reading of a text always requires more work than skimming. Tending to the needs of our tangible reality is costly. But this is why we are here. Mary's expensive perfume was purchased precisely to be poured over Jesus at his burial. Our attention is meant to be spent on those people who are intimately present to us. Indeed, these people may (and should!) include those counted among "the poor," but as liberation theologian Gustavo Gutiérrez challenges us, "You say you love the poor. Then tell me, what are their names?" Our care for anyone is only real inasmuch as that person is real flesh and blood.

Who is the real-life person in front of you that needs your attention and care today? It might even be you.

For the apostle Paul in this passage, losing everything was how he gained righteousness. He achieved perfection by letting go, by giving up. Everything he has gained, he lets go of to grasp the gift of life given to him by Christ. He talks about pressing on toward a goal, yet all his accolades and accomplishments, his excellent upbringing and character, are somehow not relevant at all. The goals and gains of the life of Christ are above and beyond these achievements for Paul. They are of an entirely different kind and require an entirely different way of pressing forward.

I wonder if the key to success here may be to stop trying. In tennis, players and coaches often talk about the dangers of overthinking and the importance of simply allowing your body to know what it needs to do. After practicing a movement enough times, thinking about it too much can actually impede it. A certain amount of letting go is required of a skillful player.

Perhaps Paul would encourage us to stop forcing, grasping, shoehorning our way into righteousness and perfection, to stop staking a claim to holiness based on our works or theological pedigree. Indeed, Paul tries to become like Christ even in his death—the ultimate giving up. So instead of scheming or striving, what would it look like to permit ourselves to loosen up, breathe deeply, and allow the muscle memory of our spiritual practices to move us into closer communion with God?

How does it feel to let go and receive perfection rather than grasp and struggle for it?

Have you ever watched a pet dog or cat snooze on the couch? Periodically, the animal will haul herself up to her feet, clicky-clack or pitter-pat to the next room over, settle into that room's respective comfy chair, and resume her nap. Sometimes she will just stand up, turn around 360 degrees, and then plop right back down in the same position and go back to sleep. What drives this behavior? What compels them to make such seemingly superfluous movements? Animals have this kind of pure will, this impulse to do what is needed in the moment without consideration for larger meaning. And while, sure, our higher level of consciousness usually requires something more of us than unbridled subservience to our id, there may indeed be something to learn from the impulsive actions of our non-human neighbors.

The prophet Isaiah says that the wild animals will honor God because God gives water in the wilderness. God provides the water, the animals drink it, and thereby God is honored. Sometimes it's really that simple. Can we respond as graciously to the simple impulses and desires that make themselves known in the course of our daily lives?

Receiving the gifts of providence that are bestowed on us is itself a practice. Receptivity is its own kind of art. Acceptance, gratitude, and moving with grace toward the next right thing—without anxiety or questioning or being overwhelmed—is not easy. But our animal friends do it so well.

We must open ourselves to the quiet needs of the moment. We must, like Isaiah's jackal and ostrich, drink the water God gives in the wilderness. We can accept the provisions prepared for us without question and without struggle.

What is the next right thing God has given you to do, and how can you move toward it in gratitude and grace?

This passage contains maybe one of the most useful but most underused commands of Jesus in the entire New Testament: "Leave her alone."

Judas Iscariot appears concerned about Mary's use of her own gifts for their purpose, but he surely should be worrying about the state of his own house.

There is, I think, holiness to be found in the skill of minding our own business. Accepting what is ours to accept and completing what is ours to complete without worry or judgment of others' affairs can be as freeing to our minds as it is edifying to our spiritual lives. This faithful attending to what God has given us requires our full attention and allows us the freedom of a singular focus, without distraction or anxiety about the work of others. Fretting over another's tasks or progress can do nothing but inhibit our own steady work.

This does not mean we cease to interact or engage with others around us. Our work, by design, requires connection to share God's love with others. We don't leave our neighbors to fend for themselves or ignore the needs we could meet. And we don't cease to hold them accountable to their commitments and calling. But there is a difference between relationship and meddling.

Instead of fussing over others' lives, especially when our attention is unnecessary and distracts us from our own work, we can simply leave them alone. We trust God to work in others' lives just as God works in ours. How that happens is ultimately none of our business. Releasing our concern for things that do not concern us gives us space to better assess our own needs and demands.

Whose work do you pay too much attention to? What has your attention that you need to leave alone?

FIFTH SUNDAY IN LENT

More often than not, acceptance and receptivity are active practices. To receive joy requires more work than, say, opening up the mailbox to see if anything good has arrived. It requires tending.

This is why the author of the psalm invokes agricultural imagery to talk about the cycles and patterns of sorrow and joy. Not only do we feel the physical labor of toiling through our emotional pain but we also have to consciously collect our joy, lest it rot on the vine or go to seed. We deserve more than simply acknowledging the appearance of joy—but that means we must dig it up. We must carry it home.

Mindfulness practices guide us in finding joy in the little things. We journal our gratitude and write thank-you notes to actively appreciate the gifts we received. We share our happinesses—great and small—with friends and family on social media. We celebrate anniversaries and remembrances with rituals, candles, and gifts. We pause at the end of the day and identify the moments of joy we have experienced since waking. The small practices we incorporate into our lives give us space to tend the joy.

These practices must be ongoing. When we cease to attend to the work of tending joy, our joy seeps through the cracks of our soul and no longer feeds us. And hoarding our joy, trying to pack our storehouses for a long winter or a famine or drought, is a futile effort. Joy doesn't keep, just as the harvest in the field or even in the storehouse will eventually decay. We must let our joy strengthen us daily, providing the sustenance we need for the next cycle of tears and joy.

What does the work of harvesting joy look like to you?

Obedience to God

APRIL 7–13, 2025 • ROBERT SCHNASE

SCRIPTURE OVERVIEW: Obedience is not my favorite word in the vocabulary of faith. I prefer to meditate on the delights of grace, love, generosity, and kindness. These appeal to me. They draw me in. I move toward them. Obedience feels heavy and hard. It prods me into places I don't want to go. Obedience offends my sense of self-determination and self-sufficiency. It challenges pride and pretension. Obedience calls me to places of vulnerability and uncertainty, requires me to give up control and to leave behind parts of myself I cling to, and causes me to choose between my preferences and God's will. This week's readings focus on the last week of Jesus' earthly ministry. They invite us to explore faithful obedience and trust in the face of suffering, injustice, and inner resistance.

QUESTIONS AND SUGGESTIONS FOR REFLECTION

- Read Isaiah 50:4-9a. Recall a time God prompted you to offer a sustaining word to someone defeated by the circumstances of their life. How did you know what to say?
- Read Psalm 31:1-2, 9-16. What does it mean to seek refuge in God? When have you experienced both threatening uncertainty and an absolute trust at the same time?
- Read Philippians 2:5-11. How does Paul's reflection that Jesus "humbled himself and became obedient" shape your faith? What does faithful obedience look like? How do we foster Christlike humility?
- Read Luke 22:14–23:56. (This reading is lengthy. Take your time.) What surprises you afresh as you read the familiar story? What touches you most personally?

The Rev. Robert Schnase is the resident bishop of the Rio Texas and New Mexico Conferences of The United Methodist Church. He is the author of *Five Practices of Fruitful Living* (Abingdon Press, 2010) and *Five Practices of Fruitful Congregations* (Abingdon Press, 2018).

Isaiah speaks from lived experience, a particular situation of emotional and physical vulnerability, a moment of anguish for the innocent. The prophet faces the violence of adversaries and describes what it's like to be deemed worthless, unseen, forgotten, and despised. The prophet does not abandon those who suffer but perseveres alongside them with an obedience that is the fruit of an essential trust in God.

This passage awakens us to the duty of those who seek to live in the wisdom and truth of God, to use our lived experience of faith "to sustain the weary with a word."

Isaiah obeys God based on an unwavering trust. God takes us to places we might never go on our own and sets us in the presence of those who suffer. God pulls us out of our comfort zone to offer a word to the weary, and in so doing, we find ourselves in situations that cause us to change our minds, or even to open our hearts, to bring a word of mercy, compassion, encouragement, and grace.

What's the most unexpected and uncomfortable place you have found yourself in obedience to a prompting call of God? Perhaps it was sitting alongside a friend who faced a fearful health diagnosis, or serving at a homeless shelter, a food bank, or in a prison ministry. In the presence of people beaten down with despair, we're invited by this scripture to step into our own vulnerability to sustain the weary with a word. We glimpse the strength of the trust in the prophet's words, a trust in God that leads to obedience. Our obedience causes us to move toward those who suffer, not away from them.

Take me to places that deepen my compassion for others, Lord. Teach me words of mercy and peace. May people hear your love in my voice and see it in my eyes so you may sustain the weary through me. Amen.

I live along the Texas border, a setting that demands compassionate response to refugees fleeing violence, fear, and despair. *Refugee* is not a word people choose for themselves. Refugees flee circumstances they would never choose.

A pastor in my area invited unaccompanied migrant children in a detention center to write their prayers on cards. The prayers are rife with anguish and fear as they ask God for help for themselves and their families. Yet nearly every youth also weaves into their pleas for relief their gratitude for all that God has given them and their certainty in the goodness of God.

In Psalm 31 the psalmist pleas for shelter and deliverance, praying, "I am in distress . . . . My life is spent with sorrow, and my years with sighing . . . . I am the scorn of all my adversaries . . . . I have become like a broken vessel." The psalmist also writes, "But I trust in you, O Lord; I say, 'You are my God.'" It's a mystery of faith how someone can feel both utterly helpless and also completely confident in God. We witness this when unwavering trust co-exists with suffering and fear.

Jesus' heart is shaped by this psalm as he turns to God during his last, dark night in Gethsemane. We see the Son of God at his most vulnerable and most human. With Psalm 31, "My times are in your hand," Jesus prays, "Into your hands, I commend my spirit" (Luke 23:46). Jesus' prayer does not connote giving up. Rather it marks a release from fear, a surrendering trust in the power and goodness of God even in the most anguishing moments of life.

Accompany me, God. Shelter me. When I feel alone, help me find refuge in you. Amen.

Jesus says, "This is my body." He does not explain or theologize. He only asks to be obeyed: "Do this in remembrance of me." He tells the disciples it is "given for you" and "poured out for you." Jesus intends his followers to repeat the gift-like quality of this solemn moment in communities of Christians to come.

When we take Christ's body into ours, we orient ourselves once more toward the ultimate revelation of God's love for each of us as we remember the life, death, and resurrection of Jesus Christ. We become, as The United Methodist Communion liturgy says, "one with Christ, one with each other, and one in ministry to all the world." The meal condemns empty quarrels among Christians.

The disciples are so consumed by the question of who is the best and who is the worst that they nearly miss the significance of the moment. They ask which of them is the greatest, jockeying for the "best disciple" award. When Jesus says one of them will betray him, they each wonder who it might be, secretly fearful it might be them. He tells Peter that he will deny him, to which Peter claims, "I am ready to go with you to prison and to death!"

Jesus interrupts their empty quarreling to remind them, "I am among you as one who serves." He calls them to humility.

Every day somewhere in the world people take bread, break it, and give it to one another to remember Christ while telling the same story. In our breaking bread, we join a company that extends around the entire world, back into history, forward into the future, and upward to eternity. When we partake of the Last Supper with humility and in obedience to Jesus, we remember Jesus' conscious commitment, gift-like, to the salvation of the world.

God, forgive our empty quarrels and divisive natures. Grant us humility. Free us for joyful obedience. Amen.

I didn't want to do it. I convinced myself that I couldn't." Susan continues, "That's how I felt when God nudged me toward work at the food bank. I said no. I struggled with the calling. I finally surrendered to it, and I've never regretted saying yes; but it took a long time to get there."

Two spiritual crosscurrents toss us to-and-fro as we struggle with our callings: the desire to say yes in obedience to God and the tendency to say no so as to avoid difficult or uncomfortable tasks. It takes time to foster the obedience that overcomes our avoidance or denial of the road God invites us to take. To trust God enough to embrace what God calls us to do rarely happens easily.

How much time passed between Jesus praying, "Father, if you are willing, remove this cup from me," and "Yet not my will but yours be done"? Perhaps Jesus knelt in Gethsemane asking to be released from what was to come and only after hours of anguished prayer arose with an acceptance of the way of the Cross with obedience and trust. Or maybe "take this away from me" reveals how Jesus felt at the beginning of his ministry, and it was only through years of obedience to the kingdom that he can pray, "Not my will but yours."

Obedience forms in us through patterns of submitting ourselves to the way of love, of doing the things that foster life in Christ. God doesn't force obedience; disciples choose to obey, imperfectly, day after day.

Obedience invites us into an unnatural humility, a trust that is hard and deliberate. Obedience suggests there are things we do, not because we want to but because God calls us to do them. What we prefer ceases to be the driving question. God's will is the center, not ours. Perhaps that's what being a follower and a disciple means at its simplest—and at its most difficult.

Unlock in me a sense of calling, and help me to perceive it, O Lord. Open me to the prompting of your Spirit. Amen.

I find no basis for an accusation against this man," Pilate says. "I have found in him no ground for a sentence of death." Pilate repeatedly refutes the crowd's shouts to sentence Jesus to death. Nevertheless, he condemns Jesus, an unjust verdict against an innocent man. Political calculation? Threats from the crowd? We don't know what shapes Pilate's decision. Scripture gives no evidence that personal conviction drove his final verdict.

Luke refuses to brush over the details of this horrific, violent murder. His explicit descriptions underline the injustice. Can we see in Pilate any of our own moral equivocation when we witness injustice and do nothing? We so easily fall into a reflexive dialogue with the expectations of others and go along with the loudest, most persistent voices. It's easy to fit into this world without even thinking, unknowingly abetting unjust systems.

The call to faithful obedience does not imply automatic, unreflective response. God wants us to exercise our free will and to choose to obey, to act intentionally in life-giving, love-revealing, justice-seeking ways.

The disciples frequently tried to protect Jesus from the raw side of life, to warn him away from broken or "unclean" lives. They caution him against eating with tax-collectors, speaking to the woman at the well, approaching those with skin diseases, touching the unclean, and interceding on behalf of the woman accused of adultery. Yet every time his followers dig a moat, build a wall, or construct a fence between themselves and those people, they'd peer through to see that Jesus is already standing on the other side, with those people.

That the Son of God suffers death unjustly stands at the core of our faith. Jesus knows unjust suffering, and this places him alongside every victim of violence and injustice.

Give me courage, God. Renew in me the desire to see and act when innocents suffer. Amen.

While playing chess at a church retreat when I was sixteen, other youth stopped by to watch. We introduced ourselves, visited a few moments, and then continued our game as the other youth moved on. I would have no memory of this except that two years later I joined a church on the same Sunday as another young person. She looked familiar—she was one of those who stopped to watch the chess game. Two years after that, she and I had our first date. Two years after that we were married.

What is the meaning of the chess game encounter? Because of what followed, the game became the moment I met my wife. And with each year of our marriage of more than forty years, the meaning of that event has changed, as our relationship and family grew. The meaning of an event is determined by what follows it.

Paul writes about the passion of Christ, but not from the viewpoint of someone who witnesses the suffering and death of Jesus. Instead, he describes the events, poetically, from the perspective of time. He sees what has followed from the life, death, and resurrection of Christ, its impact on his own life and on dozens of communities of faith and in the lives of thousands of people who have experienced the mercy, grace, and love of Christ. Paul tells us what God has accomplished through the life, death, and resurrection of Jesus Christ and its eternal consequences.

We usually witness Paul's presenting truth through intellectual exposition and crafted argument, but here he simply exhorts readers to choose humility and obedience. He invites us to empty ourselves as Christ emptied himself.

What is the meaning of your own earliest encounters with Christ? What has followed from them? How do the consequences of what God has done in Jesus Christ continue to echo through you into the lives of others?

Lord, let the same mind be in me that was in Christ Jesus, who humbled himself and became obedient to your love. Amen.

PALM/PASSION SUNDAY

L uke 23 ends Christ's Passion story by drawing our attention to intimate, less visible, and quieter obedience and trust. In what must be a risky choice, given the temperament of the crowds, Joseph of Arimathea asks Pilate for Jesus' body. He wraps it in linen and places it in a tomb. The women who had accompanied Jesus from Galilee then go home to prepare spices and perfumes for the burial. In contrast to the public shouts—first of praise, then of violence—the women prepare for the quiet, intimate, and compassionate work of tenderly caring for Jesus' body. How were they not paralyzed by fear and consumed with hate? We cannot imagine the heavy burden of grief they carried. They stepped forward, nevertheless.

My father spent the last six weeks of his life under hospice care in medical facilities. We took turns sitting at his bedside, mostly in companionable silence, as he rested. These poignant, sacred moments were sharpened by the acute awareness of the passing of time. Caregivers came and went, day and night, to feed him, listen to him, and to offer us comfort. With tenderness and compassion, they bathed him and cared for him as if he were their own. They granted dignity during vulnerable moments. They gently lifted him to heaven through quiet, intimate ministrations. I will be forever grateful for the gift of their grace.

Can you hear the weeping of the women, their softly spoken prayers, as they move unseen away from the crowds and toward the quiet tasks of compassion?

Luke gives us a moment to breathe, a respite to return us from obliterating violence to the quiet compassion seen in acts of mercy by women wrestling with their own grief. The continuing journey toward love pulls us into the most intimate moments of life.

In the quiet and unseen moments, Lord, open in me the practice of humility and the compassion of Christ. Amen.

For Us and for Our Salvation

APRIL 14–20, 2025 • EDGARDO COLÓN-EMERIC

SCRIPTURE OVERVIEW: "For us and for our salvation." This phrase from the Nicene Creed, which turns 1700 this year, sums up the heart of John's Gospel. Christ's life and work was for our sake. Everything Jesus did and experienced abounds with saving mysteries. They are mysteries because the sights, sounds, and scents of God's glory overwhelm our physical senses and intellectual understanding. They are saving because through these mysteries come gifts of forgiveness, hope, and healing. This Holy Week, John the Evangelist will be our guide to these holy mysteries. Through contemplation of the Gospel readings, we will confess with renewed vigor and deeper understanding that "for us and for our salvation," Jesus lived, died, and rose again.

QUESTIONS AND SUGGESTIONS FOR REFLECTION

- Read John 12:1-11. Can you think of a time when God's presence overwhelmed you? How did you share this experience with others?
- Read John 12:30-36. When have you missed the signs of God's presence? What helped you later realize God had been there all along?
- Read John 19:38-42. What role does divine silence play in your relationship with God? When is this silence a gift?
- Read John 20:1-18. Where do you look for and find signs of resurrection? How do you keep your hopes bold?

The Rev. Dr. Edgardo Colón-Emeric is the Dean of Duke Divinity School, Irene and William McCutchen Professor of Reconciliation and Theology, and Director of the Center for Reconciliation. Edgardo is a United Methodist elder in the North Carolina Annual Conference.

MONDAY, APRIL 14 ~ *Read John 12:1-11*

For us and for our salvation, "the house was filled with the fragrance of the perfume." In the Gospel of John, God signals salvation in large, bold, italicized, underlined, all-caps font. At the wedding in Cana when the wine runs out, Jesus provides around one hundred and sixty gallons of wine. With five barley loaves and two fish, he feeds five thousand, and there is enough left over to fill twelve baskets.

In today's reading, Mary announces Jesus' death by anointing his feet with a pound's weight of perfume, about a year's worth of wages. John's laconic description undersells the experience. The smell must have been overpowering. It must have not only filled the house; it must have soaked Mary's hair, filled every lung, and permeated every piece of food, furniture, and clothing in the room. Clearly, God wants to get our attention.

In scripture, the word *fragrance* belongs to the language of temple sacrifice. The anointing announces Jesus' crucifixion as a "fragrant offering" (Eph. 5:2). Lazarus, who had until recently been cloaked in the stench of death (John 11:39), now smells of Christ. By being around Jesus and his friends, Christians become the "aroma of Christ" (2 Cor. 2:15). For some, the smell will be unpleasant, an aroma that brings death. But for others the smell will be a fragrant aroma—one that brings life.

Mary's anointing of Jesus is a saving mystery. Its over-the-top gesture is perfectly aligned to announce the extravagance of God's love and forgiveness. The mystery empowers and examines my response to God's love. It invites me to examine my witness. Am I announcing God's presence with extravagant gestures? Or am I acting from a scarcity mindset? Am I filling spaces with the fragrance of Christ? Or am I leading an antiseptic life that makes little impression?

Lord Jesus Christ, fill our lives with your fragrance that we may be your presence in the world. Amen.

For us and for our salvation, "a voice came from heaven." Similar miraculous manifestations occur at Jesus' baptism and transfiguration. In these occasions, the voice speaks for our sake. It proclaims the identity of Jesus as God's beloved Son.

In today's reading, there is something different and more intimate. From eternity, Father, Son, and Holy Spirit live in triune conversation. The word of the Father becomes voice by the breath of the Spirit. This voice draws us into the conversation of the Triune God. We are privy to Jesus' dialogue with God. We hear our Lord giving voice to the troubled state of his soul. He could ask to be spared Golgotha. Instead, he asks that the name of the Father be glorified. We hear the Father's voice assuring Jesus and us that he has done so and will do so again.

Those in the crowd are unable to comprehend the encounter they have just witnessed. Some interpret the voice as an angel, while others hear only thunder. Unbelief constrains the mind and dulls the senses. It reduces the Bible just to religious stories, sacraments to mere rituals, and Jesus to nothing but an inspiring teacher. Faith opens the senses to non-reductive readings of Creation, salvation, and history. This is why true believers are—or should be—the most open-minded of peoples.

The voice speaking from heaven is a saving mystery. It invites us to be attentive to the many ways in which God speaks and to reject reductive readings. There is a popular version of the Bible in Spanish called *Dios habla hoy*, "God speaks today." It was the Bible I used in my first pastorate. Its simple language drew my parishioners into God's Trinitarian conversation. If we listen carefully, we can hear "a voice from heaven" today.

Lord Jesus Christ, thank you for inviting me to participate in your dialogue with God. Help me to listen for your voice everywhere and obey. Amen.

For us and for our salvation, Jesus "dipped the piece of bread, [and] he gave it to Judas." The story of Judas bears all the marks of a classical tragedy. He starts out as one of the twelve, a companion of Jesus from the beginning, the group treasurer, a friend of the poor. He ends up as a traitor.

Judas' betrayal makes no sense. Other disciples then and now have failed Jesus. But Judas' case is different. The disciples cannot accept his betrayal. No matter how many warning signs Jesus offers, the disciples explain these away. The shock of the betrayal is possibly the reason why his name and his crime always go together: Judas, the one who betrayed Jesus. An entire life is reduced to a failure.

Jesus feeding Judas and Judas selling Jesus are mysteriously related. It sounds like the connection is condemnation. After all, Satan enters Judas the moment he receives the bread. This correlation is not causation; the connection is mercy. Jesus' offer of bread is not an act of entrapment; it is an act of judgment and grace. Indeed, these go together because the proper subjects of mercy are the sick and sinners. For us and for our salvation, Jesus dipped the bread, gave it to Judas, and to all of us.

Jesus' relationship with Judas is a saving mystery. The questions it poses about predestination, divine will, and free will keep me from domesticating the gospel and taming it into a nice story. There are depths of mystery in Jesus' passion I cannot understand. What I do understand is that the tragedy of Judas is a mirror in which I consider the absurdity of my own failings and marvel at the mercies of the Lord.

Jesus Christ, Son of God, have mercy on me, a sinner. Give me the bitter medicine of grace that I may be healed. Amen.

Maundy Thursday

For us and for our salvation, Jesus "returned to his place at the table" (CEB). Among the evangelists, John is an outlier in that he does not include a narrative of the institution of Holy Communion. Instead, he invites us to contemplate the Trinitarian ground supporting Jesus' celebration of his Last Supper and the beginning of his passion—namely, love.

First, Jesus "got up from supper" in order to serve. Given what they knew about Jesus, it is surprising that the disciples were surprised by this, but they were. Jesus' holy rebelliousness overturns hierarchies both ancient and modern. By washing and wiping the feet of his disciples, Jesus gives humble hospitality a sacramental stamp. Serving is a means of grace; it helps one become fully alive.

Second, Jesus returns to his seat. He has every reason to stay away. He knows he is sowing words in hard ground. He knows his explanation of the foot washing will not make sense until after Easter and Pentecost. He knows his betrayer is at hand. Even so, he returns to the table because he loves. Tables are not only places for eating; they are places for conversation and conversion.

Jesus' return to the table is a saving mystery. His table company surprised and disturbed many. Throughout his ministry, he ate with well-known sinners, and, on the eve of his passion, he washes the feet of Judas. Jesus returns to the table to save us and give us an example. As I contemplate this mystery, I think of how his sanctified stubbornness does not give up on people because they—we—are prone to failure. I think of the times when I have written someone off and refused to serve. I too am called to return to the table.

Lord Jesus, I have failed to be a hospitable host. Show me how to serve all, even my enemies, and not count the cost. Amen.

GOOD FRIDAY

For us and for our salvation, "they crucified him." It is easy to forget that before the cross became a symbol for Christianity, it was an instrument of capital punishment. Jesus did not simply die. He was tortured and killed as a criminal.

Only three people are called out by name in the Apostles' and Nicene Creeds. All were present on Golgotha: Jesus, Mary, and Pontius Pilate. Pilate's mention in the creed spotlights the centrality of Roman politics to Christ's passion. They crucified Jesus because his life and ministry disrupted the delicate, dynamic balance of powers at work in the region.

To spotlight the politics of the Cross does not downplay its saving significance. Instead, it discloses the scandalous surprise of Golgotha. When "they crucified him," God exalted him. Pilate's mocking multilingual message "Jesus of Nazareth, the King of the Jews," became an unexpected and unwelcome affirmation of Christ's coronation. Jesus' giving up of his spirit became a little Pentecost. Its offer of judgment and mercy echoes and expands to a growing cast of crucifiers and crucified from Golgotha to Treblinka to San Salvador.

The crucifixion of Christ is a saving mystery. The contemplation of the crucified God in the faces of the crucified peoples simultaneously exposes my sin and promises grace. I too "crucified him" by my personal sins. I crucify him by playing the role of spectator, supporter, and sanctifier of the suffering of people sacrificed on the altars of cultural identity, economic prosperity, and national security gone amok. I need the grace of Christ crucified to break their hold on my soul, to forgive my sins, and to heal their consequences.

O Lord Jesus, I have crucified you. Breathe on me your spirit, that I may die to sin and live for you. Amen.

SATURDAY, APRIL 19 ~ *Read John 19:38-42*

HOLY SATURDAY

For us and for our salvation, "they laid Jesus [in the tomb] there." The days of Jesus' burial are shrouded in mystery. A strand of Christian tradition memorialized in the Apostles' Creed speaks of the harrowing of hell. Between death and resurrection, Christ descended to the dead and liberated Adam and Eve, patriarchs and prophets, and all who died in hope of heaven. The Nicene Creed refrains from speculation about postmortem preaching and simply says he "was buried."

Historically, Protestants have lifted up the empty cross. However, many Roman Catholic churches in Latin America have chapels dedicated to the dead Christ—not Christ hanging from a cross but Christ lying inside a glass casket. By the coffin, there are prayer litanies to the dead Christ with petitions for the healing of the sick, the consolation of the mourning, and the accompaniment of the lonely. The juxtaposition of images and prayers is jarring. The author of life is dead; the light extinguished. Even so, Jesus saves. The Good Friday services of Jesus' seven last words conclude in an eighth word—silence. It is the silence of God rendered speechless by the death of the Incarnate Word.

Holy Saturday is a saving mystery. The silence of Jesus' burial is a rich, resonant silence. It validates the voices of the voiceless. It heightens the senses to encounter God in the midst of desolation. Today's reading tells us that Jesus' body was wrapped in linen with one hundred pounds of spices. This extravagant gesture ups the ante on the anointing he received at Bethany. Even in death, the aroma of Christ is powerful. Contemplating the dead Christ is a *memento mori*, a reminder that death comes for us all, but more than that it is a *memento amoris*, a reminder that "love is strong as death" (Song of Sol. 8:6).

Lord Jesus, your silent body speaks without words. In the silence, may I encounter your saving love. Amen.

EASTER

For us and for our salvation, "he must rise from the dead." When Lazarus came out of his tomb, the disciples had no problem recognizing him. He was still clothed in his burial clothes, and the stench of death still clung to him. But something was different about the risen Jesus. The problem was not that he was too ethereal, as some mistakenly thought, but that he was too solid, too real, too down-to-earth. Christ's resurrection is a divine imperative. It commands us to abandon dead hopes and to allow our expectations to be transposed.

Jesus tells Mary to tell the other disciples, "I am returning to him who is my Father and their Father, to my God and their God" (GNT). Mary cannot keep the resurrected Jesus to herself. Christ's resurrection inaugurates a new "we," a new way of being. It is Christ the head and Christ the body, Christ the shepherd and Christ the sheep, Christ the gardener and Christ the garden, Christ the grain of wheat that falls to the ground and dies and Christ the Eucharist who gives life to all who taste and see. The divine imperative draws all creation to rise with Christ into new creation. For this to happen, Mary must not hold on to Jesus. She must let him go so that we too can ascend.

The Resurrection is a saving mystery. It raises our hopes from bondage to low expectations. What we really long for is not merely prosperity or long life. In the words of the Nicene Creed, "we look for the resurrection of the dead, and the life of the world to come." When we allow ourselves to be transposed by Easter's divine imperative, we find signs of eternal life everywhere around us: reconciled enemies, welcomed strangers, and clean water. It is in the density of our sinful selves, wounded histories, and groaning biosphere that Christ "must rise from death" (GNT).

O Lord Jesus, raise my hopes from the tomb of mediocrity to the heights of your mercy. Amen.

Unbelievable Truth

APRIL 21–27, 2025 • MARY CHARLOTTE JOHNSON

SCRIPTURE OVERVIEW: Humans struggle to believe the truths that God reveals. In Acts the apostles face a domineering council that has ordered them to be quiet about Jesus, but they find they cannot. In Psalm 118 we wonder at the truth that God is our salvation, and in Psalm 150 we celebrate the greatness of God. In the book of Revelation we catch a glimpse of the surprise of finding Christ's grace and peace. In John we find the apostles after the Resurrection struggling to believe this unbelievable truth without proof.

QUESTIONS AND SUGGESTIONS FOR REFLECTION

- Read Acts 5:27-32. When have you seen the world differently from those in authority? How did it feel to share a truth that others did not believe?
- Read Psalm 150. Remember a time when you praised God fully, when you sang or played an instrument or danced before the Lord or served the Lord with gladness. How do you experience the presence of God in these praises?
- Read Revelation 1:4-8. Sit and soak up God's unmerited favor and wholeness, Christ's grace and peace. Imagine it enveloping your family, your friends, your enemies and those who have brought harm to your life.
- Read John 20:19-31. What questions are you struggling with? What would you like Jesus to show you? explain to you? reveal to you?

The Rev. Mary Charlotte Johnson is a retired clergy member of the Baltimore-Washington Conference of The United Methodist Church and the Academy for Spiritual Formation of The Upper Room. Mary is married to Bishop Peggy Johnson; they have two grown sons and live in Carrollton, VA.

Some truths are just unbelievable. Often times they are too good to be true. The resurrection of Jesus is one of those truths that many have found unbelievable. Earlier in this chapter of John, Mary Magdalene could not believe her eyes when she saw Jesus. The apostles could not believe the women's report. But seeing was believing. Jesus appeared out of nowhere right before their eyes and even ate with them. Thomas, who had been absent, finds it impossible to believe. Like many, he needs proof before he can accept this unbelievable truth. Thomas needs to touch the actual marks where the nails pierced Jesus' hands and place his hand where the Roman spear entered Christ's side. Only then will Thomas dare to believe.

We are often like Jesus' closest disciples. We too have experienced the finality of death, have grieved like Christ's disciples over the loss of those dear to us. In the face of death and overwhelming grief, we wonder how resurrection can be real. Is the witness of others ever enough when the truth seems unbelievable to you? You are blessed when you have not seen and yet you believe the unbelievable.

My unbelievable truth is that I am a transgender woman. My gender transition was a resurrection from the dead into a new life. I cannot prove it to anyone. For many they need physical proof that I cannot provide. I have only my personal testimony as to what I have experienced.

We experience a variety of unbelievable truths every day. In each one of them we feel a closeness to the living God. These experiences are real and life-changing, yet all we have to share is our testimony to these unbelievable truths. Blessed are those who can believe with us even when they have not seen.

My Lord and my God! I believe what I've not seen: your living presence. Amen.

As followers of Christ, we at times struggle to believe in unbelievable truths like Jesus' resurrection. We often need time to believe. So imagine how difficult it may be for those outside the Christian tradition to comprehend, much less believe. When we speak of resurrection, our words seem crazy or even dangerous to them. The disciples believed that God raised Jesus from the dead, had exalted Jesus so that he could call us to repentance and grant the forgiveness of our sins. Others they encountered were not at that point yet.

Think about your personal journey of belief. How have you come to believe in the truth of the Easter story? What seeds were planted in you along the way? As you share your testimony to the truth, acknowledge that this truth may for others be only the first planting of a single seed. What now seems so simple and easy for you to believe may not be that simple for them. We must be patient and nurture these seeds of truth in others' lives.

Our witness is necessary but not magic. Our witness is not a once-and-done event. Others need to continually experience the reality of the living Christ through us. They need our daily prayers, they need to experience Christ through our daily acts of grace, and they need our continued witness. We live this way so that the resurrected Christ truly lives in us. In the fullness of time what Christ has begun in them will become the unbelievable truth in their own lives, in whatever way is most needed for their experience.

Holy Lord, we must live our truth. We know our words sound foolish to others: "You are forgiven." Give us perseverance as we share our witness of you with others. Amen.

In this psalm we find the unbelievable truth that God has chosen to become the salvation of Israel. When they could not save themselves, through the grace of God they were saved. They experienced God's grace as restorative, healing, and transformational.

One of the questions I am often asked as a transgender woman is, "How can you be transgender and call yourself a Christian?" They wonder how I can possibly be saved, when I have the audacity to disagree with the gender given to me by a doctor at my birth. The unbelievable truth is that God has become my salvation.

The people of Israel were chosen for salvation for God's own reasons. Israel did not catch God's attention because of their righteousness. Israel was not in any way extraordinary. They were not large and powerful. They were not extraordinarily faithful. God's grace was not due to their generosity nor their kindness to others. It was due only to God's gracious choice to become their salvation. God chose to love them and to touch their lives with divine forgiveness. God chose to be patient with them and to reveal the divine glory. This seems to be such an unbelievable truth.

I am just like every other Christian. I have the audacity to claim the unbelievable truth that God has become my salvation. God chose to save me, in spite of who I am. God does not love me because I have reached some level of holy perfection. God doesn't love me because I have tried to serve God faithfully since I was a teenager. Even though God knows everything about me and all the ways I have fallen short of divine expectations, the unbelievable truth I celebrate with the psalmist is that God alone has become my salvation.

You are my God. Your divine salvation is a gift truly undeserved, so freely given. Amen.

John shares with the seven churches of Asia and with us an unbelievable truth: Grace and peace are God's gifts to us. When we behold God, grace and peace are not exactly what we are expecting to receive. We are expecting to experience divine punishment, some sort of retribution. We will at that moment realize that we're the ones who have pierced him with our sins. We will experience the urge to fall on our knees, joining our voices with all those who will cry out before his presence for mercy. We expect God's revenge for what we have done. But what we will all experience is beyond belief: We shall receive only grace and peace.

Christ continues to be a faithful witness to the restorative justice of God. Jesus is the firstborn of the dead, the living testimony to the power of God to make all things new. This is Jesus, the righteous ruler of all, and every knee shall bow and every tongue will confess that Jesus is Lord. This Jesus is the one who sees us only through the eyes of divine love. By God's will Christ has appointed us to become a kin-dom, a community of those who share in God's glory. Unbelievably, we have nothing to fear from Christ who has in store for us only grace and peace.

We may feel that this is unfair. There may be those whom we had been hoping God would repay for all the evil they have done to God and to us. The unbelievable truth is that God loves them as much as God loves us. This grace and peace is destined for all. God does not want anyone to perish. We receive this invitation into God's kin-dom, an invitation that is also extended to every other person as well.

God, thank you for the grace and peace Christ offers to us all—even to those who pierced him. We rest freed from all our sins. Amen.

Psalm 150 is the "Hallelujah Chorus" of psalms. It reflects our heartfelt response to all the unbelievable truths that God speaks into our lives. We are overwhelmed by all that God seeks to accomplish in us and the infinite patience through which God has never given up on us. It is with unending praise that we feel compelled to express our gratitude for God's unbelievable gift of salvation, given generously to us and all of creation. We praise God for the mercy shown to us, a mercy we know that we will never fully deserve. We praise God for extending to us a forgiveness that promises to bestow upon us a fresh start each day.

The greater our awareness of all that God has done, is doing, and promises to do for us, the more our hearts are filled with joyful gratitude. Our truest praise is expressed not just in song and dance but also through our emulation of these unbelievable acts of God's grace. Each time we choose to turn the other cheek, we share an act of praise. To pray for the Lord's blessing upon our enemies is an act of praise. Every act of mercy, every time we forgive, God receives our truest praise. When we act like God in showing restorative justice, the world around us joins in the praise of the God whose presence we reflect.

Praise is our truest prayer. This praise rises from deep within our souls. Praise bubbles up when we recognize that everything God has done is extraordinarily good. Praise is a celebration of the unbelievable truth that in every act of love, God is fully present. In every act of kindness, it is God who reaches out to bring comfort. Praise flows from a realization that in every word of encouragement, God whispers the words we need to hear, transforming lives, and changing our perspective.

We praise you, Lord, showing our gratitude, and we praise you without ceasing. Amen.

The disciples were clearly warned not to speak about Jesus. They were ordered by those in authority not to speak about the unbelievable things that Christ had done. They were to say nothing of the fact that in the name of Jesus the lame could walk. They were to remain silent about the power of God to resurrect Jesus, who had been murdered. Those in authority did not want to hear about the merciful grace that Jesus extended to all, even to those who crucified him. The disciples, however, felt a burning urgency compelling them to share this good news.

Galileo looked through his telescope realizing an unbelievable truth: The earth and planets were traveling around the sun, and not the planets and sun around the earth. Church authorities commanded him to keep silent and not to proclaim such fabrications in his writings. John Wesley was commanded by his bishop to stop preaching without a parish. Wesley proclaimed the truth that the world was his parish and continued preaching. John Scopes was told not to teach the theory of evolution in his high school science class. Breaking the law, he taught what science saw as an important biological truth. He could not teach his students what was not true. He could not stay silent.

Today medical science has found that our sense of gender is found in our brains and that it does not always match our bodies. This idea is new and upsetting to those who have always thought that gender was determined by your physiology. Because of this there are those seeking to silence these new understandings.

New ideas can be frightening, the unbelievable ones even more so. No matter the resistance, though, the truth must be shared. It's how God changes the world, with one unbelievable truth at a time.

Lord, some demand silence. Yet we must obey you, proclaiming the truth. Give us courage. Amen.

Even though the disciples did not believe that the Resurrection was real, Jesus still came to them. Jesus was not angered by their unbelief. Instead Jesus breathed a word of peace upon them. Jesus did not ignore Thomas' questions about the Resurrection; instead, Jesus addressed them directly. Jesus seemed to understand that this event was forcing his followers to believe an unbelievable truth. They were slowly realizing the truth that his death upon the cross was not the end. The truth was so much more than they could have thought or imagined.

The goal of discipleship is to learn from Jesus. The best students ask the most questions. Jesus welcomed questions and answered questions with even more questions. Jesus did not cut off discussion but encouraged it. This is how we learn. We find that the older we become, the less we know because we develop the capacity to ask more questions. As we grow in understanding, new questions fill our minds, questions we never imagined asking when we were younger.

Questions are not an indication of a lack of faith. Questions lead us deeper into a more substantial faith, filled with intricacies and nuances. Questions lead to a fuller understanding, filling in some of the blanks we never even knew existed.

Thomas had not been with the disciples when Jesus appeared. He had not seen Jesus' hands and side. He had not heard Jesus speak words of peace. He only heard the other disciples tell of their experience. Thomas had questions Jesus was glad to answer. What are your questions? Seeking for answers is a spiritual quest inspired by the Holy Spirit. Your questions will never make Christ angry. Jesus says, "Peace be with you."

God, struggling to believe, my mind is filled with questions. Help me not to fear or shy away from the doubt but continue to sit with the questions only you can answer. Amen.

Deepening Devotion

APRIL 28–MAY 4, 2025 • J. DANA TRENT

SCRIPTURE OVERVIEW: Self-examination, sacrifice, love, and praise are common themes for this week's readings. Our takeaways: True, deep faith requires humility and cost. But not in the sense that we subject ourselves to an unreasonable ascetic renunciation or harmful self-punishment. Rather, the cost for us should be perpetual introspection. Contemplation is what inches us forward in our faith, connects us with God's word, and shows us God's work in the world. Deepening our devotion hinges on noticing: When has God shown God's mercy to us? What aspects of Jesus' teachings do we still ignore? How do we cling to a human stubbornness that impedes agape and praise for "worthy is the lamb"?

QUESTIONS AND SUGGESTIONS FOR REFLECTION

- Read Psalm 30. When in your life has God turned your wailing into dancing so that you could sing God's praises?

- Read Acts 9:1-20. When have you ignored Jesus' teaching in order to follow your own agenda? Consider Saul/Paul's abrupt conversion. What do you make of God's role in this story? Ananias' role?

- Read John 21:1-19. The disciples did not know it was Jesus until they ate with him. Consider a time you experienced God in fellowship. Jesus' questions to Simon Peter—and his prophecy—demonstrate the costs of discipleship. What has your faith cost you?

- Read Revelation 5:11-14. Is Jesus worthy of our sacrifice? If so, why so? When you say or sing "Worthy is the lamb," what does this phrase mean to you?

J. Dana Trent is a professor of world religions and critical thinking at Wake Tech Community College. Dana is the author of *One Breath at a Time: A Skeptic's Guide to Christian Meditation* (Upper Room Books, 2018) and *Between Two Trailers: A Memoir* (Convergent Books, 2024).

Psalm 30 is one of the most relatable psalms we have. It calls us to feel the pinch of our finite human existence, to be reminded of God's mercy, and to praise God's name.

Here, the psalmist alludes to the realm of the dead, a fearful place they call the "pit," where ancient Israelites believed that only a shadowy version of us remained, separated from the world of the living. In antiquity, without a solid notion of a joyful life to come, it's easy to understand why the Israelites would have viewed death and the underworld with despair. Death, in its certainty, brings the uncertainty of the afterlife. Would the afterlife be comprised only of hopelessness, silence, and the inability to praise God from the dusty depths of the pit?

Instead, the psalmist offers readers hope: God has lifted us out of these scary depths of death. In turn, we may trade our sackcloth for dancing garments, keen to praise God here and now. God does not leave us for dead; we are saved to sing praises, giving thanks to God forever.

Reading this psalm through the lens of the New Testament, we can see it reflect Christ's resurrection and exactly how God, in God's mercy, has saved us too. Our finite human bodies always march us to the grave. That is certain. But there is hope for our soul and spirit. "Weeping may linger for the night, but joy comes in the morning." Christ's love, teachings, sacrifice, crucifixion, and resurrection all point to devotion to God. For all our material suffering in these bodies, we are promised a spiritual life of joy through Jesus Christ.

Holy One, when we weep in the night, remind us that joy always comes in the morning. When we grieve our aging, dying bodies, remind us that spiritual life everlasting is to come. Amen.

S aul (Paul) is one of the most important historical figures in Christianity. Without Saul, Christianity would not be one of the largest world religions today. But Acts 9 shows that Saul's road to getting Christianity on the map got off to a painful start.

Saul's writing reveals his upbringing and education; his knowledge of scripture is obvious. He is a devout Jew, well-read in the Hebrew scriptures and the Septuagint, the Greek translation of the Hebrew scriptures. This education, combined with his family's status, makes him a powerful man. Saul was likely a descendant of freed Jewish slaves who remained Roman citizens. His status as a Roman citizen explains not only Saul's ability to travel easily in the Roman Empire but also how he can demand a letter from the high priest of the Jewish temple listing all who belonged to "The Way," or followed Jesus. "The Way" is a common phrase in Christianity as a sect of Judaism, as it was (and is) Jesus' own words and faith as a way of life.

These letters from the synagogue priest would have revealed first-century Jews who subscribed to these teachings of Christ and therefore were beginning to be persecuted and imprisoned in Saul's time due to their veering away from strict Judaism. Saul is on a mission: He seeks to capture Jewish Christians who have accepted Jesus as the divine Son of God.

Why would followers of "The Way" be so threatening to Saul and others? Because, like any reform movement in history, they disrupt the status quo. The beginning of Saul's story is a call for us to see the areas of our lives where we ignore our hatred, prejudice, and disdain for those who believe differently from us. It's also an invitation to be in awe of the courage Jesus' followers had.

God of us all, we confess that we have been blinded by our disdain for others. Stop us in our tracks. Shed light on our sins and turn us in the right direction. Amen.

Only when Saul had his literal vision removed was he able to see Jesus as God. And it is God, in the form of Christ, who calls Saul here.

"Who are you, Lord?" Saul questions. Because Saul is a learned man, he knows what a *theophany* is (an appearance of God on earth); it's assumed that he would have recognized the heavenly voice. And yet he does not respond with the standard, reverent response we hear in later verses from Ananias ("Yes, Lord"). The irony is not lost here. Saul, who claims to be a devout and faithful follower of God the Father, does not offer a faithful response to his theophany. Ananias, a persecuted follower of Jesus, the first bishop of Damascus, and likely a target of the letter Saul requested from the synagogue, does.

"I am Jesus, whom you are persecuting," the voice responds to Saul's question. At this moment, it's clear that Saul understands his mistake. And he is silent. Saul realizes he has been blinded literally and spiritually; he does not speak, eat, nor drink for three days. Can you imagine what must have been going through Saul's mind? Does he wonder why he has not been instantly killed by God? Does he wonder if he will regain his sight? We are not privy to Saul's internal dialogue—whether of fear, repentance, or anger.

It is Ananias, a Christian, who is called by God to go to Saul after the three days. Saul, before his conversion, would have had Ananias immediately arrested for believing in Christ. But here, it is Ananias who is chosen to help carry out God's mercy to restore Saul's sight—literally and spiritually. Saul's gift of grace comes from the very target of his persecution: Jesus and his followers.

Holy One, teach us the error of our ways. When we arrogantly believe that we have the mind of God, call us to humility. When we hatefully persecute those whom we love, call us to empathy. Jolt us from our sin. Have mercy on us. Amen.

The book of Revelation is attributed to the apostle John, one of the twelve disciples. John is the only disciple who was not martyred, but he did face exile on the Isle of Patmos during the first-century persecution of those who followed "the way" (early Christianity).

Revelation is widely misinterpreted and misused. Its genre is different from John's Gospel, which is also historically attributed to this writer. Though Revelation is often read as strictly apocalyptic literature, we are invited to consider it as an encouragement to faithful living now that leads to a joyful after-life, much like what we read in Psalm 30.

This chapter invites us to consider a vision of heaven with a wider view of who is worthy of praise. Here, we see the Lamb (Jesus) in terms that were typically reserved in Judaism for God the Father. Thus, the Father and the Son are both central figures in this vision of heaven, and each is worthy of our praise. Echoing Psalm 30, the writer reminds us that the afterlife is a joyful place.

This section is also a portion of the Doxology (blessing) that informs our devotion here and now. The church on earth is a worshiping body of Christ, and therefore the divine liturgy of "Worthy is the lamb" inspires us to be in awe and have reverence toward Christ's sacrifice in addition to God's mercy. It also serves as instruction for us today: The world is full of suffering and persecution, and we are called to the path of agape that offers the promise of abundant and eternal life, now and in heaven. One day, we too will experience the millions of angels encircling the throne to proclaim God's glory. How are we called to live this vision of heaven here and now on earth?

Agnus Dei, you take away the sins of the world. Have mercy on us. Instruct us. Invite us to wonder, awe, and reverence. May we shout, "Worthy is the lamb!" every day of our lives because you are indeed worthy. Amen.

In today's passage, Jesus appears to the disciples: visible, transfigured, and in an incorruptible body. He also reveals himself in a setting that is familiar to his disciples: fishing. The fish is a significant symbol in the Greek New Testament. Many of the disciples are fishermen by occupation; Jesus feeds the crowd with loaves and fishes. And here, the meal of fish Jesus shares with his beloved friends becomes an opportunity to reveal himself to them and a chance to reestablish his relationship with Peter.

Perhaps this meal on the beach is why the fish became an important symbol for the early church. While *ichthus*, the Greek word for *fish*, is an acronym of Greek words describing Jesus' name (Jesus Christ, God's Son, Savior), its symbolism was likely not lost on those first followers of Christ. It became the symbol the church used in its first three hundred years before the Roman Emperor Constantine declared Christianity legal to practice in the early fourth century. Before Constantine's conversion to Christianity, Christians gathered, prayed, and worshiped in hiding, with only *ichthus* as their sign to one another.

Like Saul on the road to Damascus, the disciples do not realize it is Christ who calls out to them at first. Unlike Saul's blindness, theirs is not a spiritual blindness but rather a simple and basic principle of grief. In their mind, Jesus is no longer physically with them. Once they realize who it is, though, Peter especially will not be held back.

What signs of Christ's presence inspire us to bold action? Jesus is willing to meet us where we are, but refuses to leave us there for long. We must take bold steps to follow where Christ leads.

God open our eyes to the presence of Christ and equip us to follow boldly where he is leading. Amen.

Jesus foretells Peter's upcoming death through martyrdom in verses 18 and 19. This story is a call to the disciples to embrace the sacrificial agape for God, reflected in Jesus' agape and sacrifice for them and us.

The inevitability of the death of our physical bodies we read about in Psalm 30 is reflected again here. We will grow old, and we will lose control, autonomy, and agency of our bodies. Or we may die young. We could die violently, like Peter. But Jesus is clear: No matter what happens to us, we should glorify God.

"Follow me!" Jesus instructs. We are called to surrender to the Triune God. Our aim now and forever is to praise God for God's mercy and to praise Jesus for his sacrifice. But this is a tall order. When we experience pain, defeat, suffering, persecution, violence, and hopelessness, the last thing we may want to do is praise God. When we feel scared, the last thing we want to do is be courageous. But through our love of Jesus, we shape our lives after Jesus and commit our lives to praising God and loving others, no matter the challenges we may experience.

These two verses that offered such wisdom to Peter and the disciples speak to us today. We are not in control, and to love Jesus and follow Jesus is to give up control. Yet this was the commitment Peter made when he declared his love for Jesus three times. It was not only with his words that Peter proclaimed his love but with his actions that followed (told in the book of Acts). The same is true for us: Our words of love and praise for Christ go only so far. It is only when our lives are lived in love and praise of God that we truly live out the call to follow Jesus.

Triune God, even as we long for control and feel the pinch of our finitude, you remind us that to follow you is to give up control and live a full life of love and praise. Amen.

We end this week's readings by coming full-circle back to the Psalms. Psalm 30 provides opportunity for deep self-reflection. How has God pulled you from the depths? How has God shown you mercy in your spiritual blindness? In what ways are you being called to agape? How will you respond to Jesus' instruction to follow him?

Psalm 30 was a good place to begin our week, and it's a fitting way to end it. Praise is always where we should land. And Psalm 30 shows us the way. The psalmist praises God for deliverance in times of distress. We should do the same.

Psalm 30 is a reminder of the power of having faith and trusting in God even as we face the darkest of times. It is an invitation to remember how God has heard us, healed us, and brought us up from the depths. It is a reminder that even when we feel like all is lost, God lifts us from the pit.

Finally, Psalm 30 is also a strict imperative: We were made for praise. We are called to praise. The psalmist ends with this commitment to praise God forever. We should take note and join in, trading our wailing for dancing and our sackcloth for garments of delight. Our bodies will fail and fade, but our spirits will delight in God forever.

Read Psalm 30 silently or aloud. Examine. Notice. Are you committed to a true, deep faith that transcends the deepest of pits? Are you driven to devotion that requires humility and sacrifice? Remain committed to observing: What aspects of Jesus' teachings are you still ignoring? What are you clinging to that impedes your agape, your discipleship, and your praise for "Worthy is the lamb"?

God who is worthy of my praise, thank you for lifting me out of the depths and healing me. I praise you for your faithfulness and mercy, and I will sing your praises forever. Amen.

The Righteous Shepherd

MAY 5–11, 2025 • BRIAN R. BODT

SCRIPTURE OVERVIEW: The familiarity of these passages should not lull us into complacency about their blessings and expectations. The psalmist's words about the shepherd who comforts also leads to paths that challenge us to seek moral uprightness and justice. In Acts, Luke presents Tabitha as an example of one such disciple, whose restoration to life is the fulfillment of the psalmist's promise. Revelation reminds us that the righteous life is not lived without struggle, but that the promise of redemption overcomes the worst that we encounter. John shows that even Jesus, the Lord who is the Shepherd, faced critics of his good works. Yet those who desire righteousness hear Jesus' voice, he knows them, and "no one can snatch them out of [his] hand."

QUESTIONS AND SUGGESTIONS FOR REFLECTION

- Read Psalm 23. What are the "paths of righteousness" into which you need to be led?
- Read Revelation 7:9-17. Who do you think stands "before the throne of God?" When? Why?
- Read Acts 9:36-43. To what "good works and acts of charity" are you called? How do you guard against righteousness becoming self-righteousness?
- Read John 10:22-30. How do you discern Jesus' voice from the cacophony of voices that daily surround us? How is it different? To what does it call you?

The Rev. Brian R. Bodt is the pastor of Woodbury United Methodist Church in Woodbury, CT, and the pastor of community care at Greenfield Hill Congregational Church in Fairfield, CT. Staying in love with God and blessed in human loves by his wife, Carol Galloway, and their children and grandchildren, Brian skis, runs, and plays with all kinds of trains.

What more time-honored and cherished words of scripture are there than the Twenty-third Psalm? They are *de rigueur* at many funerals, often printed on remembrance cards; a memory requirement for some confirmation students; and, for some of a certain age, perfected only in the King James Version of the Bible.

The images of shepherd and sheep would have been familiar to the first readers of scripture, but to us? What do we really know about shepherding and sheep? If you're like my friend Roni, you know a lot. I once spent time with Roni and her husband, Mike, on their farm, and I learned that sheep are not as dumb as is sometimes supposed. In fact, they are smart. When Roni fetched grain to feed them, they knew how to open the door of the granary. They come when called, recognizing the shepherd's voice (see John 10:27). They recognize up to 100 faces, sometimes better than many of us who see faces (and try to remember names) for a living. They are social creatures, peaceful and gentle.

Then why do they need a shepherd? One reason is they tug at grass rather than chomp it, so they will destroy a pasture as they pull the grass out by its roots. As a result, they need to be led to green pastures. Moving water is a cause for fear of drowning, so they need to be led to still waters. While they are social creatures, they sometimes wander alone and need to be led back to the nurturing and loving community that seeks equity and justice.

Sound like anyone you know?

Shepherding Lord, help me to trust and follow you. Restore in my soul whatever has atrophied from the abundance you envision for me. Allow me to embrace my virtues and recognize my limits so that I will be better enabled to follow. Amen.

The joke among my friends is that I'm failing retirement. Six months after retiring in 2018, I took a six-month interim parish appointment that lasted thirty months, including fifteen months during the worst of the COVID-19 pandemic. After re-retiring for 15 months, I became a part-time pastoral care staff member in October 2022 where I have served since.

Why? The professional (and amateur) psychologists will doubtless have a good time assessing my inner motives, and there are temporal considerations including the continuing full-time work of my spouse. Still, I truly believe that my yearning to serve comes from hearing the Shepherd's voice. There is no personal virtue in this, nor veiled criticism of my colleagues who are more adept at retirement than I. They also find ways to respond to Christ's call to serve.

To hear Jesus' voice, to belong to his sheep in the community we call the church, to make a difference for those who are "walk[ing] through the valley of the shadow of death" (Ps. 23:4) are profound privileges. While my own self-interest may obscure other motives, the voice of the Shepherd is unmistakable.

Jesus' critics in this passage miss two important messages. Jesus tells them who he is and they don't believe. Jesus also tells us who he is. Do we believe? Jesus then shows them who he is. We too see his works: healing, feeding, visiting, loving, serving, praying. These works testify to him in scripture and in the life of his body, the church. May we do these works also and be the sheep that "no one will snatch . . . out of [Jesus'] hand."

God, we are your sheep who yearn to follow. May the witness of your voice and your works help us do just that. Amen.

With apologies to William Shakespeare, a gazelle by any other name is still a gazelle. *Tabitha* is Aramaic for a female gazelle. Perhaps, like my almost-six-year-old granddaughter Eva, Tabitha was a jumper, full of energy, quick on her feet. The name Tabitha recalls to me Frances Havergal's lyric to "take my feet and let them be swift and beautiful for thee."

More importantly, Tabitha was consecrated to "good works and acts of charity." Her mourners showed Peter the garments she had made while alive, tactile testimonies of a life of giving and serving. The prayer shawl ministry of my former church was such a ministry, knitters faithfully and lovingly creating blankets to convey God's comfort.

Of course, temporal life ends. As my former church treasurer quips, "None of us gets out alive." Yet too often we act—or neglect to act—in ways that belie this simple truth. Our capacity for righteousness, for being good and doing good, is underutilized in our time on earth. We could do far worse than to inventory our gifts. What gifts can we offer, or continue to offer, to bless others?

Yes, Tabitha's story shows the power of God through prayer. She was indeed restored to life. Who among us has not prayed the same for those who are dear to us? We are glad Peter's prayer was answered: for Tabitha, for the widows who mourned her passing, and for the evangelical witness that "many believed in the Lord."

Yet death comes, even to Tabitha. So let us who are sheep, who follow the Shepherd, become Tabitha for today, gazelle-like in our quickness to do good.

Jesus, in the Apostles' Creed we affirm that you "come to judge the quick and the dead." Grant that such judgment is tempered with grace, so that we are inspired and invigorated to live lives of righteousness worthy of you. Amen.

Eighty years ago today World War II ended in Europe. As I am writing this in early 2024, the Russian invasion of Ukraine nears its two-year mark, the 2023 Sudanese war reaches its ninth month, and Israel's response to Hamas' surprise October 2023 attack nears its three-month mark. Domestic US gun violence continues unabated.

The vision of the writer of Revelation is as relevant today as it was at the end of the first century CE. Those "who have come out of the great ordeal" have the promise of being "before the throne of God." For John of Patmos, the vision's author, they are the church persecuted by imperial Rome for refusing to address emperor Domitian as "Lord and God." Today, those experiencing "the great ordeal" are all who are victims of hate and violence, extremism and terrorism, war and death—expressed through the barrel of a gun.

The search to determine the identity of the 144,000 (7:4) ensnares some Christians. The answer is irrelevant in the light of the welcome given "a great multitude that no one could count, from every nation, from all tribes and peoples and languages." God's welcome, on earth and beyond earthly travails, is often wider than our own. Their white robes and palm branches, symbolizing righteousness and victory, are the mantles suffering affords. In John's vision, it is a beatific life with God.

Let us pray this is so. How will we account for our lives to the Shepherd who is now the Lamb? He promises no more hunger, thirst, or scorching heat. He promises the refreshment of the "springs of the water of life" in the life to come. In the meantime, we who remain here on earth—often comfortable, often privileged—have similar marching orders. See Matthew 25:31-40 as we head to the mission field.

O Lamb of God, who taketh away the sins of the world, have mercy upon us. Amen.

John's triumphant victory song defies words to fully express its power. Consider listening today to any musical interpretation of "Worthy is the Lamb that was slain." My favorite is from G. F. Handel's *Messiah*, with its soaring chorus, dramatic pauses, and decisive "Amen." Or find another musical genre that appeals to you. It will move your heart as well as your mind as you embrace John's visionary promises.

They are indeed visionary. The Wesley Covenant Service reminds us, "My own righteousness is riddled with sin, unable to stand before you." John Wesley, Methodism's founder, knew this well, as his journal entry from May 24, 1738, witnesses. For him, the striving after a life of being perfect was a dead end. It was when he felt his "heart strangely warmed" by the grace of God that he came to understand Christian perfection as perfection in love. God's love, freely given—grace—is the true basis for our efforts to do good.

Doing good is its own reward. My late father, a committed churchman and law enforcement professional, sometimes questioned the notion of grace. He had seen enough bad actors to wonder about this God who loves us unconditionally. He would say, "If God loves me anyway, why be good?" I answered, "Dad, you don't have to be good. You can be 'bad' any time you want. But it is in your nature to be good; and it is in God's nature to be loving and gracious." I don't know that I ever fully convinced him, but he did seem to acquiesce to the analogy.

Ironically, the Shepherd has become the Lamb that was slain. We are forgiven by the power of his life and love, redeeming us to do good. Thanks be to God!

O God, thank you for Jesus the Lamb. Grant me humility as I remember and seek to live your redemptive love. Amen.

A challenge of John's Gospel is the phrase "the Jews" to describe Jesus' detractors. Many scholars believe John intended to refer to the religious leadership of Jesus' time, since Jesus and the earliest followers of "The Way" (as Christianity was first called) were all Jews.

This intent does not erase the ugly and violent history of antisemitism in general or of Christian persecution of Jews in particular. Since the Roman emperor Constantine converted to Christianity, Christians have done unspeakable things in God's name to Jews, other Christians, siblings of other faiths, and those of no particular faith. Both antisemitism and Christian nationalism are on the rise in the United States.

The dialogue between Jesus and "the Jews" in today's reading should give every Christian pause. "I have told you," Jesus replies to the demand to declare his identity as Messiah, "and you do not believe." *Pisteuo* in the Greek New Testament is the word for conviction or belief. This word appears ninety-eight times in John's Gospel, conveying not just intellectual assent but trust. We can easily substitute "the Christians" for "the Jews" in the dialogue. How do we fail to trust who Jesus says he is? If we fail to trust him, how are we disobedient in following? Will he know us?

One way to pursue righteousness is to examine our discipleship for its fidelity to Jesus. This is not only a personal examination but also a review of the ways Christianity has been unfaithful to Jesus. Another way to pursue righteousness is to promote interfaith understanding: as simple as getting to know a person of another faith and as complex as organized interfaith dialogue. These are ways to truly follow him.

Jesus, free us from the idolatry of orthodoxy. Help us to see the gospel witness of your works of love. May we show your love by doing our own works of love in your name. Amen.

We end the week as we began it: with the lyrical stanzas of Psalm 23. Though its cadences are often set to music, many of us speak of this psalm with a lyricism of the heart, a story we tell of how this psalm saw us through adversity.

Thirty years ago I stood in a line of tourists at Mesa Verde National Park in Colorado. The ranger leading our group advised us that the gate would be closed behind us as we entered the climb to the Native American cliff dwellings. The closed gate signaled to groups following that a group was ahead of them. He then turned to me and said, "Would you please be the last to enter and close the gate?"

"Sure," I chirped, not realizing this meant that I would be the last to climb. While the other tourists climbing the near-vertical ladders to reach the cliff dwellings had someone behind them to aid them if they stumbled, I did not. Nor did the ranger know I have a fear of heights. So, as I ascended rung by rung, I whispered Psalm 23. My fear subsided, but I was too embarrassed to confess how alone and inadequate I felt.

What inhibits our pursuit of righteousness is fear—of the unknown, of failure, of rejection—and trying to go it alone. Both are answered when we renew our belief in Christ as our Shepherd and live out that belief in the faith community we call the church. We belong to Christ and the church. The Shepherd's voice calls us to *ora et labora*—pray and work—for the justice and peace that is the path of righteousness. May this journey be ours.

O Jesus, grant me faith to trust your guidance as my Shepherd. Comfort me, but speak also to me of a holy calling to care for others, that the justice and equity that is your yearning may truly come. Amen.

Letting Love Guide You

MAY 12–18, 2025 • ANGELA D. SCHAFFNER

SCRIPTURE OVERVIEW: This week we focus on love. Through the psalm, we reflect on ways to engage with the external world of creation in order to refresh and renew our love for ourselves and for God. The passages from Acts and Revelation help us to take an internal look at ourselves, to acknowledge what we like and don't like, and to embrace all of it. The words of John's Gospel call us to turn outward and extend love to others. Indeed, love is the way others will know we are disciples of Jesus. Let love guide you through your journey this week.

QUESTIONS AND SUGGESTIONS FOR REFLECTION

- Read John 13:31-35. What is your definition of love? How do you love others, and how do you love yourself? What is the balance in the energy you give to others versus the energy you give to yourself? How do you feel about it?
- Read Acts 11:1-18. Are there aspects of yourself that you consider "unclean"? Could you give yourself more permission to allow all parts of yourself to be seen and loved?
- Read Psalm 148. What are some ways you can connect more deeply with God through creation?
- Read Revelation 21:1-6. What do you understand about this image of "a new heaven and a new earth?" What seems beyond comprehension or unknowable?

Dr. Angela D. Schaffner is a licensed psychologist practicing in Atlanta, GA. Angela specializes in helping clients with eating-related concerns and leads a martial-arts therapy group. She enjoys taekwondo, hiking, and spending time with family and friends. Angela attends Oak Grove United Methodist Church in Decatur, GA. She is the author of *Revealed: What the Bible Can Teach You About Yourself* (Upper Room Books, 2019) and *Gather Us In: Leading Transformational Small Groups* (Upper Room Books, 2020).

During my graduate training to become a licensed psychologist, I learned early on the importance of starting with a curious, loving stance with my clients. As budding therapists, my classmates and I were taught to foster an environment of safety and non-judgment as the foundation of all our work. We could be skilled at implementing the most complex interventions, but if we couldn't create safety through unconditional love all our other efforts would be fruitless.

Inevitably, our judgments surfaced. As we courageously named our biases in the light of a conversation with a supervisor, however, our competency improved. Once we could name our honest feelings and reactions to clients, we were free to love more fully and make better clinical judgments. We could show up for clients in a more unconditionally loving way.

Unconditional love flows most genuinely from our hearts into the lives of those around us when we understand that we too are deeply loved. One way we get to that understanding is by allowing safe people in our lives to see all parts of us. For us students, when a skilled supervisor witnessed our judgments, insecurities, and missteps, and then responded with grace and compassion, we felt seen and supported and could offer the same grace to our clients and others in our lives.

Jesus' commandment in today's scripture is to love one another. In fact, this is how others will be able to identify us as his disciples. But love is more than a feeling or an emotion. Love is active, and it's best expressed in honest relationships. Those I know who love others best are willing to address their biases and see other people through a clearer lens, and they allow themselves to be seen as the whole person they are. It takes both elements—of seeing and being seen—to truly love.

How am I letting people know and love me so I can more fully love others?

I spent much of my early adult life striving for degrees, accomplishments, praise, and approval from others. Though I followed my passions and genuinely loved many of my pursuits, my sense of peace was often lacking as I rarely paused for very long to really be still and breathe in the pleasure of living in these moments. Often it felt as though peace were a destination to which I'd not yet arrived.

Now in my forties, I'm considering a broader range of goals. My most meaningful pursuits are deeper and more relational in nature and less marked by a degree or formal celebration. I have more internal celebrations, knowing and recognizing when my choices reflect alignment in my relationship with God. It's easy to be pulled away from this alignment when we are chronically externally oriented to the many needs and perspectives of others or to the demands of our roles, responsibilities, and work.

Stepping into creation can be a way back to alignment within ourselves and with our Creator. The psalmist calls upon nature to praise the Lord, a personification of plants voicing a spiritual message. The cedars and fruit trees may preach the best sermons available to us if we are willing to visit them and be still. If we open our spiritual eyes and ears, we may hear their praise of love and truth. The truth is available to us in many places—through a gentle breeze that reminds us to be still and soothed in her softness, or through a cedar tree's strength, firmly rooted in its place during the storm with no shelter other than the companionship of neighboring trees. Creation is medicine for us, bringing truth to our souls. She is preaching the truth to her listeners.

Holy Creator, in the stillness of the trees, in the mountains and hills, my heart is revived by the truth. Thank you for this simple truth. Amen.

In my work, I help trauma survivors experience healing. Sometimes after experiencing a trauma, a client feels 'unclean' and undeserving of positive life experiences, limiting themselves and keeping their world small. They may associate with only a few people or limit the places they visit, or even limit the types of foods and pleasurable experiences they grant themselves, missing so much of what a full life has to offer.

As a trauma survivor myself, I worked hard to expand my world, allowing myself to be pulled further out of my comfort zone and to experience more of what life has to offer. I practiced meditation and mindfulness to become more present moment-to-moment rather than numbing myself through a jam-packed schedule and too many responsibilities. I allowed myself to bring all my questions, awkwardness, and fear into the light of God's and others' healing presence. Through God's radical permission and love, I found more of myself.

At the time of Peter's experience as told in Acts, the early growing church was struggling with who was in and who was out. Peter understood his vision to be telling him that exclusionary practices were not God's will for the community of faith.

Today, we likely have more difficulty accepting ourselves than we do others. I haven't always felt comfortable with what I witness in myself, but God gave me permission for all aspects of my identity and preferences to be named, seen, and known. My core sense of self came into the light and God called me *good*. I can approach myself with more curiosity and less judgment, have more courage stepping into the unknown, and grant myself more permission to live a full life. As we examine the ways we set unnecessary limits on ourselves and our experiences, we can embrace permission to live a full life, knowing we are loved.

God, embrace me as I step into the light; open my heart to receive permission to live a full life. Amen.

I love stepping into my backyard in my bare feet at night, walking through the grass and catching a glimpse of the moon through the branches of the large tree that stands just beyond our driveway. Sometimes it's a small crescent, barely visible, and other times it glows brilliantly and full, hanging low in the sky. Though the moon appears different each night, I know it is a constant. In viewing the moon and noting the moon's phases, I acknowledge the cyclical passage of time. I take it as an opportunity to reflect on my life as both deeply significant and as a part of something larger and more powerful going on around me.

As we follow the cyclical rhythm of our lives, we can orient ourselves both to what is constant and what is changing, knowing that we too show up differently day to day. Sometimes we reflect more light or less light to those around us depending on our feelings and circumstances. Notice how you feel about the moon; do you judge according to how much light is reflected, or can you see the beauty in each phase? We may benefit from approaching ourselves with the same grace, allowing ourselves to reflect more or less light to those around us in various seasons, but knowing our love and faith in God remains constant nonetheless.

Step outside to view the moon tonight and ask yourself a few questions. What is changing for you, and what is still the same? What are the cycles you see yourself repeating? Is there something you are needing to let go of during this season? Is there something new you're ready to embrace? As the psalmist notes that all of creation praises God, allow yourself to notice how the moon, the sun, and stars may be inviting you into a new way to worship and praise.

What do I most need to embrace, and what do I most need to let go?

John shares his powerful vision and paints a picture for us of a new heaven and a new earth, where God will dwell among us close enough to wipe away our tears. He describes a time when mourning, crying, pain, and death will no longer be a part of our experience.

We are all familiar with tears associated with mourning, pain, and sadness, even if we try to run or hide from them. But we need to feel emotional pain if we are to heal. We need to move toward painful feelings rather than avoid them. Most of us resist this, either consciously or unconsciously. Sometimes we numb ourselves through work, substances, distractions, or other activities we devise to avoid feeling discomfort. But when we avoid the pain, we often also lack true joy.

Hearing that God "will wipe every tear from [our] eyes" is a powerful image for all of us who have experienced the pain of life. When was the last time you cried? Recall the circumstances or feelings that prompted your tears. Were you alone or with someone? Did you fully release your tears or try to restrain them? How did you feel after you cried?

John's vision of a "new Jerusalem, coming down" insinuates that this holy city in which we will commune with God isn't some far off place but instead will become a reality in the world we know now, transforming this world. And in Christ, we know we can experience this new creation right here, right now. We can allow our tears, and we can allow Christ's presence to soothe us in our sadness.

God, be present with me as I allow my tears to flow, and help me experience your soothing relief as you and others comfort me in my sadness. Amen.

The promise of a new heaven and a new earth means we will experience change from what currently surrounds us. But John's apocalyptic words are not intended to comfort us about what is to come. His vision is an attempt to point out what is so very wrong with the world around us and to call us to change.

Doing new things has a lasting impact on our brains. We know a lot more about the brain than we did even twenty years ago, and one major recent finding is that we can impact the way our brain functions and rewire the brain through activities like meditation or simply thinking about things in a new way. Through repetition and focused attention, we can change the patterns in our brain and the way we automatically think about things. Many of our problems exist or are made worse by rigid thinking patterns and inflexibility. When we do new things or think about things differently, we open ourselves to the potential power in Christ to change the world around us.

Making changes can be difficult, however. Our brain likes to take shortcuts and default to its usual ways. By maintaining a focus on God's vision of a new creation, however, we can be encouraged to make small adjustments in our thoughts and behavior that bring us closer to God's vision. With practice, these small changes grow and grow, allowing God to work through us to bring about this new creation here on earth.

It may take some intentionality and repetition to make changes. Sometimes we stick with what feels comfortable because it feels safer or easier. Being willing to do something new or say something different is only the first step. God is moving and active in our lives, and we can safely move into new places too.

God, you are making all things new. Nudge me toward change that helps me participate in your work to bring change to our hurting world. Amen.

How do you know that someone loves you? Is it the words they say, the commitments they keep, the affection they show to you? Or maybe it's in the ways they've been there for you like no one else has, seeing you through some of your most vulnerable moments and standing by you, extending warmth and kindness. Maybe they have shown great patience and understanding. Maybe they have stuck by you when others have bailed.

We experience love in many ways, and we differ in terms of what feels most loving to us. I can recall countless times when a friend sat with me over coffee or dinner and listened, cried with me, or offered a kind of gentleness that invited me into more gentleness with myself. To me, that is love. Love is more than a kind intention, a warm thought, or a feeling. Love involves action that matches our feelings and commitment. Love stands as the greatest attribute and evidence of our faith.

When Jesus gives us a new commandment to love one another, he is issuing an invitation into his active ministry. To love as Jesus loved, we must sacrifice our self for the benefit of another. When all of us in community with one another love as Jesus loved, we all then become the recipients of a life-changing love that shapes how we see ourselves and how we interact with others. It is through this community of mutual love that others can see Christ.

Reflect on the deepest expressions of love you've received, and practice extending the same love to others. Our spiritual journeys wind through difficult terrain, but love steadies us. As we seek wisdom when we endure hardship, love grows. Love opens our eyes to the perspectives and challenges of others as we encounter our own. Our acts of love allow Christ's love to permeate the world around us.

God of love, help me love others as you have loved me. Amen.

Not as the World Gives

MAY 19–25, 2025 • BENJAMIN J. DUEHOLM

SCRIPTURE OVERVIEW: In this week's Gospel, Jesus is preparing his friends for his departure by promising them the Holy Spirit, who will guide them through the inevitability of loss and confusion. In Acts, we hear a story of this Spirit at work in the concrete choices faced by the early missionaries. The Spirit also grants John, the author of Revelation, a vision of a city that has been restored and redeemed by God's grace. In these passages, the Spirit is both a source of hope beyond our own perception and an aid to our own necessary decisions. Like the psalm's appeal for God's countenance to shine on us, the Spirit leads us into seeking and yearning for more.

QUESTIONS AND SUGGESTIONS FOR REFLECTION

- Read John 14:23-29. What more do we need to hope for? What gifts do we need that the world cannot give?
- Read Acts 16:9-15. What choices do you invite the Spirit to help you make? When has the Spirit shown up uninvited to your decision-making?
- Read Revelation 21:10, 22–22:5. Where do you see God at work redeeming or transforming your own community? Where are gates open, and where are they closed?
- Read Psalm 67. What do we hope for and work for on behalf of those we don't know or love? What should we hope and work for?

The Rev. Benjamin J. Dueholm is the pastor of Christ Lutheran Church (ELCA) in Dallas, TX. Ben is the author of *Sacred Signposts: Words, Water, and Other Acts of Resistance* (Eerdmans, 2018). He lives in Richardson, TX with his wife and three children.

In my years of ministry, I've often felt that I don't really know what I'm doing in the big picture. Perhaps you've felt this way too. But then, unexpectedly, I'll meet someone needing something that I am unusually well-prepared to provide. It may be a word of grace, a recognition of their unusual circumstance, or just the answer to a question I can give. Even when I feel lost and unsure of my work in the world, God grants me moments when I think *I'm glad that person happened to reach out to me in particular.* Have you experienced this alignment of your offering to someone's need? I try to treasure those moments.

When I hear Jesus say, "I do not give to you as the world gives," I think about those occasions when I feel particularly able to serve. Jesus' statement is a rather frustrating negative without a clear affirmative. How does the world give? It gives, we might say, by reliable and repeatable processes, by cause and consequence, by payment and benefit. How does Jesus give? Not like that.

Yet these are words of comfort for people destined to be tempted by perplexity. Jesus promises his friends an Advocate, or Helper, who will guide them through what will be an interminable wait for Jesus' return. We might follow Paul and say that the Holy Spirit advocates for us before God. But the Spirit also advocates for us before the world and its ways of giving. Maybe the Spirit also advocates for the world before us, to better enable us to navigate the world with wisdom and charity.

Jesus does not give to us as the world gives. But Jesus does give us the world in his own way—as a ground of serendipity, as oases of joy, as a place for us to give our best even when we can't imagine how we came to have the chance to do so.

Dear Jesus, as you give differently than the world gives, help me to receive your gifts as you wish them to be received, and help me to see your gifts where I am not accustomed to looking. Amen.

Not as the World Gives

Perhaps you've had this experience: In a dilemma, the right choice presents itself because the other options have become impossible. Before Paul's night vision of the Macedonian pleading for help, the disciples have been barred by the Spirit from proclaiming in the south and traveling to the north, so they take the road left to them, across the sea from Troas to Philippi.

While the first part of the chapter tells of a place where the churches "increased in numbers daily," the visit to Philippi at first feels like a shaggy dog story. Troas to Samothrace, Samothrace to Neapolis, there to Philippi, and after a few days, to a riverside place where Jews might be expected to gather on the sabbath (if the city didn't have a synagogue). There they find one person whose heart is opened and who listens eagerly.

Here's the wiliness, or maybe the thriftiness, of the Holy Spirit: closing door after door, elongating the remaining passage, and delivering her followers at last to one stretch of riverside and one listening soul. Lydia, she's called, a dealer in luxury goods who is originally from the very region where Paul and company have been unable to preach. In her zeal, she sees to the baptism of her whole household.

We have no indication that Paul had any resentment about crossing a sea for one believer. If, as seems plausible, there were second thoughts and moments of dejection on the trip, we must imagine them ourselves. Jesus does not give as the world gives, but he gives pearls of great price. It was the last thing to do, and the right thing, and it worked by the Spirit's own mysterious reckoning.

Gracious Holy Spirit, lead me and guide me where the path is uncertain and the future unclear. Help me to trust in your calling and rejoice in the people I meet through it. Amen.

Check out Pieter Bruegel's *Tower of Babel* paintings. They are late-medieval imaginings of the story from Genesis 11, when humanity attempts to scale heaven. This becomes the origin story for the diversity of languages, as God frustrates the plan by rendering the people unintelligible to one another.

Bruegel pictures a time before the disruption. In the version that hangs in Vienna, a ruler and subjects stand in the foreground of a majestic spiraling edifice. It's a doomed building, its pillars destined to crumble (and seem already to be doing so). Yet you can see scores of people still busy at work, far up in the structure. And the king, receiving the submissive gestures of the perhaps skeptical workers, is undeterred. Brilliant and accomplished but off-kilter and destined to fall short: here's the life of humankind in one image. Before Babylon or Rome, Bruegel seems to say, the paradigm of the great city had been attempted.

Images of redeemed cities are rarer. In Revelation, John is "in the spirit" when he sees Jerusalem descending from God. This city needs no lamps or places of worship because God is in its midst. Its gates will never close, the peoples and rulers will flow there to bring praise and tribute, and nothing wicked will enter. Even its flora will give grace.

I can't help but feel fondness for and even pride at the hopeless striving of the people in Bruegel's *Babel*. Storming heaven is the world's occupation, and why not? What marvels we can make in our attempts! What beautiful and terrible gifts we extract from the world!

But Revelation reminds us that God does not entice us up to heaven with ever-greater ingenuity. Rather, the redeemed city comes down from heaven to earth.

God of all the nations, remind us that we all have our source and end in you, and that your blessings will always exceed what we seek to gain with our own might. Amen.

Most of us like attention, even crave it; to be beheld can be a powerful experience, especially if we perceive the beholder as someone whose attention is discriminating and hard to hold. When the psalmist asks for God's "face to shine upon us," it is a recurrence of a figurative theme throughout the scriptures. Even Moses does not see God's face directly. But it is the summation of a yearning. It is the primal desire to be known and to know, to bask in the light of the One who cannot be truly known except through self-revelation.

This is different, however, from the manipulative gaze people sometimes employ on one another. People with narcissistic personalities hide their toxicity by making others feel special with their attention. It is challenging to see the toxic behavior for what it truly is because we want to be seen. While the yearning may feel the same—who has not longed to be gazed upon with a fervor like that of faith?—God's gaze is undiminished regardless of how many it falls upon. Shine your countenance upon us, not so that we may feel special but so that "your way may be known upon earth, your saving power among all nations."

Can we imagine attention without rivalry? Christians have often struggled to reconcile the belief that we have received grace and vocation in a particular way from God while also being part of God's universally beloved humanity. It's the logic of the world. For one to have, another must lack.

But as Jesus says, "I do not give to you as the world gives." In the economy of the psalm, there is no competing for God's attention. It may shine, at God's good pleasure, on the just and unjust alike, for God's own purpose of cultivating praise and salvation wherever it may grow.

O God, make your face shine upon us, that we may help your mercy grow and be shared with all nations. Amen.

Every Wednesday during the school year, my divinity school hosted a service in the small chapel on campus. It was a sparsely-attended affair all fall and winter until we got to Ash Wednesday. Then a big crowd would show up for the prayers and the ashes. The next week, they were gone again.

There's something about the ashes on the forehead that attracts us, I think. It is an intimate but also public gesture, a sign of humility stamped on the seat of our very personality. Everyone can see it but us. We are reminded of its presence on our own brow by seeing it on the faces of others.

"They will see his face, and his name with be on their foreheads," the visionary says. This line has the rhythm of the Hebrew scriptures: I will be your God, and you will be my people. The light of God's countenance will shine on them—for in them will be fulfilled the primal desire of beholding God face to face—and, somehow, they will be marked and identified with God's own name on their foreheads.

The desire to be seen and known brings with it the desire to belong: to see myself reflected in the other, and know that the other is reflected in me too. I don't picture anything as crude as a literal written brand imposed on the heads of those who have swarmed into the New Jerusalem. Rather, I imagine a revelation. The citizens see beyond the surface into the real self to find the name of their Creator and Redeemer etched there more deeply than words.

God of new creation, enlighten my heart so that I may see your name etched in me. Mark my life so that I may be seen and show forth the light of your face to the world. Amen.

Have you ever been the recipient of impulsive or unexpected hospitality? When I was a young English teacher in Taiwan, a mother of two helped rescue my credit card from a payphone that didn't want to give it back. Before I knew it, I was sightseeing in her hometown and getting an impromptu tour of her husband's dental practice. I was grateful but vaguely embarrassed. It seemed rather excessive.

Lydia, the newly baptized merchant in Philippi, "prevailed upon" Paul's traveling party to accept lodging and hospitality, Luke says. Perhaps I am reading the apostles' reluctance into that translation, picturing a full-press persuasive effort by Lydia where none is implied. Nevertheless, hospitality (especially in their world) creates a relationship and obligation that one might not wish to enter lightly. A little later in the book, Paul attributes to Jesus a claim that will become proverbial, that "it is more blessed to give than to receive" (Acts 20:35). But here, the hard work is to receive what is offered.

Jesus has a lot to say to his followers about giving things away and almost as much to say about going without. But he also stresses something that is easy for Christian preaching to leave out: the duty to receive joyfully what people give you. Indeed, he promises his friends that they will receive in return a hundredfold of what they give up in the form of unexpected blessings and new relationships that come as if from Jesus' own hand (see Mark 10:30).

Lydia prevails upon them to receive what she offers. The proud and dignified thing would be to say, "No, thank you, we're fine." But the godly task is to accept a new relationship, even on the spur of the moment, and accept its gifts with rejoicing.

God of unexpected gifts, help me to receive with joy even as I long to give with grace. Open my heart to those in a position to do me good, and help me to receive as from your own hand. Amen.

We started the week considering the opportunities we've had to provide something needed by another. Coming full circle, we now consider the times we have been on the receiving end. At times I have found myself in some kind of trouble, whether stuck in a plan that was failing, lost on the road, or just isolated and bereft in a place where I didn't know anyone. And somehow I got help from an unexpected source: a person I'd never met, or a chance encounter that offered precisely what I needed in the moment. My larger problem was not necessarily solved, but it was a relief to think, "I'm so glad I happened to run into this particular person."

"I do not give to you as the world gives." We take on projects, chase the gaze of the beloved, try to depend on ourselves and not the hospitality of strangers. And all of this can work. Just because we can't build the New Jerusalem ourselves doesn't mean that we can't build beautiful things together. Just because human attention falters and strays doesn't mean that we can't see and know one another in good and meaningful ways. We glimpse God's goodness in these things.

But Jesus insists that his way of giving is different. It is unexpected, undeserved, and not always easy to accept. We are placed in relationships with people we did not plan to encounter and made to depend on blessings we did not know to look for. With prayer and hindsight, we may note the hand and voice of God in them. Jesus assures his friends that the Advocate, the Holy Spirit, will not just lead them into new situations but will remind them "of all that I have said to you." To receive from God is to remember, so that all our new arrivals are also homecomings, and all our new faces are portals to God's countenance.

Dear Jesus, thank you for the gifts you give and the ways you give them. Attune my heart to remember, to be grateful, and to look forward with hope. Amen.

Transformation as Salvation

MAY 26–JUNE 1, 2025 • JULIE O'NEAL

SCRIPTURE OVERVIEW: Across these verses, a rich journey unfolds, weaving together themes of identity, transformation, faith, and unity. Acts portrays powerful shifts in identity as a young enslaved girl and a jailer are given new opportunities. In the psalms, we read how people empowered with God's righteousness and justice can transform communities. Revelation helps us remember the early church and how tradition continues today. John underscores unity among believers, praying for oneness through faith, mirroring divine unity. Collectively, these scriptures showcase how individual identity, nurtured by faith and transformation, unites people with God and one another, fostering cohesive unity and shared purpose.

QUESTIONS AND SUGGESTIONS FOR REFLECTION

- Read Acts 16:16-34. When have you experienced unexpected transformations that have challenged your sense of identity and self-perception?
- Read Psalm 97. How does recognizing the presence of something greater than yourself inspire in you gratitude and a desire to contribute to your community?
- Read John 17:20-26. What signs of division do you see in your community? How can you work toward the oneness to which God calls us?
- Read Revelation 22:12-14, 16-17, 20-21. Who is invited into the kingdom? How does this reshape the way you view the invitation to the sacraments?

Julie O'Neal is a fifth generation United Methodist, and her family has lived in Arizona for four generations. Julie is a Korean American adoptee who enjoys traveling and spending time with her family, friends, and two dogs.

The story of Paul and Silas being sent to prison focuses on the actions of Paul and the anger of the enslavers. Yet within this story exists a girl possessed by a spirit of divination that clouds her genuine self. After we read of Paul's casting out of the spirit, we are left with no resolution to her story. We instead follow Paul and Silas to the jail.

We can only imagine the impact and consequences for the girl in the aftermath. We can assume that when Paul removes this spirit, it disrupts the girl's reality, opening the door for a tumultuous shift in her existence. She is set free. She becomes human again. Perhaps it brought confusion, shattering the familiar but false identity that the spirit imposed. It certainly destroyed her worth in the eyes of those who had enslaved her. What did she do in the days and weeks after this transformation? I wonder if she had any further interaction with Paul or the early Christian community. Did the community around her accept her, finding a place for her to thrive in this new identity?

In our own lives, we may experience transformation that reveals an unexpected truth about our own identity. This process may challenge our previous perception of ourselves and open a new chapter in understanding who we are, bringing with it a myriad of contradictory emotions. Others may wonder about and even be uncomfortable with our process of revelation.

Transformation as a characteristic of the life of faith means that our identity is ever evolving. Instead of avoiding or fearing growth, we can acknowledge the complexities of our identity as children of God and soak up the reassurance of God's guiding light in times of personal transformation.

Holy One, grant us the courage to confront and overcome the forces that cloud our genuine selves. Help us discern the illusions that hinder our true identities and block our path to growth. Amen.

We continue the story with Paul and Silas who are now imprisoned for their unwavering commitment to spreading the gospel. Rather than feeling defeated or giving up hope, they wait patiently for God's action, singing and praying as they wait. They exhibit a deep and unwavering belief in God's liberating love and saving grace. Their actions offer the other prisoners—and us—a different way of dealing with tough times.

Because of Paul and Silas' response to their imprisonment (singing and praying), we clearly see the earthquake as God's divine intervention. We don't know why Paul or Silas or, apparently, any of the other prisoners do not escape once the prison doors are opened. Perhaps they are as surprised as the jailer is fearful. He has failed to do his job, and fears the consequences. However, he is surprised to learn all the prisoners are still inside. Their integrity overwhelms the jailer, and he begs Paul and Silas to explain how he can be saved.

Paul and Silas are quick to explain that God's salvation is for all, including him and his household. They invite the jailer to embrace divine love, an act that profoundly changes his life and the lives of those in his household.

God's salvation extends beyond anything and everything that defines any of us. Another example of the expansive love and inclusion of God, it highlights the work of unyielding faith, unforeseen hope, and the promise of redemption. These transformational experiences of faith are available to all who are willing to have God radically alter the course of their lives.

God of grace, help us, like the jailer, embrace the liberating truth of God's salvation. May it redefine our identity, enabling us to extend love, grace, and compassion to others through the extraordinary power of the gospel. Amen.

In the musical *Hamilton*, Eliza Hamilton asks her husband, Alexander, to acknowledge the joy of simply being alive in the moment with one another. She wants him to be content because his efforts to build a new world and leave a legacy threaten his life. Her heartfelt words capture how simply being present with each other is fulfilling and satisfying enough. Yet Alexander is not satisfied. He has an internal drive to create this new world he envisions, and he sees it as his responsibility to make this vision a reality for his family and for his country. The conflict between the two characters fuels much of their interaction throughout the musical.

What is the balance between progress and praise? In Psalm 97, the psalmist affirms God's righteousness and justice as an ever-present reality, the ultimate refuge and source of true happiness and life. Because of God's rule in the entire cosmos, there is a right ordering of society that excludes no one from access to provision for life and future. This praise seems to indicate that all is right, that God's envisioned future has come to fruition. Yet clearly not all is right with the world. War rages, children go hungry, political division digs us deeper into a standstill. How do we praise God knowing so much suffering abounds?

Returning to the psalms of praise is not an invitation to ignore the realities of our world or to be satisfied with the injustice we see. Rather, the psalms invite us to seek that balance between praise and progress for ourselves. We can confidently praise our Creator for the existence of a righteous and just foundation, while allowing God to work through us to establish that foundation here on earth.

Creator God, we acknowledge your presence as the ultimate refuge and source of true happiness and life. Guide us to create a society where every individual has access to a dignified life and a promising future. Amen.

ASCENSION DAY

Over the course of history, artists have rendered their interpretations of the Divine through various mediums. From oil paintings to clay figurines, artists can manipulate the various materials to show their vision and imagination, offering a window to let God's light shine through.

At the Basilica of the National Shrine of the Immaculate Conception, located in Washington D.C. (USA), there is a mosaic that portrays the ascension of Jesus. I am struck by the vividness of the color of the sky and the depth of the neutral-toned clouds and Christ's scarlet robes. While the complexion of Jesus conveys a euro-centrality that causes me to pause, I still marvel at how the artistic manifestation can foster connection and introspection, stir devotion, and nurture a deeper spiritual resonance.

The culmination of Jesus' earthly journey at his ascension, along with the successive arrival of the Holy Spirit, sparks the inception of the disciples' own profound ministry. It marks a pivotal shift of leadership. Empowered, they embark on a sacred duty: to reassemble and rekindle the fragmented community. Their ministry, a symphony of teaching and service, aims to create a unified body guided by Jesus' teachings. They become custodians, nurturing a collective of people bound by faith and compassion, using the teachings and tools they have been given along the way, just as artists use their tools to draw viewers in and move them to a new place. Today, Christians follow in the footsteps of the first disciples, piecing together the body of Christ into one beautiful image.

Creative God, may our artistic expressions invite all to experience you in new and beautiful ways and deepen our understanding and expression of you. Amen.

When I was in seminary, a wise professor often emphasized, "If it's repeated, it must be important." It was a clue to what might be coming. Psalm 47 is one of those places where repetition invites us into a melody of praise that transcends boundaries. It feels like a catchy song that repeats its chorus, inviting all nations to clap their hands and raise joyful shouts to God. This psalm has no limit: either in geography or language. It repeats the message that God is in charge of everything, including us. The power of repetition is a rhythmic reminder to weave a cadence of adoration into the fabric of our daily existence. In the constancy of our praise, we echo the steadfastness of God's work in the world.

Yet making this a reality requires intentionality. It invites us to infuse our days with simple moments to praise God. And even then, it will take some practice. We might scribble a reminder on a piece of paper or set an alarm on our phone. We might repeat a short, one-sentence prayer throughout the day. We might allow ourselves to be cued by the ordinary, recalling ourselves to praise while standing in line at the store or when taking a short walk. Amidst the whirlwind of obligations and responsibilities, integrating repeated praise becomes an affirmation of our identity.

Like a variety of instruments coming together to create a beautiful harmony, let us, in our weariness and diversity, join the chorus of Psalm 47. May the recurring notes of our praise reflect the unchanging nature of God and remind us of our identity as beautiful parts of God's creation.

God, through our continual praise, may we resonate with your unchanging presence, affirming our identity as your beloved. Amen.

Bread of Life, given for you. Cup of Hope, poured out for you. At the core of the church's purpose is a constant exploration of what it truly means to live out the teachings of Christ. One way we do that in the life of the church is through ritual. These practices continue the traditions that Jesus shared with the disciples. When we take part in the sacrament of Holy Communion, we participate in remembering Jesus' words, life, and sacrifice. We gather as those who have witnessed Christ's influence in the world. We praise God's love for humanity. And we celebrate and affirm the connection among believers.

Yet our inclination is to define who is worthy and who falls short of receiving the gift. We skew the understanding of redemption and grace. As much as we may not want to admit it, the invitation is not ours to extend. We do not get to create the guest list. The Spirit and the Bride are the ones inviting us to this holy party, and Christ is the host. The rest of us are merely guests. Although not everyone chooses to attend God's party, everyone is invited. After all, who isn't thirsty? Who doesn't need Christ's life-giving water? We do not have to fight to be the first in line. There is plenty of God's love and abundant life to go around.

God, you have promised the gift of living water. May we be quick to accept your invitation, wash our robes, and sit at your holy table. Amen.

Written in 1988, the hymn "Ososo" (TFWS #2232) petitions God to reconcile the divide between North and South Korea. Today it is sung to ask God for wholeness and healing in all places of conflict and harm.

It is not hard to imagine a nation in turmoil, torn apart by deep-rooted division. Political, cultural, and historical fault lines fragment its people. The imbalance of power, resistance to change, lack of trust, and unwillingness to forgive stand in the way and cause resistance.

In the heart of such a tumultuous landscape, whispers of unity begin to surface. Voices from everyday people, weary of discord, start conversations that reveal shared worries and aspirations. Leaders begin complex and delicate negotiations to broker a ceasefire and work toward peace. Regular people offer a kind smile or a helping hand across "enemy" lines and begin to build connections with one another. Children, with no record of the past, bridge chasms no one else could. Slowly, things can shift. Communities band together to confront common challenges, realizing the strength that comes with unity. Fractures begin to mend, and healing guides a path forward.

Today the fracture between North and South Korea, as well as countless other communities and countries, is as wide as ever. But Christians still pray "Ososo" together. There is profound unity between two supposed enemies in their prayer for reconciliation. They embody Christ's prayer in John 17 that if Christ is in us we will be made one in him.

Prince of Peace, healer of all, may we be inspired to imagine peace and to work toward reconciliation in our communities and the world at large. Amen.

The Promised Holy Spirit

JUNE 2–8, 2025 • RHODA MANZO

SCRIPTURE OVERVIEW: The passages for this week talk about the coming of the promised Holy Spirit. In John's Gospel, Jesus promises to send the Advocate, the one who will teach the disciples and help them remain connected to Christ. The psalmist praises God for how creation is renewed through the Spirit. Paul reminds readers that those led by God's Spirit are God's children. In Acts, the disciples wait for the promised power that will help them become effective witnesses. They receive that promise fulfilled on the day of Pentecost, turning them from people of fear to people of fire. Through our exploration of the Holy Spirit, we learn this Helper is not just an idea or a reminder but a manifestation of God's presence who will guide us in truth, advocate for us, and give us peace.

QUESTIONS AND SUGGESTIONS FOR REFLECTION

- Read Acts 2:1-21. Why was the outpouring of the Holy Spirit on the day of Pentecost important for the church?
- Read Psalm 104:24-34, 35b. When you look at the natural world around you, what does it tell you about God?
- Read Romans 8:14-17. What assurance does the Holy Spirit give us?
- Read John 14:8-17, 25-27. How often do you seek the help of the Holy Spirit?

The Rev. Dr. Rhoda Manzo is a pastor and a trained teacher with The United Methodist Church in Nigeria.

Waiting is always a difficult task. The disciples were commanded by Jesus not to leave Jerusalem but to wait there for the promise of God. It must have been difficult for them to wait, not knowing when this promised help would arrive.

Ten days after Jesus' ascension, about 120 of his followers were praying together and waiting for the gift of the Holy Spirit that Jesus had promised. It was the Festival of Weeks, an annual Jewish celebration of the giving of the Law at Mount Sinai, where the first fruits of the harvest are offered with joy and thanksgiving accompanied by the recitation of Deuteronomy 26:3-10. This festival takes place fifty days after Passover, and Jerusalem was crowded with Jews who had come from many countries to celebrate. Into this setting the Holy Spirit arrives. When the foreign Jews hear the local Galileans praising God in all their native languages—at least fifteen are listed—a great crowd gathers in bewilderment. "And how is it that we hear, each of us, in our own native language?" they ask in amazement.

The Day of Pentecost is an interesting time for Jesus' followers to be empowered to fulfill their commission to continue his ministry on earth. The miraculous arrival of the Holy Spirit is more widely experienced because the disciples are surrounded by Jews from "every people under heaven." Jesus' followers are not only filled with the Holy Spirit but with the ability to speak the languages of the nations present. This is one of the first signs that the gospel is intended for all nations of the earth. God does not want anybody to be left out; the Holy Spirit is still available to all who desire the Spirit's indwelling presence and power today.

Thank you, God, for your great gift of the Holy Spirit which you have poured out freely. Amen.

Jesus promised that the disciples would receive power when the Holy Spirit had come upon them. Sure enough, Peter, who a few weeks before had been afraid even to admit to a servant girl that he was a follower of Jesus, now stands up and preaches a powerful sermon to a great crowd that has gathered. "These people are not drunk, as you suppose. It's only nine in the morning!" he thunders. "No, this is what was spoken by the prophet Joel: 'In the last days, God says, I will pour out my Spirit on all people'" (NIV).

When the Holy Spirit was poured out on them, a divine reinforcement took place instantly. They appear to become new people doing a new work. Although the Holy Spirit was clearly at work in the lives of God's people in the Hebrew scriptures, the prophet eagerly looks forward to a far greater and more extensive work of the Spirit as promised. This is the promise the prophet Joel reveals. The great gift which God had reserved till the last day was being poured out freely now.

All were to know the touch of the Spirit of God. We see God moving out beyond the boundaries of the Jewish people to offer to all people that relationship which is at the heart of eternal life. The Holy Spirit living in each believer constitutes a living link binding each individual to other believers, forming a worldwide community. With the coming of the Holy Spirit on Pentecost, the nature of the relationship between God and God's people changed.

God, thank you for your gift of the Holy Spirit, our source of power. Help us to be effective witnesses and to proclaim the gospel of Christ. Amen.

Reading through this psalm brings to mind my experience visiting Nyanga, Zimbabwe. We took a hike up the mountain, and I found a top stone and sat down to see the view. It was absolutely majestic! It was a beautiful sight to behold. Like the psalmist, I was reminded that all the beauty and splendor of the universe come from God's creative hands.

We can rejoice in the marvels of nature, at the sparkling waterfall and the soaring eagle, because we know they are the handiwork of God. All creatures, great and small, depend on God as their parent figure, and they are members of God's vast family. God's sustaining care is the ultimate source of their food supply. The power of life and death is in God's breath.

Everything God created is a gift. Any effort to save the earth should arise from our worship of its Creator and our knowledge that we are called to responsible stewardship of this gift. While secular poets describe nature in beautiful and fascinating ways, the psalmist rightly gives credit where credit is due. Everything that exists is made by God. We can and should praise the Creator.

This psalm brings to mind the hymn "How Great Thou Art" by Stuart Hine (UMH #77). The first two verses of this hymn extol the majesty of creation, and the chorus echoes into glorious praise as a result of viewing this creation: "Then sings my soul, my Savior God to Thee; / how great thou art!" Whether through praying the psalms, singing hymns of praise, or writing our own words of acclamation, our experiences in God's creation can only direct us to a place of praise and thanksgiving.

Lord, thank you for creating all creatures both great and small. We praise you for your sustaining care. Amen.

Paul's message in the eighth chapter of his letter to the Romans necessarily calls to mind the Exodus story of the Israelites leaving Egypt. God led the Israelites out of Egypt, away from a life of bondage and slavery into an inheritance of land and prosperity. Paul says God is leading those of the new covenant in this new day. Just as the Israelites were claimed by God as God's children, so too are followers of Christ claimed as God's children.

Under Roman law a person could be adopted at any age to possess all the rights of an heir born into the family. Paul uses this analogy to express important theological principles. Christians become the children of God through God's own initiative through faith in the person and work of Jesus Christ and by being conformed to the likeness of God's son. Christ is the son of God by nature and high relation, but Christians are God's children by adoption. As children of God, we receive privileges such as redemption, the removal of condemnation, and the full rights of an heir.

Paul concludes this section with a reminder of what it means to be a full, fellow heir with Christ. It's not all benefits. When Christians become children of God, there are certain responsibilities involved. We are expected to live according to the Holy Spirit and the new nature, to put to death the misdeeds and work of the flesh, to share in Christ's sufferings, and to follow God's Spirit and will.

Dear God, thank you for granting me the full rights to eternal inheritance. Amen.

Have you ever struggled with a deep sense of inferiority? Have you felt like your life was amounting to nothing? As a child I often found myself struggling with this feeling. I grew up in a culture where preference is given to male children over female children. The male child is seen as the one who will carry on the family lineage, so all privileges and rights go to him. The female is expected to marry into another family and help her husband carry on the lineage of that family. As a result, she is considered less important. Even though things are changing now, this societal norm affected me badly.

But when I gave my life to Christ, everything changed for me. I moved from inferiority to adequacy. The Holy Spirit gave me the assurance that I have been "accepted in the beloved" (Eph. 1:6, KJV). No matter how little worth the world may see in me, God has proclaimed my value through adopting me as God's child. God loves me for myself alone; as our text for today puts it, a "joint heir with Christ."

What does it mean to be a child of God? No good work can earn this position. We are each dear to the Almighty as God's own child. And if we are a child of a king, how can we feel inferior? Words alone cannot move this truth from our head into our heart. But we can lean on the Holy Spirit for support in understanding and accepting this truth.

Every person is dear to God, not because of what they do but because of who they are as a child of God. Can anything be more wonderful than to know beyond any shadow of doubt that we belong to God and are heirs and joint heirs with Jesus Christ? It is the Spirit who helps us believe we are known and loved.

God, I am grateful for your Spirit that bears witness to my position as your child. Amen.

The disciples of Jesus are distressed and confused in the upper room as they listen to Jesus trying to prepare them for his coming death and departure. "Do not let your heart be troubled; I will not leave you orphaned," Jesus assures them (John 14:1, 18). Then he promises that God will send them an Advocate to be with them forever. The Holy Spirit will come and be with them as their constant companion.

The word that catches my attention is *advocate*. The Greek word is *parakletos,* translated literally "one who is called to one's aid" and can be translated as "exhorter" or "encourager." An advocate is a legal representative who is required to do their best for their client and plead their cause; they are someone called in to help in time of trouble or need. In the Holy Spirit we have an advocate who operates on a higher level. The Spirit is Jesus' personal representative and substitute, enabling the disciples to carry on Jesus' ministry without his physical presence on earth.

The Holy Spirit is an advocate who does not merely support us but is the manifestation of God's presence with us. The Holy Spirit is the Spirit of truth who pleads the cause of truth in our heart against every argument that sin can devise. Similarly to the way we engage the Christ, the original *parakletos*, we choose whether we receive this gift of the Holy Spirit. Like Christ, the world will reject this Advocate, but Christ's followers will know the Holy Spirit living within us.

Triune God, thank you for providing for me an advocate who is always there to guide me. May I be open to the Spirit's nudges, following where she leads. Amen.

PENTECOST

We continue to look at the ministry of the Holy Spirit. These verses convey Jesus' final message to his disciples as recorded in the Gospel of John.

He speaks of the Holy Spirit as a teacher who will teach us all things. The Spirit will lead Christians deeper and deeper into the truth of God. The Spirit will remind us of the teachings Jesus has already given. In matters of belief, the Holy Spirit is constantly bringing us back to the things Jesus said and taught (see 1 Cor. 2:13).

In addition, the Holy Spirit will keep us right in matters of conduct. At times when we are tempted to do something wrong, we may recognize in the back of our mind a saying of Jesus, a verse in a psalm, or some teaching we received when we were young. In a moment of temptation, these things might flash unbidden into our minds. We can identify that as the work of the Holy Spirit.

Jesus finally speaks of his gift of peace. In Hebrew the word for peace is *shalom*. This is not simply the absence of trouble. It means everything which makes for our highest good. The peace which the world offers us is never complete: It is the peace of escape, the peace that comes from avoidance of trouble and from refusing to face things. But the peace that Jesus offers us is the peace of wholeness. No experience in life can ever take this peace from us, and no sorrow, no suffering can make it less. The peace that Christ gives banishes fear and dread from the heart.

Thank you, God, for sending the Holy Spirit to give us the assurance that you will always fulfill your promises. Amen.

The Gift of Divine Connection

JUNE 9–15, 2025 • SARA COWLEY

SCRIPTURE OVERVIEW: The Holy Spirit is God working in our lives to create sacred connection within our shared human struggle. The psalmist is overwhelmed by the splendid work of creation in Psalm 8. Paul writes in Romans about the powerful love we can find in the presence of the Holy Spirit. The Gospel of John echoes this sentiment by seeing the Holy Spirit as the messenger of truth. And finally, Wisdom, expressed as a female personification of God's divine attribute, cries out from the city gates in Proverbs. The workings of the Holy Spirit create within us the space to hear the voice of God. As Wisdom cries out sacred truth, so should we continue to listen for the promptings of the Spirit.

QUESTIONS AND SUGGESTIONS FOR REFLECTION

- Read Psalm 8. How do you feel the presence of God when you express your creativity?
- Read Romans 5:1-5. What does the gift of the Holy Spirit mean for your everyday life?
- Read Proverbs 8:1-4, 22-31. In what ways have you been speaking out against injustice in your community?
- Read John 16:12-15. How does the concept of integrity relate to your experience of God?

Chaplain Sara Cowley is a certified candidate for ministry as a deacon in The United Methodist Church. Sara is a member of St. Stephen UMC in Mesquite, TX.

The psalmist compliments "the work of [God's] fingers" in verse 3, and I envision the first quilt I made. While not as majestic as the heavens or the stars and moon, I created this quilt with my own hands. I stared longingly at the fabric wall at my local sewing shop and imagined what beauty I might create. My eagerness to select the perfect colors and my final fabric and thread decisions were made based on the hope that I might transform those raw materials into something beautiful. The base fabrics were there, but it was up to me to turn them into something marvelous.

Creativity is a gift from God's power, an indication of the divine spark within us. The beauty we find in nature comes from our reflection and admiration of God's handiwork. From the bright noonday sun to the glow of moonlight, God's completed work shows we share the same intentions that I had at the fabric store: the hope and the potential to create a thing of beauty.

My first quilt was not perfectly constructed, but its uneven lines remind me of the time and love I invested in the project. Looking at my quilt reminds me of how God put similar care and love into the act of Creation, a much larger project. Humanity's desire to make new things is one that comes from the Holy Spirit's influence on our lives, driving us to mirror God's precise construction. Whether it is a quilt, a painting, a dance, a poem, a building, or a loaf of bread, we honor our Creator by modeling the hope and care God has gifted us.

Creator who shaped the stars and moon, we praise your majestic name! Help us create in ways that honor the divine spark within us. Amen.

TUESDAY, JUNE 10 ~ *Read Romans 5:1-2*

When I am really excited about something, I can't sit still. I become so invested in what I am passionate about that I cannot stop talking about it. When I began seminary, it was all I could think about. It became my whole identity almost overnight. My friends certainly became incredibly well-informed of my excitement at starting a new path. It was the first step in a journey that got me closer to becoming a hospital chaplain, and I would enthusiastically expound to anyone willing to listen where I felt God was guiding me.

Here in Romans, Paul is also encouraging us to boast. We are taught from an early age that boasting should be avoided because it is selfish. But the Greek root does not mean boasting in the sense of bragging; this root can also mean *rejoice* or *glorify*. Imagine being so excited by your faith that you jump at the chance to talk about the "hope of sharing the glory of God." How thrilling to finally feel the grace of God working inside you!

My enthusiasm at starting seminary was the same. I was so happy to finally be stepping into my call. And even though it was scary and I was full of my own insecurities, I found the entire process exhilarating. I was full of hope.

You do not have to go to seminary to discover how your connection to God is changing your life for the better. You only have to be willing to see the Holy Spirit working in your life and to appreciate the grace you have been given as a child of God. No matter the glory of God that we have received, we can boast in our hope joyfully.

Holy God, we ask for your help to boast in gratitude for the many gifts you have given us. Encourage us to rejoice in your hope. Amen.

In times of great turmoil, I feel the presence of God. Not everyone does, and I think this is because we as human beings are often distracted by our own pain. In my work as a hospital chaplain, I see how very easy it is to forget the care God provides and the love "poured into our hearts." I often sit on the oncology floor with patients who are experiencing heartbreaking and unfathomably painful situations. Many of them have already resigned themselves to a hard death, one full of pain. In these situations, Paul's words are not helpful to them.

Not to say that this part of Romans is inaccurate. Suffering does produce many profound things, including endurance and character. But not all those who suffer boast of or joyfully glorify God in their pain in obvious ways. Sometimes there is no silver lining to pain. Just because you, the spiritual caregiver, see hope in the situation does not mean the patient in front of you does. The best response I can offer in these moments is to listen. Listening is a sacred gift of the Holy Spirit.

I witness these painful moments in the lives of others constantly. Chaplains hold space for the intense negative emotions of their patients and also hold space for hope, keeping these feelings in tension with one another. Our patients feel God's love when they are given space to be open and honest. For many of my patients the first step to feeling the presence of God is being able to express their pain aloud and to be heard without yet expecting to find the redemption that will one day be there.

Healing One, comfort those in pain so that they can feel the strength of your love poured into their hearts. Guide us in supporting those who may simply need us to listen. Amen.

Wisdom calls out to us, her people. From her vantage point at the town gate, she sees the frustrations and difficulties of her community, and she empathizes with them.

I experience a feeling of unease in the pit of my stomach when I watch acts of injustice unfold around me. Before I became a Christian, I might have called this unease a "gut feeling." But it isn't just disgust or discomfort at specific situations. I believe it is the Holy Spirit sounding the alarm within me. We must consider these feelings and reflect on the empathy of Wisdom, not ignore these promptings of the Spirit when they occur.

When we witness discrimination toward another, it's easier to ignore our own discomfort than confront the situation head-on. After all, it's not about us. Who are we to step in? But that's not what Wisdom asks us to do. She raises her voice at the very center of town, demanding that she be heard. When we see injustice happening around us, we must do the same. It is never okay to stay silent in the face of oppression. It is up to us to speak out when we feel injustice crying out from inside, when we feel that prompting from the Holy Spirit to stand up and raise our prophetic voices against prejudice (see Prov. 8:6-7).

Wisdom stands at the town gates for a reason. She will not be ignored. Her exhortations are public and loud. Hearing Wisdom's cry is not enough. It is not just our job as Christians to listen; we must also act! We must stand with her at the town gates and scream for God's justice to be done "on earth as it is in heaven" (Matt. 6:10).

God who hears the cries of the marginalized, help us find our prophetic voice. Help us cry out with Wisdom on behalf of those suffering injustice so that we can work toward a better world together. Amen.

I am an only child. My parents constantly joked that "if we had more kids, we would have gotten the child we actually deserved," because I was, in their words, an "angel" growing up. I was high-achieving at school, polite, shy, and never gave my parents a reason to worry about me. This persisted all the way until my preteen years, when things changed. My parents struggled to reconcile that children grow up and make their choices, and parents must live with hope that they have instructed their children as best as they could. These growing pains are difficult for all involved.

Humanity may represent God's children. But we certainly are, over our time on earth, growing up and making our own choices. We look to our faith to help guide us, and we look to what we learn from our Infinite Parent so that we can be stewards of the earth. The fulfillment of our vocation to love God and love neighbor is challenged constantly by the sinfulness of our environment. Like the growing pains I experienced as a preteen, these are growing pains too.

Wisdom rejoices in creation and spends time "delighting in the human race" because God's inhabited world, despite all its sinfulness, is still a place to celebrate. We are God's children, and with that comes responsibility. Can you delight in the human race even when it makes mistakes? Wisdom can, because she is one of God's greatest attributes. Wisdom is being able to see humanity as multifaceted and still maturing. The ability for us to see humanity as complex, yet delight in it all the same, is the very heart of our identity as children of God.

Infinite Parent, help us mature in you so that we can continue to rejoice in the world's shared humanity. Amen.

The Spirit of truth, the Advocate that Jesus promises to send, is a presence we can trust. The Holy Spirit functions as a bridge of communication between God and humankind, and we should rejoice in this shared connection with our Creator. At the same time, truth is a double-edged sword. "All the truth" means we will hear messages good, bad, and in-between about what is to come. How can we live in this complexity?

When my husband, Cameron, and I went on our first date, we were just starting the process of getting to know one another. But the principle that guided us in cultivating that relationship and learning more about one another was honesty, both with each other and ourselves. This led to more dating and finally a marriage that has thrived in mutual respect and care. There have been bad days, lean years, and much change, but our love is strong. Honesty and truth can be painful, but through them relationships grow and thrive.

When I became a Christian again after many years of seeking something else, reconnecting with God felt even more tentative than that first date with Cameron. I didn't know exactly what I wanted out of my relationship with God. But I did know I wanted truth, even when the initial getting-to-know-one-another-again was not going well. I knew at that time that my commitment had to encompass honesty, especially honesty with my own failings and insecurities. When I accepted the truth of who I am, the Holy Spirit led the way. The Spirit of truth solidified my new identity as a Christian.

God, through good times and bad you provide us a path to live with integrity and to follow you. Help us appreciate the gift of prayer and communicate to you and to one another with open hearts. Amen.

TRINITY SUNDAY

When Wisdom yells, "My cry is to all who live," she is breathing divine grace to us. That grace is wisdom. Wisdom is a divine attribute of God. Wisdom does not favor one group over another. Its secrets are not gate-kept. Rather, it is the great equalizer. Wisdom is fully inclusive of all the people on earth because, like the first breath of a newborn, we all need it to survive and thrive. The call to wisdom is one to universal understanding that comes from the city gates, the very center of activity in the ancient world. And though this might sound like a cry from the past, Wisdom continues to actively call humanity to her side. "I love those who love me, and those who seek me diligently find me" (Prov. 8:17) is a solemn vow, one that rings throughout time.

My first year of seminary, I mixed up Proverbs with Ecclesiastes on a final exam. I put Wisdom where she did not belong. My professor responded by subtracting points. When I did the quick math reading through his subtractions, I realized this mistake would cost me a full letter grade on the exam. I was devastated. I was sure this simple mistake would drop my final grade in the class as well.

Then I saw in his final comment that he had given me grace and rounded my grade back up. He included a personal note that wished me blessings on my future ministry. I cried tears of relief for my grade and for my professor's compassion. I know now that true wisdom is giving others the same grace God shows us.

God of compassion and grace, thank you for always forgiving our mistakes and leading us toward greater learning. Amen.

Navigating Life with God

JUNE 16–22, 2025 • ERIN BEASLEY

SCRIPTURE OVERVIEW: In this week's readings, individuals long for God's grace and receive it, being transformed for service to God as a result. Psalm 42 reflects the deep longing of the soul for God's presence, a sentiment echoed in the verses from First Kings where Elijah seeks guidance in a moment of despair. Both are revived through God's faithfulness. In Luke's Gospel, the healing of the man possessed by a demon showcases Jesus' power over spiritual forces and his ability to heal and transform. Galatians emphasizes the grace given to all, transcending all backgrounds. Together, these verses highlight the human need for God's guidance, the transformative power of faith in Christ, and the inclusive nature of God's love and grace.

QUESTIONS AND SUGGESTIONS FOR REFLECTION

- Read Psalm 42. Consider what you find most challenging about being transparent with God. How might opening up to God deepen your relationship?

- Read 1 Kings 19:1-15a. When facing challenges or moments of uncertainty, how can you cultivate a receptive heart to better discern God's voice?

- Read Luke 8:26-39. Reflect on a time in your life when you felt bound by something. How did encountering Jesus and his transformative power help you break free?

- Read Galatians 3:23-29. Consider the truth that in Christ, you are a child of God. What does this statement mean to you?

The Rev. Dr. Erin Beasley is a pastor at The Vine UMC in the Tennessee-Western Kentucky Conference of The United Methodist Church. Erin is one of the authors of *I'm Black. I'm Christian. I'm Methodist.* (Abingdon Press, 2020).

Psalm 42 reminds us that we have the freedom to be honest with ourselves and with God. The psalmist's words invite us to reflect on the importance of sharing our true feelings with God, even when those feelings are filled with despair. God gives us room to lean into our feelings. We don't have to pretend that we are okay: God always knows, and God cares.

The opening verse illustrates our need for God with the image of a deer panting for water. Through the psalmist's willingness to be vulnerable, we see that the need for God is not optional. Like water, God is necessary for life.

As the psalmist expresses a desire for God, we begin to understand the feeling of being separated from God. Though the reason for the separation is unclear, we see clearly the psalmist's deep desire to be reconnected with God. The plea for reunification reminds us that being a person of faith doesn't mean that our path will be easy or that we must view our experiences with rosy glasses, pretending or presenting to others that everything is fine. We have been given room to express our needs and concerns. When we confront the things that burden us—even if that burden is feeling disconnected from God—we create space for God to work within us to bring transformation.

Notice how the psalmist turns from anguish to hope. Time is taken to reflect on the reality of the situation, then hope emerges. This emotional journey shows the power of honest dialogue with God. When we allow ourselves to be vulnerable with God, we discover that God meets us where we are, transforming our doubt into certainty and our pain into peace.

Gracious God, thank you for the freedom you've given us to approach you earnestly. We find comfort in knowing that we can cast our cares upon you because you love us. Thank you for always meeting us at the point of our deepest needs. Amen.

There are moments when we each yearn for God's presence. Spiritual thirst is a common human experience. We can find comfort in knowing that God is always able to quench our spiritual thirst, but we must be willing to acknowledge our need.

When we find ourselves disconnected from God, we must choose to turn back to God by remembering previous encounters and breakthroughs. Remembering God in desperate times can be healing and transformative.

I'm always struck by the story of the Israelites' grumbling over their need for water in the wilderness (see Exod. 17:1-7). It's striking because they apparently fail to remember the miracles that led to their deliverance from slavery in Egypt. Their physical thirst became such a distraction that they became spiritually thirsty as well.

We must understand that remembering God's faithfulness is an integral part of faith. Recounting the ways God's power and presence have been revealed reminds us that God has never left us estranged. Keeping a gratitude journal is a great spiritual practice that enables us to hold previous experiences with God close to our hearts and minds. Reviewing old entries during challenging seasons can be incredibly meaningful by reminding us that God has never abandoned us, even when we felt disconnected.

The psalmist bravely cries out for God's presence and recounts times of closeness with God. Whether we are yearning to feel God's presence or feel securely wrapped in the arms of God, we can recall and express gratitude for the ways God has provided for us.

Dear God, we rejoice and give thanks as we remember your faithfulness. We are grateful for the many ways you reveal your love, power, and presence to us each day. Amen.

The powerful prophet Elijah has just defeated the prophets of Baal. Yet when Queen Jezebel threatens his life, he flees to the desert in fear and despair. Elijah, who stood with so much strength when facing the prophets of Baal, is now terrified. After traveling for a while, he longs for his death, pleading with God to take his life. Instead, God tells Elijah to get up and eat something. The prophet does what he is told and is sustained through forty days and nights traveling through the wilderness.

A humorous interpretation of this story emphasizes the need for self-care: When all seems lost to Elijah, a nap and a snack make everything much better. On a more serious note, Elijah's story teaches us the importance of not just listening to God's voice but also obeying. As our creator, God knows us better than we know ourselves and understands our needs better than we understand them. Even when we think we know the right solution to our problem, listening for and following God's guidance is a better path forward.

No matter how qualified we are or how we have overcome obstacles in the past, we will all find ourselves in the raging storms of life or isolated in deserted places. Nothing will keep us from these challenges, and when they come, we must pause to give God room to speak. Listening to the voice of God requires slowing down to receive God's words of wisdom and guidance. God is always speaking. Are we truly listening?

Dear God, we know that when we seek you, we will find you. Open our hearts, our minds, and our ears to receive your wisdom. Amen.

Elijah's struggle in the desert is an example of the humanity of God's servants. Elijah is revered as one of the most faithful people in the Bible, on par with Moses. His later assumption into heaven without experiencing physical death seems to place him on a different level than other human servants of God. Yet in today's passage, we see Elijah's full humanity.

The prophet is fleeing for his life, overwhelmed by fear and questioning his purpose despite all that he has accomplished for God's glory. Elijah is ready for God to take his life. Here, this prophet who has experienced the height of triumph in his service to God experiences the lowest of lows. Elijah is certainly terrified for his life. Is he burned out? Is he depressed? Does he doubt the faithfulness of God in the face of this new level of challenge? Whatever brings Elijah to this point of despair, we see in his situation the eternal truth that even the most faithful can and will experience moments of fear and despair.

Interestingly, God responds to Elijah's plea without condemning him for his emotional state. It would not be surprising for Elijah to receive a holy condemnation for his—let's face it—whining. "Get up!" we might expect God to shout in the winds. "Get out of this cave," we might anticipate God to hiss while ushering Elijah out with the fire. Or "Don't you remember who I am?" as God reminds Elijah of the heavenly power in the earthquake. But God's voice is in none of these powerful forces of nature. God, instead, arrives in the silence, the calm voice reminding Elijah of his calling. Perhaps God sees the depth of Elijah's struggle beyond his words and responds with the grace and nourishment Elijah really needs to get up and move forward.

Creator God, thank you for the blessing of being human and for the stories of your grace that remind us how much you love us. Amen.

Luke recalls an encounter between Jesus and a man possessed by a legion of demons. On display in this passage is God's ability to bring about transformation in the most unlikely and hopeless of situations. As soon as Jesus arrives in the region of the Gerasenes, he is met by a man who is living among the tombs, homeless and tormented by a legion of demons. His situation symbolizes the misery that can consume our lives. Yet in this dark moment, God's power breaks the stronghold of suffering.

Jesus commands the legion of demons to leave, and they enter a herd of swine, which then rushes into the lake and drowns. A man once tormented by demons is now "sitting at Jesus' feet, dressed and in his right mind" (NIV). God's power to transform has no boundaries. We are not bound to the things that oppress us.

Change is always possible with God. Our circumstances can change. We can change. This story from Luke teaches us that we should never question God's ability to transform our lives and the lives of those around us. Let us also remember the transformative power that comes with God's grace. Our Lord gives us opportunities to forgive ourselves, learn from our mistakes, and make better choices. God cares about the broken places in our lives and has the power to fix them. God can restore us to wholeness by filling every void.

> *Transformative God, we are relieved that we are not bound to situations in our lives that cause suffering and hopelessness. We are grateful to have found confidence in your power to fix what we cannot. We ask you to continue to mend the broken places that so desperately need you. Send forth your peace, wholeness, and restoration. Amen.*

In Luke 8, Jesus miraculously restores a man possessed by demons to wholeness. Now the man can live among the others in his community. Now he can live freely, no longer bound to the chains of suffering. As Jesus is leaving, the healed man begs to accompany him as one of his disciples. Jesus instructs him to go home and tell others what God has done for him. Luke tells us that he does as Jesus instructs, proclaiming how Jesus healed him.

It is important for us to proclaim how we have seen God at work in our lives. Sharing our testimony is an integral part of our faith. There are numerous occasions in scripture where Jesus instructs people to tell others how they have seen him at work. Our encounters with God have more power than we often realize. Our stories offer hope to people who are still waiting to hear from God, wondering if there is an answer to their prayer. God uses our stories to answer others' prayers. Someone may be experiencing a situation that you just overcame. There's someone who needs to know that a breakthrough is possible because you've already experienced it.

Others can discover the true loving nature and character of God simply by hearing our testimony. The healed man's story would not only be a source of encouragement to those who knew him but also a witness to his entire community. Through his testimony, he became a living example of the transformative power of God, and his story served as an invitation to seek the same transformation.

Dear Lord, thank you for revealing your power and presence. We have heard your call to offer our witness to others. Empower us to share our beautiful testimonies with those who would be encouraged by them. Amen.

When I was growing up in the church, adults would say to me, "Never forget who you are and whose you are. You are a child of God." I felt so big and proud when hearing those words. Now, as a pastor, I've often found myself sharing those same words with parishioners who, for the most part, are old enough to be my parents and grandparents. It doesn't matter how many times I say it; something always shifts in the room. Regardless of our age, the affirmation that we are all children of God touches us in a similar way.

This affirmation speaks to our dignity as human beings. Today's passage from Galatians teaches us that we are worthy, seen, and valued. Our backgrounds don't define us. Jesus Christ defines us. As children of God we are loved beyond measure. It is Christ's endless love that has afforded us grace and salvation. It is Christ's love that makes way for new life, despite previous challenges and shortcomings—or even those challenges and shortcomings we still continue to face.

As God's children, we are clothed in Christ, which means we have been given what we need to change and cultivate righteous lives. We are called to live according to Christ's example, loving God and loving others as we love ourselves. Let us rejoice and give thanks that we are valued by God and empowered to become the best versions of ourselves for God's glory.

Dear God, thank you for claiming each of us as your own. What a joy it is to know that we are your children, valued and worthy of your love. As we have been clothed in Christ, we seek to exude his true character. We offer our lives to be advocates for your glory, upholding the dignity of all people and serving as your light in dark places. Amen.

Determined Discipleship

JUNE 23–29, 2025 • KIRA AUSTIN-YOUNG

SCRIPTURE OVERVIEW: Both the reading from Second Kings and from Luke portray the challenges and the rewards of discipleship. In Elisha's case, his determination to be by Elijah's side is rewarded with receiving the mantle and the powers of the great prophet, displayed in the parting of waters. For those following Jesus on his way to Jerusalem and the cross, Jesus requires single-minded focus and rebukes those who are not fully committed. The reading from Galatians lists the fruits of the Spirit and encourages us not to abuse our freedom in Christ but to use it to serve others. And the psalm reminds us of the might and faithfulness of God, even in the midst of personal distress and trouble.

QUESTIONS AND SUGGESTIONS FOR REFLECTION

- Read 2 Kings 2:1-2, 6-14. What spiritual mentors have you had in your life whose gifts you would hope to emulate?
- Read Psalm 77:1-2, 11-20. When have you reached out to God in a time of personal trouble? How are God's mighty deeds of the past comforting to you today?
- Read Galatians 5:1, 13-25. How have you experienced subverting your personal freedom in order to serve others?
- Read Luke 9:51-62. What excuses have you made to avoid the difficulty of following Jesus to the cross?

The Rev. Kira Austin-Young is an Episcopal priest currently serving at the Episcopal Church of St. Mary the Virgin in San Francisco, CA. Kira is a contributing author for publications from the United Methodist Publishing House, Forward Movement, and Westminster-John Knox Press.

This passage marks the conclusion of the story of the prophet Elijah, who was active in the Northern Kingdom of Israel throughout the reign of Ahab in the ninth century BCE. Elijah's faithfulness as a prophet stands out against Ahab's unfaithfulness and apostasy, but now a time for transition has come: The focus shifts to Elijah's protégé, Elisha.

Despite Elijah's warning to Elisha not to follow him across the Jordan, Elisha insists. Even given the difficulty and heartbreak inherent to the prophetic vocation, Elisha asks to inherit a double share of Elijah's spirit, to succeed Elijah. After witnessing Elijah being taken in a miraculous manner, Elisha's determination and faithfulness is rewarded. Using the mantle that had fallen from Elijah's shoulders as he was swept up into heaven, Elisha demonstrates his new position by parting the waters of the Jordan and crossing back over.

I have been in ministry long enough now that my spiritual mentors from early in my formation as a clergy person are retiring and even dying. These transitions took on a poignant resonance a couple of years ago when I took on a seminary intern to mentor at my church. Suddenly, I had switched from being the mentee to the mentor. It was an adjustment to realize that I had my own breadth of experience and wisdom to offer.

Transitions between generations, transitions from one life-stage to another, and transfers of power within governments are not easy and require deliberate care and attention. While the story of Elijah and Elisha contains powerful, supernatural elements, it is also a story of dedication, devotion, and discipleship during a transition as Elisha sees in Elijah the prophet of God that he hopes to be himself.

God, we give you thanks for the mentors you have placed in our lives. Help us to be faithful disciples in the midst of transitions. Amen.

Paul's letter to the Galatians is notable for the very strong language he uses to tell the Gentile Christians that it is not necessary to follow the Hebrew law, particularly undergoing circumcision. Though Paul rakes them over the coals, I have a soft spot for the Galatians because of their desire to do the right thing, to get an A-plus at being Christian. What they don't fully realize is that there is nothing they can do to justify themselves before God because Jesus has already done that for them. I recognize in them my own longing for approval, even for things as silly as getting through the airport security line efficiently. Especially when I am new to something, I want to do it the "right" way, to learn all the rules and follow them diligently as the Galatians do. If I am honest, I know that my desire to do things "right" does not come from a desire to please God but to receive recognition and esteem from others.

Paul is correct to attribute this desire to the flesh, by which he means not just the physical body but the whole self under the power of sin. These self-serving desires and motives are never satisfied; there is always more power, wealth, and pleasure to obtain. He instead encourages the Galatians to lean into their freedom in Christ. He notes that this is not only a freedom from the law, a kind of free-for-all or libertinism. The freedom we have gained through Christ is a freedom for service to one another.

Freedom can be scary. It is much easier and more comforting for someone to give us the rules and boundaries so we can then behave accordingly. Even when the rules are difficult to follow, it gives us something to structure our lives around. The law of love often feels too vague, too immeasurable. And yet it is this law of love for one another and for God where we find true freedom in Christ.

Holy Three-in-One, help us find our freedom and our rest in you, that we may love our neighbors as ourselves. Amen.

Early in the COVID-19 pandemic, when many places in the United States were under stay-at-home mandates, I was inexplicably drawn to learning about other times in history when people suffered from pandemics. Hearing stories from the Black Death in the mid-1300s, the yellow fever epidemic in Memphis, Tennessee, during the 1870s, and the Spanish Flu epidemic from 1918-1920 comforted me and made me feel less alone, knowing that humanity had suffered in this way in the past. While people dying from disease en masse is certainly a tragedy, for many others, life continued. The sun rose and set, and the world kept spinning. Babies were born, people went to work, fell in love, prayed, and eventually those epidemics ended.

I think I was in good company with the psalmists, who find themselves in personal distress and call out to God seeking help and relief. The psalmists place their individual struggles in the context of God's mighty deeds and works in the past, trusting that God's past faithfulness extends to the present and the future.

As Christ's disciples, we gather in community every week to tell the story of God's action in the world through scripture, hymns, and prayer. God has acted mightily in the past on behalf of God's people, and we trust that God will be faithful in bringing all of creation to fulfillment, even as we face personal and collective difficulties and griefs. The same God who brought the Israelites out of slavery into freedom and raised Jesus Christ from the dead will redeem each of us and all of creation.

While the psalmist recalls God's mighty deeds in the past on behalf of the Israelites, God is also active today. When we find ourselves in moments of distress, let us recall the ways in which God has acted powerfully both in history and in our own lives.

God, help us to see where you are working in the world and to share your powerful deeds with others. Amen.

The story of Elijah and Elisha contains scriptural resonances that echo forward and backward through the Bible and Christian teaching. The crossing of the Jordan, first by Elijah and then by Elisha, is reminiscent of Joshua's crossing of the Jordan (see Josh. 3:14-17). Elijah's striking of the water with his mantle and the parting of the waters is an obvious reference to Moses' parting of the Red Sea and leading the Israelites to safety (see Exod. 14:21-22). Less obviously, Elisha's dedication to Elijah and his determination to follow him despite discouragement is reminiscent of the love and commitment between Ruth and Naomi in the book of Ruth.

It behooves us to be familiar with Elijah because he serves as a way that people during Jesus' lifetime understood the ministries of Jesus and John the Baptist. The prophet Malachi prophesies Elijah's return (see Mal. 4:5), which explains why, in the New Testament, John the Baptist and Jesus are asked if they are Elijah. As a representative of the prophets, Elijah also makes an appearance at Jesus' transfiguration.

Elijah's departure from earth without dying is only the second time this occurs in the Bible; the first being Enoch in Genesis. We know little about Enoch except that he was a man of great faith, and we can take from this that Elijah was also being rewarded for his great faith. Forty days after his resurrection, Jesus ascended to heaven in a similar way, and certain Christian traditions hold that Mary, Jesus' mother, also was assumed into heaven directly.

The connections throughout the biblical canon and Christian tradition add depth to this narrative and help illuminate the ways in which God acts.

God of all history, we thank you for your witness throughout scripture. Help us to read, mark, learn, and inwardly digest the record of your saving deeds throughout history. Amen.

Jesus' act of "set[ting] his face to go to Jerusalem" marks a turning point in Luke's Gospel as the disciples realize exactly what might be required of them in following Jesus. Just as Elijah set out for Gilgal, Jesus sets his face toward Jerusalem. This shift takes place shortly after Peter, John, and James witness Jesus' transfiguration, a manifestation of Jesus' divine glory and his company with Moses and Elijah. I imagine that the disciples are filled with dread by Jesus' resoluteness in heading to Jerusalem, not only for what might happen to their beloved teacher but what might happen to them. At the same time, three of them have just been exposed to the fullness of Jesus' divinity, which they will keep in mind throughout the journey to the cross.

My spouse jokes that when I have made up my mind about something, it is best that he get on board because there is little that will deter me. While he takes his time making big decisions, I do a lot of information gathering on the front end, so that when an opportunity arises, I'm ready to go for it. Like the disciples, I can also get a little carried away.

When Jesus and his followers are rejected by the Samaritan village, the disciples immediately escalate the situation. In a reference to Elijah calling down fire upon a king of Samaria and his party (see 2 Kings 1), the disciples ask Jesus to let them incinerate the village. Differentiating himself from Elijah, Jesus' ultimate mission is to save and reconcile, not destroy. This incident foreshadows Jesus' response to rejection in Jerusalem. Rather than fight fire with fire, Jesus shows us a new way to overcome hatred and resistance—with love that is stronger than death.

Determination and single-minded focus do not preclude our obligation to love even those who seem to stand in the way of what we believe is right.

Jesus, help us deal gracefully and lovingly with those who oppose the things we deeply believe in. Amen.

As followers of Christ, Paul encourages us to live according to the Spirit rather than according to the self that is under the power of sin, the flesh. In his list of works of the flesh, we might be most familiar with the ones that require a certain kind of purity like "idolatry" and "drunkenness," but notably, a good portion of them involve life in community and how the works of the flesh lead to unhealthy conflict and disordered relationships with one another. Both the works of the flesh and the fruit of the Spirit occur not only on the individual level but in communal life.

Once again, I am sympathetic to the Galatians who are so excited about the Christian message that they want a tangible, public marker of their faith journey in circumcision and table practices to demonstrate their piety and discipleship. As opposed to choosing a big gesture and one-time act like circumcision, the work of the Spirit is a slower process. Being transformed by the Spirit is a process that leads us to be more loving, kind, joyful, and peaceful. Unlike circumcision or table practices, the development of the fruit of the Spirit take time and are not always readily visible.

The work of discipleship is the work of being transformed, not through trying harder or following more rules but by leaning into God's power of grace and love so that the fruit of the Spirit become evident in our lives and our communities. When we bear one another's burdens, when we love one another as Christ loves us, we are living out the transformative power of the Spirit that is given to us in baptism. The Spirit is at work in each and every one of us, helping us to walk in the footsteps of Christ and fulfill the commandments to love one another.

Loving Spirit, by your power transform us so that our lives may show forth your fruit. Amen.

Jesus makes it very clear in this passage that following him is an all-consuming task and that not everyone is up to it. Using three would-be followers of Jesus as examples, their responses show that they have not understood the demands of discipleship and are not prepared to give it the priority that Jesus demands, especially knowing that the Crucifixion approaches.

The first one animatedly announces that he will follow wherever Jesus goes, but Jesus knows he is going to the cross and glib enthusiasm is not enough to counter the rejection that Jesus and his followers will face. The second asks to bury his father before following Jesus, a duty of all faithful Jews. Jesus' response is harsh, communicating that the priority of proclaiming God's kingdom is over every other priority, even justifiably good ones.

In another reference to the Elijah-Elisha narrative, the third example asks to bid farewell to his family. When Elijah calls Elisha to follow him while he is plowing in 1 Kings 19, Elisha asks to kiss his parents before following Elijah, and this is permitted. Again, Jesus' demands may read as overly harsh regarding the unconditional demands of discipleship. But knowing he is on his way to the cross, there is no room for confusion or misunderstandings about the cost of following Christ.

Much of modern Christianity privileges family relationships, so Jesus' response to those who want to attend to those relationships might offend us. We all face obstacles to following Jesus, and some of those obstacles are objectively good things. We should not delude ourselves that being Christ's disciples is without sacrifice or that it is something we can commit to without counting the costs. Following Jesus changes us. Proclaiming the kingdom of God might lose us family and friends. But none of this is counted as loss at the cross where all is set right.

God, remove the obstacles that prevent us from being faithful disciples. Amen.

Doing It God's Way

JUNE 30–JULY 6, 2025 • RACHEL GILMORE

SCRIPTURE OVERVIEW: I may have many gifts and strengths, but navigation is not one of them. I don't know how I survived before the dawn of Google Maps. Daily, I follow the guidance offered by that little app because without it I would be hopelessly lost. The lectionary readings for this week are a reminder that we were created to follow, daily, in the way of God. Naaman sought healing but could only receive it when he was obedient to God's way of restoration. The psalmist sought help and healing after suffering and struggle but had to wait on God's way to reverse the situation. In Galatians we learn about the cause and effect of following God's way as those who sow to the Spirit reap a different result than those who sow to self. In Luke, Jesus sends the disciples out in pairs to go God's way, the way of peace for provision and healing. May we take time this week to evaluate our journey of faith and see if we are living life our way or God's way.

QUESTIONS AND SUGGESTIONS FOR REFLECTION

- Read 2 Kings 5:1-14. When has healing come to you in unexpected ways?
- Read Psalm 30. Think of a time when God turned your mourning into dancing, and give thanks.
- Read Galatians 6:1-16. When you grow weary of doing good, what helps you take the next right step?
- Read Luke 10:1-11, 16-20. "The harvest is plentiful, but the laborers are few." Who could you invite to go with you as you share the good news of God's peace and love with others?

The Rev. Rachel Gilmore is the director of New and Vital Faith for the Desert Southwest Conference of The United Methodist Church and co-founder of Intersect: a Church Planting Network. She is the co-author of *Where We Meet: A Lenten Study of Systems, Stories, and Hope* (Upper Room Books, 2023).

Naaman had it all, almost. He was a successful army commander who had a wife, servants, and the respect of the king. But he also suffered from leprosy. So when he heard of a prophet in Samaria who could help, he spoke to the king and went on his way to seek healing. Where did this good news of the prophet come from? Naaman heard it from a young girl from Israel who had been taken captive on one of their raids.

Naaman eventually ends up at the doorstep of Elisha with all of his horses and chariots. Naaman's power halts at the door of healing, and yet Elisha doesn't come out to greet him. Instead, a messenger brings the simple steps that Naaman must undertake to be healed. Naaman is furious because the healing doesn't happen the way he expects or where he expects. In a rage, he turns away. But his servants remind him of how easy healing could be if the commander would only obey the simple orders that have been given to him.

So often the good news, the healing that awaits us, comes from unexpected places. For Naaman, it comes from a captive girl whose voice eventually leads to Naaman's flesh being restored "like the flesh of a young boy." It comes from messengers and servants, those who aren't always seen by society, those who are marginalized or forgotten but who offer the good news anyway. It comes from simple acts of obedience. I read this story, and I know there are many times when the journey of healing is long and arduous. But other times the journey is easy if I just step away from my preconceived notions and do it God's way.

God, help me hear the voices that are so often silenced. Keep me humble, lest my pride prevent my healing journey. Teach me to leave my power at the door and trust in yours. Amen.

Sometimes our assumptions get the better of us. The king of Israel receives a letter from the king of Aram, who has recently beaten him in battle. The letter explains that Naaman is there to seek healing, but the king of Israel panics and tears his clothes in distress, convinced that this is some kind of trap, sure he will be punished in some way for not having healing powers.

There are times, especially when we feel beaten down by our enemies, that we isolate ourselves and think it's up to us to handle everything that comes our way. There are times, especially when we get unexpected news, that we jump to the worst possible explanations or outcomes instead of trusting in God, who promises to be with us. Part of the beauty of the community of faith is that we all have unique gifts that we bring to the wider body of believers so that God can be glorified through us. What the king of Israel saw as a horrible situation, Elisha saw as an opportunity to show God's healing power to a man outside of the family of Israel.

When we turn to others in difficult times and let them use their unique gifts, it can have eternal impact. Naaman didn't just receive physical healing. Later in this passage, he goes on to proclaim his faith in God and his desire to serve others. When the trials of this world seek to isolate us or lead us to assume that we are alone in our desperate situation, we can turn to God and God's people to remind us that all hope is not lost.

Gracious God, keep us from jumping to reactions that may not be grounded in reality. Help us to turn to you and to one another when we feel inadequate in the moment. Amen.

Ten years ago while serving in the Peace Corps, I had the opportunity to travel to Egypt and climb to the top of Mt. Sinai to watch the sunrise. I spent hours walking the long, dark trail in bitterly cold weather before reaching the 750 steep steps required to reach the top. Being an uninformed tourist, I had stupidly worn flip-flops and forgotten a flashlight, so I kept stubbing my toe on the trail. I finally reached the top and collapsed on a rock to wait for the sunrise, but the clouds were too thick to let the light through. I waited and waited and waited and, just as I had turned to leave, the sun finally began to break through the cold night, and I saw the mountain illuminate with warmth.

The words of the psalmist are a reminder that tough times don't last forever. We might feel like the difficult situation we face will never end, but we know that our story doesn't end with suffering and struggle. We serve a God who brings joy after weeping, dancing after mourning, sunrises after long nights and steep steps.

Psalm 30 overflows with words of thanksgiving, but it doesn't leave out the words of struggle. We are people of faith in a world full of brokenness, and it's important to share that our lives aren't always perfect. We face long and difficult journeys. We cry out to God for help, we walk in the dark unprepared, and then we wait for the situation to change—for God to bring help and healing. When we question what kind of God we serve, the psalmist's words remind us of the faithfulness of God, who shows up and restores us and our stories.

God, may we reflect on the painful and promising chapters of our lives and give thanks to you for redeeming every page with your unfailing love. As we wait for the sunrise, may we do so knowing that you are faithful to us every step of the way. Amen.

We've all met people who do not reap what they sow. The young father who has never smoked a cigarette, eats organic food, and runs marathons dies of aggressive lung cancer. The retired CEO who was a kind and fair boss loses her entire life savings in a Ponzi scheme. The extremely mean and angry family member lives to be 110 as the thorn in the flesh of others. But what if the author of Galatians isn't talking about some kind of cosmic karma? What if these words are a reminder that every day we can chose to move closer toward the heart, mind, and actions of God, or move away from God's plan and toward other things?

In October 2006, a man in Pennsylvania walked into an Amish schoolhouse and killed five children, injuring five others before taking his life. The response from the Amish community that had lost innocent lives shocked the world. They immediately reached out with words and actions of love and forgiveness. As a mother of two school-age children, I wonder if I would have the capacity to immediately respond to violence and traumatic loss with love and forgiveness.

The words to the church in Galatia are a reminder that our capacity to love and forgive aren't formed in an instant. They are seeds of the Spirit that we intentionally cultivate each and every day. The Amish community was able to forgive because they live out forgiveness every day, month after month, year after year. What if the harvests we are meant to reap aren't ones of health and wealth but of forgiveness and grace and radical love?

God, help us sow seeds of the Spirit each day so that we might reap a harvest of forgiveness, grace, and radical love. Amen.

Our desire as humans to find a place to belong can lead us down the wrong path. The church in Galatia isn't so different from many churches today. A group called the Judaizers wanted to define what it meant to follow Jesus. But they added steps or marks of faith that weren't prescribed by Christ, and they thought their rules about who was in or out of the Jesus club were the only ones that mattered.

We see churches today who like to create rules for what it means to be a Christian. I went to a Christian college that forbade dancing, alcohol, shorts, tank tops, and screen-printed T-shirts. And if a female student became pregnant, she was expelled from the school, while the father of the child remained enrolled because no one could tell he was expecting a child too.

Paul points out two problems with creating these kinds of rules. First is the hypocrisy of the rules we create for others that we don't abide by ourselves. We focus on whether others are doing the right thing, while we fail to do the right thing ourselves. The bigger problem is why we design these systems in the first place: to feel like we belong. But following Christ means we don't fit in to anything except the invitation to be a new creation, living in the world but not of the world.

Have you ever met someone who lives as a new creation? Maybe they wear shorts and screen-printed T-shirts. Maybe they drink alcohol. But when you see them, you see a life overflowing with the fruit of the Spirit. We see followers of God expressing love, joy, peace, patience, kindness, goodness, faithfulness, gentleness, and self-control—regardless of what they wear!

God, help me focus more on you and the life you offer than the rules I want others to live by. May my goal be to fit more into your loving community than one I design for myself. Amen.

In December 2021, I was blessed to participate in a Kava ceremony for the dedication of a new cooperative parish in the Las Vegas area called Pasifika: a United Methodist Community. While I had visited a Tongan celebration before, this was unlike anything I had ever seen or tasted. I was overwhelmed by the hospitality and inclusion that I felt in that space.

As I ate the delicious food, I was reminded of Jesus' command to the seventy-two disciples in Luke to eat whatever is placed before them. These travelers throughout Samaria were going into homes that might embrace different cultural nuances or customs. Jesus' followers were encouraged to accept the hospitality that was offered to them and not move around from house to house within one community. They weren't to leave a Samaritan home to look for those with more traditional Jewish practices they were accustomed to.

Many of our church histories and traditions are steeped in colonialism. We showed up at the homes of others and told them what kind of food Christians eat, what kind of music they sing, and what color carpet they need in the sanctuary. We weren't good guests. We expressed conditional hospitality, and it's why many in the church are still repenting and seeking to repair the harm done by these colonizing ways. The seventy-two followers were told to stay in homes where they experienced peace upon entering, not control or reverse assimilation. What if our goal when encountering others was to seek relational harmony, rather than "win souls" or build a Christian empire? What if we took the role of being a guest seriously? Maybe then we would come back with stories of wonder and awe at a God who works through our humility and offers hospitality without condition.

God, forgive our colonizing Christianity, and help us to learn the art of receiving the hospitality so generously offered to us by others. Amen.

God's good news is for everyone, but that doesn't mean everyone wants to hear it. Jesus sends the seventy-two into vastly different conditions than he sent the twelve disciples in Luke 9. The disciples were sent as messengers to Jerusalem, but this group is going ahead of Jesus into Samaria, a place of tension and hostility for these Jewish travelers. Jesus is clear that the conditions are not safe and that they will not encounter peace in every home they enter.

Perhaps they are directed to withhold their greetings as an added layer of protection: If they don't identify themselves, they might be safer. Leaving their sandals at home is a reminder that they are still on holy ground. As these barefoot messengers journeyed through Samaria, perhaps they were reminded to see everyone as a neighbor they should love and every home as a sacred space where they could encounter God. The seventy-two messengers had to go on this journey God's way, being obedient to the commands that certainly made them uncomfortable and vulnerable—vulnerable feet with no sandals, vulnerable bodies with no cloak, vulnerable voices with no greetings to share on the way.

When we bring the good news with nothing else to lean on but the message, we reflect the same vulnerability they felt—the vulnerability of being hurt by the church or by those who identify as Christians; the vulnerability of being hurt by a world that doesn't value us or include us; the vulnerability of wanting to belong but not knowing how to find our place at the table. May we walk roads with our shoes off and our hearts open, knowing that if we are following in God's way, the place where we walk is holy—and the journey is as well.

God, help me remember that you came to this earth in human form, not as a powerful king or mighty warrior but as a vulnerable infant in a manger. Help me lean on you for all I need in the journey to share your good news. Amen.

Measuring Life in Mercy and Love

JULY 7–13, 2025 • JES KAST

SCRIPTURE OVERVIEW: Amos and the psalmist speak of the divine judgment of God. For Amos' audience, judgment will come because they have ignored God's warnings. The psalmist warns of judgment against those who oppress the weak and needy and fail to protect them from the wicked. These passages leave us with an understanding that human righteousness falls short of God's expectations. When we read the Luke and Colossians passages in light of the Hebrew texts, we see hints as to what the rule of judgment should be—mercy and love. Live in the way of mercy and love, and you will be filled with all spiritual wisdom, as Colossians proclaims. This is the measure of a good society: mercy and love.

QUESTIONS AND SUGGESTIONS FOR REFLECTION

- Read Amos 7:7-17. Look for God's plumb line in the world. In what ways is the ground you stand on askew?
- Read Psalm 82. If you sit on the council of the Most High, how does this change your perspective on the world?
- Read Colossians 1:1-14. Prayers of mere words are just the beginning of prayer. To what prayerful actions do your prayerful words call you?
- Read Luke 10:25-37. Consider how you live out Jesus' call to love your neighbor.

The Rev. Jes Kast is an ordained minister of word and sacrament in The United Church of Christ. She is the pastor at Faith United Church of Christ in State College, PA. After living in New York City, Jes finds a theological fecundity in the agrarian lifestyle of Central PA.

In chapter seven of Amos, we read about three of Amos' visions, which emphasize prophetic intercession for Israel. In today's passage we read the third vision. We are given a striking image of a plumb line that God uses to measure Israel's moral and political life. A plumb line is a device used to determine a vertical reference point. At the end of a string there is a heavy weight, often with a point, to provide the most accurate vertical measurement. In ancient cultures, plumb lines were necessities in building taller buildings. As a building was built, it was crucial that the plumb line provide the most accurate information for a straight, vertical point.

The image of God using a plumb line to measure Israel is an arresting image that demands our attention. With this image, God is saying that the ethical life of Israel is not being built to measurement. As a result, the high places will be made desolate and the sanctuaries laid to waste. The plumb line has measured that their life together has been built crooked.

In *Birmingham Totem* artist Charles White uses ink and charcoal on paper to draw a young African American boy shrouded under a large blanket as he looks at the debris of a collapsed building he is standing on. In his left hand he touches the brokenness, and in his right hand hangs a plumb line right in the middle of the devastation. White created this piece in response to the bombing of the Sixteenth Street Baptist Church in Birmingham, Alabama, on September 15, 1963.

Both White and Amos draw a strong visual for us emphasizing moral development. Morality is not hidden away in a Sunday morning worship service; morality is every facet of our lives. Our lives are to be built on the righteousness of God's justice.

God, measure our lives with your holy plumb line, and correct us in your mercy as needed. Amen.

I used to live and minister in New York City. I loved my life there, but as I saw the growing divisions in the United States, I began to hear a call from God that I could not stay in NYC. I now minister in Central Pennsylvania where the rural life of farmers informs much of my life—and my dinner table.

I think of this change in my life when I read Amos. If Amos were alive today, he would probably feel most comfortable in the small-town farming communities that I know so well in Central Pennsylvania. After all, he was a farm boy and a herder. He saw how the opulence of the cities of the Northern Kingdom would "trample the head of the poor into the dust of the earth" (2:7). Amos, however, was called by God to proclaim a different vision of the world.

This small-town farmer had visions from God about justice, righteousness, and social equality that were concerned for the welfare of the poor and not just the elite. He himself was not concerned with stature. He even acknowledges in this passage that he doesn't consider himself a prophet but a herdsman. He's just a humble guy from a small-town village that the Lord took from his flock to prophesy to the people of Israel.

The book of Amos has some of the most roaring justice passages in scripture. These passages have been used in various art pieces and sermons to rouse people from complacency. For all the success and longevity of Amos' prophecies, he was not concerned with success. Amos knew he was a farmer, and his humility in both his self-knowledge and his openness to God were the doorway to becoming a prophet.

That humility in Amos is something that speaks both to my city soul and to my now small-town living soul.

God, use my life, like Amos, to point our world toward your passion for justice and social equity. Amen.

The church I serve is across the street from Penn State University. I have a lot of academics in my community, and when I read this story from scripture, I think of them. Academic settings are full of rigorous questions and friendly debates. In that setting, this story shifts to show two professionals searching for truth in a friendly debate.

The lawyer's profession would make him concerned with the rules and laws of his society. His question can seem reasonable in this context. Jesus' response—with a question—seems reasonable as well. "What is written already?" Jesus asks like a professor turning the question back to her student. The learned lawyer responds from the scripture, "You shall love the Lord your God . . . and your neighbor as yourself." Jesus commends him and says to go and do likewise.

But like so many academic debates, the lawyer presses harder: "And who is my neighbor?" Jesus responds with a story of a Samaritan who helps a man in a troubled spot after societally privileged people pass by. Like a good professor, Jesus then asks his student which example from the story answers his question—who is the neighbor? The smart lawyer responds correctly, "The one who showed him mercy." While the text doesn't say Jesus smiled, I like to think he did as he tells the lawyer, "Go and do likewise."

We often understand this story to show the lawyer antagonizing Jesus. But from my place within an academic community, I see in this story a person pushing hard to discover truth, being changed by the truth he learns, and then going to live in the way of that truth: mercy. Let us go and do likewise.

God, may you welcome the questions we wrestle with just as you welcomed the lawyer's pushing. Remind us that the greatest measurements of the law are mercy and love. Amen.

Have you ever met someone who loves rules? I don't consider myself a rule lover, but I value good bylaws. This feels like an embarrassing thing to admit, but let me tell you why. Good bylaws help organizations function better. When we are clear about the boundaries of a mission, we are given better guidance on how to measure how we live together.

I like bylaws—except when I don't. Bylaws are helpful until they are held as more important than the actual people they are supposed to serve. At that point bylaws need to be reevaluated and updated, or those in leadership need to reexamine their priorities.

The lawyer and Jesus have a discussion about the religious bylaws. Jesus knows he is talking to a "rule guy." Jesus uses a story of people who were following their religious laws as examples of what not to do when someone is in trouble. The rule that guides all rules, Jesus outlines, is mercy.

Mercy is the ability to acknowledge that our complicated human lives often require a soft place for our hearts to land to find healing and be able to change. Rules are good. They help us live in harmony with one another. But when rules get in the way of our humanness and our ability to love one another with our whole hearts, we must faithfully reassess those rules and how we measure our lives.

The measurement of ethics for Jesus is showing love to friend and foe. As followers of Jesus, the way of mercy trumps strict adherence to the rules. Consider how much more compassionate our society would be if we suspended our judgments and instead acted on mercy. Imagine how much more we would be able to love our neighbors.

God, you have consistently been merciful to me. Help me to be merciful to others, even when I don't think someone deserves it—when mercy is needed the most. Amen.

After some sterner words on the measurement of divine judgment this week, this passage reads like a fresh bouquet of beautiful flowers. I have used verses from the opening of Colossians many times in pastoral letters to express my fondness of the one I am writing to.

The writer says, "In our prayers for you we always thank God, the Father of our Lord Jesus Christ, for we have heard of your faith in Christ Jesus and of the love that you have for all the saints." What a beautiful thing to say to someone whose faith and love are the markers of their reputation. I wish I could jump back in time to meet the people at the church in Colossae. What about them made their faith precede their reputation?

We can read Colossians to get a glimpse of the people of God from long ago, but we can also look for those sparks of divine love in the people we know today and be quick to tell them too. I think about a retired minister in my congregation whose whole life was dedicated to the gospel of mercy. At his funeral his stole lay on top of his casket, a visual reminder of the faithful life he led. His faith in Christ Jesus and his love for all the saints inspired me, even at his funeral.

There are ordinary people in our lives whose faith inspires ours. My mom is another one of those people. Her long life of faithfulness in very simple ways and her deep love for all people never ceases to inspire me. Who are the people in your life who inspire your faith? When have you last told them so?

This passage reminds us that the measurement of our lives is lived in our faithfulness to Christ Jesus and the love of all God's people. We know people like this. We can be people like this.

God, the people in the book of Colossians were known as people with rich faith and love. I want to be one of those people. Amen.

In a September 2023 *Atlantic* article by David Brooks titled "How America Got Mean," Brooks asks two questions. Amidst outlining statistics of increasing depression rates, he asks: "Why have Americans become so sad?" His second question, rooted in stories of people leaving professions because of challenging interactions with people in public, asks: "Why have Americans become so mean?" After considering many different theories, from technology to demographic inequalities to economic challenges, Brooks makes a case that the reason for these challenges in America is the lack of "moral formation" in the U.S.

Understandably, even Brooks states that the phrase "moral formation" sounds a bit stuffy. Yet when we look at this through the lens of Colossians, we hear echoes of this sentiment.

The biblical writer prays that the Colossians will be "filled with the knowledge of God's will in all spiritual wisdom and understanding." Spiritual wisdom is part of moral formation. Spiritual wisdom guides us in how to measure the effectiveness and the goodness of a society.

When I ask college students what they want to be, they respond with titles and roles that speak to stature in their hoped-for jobs. Usually there is money attached to that hope. What if, however, we were better at moral formation? Would their responses reflect more the type of person they want to be rather than the job they want to hold?

Being filled with spiritual wisdom brings "good fruit." Good fruit is not about how much money we make, but it is about the character of the persons we are. In a culture that values money over morals, we must remind ourselves to seek true spiritual wisdom as we seek to "live lives that are worthy of the Lord" (NIV).

God, wisdom is worth more than a bigger bank account. No matter the job I'm called to today, help me to be filled with your spiritual wisdom that brings good fruit. Amen.

It was 1996. It was my first winter-holiday vacation of middle school. It was also the first time in my life that I cheated on an exam. I did not rest easy during that vacation.

I had put so much pressure on myself to succeed on my science exam that I cheated. I was so scared of failing the exam that I had failed my own moral judgment. I remember feeling the daily shame during what seemed the longest break of my life. I couldn't wait to get back to school because it was eating me up. I had to confess.

The new year came and I counted down the days until school resumed. I was the first one in my science teacher's class that day. I was terrified. What did this say about me, a cheater? Would my teacher fail me? The spiral of shame is ugly.

My hands were so sweaty as I told my teacher how I had cheated. He listened to me without interruption. After my confession, he lovingly said to me how much he appreciated my honesty and that he would allow me to take the test again at the end of the week by myself. Mercy!

I have never cheated since that day. Mercy is powerful and transformational. It is why Amos prophesies with mercy in his heart. It is why Jesus reminds us that the greatest among us is the most merciful. It is why the psalmist reminds us that divine judgment rests with our merciful God. And it is why Colossians speaks of a faith measured in love. May our lives be lived with flowing mercy.

Divine Judge, your loving-kindness is the measure of mercy. Mercy transforms us to do more kindness. Help us to accept your mercy and to be merciful to others. Amen.

The Justice of Reconciliation

JULY 14–20, 2025 • NICOLAS IGLESIAS SCHNEIDER

SCRIPTURE OVERVIEW: The texts for this week have common messages around reconciliation and justice. Human beings have distanced themselves from God's project, which is based on love and justice for all created things. This project that Jesus defines as the "kingdom" encompasses the restoration of interpersonal, community, and ecological relationships. Some of the passages for this week challenge us to see how human beings have created unjust ways of living with one another. God does not forget those who suffer or those who live in poverty. God is also no stranger to evil. By integrating these lessons into our daily lives and communities, we can live an authentic faith that seeks justice, trusts in God, collaborates as a team, and reflects the love of Christ toward all human beings.

QUESTIONS AND SUGGESTIONS FOR REFLECTION

- Read Amos 8:1-12. How can we echo the prophetic attitude inspired by the text of Amos at both our individual and community levels?
- Read Psalm 52. What experiences do you have in your daily life trusting the steadfast love of God?
- Read Luke 10:38-42. How can we work more as a team and value different ministries in our church and community work?
- Read Colossians 1:15-28. How can you discover the image of God in your neighbor? How can you live in unity and harmony in the midst of conflict and violence?

Nicolas Iglesias Schneider is a social worker for The Methodist Church in Uruguay and coordinator of the project on Faith and Human Rights at Fe en la Resistencia.

This is the fourth vision of the prophet Amos, where he denounces the greed of the rich. We read that God does not forget those who experience injustice or those who oppress the poor and take advantage of their position. The prophet says that a day will come when those who feast on the suffering of their neighbors will thirst for the word of God and will not find it. To those who do not have time to listen today because they are too busy with their wealth, the day will come when they will seek comfort in the word of God and it will not be there.

During the COVID-19 pandemic, I experienced God calling me to a new opportunity. I worked with a group of young people to open the church and provide support for persons experiencing homelessness. We provided food, recreation, and a safe, temperature-controlled place to be, especially in winter. Through this work I heard the story of hundreds of people who were on the streets for numerous reasons. They each had nothing more than their life and the clothes on their backs—and oftentimes some faith and hope that tomorrow would be a better day.

When reading the harsh words of the prophet, I am reminded of a desire I often hear in response to the problem of homelessness: We should make the poor disappear because they are uncomfortable to look at. We blame the persons experiencing homelessness, saying they must be lazy, but we rarely explore and blame the underlying systemic structures that leave people without homes. Hearing the stories of individuals in this situation has helped me see the error in this way of thinking.

Amos' vision is hopeful in that God does not forget the poor. It also invites us to act to break the chains of injustice while we pray that those who worship only their wealth will return to God.

"Is not this the fast that I choose: to loose the bonds of injustice, to undo the straps of the yoke, to let the oppressed go free, and to break every yoke?" (Isa. 58:6). Amen.

The psalmist is angry with injustice and with the wicked always planning and executing injustice. The psalmist anticipates a time when God will punish the oppressor and bring the fall of an unjust system. The sin of injustice is not limited to what an individual does alone, but rather it is the whole of a system and a culture that sustains oppression against those living within it. The psalmist finds the central point that seems to be the root of change: the love of God.

Perhaps the answer to injustice is not in taking sides, even with the supposedly good, with those who believe they are in the right. Perhaps the appropriate response to injustice is seeking personal and social change based on love. If hope is in the love of God, it is not in vain.

At all levels of conflict, from international to community to family, we often operate with the belief that problems will be resolved when one position takes precedence over that of the other. This is the understanding that underlies the court system in the United States and other countries around the world. If one of the parties wins, at least temporarily, the conflict is solved.

Yet God's invitation is to have our trust be in the love of God and not in the punishment of our opponent. The challenge is to recognize that in Christ we are all united. Even the neighbor whom I may temporarily consider my enemy is also made in the image and likeness of God. Although their presence or their ideas may bother me, they also have the opportunity to be redeemed by the love of God. They are so loved like me that I cannot believe myself to be the sole owner of truth, faith, or reason.

> *O God, help us to trust that your love sustains us. Help us discover in those whom we see as enemies persons created in your image and likeness. Amen.*

Many times we read the passage of Mary and Martha as if there is a correct attitude and an incorrect attitude—that Martha is wrong and Mary is right. Indeed, it is a struggle to interpret what Jesus really means when he says, "Mary has chosen the better part." But Jesus doesn't play favorites elsewhere in the Gospels, so why would he here? Perhaps both tasks are important in the home and in the church of the followers of Jesus.

Both disciples are important in Jesus' ministry. We know through other stories that Martha and Mary, along with their brother Lazarus, were very close to Jesus. In John 11 we see that Martha exhibits a more theological attitude by going to talk with Jesus about the death of her brother and Jesus' potential response. According to the interpretation of important theologians such as Xabier Pikaza, Martha is a "bishop," meaning she is a witness to the faith and a servant of the church. Mary is "beloved," as is the beloved disciple of John's Gospel.

The complementary functions of Martha and Mary have been little highlighted in *conjunction* with each other as opposed to in *contrast* to one another. We want to determine which sister is right, rather than look to how they are both responding to the moment in front of them. We often speak of this scriptural story by identifying with either Mary or Martha. But at different moments in our vocation, we will find ourselves fulfilling different needs and serving in different ways. The fundamental message is that we are not to be distracted from the ministry at hand, not to lose focus on what is in front of us. And in the moment, in an alternative version of what Jesus tells Judas in John 12 when Mary anoints him with perfume, we will always have the work with us, but we will not always have Jesus.

God, give us the wisdom to see the important work that is before us in the moment and to choose what is most right in serving you. Amen.

I live in Uruguay, a few kilometers from Brazil, a country where churches occupy a very important place in people's daily lives. In the last four decades, the number of evangelical churches and Christians has grown exponentially. Yet this growth has not brought unity among believers. Due to the partisan political involvement of some pastors and the polarization of society along political lines in recent years, faith communities have experienced greater division and even acts of violence. In some churches, those who did not vote the same as the pastor suffer public ridicule.

In situations like these, it is clear we have become confused about Christ's role as head of the church and king of all creation. According to today's passage from Colossians, Jesus is the image of the invisible God. Our ultimate loyalty should be to Christ, and all our actions should reflect this relationship we have with God. Through Jesus, God became closer and more comprehensible to us. Our job is to follow Jesus' way of living, to live as redeemed people. That identity must imbue all aspects of our lives, not just the times we find ourselves within the walls of a church.

We live in a world that is divided, but God in Jesus came to reconcile. At the time this letter was written to the Colossians, there were as many divisions as there are today in our communities. We cannot allow conflict and division to cause us to lose focus on our unity in Jesus. We are reconciled through the Cross, and God invites us to root ourselves in love, not to pitch our tent on grudges, lies, or partialities.

God, may my faith in Christ be a reason for love and service to those I agree with and to those I don't. Amen.

The core of the division we experience in our world is because we fail to recognize our neighbor as a beloved creation of God. The prevailing logic is that of animosity, that others are out to get us, and that we must look after ourselves only.

In Colossians 1:21-22, we read that although we were once strangers or enemies, today we are reconciled through Christ. In him and in the condition of creatures created by a loving God, we are connected to one another. In that same sense, the psalmist invites trust and gratitude, implying that if we live in love, we grow like a green olive tree.

The prophet Amos shares this understanding that we are interconnected with one another. The book of Amos is topical today as we face ecological crises and profound social injustices, where millions are exploited, displaced, and unable to live in a dignified way. Amos' text is harsh because it not only challenges the individual actions of the wicked but also denounces the creation of and participation in systems that are sinful and unjust. It condemns a society where banking fraud, exploitative selling of crops, and trafficking of humans is present.

Amos' world and our world are both systems built not by the logic of love but by calculating the utility of others and the planet to serve oneself. Theologian and economist Franz Hinkelammert in his book *Lo indispensable es inútil* (*The Indispensable Is Useless*, 2012) makes a profound criticism of utilitarianism and the market as a form of religion that distances us from God. "What is indispensable for life is useless for the market," says Hinkelammert. The most important things—to live well and live with abundance and joy—do not have an economic value in the market.

O God, help us remember the importance of cultivating things that do not have a market value: relationships, time together, love, and the practice of mercy. Amen.

God's grace is a fundamental concept that guides our faith and practice. Grace reminds us that we cannot earn salvation through our works but that grace is a divine and undeserved gift. In Luke 10:38-42, we see Jesus praising Mary for choosing to listen to his teaching. This story teaches us that our relationship with God and knowledge of God's word are essential and that grace calls us to rest in God.

In Colossians, Christ is presented to us as the center of all creation and the church. In the letter to the Galatians, Paul emphasizes that in Christ there is no gender distinction: "There is no longer Jew or Greek; there is no longer slave or free; there is no longer male and female, for all of you are one in Christ Jesus" (3:28). The apostle highlights the importance of empowering all people, regardless of gender or status, to fully participate in discipleship and service.

Putting into practice this teaching that Christ is the head and we all are equal before the Creator, the Methodist Church in my country has been a defender of gender equality. Within its ranks is Pastor Ilda Vence, the first woman ordained in Latin America. Following the tradition of women following and serving Jesus alongside men, we have many women who lead churches and serve throughout the connection and the country in a variety of ways.

God's transformative grace and generosity are central aspects of the tradition of faith. Through a deep relationship with Christ, we can embrace God's grace, empower one another, and work together in service to God's kingdom.

God, empower us to hold gender equality as a central value in our faith, remembering that we are all one in Christ Jesus. Amen.

SUNDAY, JULY 20 ~ *Read Amos 8:1-12*

How can we denounce, like the prophet, the greed, exploitation and oppression of the most vulnerable in society? How
do we prioritize the call to be peacemakers that Jesus gives us
in the Sermon on the Mount? From a Christian perspective, we
are called to address these problems not through violence but
through peace and justice.

Amos, a prophet of God, raises his voice against exploitation
and injustice in the society of his time. He denounces those who
oppress the needy and enrich themselves at the expense of the
poor. This passage reminds us that injustice and exploitation are
unacceptable in the eyes of God.

As peace-seeking Christians, we follow the example of
Jesus, who called us to love our neighbors as ourselves. Non-
violence is a fundamental principle in our faith. In the face of
injustice and oppression, our response is not violence but peace.
We seek to build a world in which the dignity of every human
being is respected.

Exploitation and oppression perpetuate the cycle of violence
and suffering. But instead of responding with violence, as followers of Christ we seek peaceful and just solutions. We seek
reconciliation and restoration rather than revenge. We believe in
the ability of God's grace and love to transform lives and societies.

In Amos 8, we see a vivid description of economic exploitation and corruption. This prophecy reminds us that God is on
the side of the oppressed and expects us to act with justice and
compassion. We see that our faith becomes alive and credible
when we address injustice through nonviolence, the promotion
of equality, and the defense of human rights.

*God, help us to be agents of peace and justice in a world full of
oppression. Guide us to respond to injustice with nonviolence
and love. May justice and compassion prevail as we follow the
example of Jesus. Amen.*

God's Extravagant Generosity

JULY 21–27, 2025 • ROLF NOLASCO, JR.

SCRIPTURE OVERVIEW: This week our meditations take us on a journey where our spiritual infidelity and impoverishment is met with God's steadfast faithfulness and diffusive love. It starts with God's pronouncement of restorative judgment toward Israel's unfaithfulness in Hosea. We then turn to Psalm 85 which describes in vivid and soul-nourishing ways what this promised restoration looks like. The theme of God's extravagant and generous character carries us to Luke's Gospel and Colossians, where we see it exemplified fully and incarnationally in the person of Jesus Christ.

QUESTIONS AND SUGGESTIONS FOR REFLECTION

- Read Hosea 1:2-10. What does it mean to be faithful to God in this current moment of our personal and collective lives?
- Read Psalm 85. How have you experienced God's faithfulness and restoration?
- Read Luke 11:1-13. How has praying regularly changed you? If you do not pray regularly, start a practice now. Look for the ways it changes you.
- Read Colossians 2:6-19. How might a life lived in the fullness of Christ influence a world mired in spiritual bankruptcy?

Dr. Rolf Nolasco, Jr., is the Rueben P. Job Professor of Spiritual Formation and Pastoral Theology at Garrett-Evangelical Theological Seminary. Rolf is a member of Edison Park United Methodist Church.

Most of us live under the glare of social media. With every post comes a slew of comments, often tinged with negative judgments, mostly of a personal nature. God's judgment is of a different kind. It is never meant to ridicule, shame, and induce toxic guilt, as we humans usually do with one another. Instead, the judgment God gives is restorative, empathic, and comes from a place of deep love and intimate regard for the other—never impersonal and certainly not judgmental.

Integral to God's covenantal love and restorative judgment is the naming of Israel's spiritual idolatry, unfaithfulness, and betrayal of their relationship with God. As a stand-in for the people of Israel, the prophet Hosea used the symbolic action of marriage and naming children to signal a kind of intimacy shattered into pieces by Israel's wayward ways. And like a jilted lover, the deep hurt God feels comes out in fierce anger. This is a side of God we tend to bypass. Yet there might be wisdom in staying with the forcefulness and seemingly retaliatory response of God, if only to discover the sheer power of our own actions and their subsequent impact on God. God is never unbothered by us but is moved quite powerfully by the choices we make, for ill or good. And as we shall discover later on, God's fierce anger is cradled by God's steadfast love, which faithfully renews us every morning.

Hence, the warning the people of Israel receive of the dire consequences of willfully severing their ties to God can be seen as a two-fold invitation. First, it is an invitation to ready themselves to face the consequences of their actions. Second, it is an invitation to remember that despite their betrayal, God's faithfulness toward them remains.

God, thank you that in times of our unfaithfulness you remain steadfast and deeply committed to restoring our relationship with you. Amen.

When we come face-to-face with our acts of betrayal and unfaithfulness, we would rather deny, justify, and assign blame to someone else. At times, we may also prefer to take responsibility so as to let larger structures and systems off the hook. In other words, we would rather stitch leaves to cover our sins, personal and collective, than admit with humility our "extra-spiritual affairs" that injure ourselves, our relationships, our communities, and God.

With God's covenantal love and restorative judgment in the background, we hear Hosea's message as an invitation to name and confess the ways we wound the very heart of God. We engage in adulterous relationships with the world by succumbing to worldly desires that serve only personal gratification and selfish interests. We participate in idolatrous behavior by investing time, energy, and resources in the accumulation of prestige, power, and possessions without regard for the well-being of others or our planet. Capitalism is king and consumerism is its servant. We commit violence in the discrimination and oppression of our Black, Brown, and LGBTQ+ siblings, along with other marginalized persons, using the name of God to justify these heinous acts. We show spiritual apathy by ignoring the material conditions of the poor among us, the disproportionate number of communities who do not have access to basic needs like health care and clean water. We participate in the degradation of our planet. We remain silent on issues of social justice, racism, gender-based violence, mental health, immigration, violence, and war.

Before we can move forward, we must acknowledge our complicity and contribution to the harm. We must confess these sins, and many more than can be named here, in order to begin to rebuild our relationship with God.

God, have mercy on us. Enliven in us the desire always to choose you, and you alone. Amen.

Having been assured of God's faithfulness in response to our naming of our acts of unfaithfulness, we are now invited to share our deepest longing for relief, restoration, and redemption to God who watches and waits for our return home.

The psalmist offers us a litany of remembrances, memories that breathe life into the present moment. Psalm 85 vividly reminds us of God's steadfast companionship throughout the twists and turns of our lives. Engaging in the spiritual practice of repentance is especially significant as it counters our inclinations to linger in shame, pain, and guilt, preventing us from getting entangled in the quagmire of our own creation.

Therefore, we accept this invitation from God, the one who is our constant across yesterday, today, and tomorrow. Like the people of Israel, we too yearn for divine presence and provision.

Like the people of Israel then, we too yearn for forgiveness and mercy for those times when we participate in stealing what does not belong to us and diminishing the inherent dignity and worth of those different from us.

Like the people of Israel then, we too yearn for restoration of joy and peace instead of experiencing Divine anger.

Like the people of Israel then, we too yearn for vitality as we have been numbed by the illusory comforts that this world offers and the drive to fill our egos often at the expense of those around us. We also hunger anew for a love that is unconditional and that will never fail us.

As we express these deep longings, we will incline the ears of our hearts and claim the divine promise of peace, presence, and provision wherever we may be so that we can bear the fruit of love, faithfulness, right living, and experience God's favor surrounding us on every side.

God, may it be so! Amen.

Our text for today begins with a teaching on how to pray, the words of which have become a staple for communities gathered to worship God. The second section contains a parable full of exaggerated imagery to underscore God's extravagant generosity toward those who express their innermost longings and desires with such unabashed boldness.

But there's a twist. If we flip the order of our exploration by starting with the second section, we see that it acts as a chalice that holds our petition in the form of the Lord's Prayer. Expressed differently, it is God's extravagant generosity that compels us to pray with confidence. What matters the most is "how we pray," not simply "what we pray for."

The "how" starts with an attitude of hospitality and persistence, exemplified by the protagonist's determination to meet the needs of their unexpected visitor. Their unwavering insistence, even after an initial refusal, results in their receiving what they ask for.

In this passage, we discover that praying requires an openness to receive the needs of others and to pour them out in the same character as God's extravagant love, with unwavering and persistent faith.

To drive the point of "audacious praying," Jesus uses the action verbs of *asking*, *seeking*, and *knocking*, resulting in receiving, finding, and door opening. In simple terms, audacity is met with the availability of God who is always ready to listen, hold, and respond to the attitude and requests of the one who prays.

In praying persistently, we encounter God, whose first and only response is to give generously and extravagantly.

God, help us to be outrageously persistent and audacious when we pray. Amen.

It is the example of Jesus praying that prompts Jesus' disciples to ask him to teach them to pray. Through this display, we see that God's generosity precedes the first utterances of our prayers. Jesus responds by offering a pattern for prayer that is both simple and profound. Followers of Christ have taken this example and speak it individually and collectively as the Lord's Prayer. But looking at it as a pattern instead of a script allows us to see the attitude that should undergird our prayer as well as key teachings from Jesus about what it means to pray to God.

Praying is an act of consenting to an offer of intimate connection with God. Responding to this invitation to deepen intimacy with God through prayer results in an attitude of reverence and awe toward God who is holy and sacred—distinct from all of creation yet intricately part of it at the same time.

Praying emboldens us to be audacious and persistent in our dependence on God's provision and care, not for what we need in the foreseeable future but for today's immediate sustenance. Asking for daily provision indicates the confidence that God will show up for us again and again.

Praying makes us acknowledge our tendency to harm others. Receiving God's forgiveness is a gift that keeps on giving. We offer forgiveness to those who have wronged us in gratitude for what God has done for us. Praying also recognizes our vulnerability to fall from grace, to succumb to life's challenges, to turn away from God and cave in to temptations that surround us. And so, earnestly and eagerly, we plead for guidance and protection through the vicissitudes of life.

Praying the Lord's Prayer is ultimately about being transformed into the likeness of Christ—dependent, unwavering, and audacious.

God, guide me not only in what to pray but also in how to approach my prayers. Amen.

A recent Pew Research Center study projects the percentage of Christians in the U.S. might decrease from 64 percent to between 54 and 35 percent by 2070. At the same time, the number of religious "nones" is expected to rise from the current 30 percent to somewhere between 34 and 52 percent.

Christianity faces a multitude of challenges that are causing its decline, such as the surge of secularization, the politicization of the faith, unremitting instances of clergy sexual abuse and scandals, disillusionment with religious institutions, and a perceived disconnect from the demands of modern life.

The challenges faced by the Colossian Christians mirror those encountered by contemporary Christians. The admonition of the apostle to the Colossians remains relevant to us today.

The anchor that will keep us steady during these times is our deep, abiding, experiential, and intimate knowing of Christ. The choice is not about believing in another dogma, doctrine, philosophy, or spirituality, but about choosing to ground our lives in Christ, to grow, and to be grateful for his transformative work in our lives. This is an active form of cultivating our faith—tending the interior garden of our heart in prayer, silence, solitude, and expectant encounter with the Word. It is also about growing our faith—seeking after and thirsting for a deeper connection with Christ, patterning our lives after him in a way that impacts the lives of others, and engaging in changing the conditions in which others live. To grow in Christ is to be like Christ—living and loving out loud practically for the sake of others, overflowing with deep gratitude.

God, help us to stay anchored in Christ and to live like Christ. Amen.

In my early life as a follower of Christ, I embraced the familiar understanding of creation (God created everything good), fall (humanity sinned), and redemption (Christ's death provided rescue from sin). However, this understanding produces a rather troubling image of God—a vengeful God whose demand for retribution presupposes vengeance through violent means. It also produces moralistic or legalistic interpretations—good Christian behavior is privileged as the rightful response for the bloody sacrifice rendered on our behalf. As a queer person of color who desires to follow Christ, this implies "straightening" my so-called disordered queer life. Through this interpretation, I am compelled to live inauthentically and contrary to being God's beloved queer.

This reading also trivializes the impact of the revelatory and transforming death and resurrection of Jesus Christ. Christ willingly subjected himself to experience humiliation by occupying the place of shame on the cross, not to appease God's vengeful intentions but to make plain our own cruelty and violence toward one another. He accomplished this not to make us feel guilty but to grant us unqualified forgiveness so we can begin to live differently, to stop the cycle of violence, to truly treat one another as image bearers of a loving, forgiving, and compassionate God. This new way of being together confirms our participation in God's extravagant generosity.

The Incarnation of Jesus Christ is about God choosing us. There is no other place that God would rather be than with each of us, embracing the concreteness of our lives. This choice is a vivid display of God's intention for us to flourish, encouraging us to be awakened persons and communities who are lovers of God and lovers of all.

God, we thank you for your extravagant generosity. Help us to extend that same generosity to others. Amen.

Redeemed Community

JULY 28–AUGUST 3, 2025 • ELIZABETH MAE MAGILL

SCRIPTURE OVERVIEW: We find redemption in a community that accepts all. Hosea makes clear God's love for the people gathered. It is not individuals who are redeemed but a community brought home by God. God's love and caring show up again in the psalm's celebration of the redemption of a people lost in desert wastes. When they cry out, it is God who brings them to a town with other people. Renewal is found in the community of that town. The Colossians text reminds us of strategies for living in community: Don't do things that hurt others. Because we are redeemed together, our actions must show respect and concern for ourselves, for others, and for the God who has renewed and redeemed us. As the community is redeemed, Christ is revealed within us. In Luke we are reminded that Christ cannot be revealed if we are hoarding resources for ourselves—do not store excess resources but use them for the good of our community.

QUESTIONS AND SUGGESTIONS FOR REFLECTION

- Read Hosea 11:1-11. Consider God as the parent of your community, raising you up, teaching you to walk. How does that change your community's story?
- Read Psalm 107:1-9, 43. When have you been alone in the wilderness of loss, suffering, or doubt? How were you supported by a community in this wilderness time?
- Read Colossians 3:1-11. What on this list is hard for you to let go? What can you do to let go?
- Read Luke 12:13-21. What are resources you tend to hold on to, even when you have more than you need? What can you do to let these go to the community around you?

The Rev. Dr. Elizabeth Mae Magill is the pastor of the Small Church Collaborative in Ashburnham, MA and Rindge, NH. Liz is ordained with the Christian Church (Disciples of Christ) and the author of *Five Loaves, Two Fish, Twelve Volunteers: Growing A Relational Food Ministry* (Upper Room Books, 2020).

Who are the people you don't respect? Who are the people you or your friends constantly cut down as not really understanding what is right and what is wrong? Who are the people that, to your way of living, do not have the right culture or attitude or civility? I know that I have people who fit that category. They are generally not people I know or engage with every day but people I read about in the news or on social media.

Those we deem uncivilized or out-of-touch are the barbarians this passage is talking about. Barbarians are not just a neighbor we disagree with over lawn mowing or our property line but outsiders that we are certain will ruin our society. Scythians were barbarians but worse—over the line of decency.

The writer to the Colossians is suggesting that barbarians and Scythians are included in the dividing lines that go away in Christ. We don't talk about this text as often as Galatians 3:28, perhaps because it is not as poetic, or perhaps because the dividing lines between male and female, race, and slave and free are more comfortable to consider. But the idea of grouping ourselves with barbarians is not.

Christ is offering to renew—to redeem—our community, and that includes everyone, even barbarians. Our differences should not divide us. For that to be true I need to learn to care for these people that I label "barbarian." And caring for people is not about requiring them to become the same as I am; somehow, I must learn to appreciate other people as they are.

The writer reminds us that Christ is all, but also that Christ is in all. If Christ is in barbarians, shouldn't I learn to love them? To love as Christ, we must look for Christ within the people we most dislike. It's hard work.

Consider the people in your life you do not respect or get along with. Look for something about them that proclaims Christ in the world.

Hosea's images can be overwhelming, showing God as destructive and punishing. But Hosea also reveals the tenderness of God and the hope that God is with us even as the world falls apart.

The "son" in verse 1 is the nation of Israel. God is the parent of an entire community; the community is God's child. In Hosea's time people are sacrificing to other gods, Baals. In our time we are sacrificing to money, to our nation, to greed, and to power, to standing with "our people" as something separate from "those other people." The consequences described are harsh, but still, we find other gods—money, career, popularity, sometimes just the tediousness of life. We turn away from our home.

You can hear God crying in Hosea's words. God remembers teaching us to walk, leading us with kindness and love, bending down to feed us. Can you remember the times that God felt that close? What was going on? Why was God nearby? Was it a time of healing from a loss, or a time of finding a new community, or a time of being filled with the fullness of God? God wants us to remember the feelings we had at that time. God wants us to return to those moments of home.

God cannot, and will not, give up on us. Despite all that we do, our community will be redeemed by God. God cannot forget that God loves us. God remembers those times we were close and insists on staying engaged with us. God's work, in the end, is mercy and redemption, not destruction and punishment. God's promise is that, with all the ways we have turned aside, God will return us to our homes.

Holy parent, we give thanks for your gracious patience as we struggle to find our way. We give thanks for the ways you bring us home. Amen.

I am a quilter, and like many quilters, I have a fabric stash, a collection (or rather a massive pile) of fabric that I have bought without a plan. This is in addition to the scraps remaining from other quilts. If I were to make a quilt each week for the rest of my life, I would be unlikely to use all that fabric I own.

I have conflicted feelings about my fabric stash. I worry that it will be a burden to dispose of when I am gone. Yet if someone were to come and say, "Let's split your fabric, so I can take half," or even if they only wanted a third, I would be slow to let it go. Like the person in the crowd asking Jesus for help, I want to hang on to my share of this fabric. I expect a heavenly reprimand for this.

But Jesus doesn't want to be part of deciding how to split private property. He is not willing to discuss how best to distribute the resources we have. Jesus instead calls us to be on guard against greed. It is greedy to hang on to an abundance of possessions, even beautiful possessions like fabric.

Jesus' objection here is to greed and abundance beyond what we need to get by. Jesus is objecting to the focus on care of oneself rather than care of the community. Life is not about the things we own.

What then is life about?

If we are to be a redeemed community, then we are called as a community to share our possessions freely, to be sure that everyone in the community has what they need, to build an abundance of love and caring rather than an abundance of stuff.

Abundant God, help us to focus on contentment when we have enough, and move us to share what we have with the community around us so that all have enough. Amen.

Abundance is used in the Gospels both positively and negatively. In the feeding of the multitudes, the baskets of leftover food point to the bountiful excess of God's rule (see Luke 9:10-17). And in this story of a rich man, the land that has produced abundantly and the crops that are stored are a warning against individual abundance. The big difference between these two stories is whether the excess and abundance are for the community or for oneself. The baskets left over are shared among thousands; the storage barn is for one person (or perhaps one family). Central to this text is the idea that an excess of resources means you have failed to care for the community. God provides more than we need, but it is not meant to be hoarded.

Those listening to Jesus would have understood the cultural imperative to share within the economy with those who had less. Anyone with more than they needed for housing and food was supposed to use the excess to make purchases from vendors, service providers, and other artisans. Having extra money meant someone kept money from those workers—by not having more letters written, or buildings built, or pots made, or cloth formed into garments. The purpose of money was, and is, to spread it around to all the people dependent on this economy.

Since I have money set aside for retirement and am approaching the time for relaxing, eating, drinking, and being merry, I want to know where my own storing up of resources fits into the gospel. There is nothing in this text that argues against providing for my own family's needs, but excess should not be stored; it should be shared. That is how we are rich toward God.

And so, I must consider how much of what I have stored for retirement is what I need and how much I am to share.

God of abundance, forgive me for storing up savings beyond what I need to care for my family. Help me to be someone who shares with my community, and to be rich toward you. Amen.

If you have been raised with Christ, you have new life and will seek the things that are with Christ. You will focus on God's things, not on your own things. Christ is your life, and when that is revealed, you will find glory with Christ.

Many of us have been Christians for a long time. This idea of a new life feels connected to having a sudden conversion. Perhaps instead of a moment of revelation, we have had a slow blossoming of our faith. For others we had a born-again moment, but it was years ago. We've had our "new life" for a long time now. It is easy to forget that newness, easy for the joy of a life in Christ to become ordinary. Today's text is an invitation to restart our faith with the wonder and excitement of life started over.

How do we do this? The writer of Colossians states that we are raised with Christ now—in this moment, today. This is not about life eternal after we die. The writer suggests that we have died to our old life. For those of us who have been living this life in Christ for years or decades, we must do this dying and being resurrected again and again. The gift of this is being "hidden with Christ in God."

Try on a moment of renewal. Throughout our day are many things we could choose to lose, to die to. What do you die to today, or what are you willing to let go from your life? Can you feel the excitement in that choice? Can you feel Christ's presence?

Our church communities need much renewal, but the most important part is for us to be renewed in our faith. The possibilities grow when we set our minds on God's ways. See if you can find that new faith excitement today.

Redeeming God, we give thanks for the promise of new life and ask that you guide us to let go of the parts of our life that are not serving us well. Help us to be renewed and redeemed again and again in the Christ who lives within us. Amen.

If you aren't angry, you aren't paying attention! There is much going on in our world that makes me angry. Sometimes anger moves me to action, which is a good thing. Often anger consumes me. It keeps me from sleeping, from focusing, from engaging with people who are different than me.

The letter to the Colossians tells readers to stop many behaviors because they are earthly. Instead, we are called to be Godly in our actions. Earthly actions harm others; Godly actions unite despite differences. We must avoid behaviors that hurt our community, hurt our neighbors, and hurt ourselves. For me, the earthly actions that harm others come from my anger.

This is not about my inner feelings of being violated and provoked to anger; there are no rules against having feelings. But it is not okay to lash out in response. It is not okay to let the feeling simmer through the day. When I hear news that makes me angry and am still hot hours later, this has not helped me to engage the issue. The heat does keep me from engaging people who think differently than I do. If I start calling others barbarians, my anger hurts my community.

The writer has good advice: "Seek the things that are above." While I don't believe that God is literally above us, I do find that looking up as I take a pause and count to ten helps me to focus on what God wants for me. Hands open to the space above or clasped in prayer help me to release some of the anger. Letting go of my need to figure out the solution right here and right now and trusting that God is part of the solution helps too.

To develop a redeemed and renewed community requires that I work, over and over again, to be a healthy member of that community, to be part of God.

God of all, help me let go of that which harms the community and to see Christ in those around me. Amen.

Can you remember a time you were in trouble and God came to the rescue? A time you felt hungry, thirsty, but most of all lost? What was or is the "desert waste" in your life? While I haven't been to a place full of sand, I definitely find deserts in my heart. The psalmist describes it as a place with no inhabited town. Perhaps it is the heart of loneliness. It is certainly when we just don't have what we need.

I once drove across North Dakota, from Jamestown to Williston, with my brother, his wife, and their baby Erin. We had finished our car snacks and wanted lunch—actually, we had wanted lunch an hour before. The sun bore down on a treeless landscape, yet we didn't want to stop until we got to a town that had a restaurant. The blank horizon felt far, far away.

An inhabited town provides hope, welcome, and community—for us that meant a restaurant with air conditioning. In the psalm, the psalmist is possibly describing a homecoming after the Babylonian Exile. The inhabited town the people are led to is home. They are returning to a place with great memories.

In the psalm, members of the redeemed community gather from all over to give thanks to God. People come from their separate lives, separate problems, separate cultures, and join together in this celebration of redemption. It is not our differences that make us one but our shared experience of moving from being lost to being home. We have been redeemed! God's steadfast love always redeems our community! Praise God! As a community we collectively give thanks and praise. Even though each of us has a different experience, what we have in common is the way that God has shown steadfast love. Our praise is for the way God has brought us home.

God of redemption, be with me when I am in the wilderness. Show me the way. Thank you for guiding me home. Amen.

Aligning Faith and Action

AUGUST 4–10, 2025 • CHARLIE BABER

SCRIPTURE OVERVIEW: The Hebrew scriptures act as the voice of God declaring that faith must align with behavior. To worship God without forming one's life around justice is to bring empty and hypocritical words to the altar. While God delights in the praise of the people, God delights only when that praise is met with a life aimed at justice and mercy. The epistle reading harkens back to the heroes of old, whose faith in God's promises led them to get up and follow. In the Gospel, we hear the words of Jesus giving us the kingdom of heaven now. We receive a call to readiness for whatever may come next.

QUESTIONS AND SUGGESTIONS FOR REFLECTION:

- Read Isaiah 1:1, 10-20. Do you ever worry whether God really listens to your prayers? How do your prayers reflect your life lived in faith?
- Read Psalm 50:1-8, 22-23. Are there things in your life you'd prefer to keep hidden? What would it look like for God's light to shine in your darkest corners?
- Read Hebrews 11:1-3, 8-16. How would you describe God's promises? How do God's promises motivate your actions?
- Read Luke 12:32-40. Do you ever find yourself aimlessly wandering through life? What steps could you take today to be more alert to God's presence and love for you?

The Rev. Charlie Baber is a deacon in The United Methodist Church serving as the youth pastor of University UMC in Chapel Hill, NC. Charlie is the author of a weekly web comic following John and Charles Wesley (wesleybros.com) as well as the books *Submitting to Be More Vile* (Abingdon Press, 2019) and *Incompatible* (Cascade Books, 2023).

What a way to start a week! You've just poured your coffee and want some quiet time with the Lord and we give you *this* scripture to read. You're just looking for some encouraging words to get you through the day, and instead you read that God is fed up, repulsed, hiding, and not taking calls right now.

This is not a text that allows us to sit back and relax. No, Isaiah is lighting a fire under us with a call to action. There's no room for a case-of-the-Mondays here, friend. We've got work to do this week.

With such strong language, it's easy to think Isaiah must be talking to someone else. I mean, I'm no leader of Sodom and Gomorrah. Surely God loves my praise and worship and is extremely dissatisfied with someone far more disreputable. But let's invite the possibility that our love for God is deeply tied to how we love our neighbor. God wants our faith and our actions to align. What if God is calling us to a realignment?

Verses 16-17 are the real call to action, a call to justice for the oppressed, the defenseless, and the vulnerable. Now I know that's a tall order, so let's spend some time asking for eyes to see. Where can your hands lift up the lowly this week? When can your voice speak up for someone that nobody listens to? Who can you spend time with to remind them of their dignity and worth?

Merciful God, your love and grace extends to us all, even when we feel alone and forgotten. Forgive us where we have failed to seek justice. Open our eyes to see the worth of our neighbors, especially those most in need. Move our faith into action this week for your honor and glory. Amen.

Sin is a bloodstain on the soul—scarlet, red, crimson, a stain that cannot be removed. But speaking as the voice of God, the prophet declares an incredible gift: God will do the cleaning. God will make them new.

The sin in question is the failure of the people of God to stand up for the oppressed, the orphan, and the widow. Should the Israelites obey God, they would find abundance in the Promised Land. Should the Israelites disobey, they could expect destruction—but destruction would not be the end.

God always promises to offer forgiveness and restoration, no matter how dark things get. This promise in particular was important in helping Israel process how they could be God's covenant people and yet experience exile in Babylon. Their exile was not God's failure, and wasn't the end of their story. Crimson sins can become like wool.

Have you ever stopped to ask who this God really is? This God who is more concerned with how religious people treat the poor than how religious people are, well . . . religious? This God of second chances who holds us accountable but also stands at the ready to forgive and make us new? This God who seems to care so deeply about how human beings treat one another and yet allows us the space to either mess it all up or learn and grow in love?

This promise of forgiveness is part of our realignment, where faith in a just God causes us to act justly toward our neighbor. God really does give us a fresh start, from scarlet to snow. And the idea is that this fresh start will grow, maybe like a snowball rolling down a hill, getting bigger as it goes. Forgiveness is the beginning. What comes next is up to us.

God of new beginnings, refresh me today so that I can bring your refreshing grace to those who need it most. Amen.

This psalm is a call to inspection. Like the rising of the sun, God's light is on the rise. When God's light shines, all will be revealed. This inspection is specifically for people of faith, the ones who have made a covenant with God. Faith and action must align if God's covenant people hope to pass the inspection. When read in its entirety, the psalm complains that the community has performed the ritual of worship without allowing it to transform their actions or attitudes. They have brought sacrifices hoping to appease God without a spirit of thanksgiving for what God has given. They have claimed beliefs about God without taking care of the people God cares about. This inspection is not going so well.

The psalm is full of light imagery. Light is usually a comfort, guiding our way when it's dark, providing warmth and safety. But nothing can hide when God's light comes to shine. We are called to stand in this light, to remain in this light, to walk in this light as if nothing were hidden. The faithful community, whether it be Israel or the church, is the community that integrates its practices with its beliefs. Faith and action go hand-in-hand if one is to follow the God of Israel.

The psalmist also relies heavily on the idea of sound. God speaks, calls out, won't keep quiet. God is in the middle of devouring fire and raging storm. Not only do we serve a God who shines the light of truth, we also serve a God who speaks the word of truth. To follow this God is to open oneself to inspection, to let go of partial truths and lies.

Light of the world, shine on my darkest places and speak the truth to me. Align my practices with my love for you, that your light may shine through me into this world. Amen.

Though we don't know who wrote the epistle to the Hebrews, the author gives us the most famous definition of faith in the Bible: "Faith is the reality of what we hope for, the proof of what we don't see" (CEB). Other translations say that faith is the "confidence" (NIV), the "firm foundation" (MSG), or even the "assurance" (NRSVUE) of things hoped for. A closer inspection of the original Greek text reveals this word used to define faith—commonly transliterated as *hypostasis*—most literally means "standing under" and was used as the Greek word to describe a title or contract which proves property ownership. Just as holding the title gives me ownership of my car, faith is the reality, the assurance, the confidence, yes even the certainty, that I can live into God's calling.

The rest of the chapter gives the context that helps us understand this definition of faith. The author of Hebrews calls our attention to Abraham and Sarah, the parents of the people of Israel, to describe what faith as *hypostasis* looks like. Abraham obeyed, he went out, he lived, he looked forward. Sarah conceived and bore a child. They took action. They not only held the title to the car, they took the car on a road trip. Their faith in an invisible God was made visible when they got up and followed.

The great news about Abraham and Sarah's examples is that they were both completely human, like you and me. Their story of faith is littered with questions and doubts, even to the point of Sarah laughing at God because the promises seemed so unbelievable. To have faith in Christ does not end or eliminate questions or doubts. Faith, instead, empowers us to get behind the wheel anyway, to start moving forward until that which was invisible becomes tangible to us.

Invisible God, with a word you made the visible universe. Open my ears to hear your calling today. Steady my feet to follow. Put my faith into action. Amen.

In today's passage, we can picture faith as a family packing everything they have into a U-Haul. After a litany of heroes of the faith, the author of Hebrews gets to the point: Faith looks like emigration, relocation, "looking for a homeland" (CEB). Abraham and Sarah trusted God so much that they uprooted their lives in search of a Promised Land. Faith kept them moving even when God's promises felt out of reach.

A common thread in immigration stories is a parent's desire to provide a better life for their children. So they get in the boat. They cross the river. They learn a new language. They start all over from the bottom. It takes a combination of humility and courage to uproot everything for the simple hope that life could be better. This is the example of faith we see in the book of Hebrews. It is trusting that even when God's promises seem out of reach, they are worth pursuing. When all of that longing for a better country, for a real homeland, motivates you to action, that's when your faith finds meaning.

Perhaps this definition of faith is frustrating. Shouldn't faith lead to answers and solutions? Shouldn't faith lead to prosperity and perfect health? In Hebrews, faith looks more like wandering than settling. Faith looks more like moving away from what was known and finding yourself in a strange and foreign land. Perhaps this is the most realistic picture of faith: When life leaves you feeling like a stranger in a strange land, faith provides the courage and the humility to pick up the pieces and keep moving.

God of great promises, remind us once again of your eternal goodness. May we delight in your love as you delight in us, so that we can be refueled for the walk and the work ahead of us. Amen.

In high school, my friend drove a beat-up Honda Accord with the bumper sticker, "Don't be fooled, my treasure is in heaven." It was funny because of how terrible her car was. But if that same sticker had been on a fancy sports car, it would have felt disingenuous to me.

When Jesus talks about "a treasure in heaven," it is in the context of selling off possessions to give to the poor. Just as Abraham and Sarah left their country behind to pursue God's promises, the disciples left homes and careers to follow Jesus. Jesus told his disciples not to worry about where food or shelter would come from, not to concern themselves with collecting wealth to provide for their journey.

In verse 32, the reason Jesus gives for releasing our fear is a matter of faith. The word "delights" (*eudokeo*) is the same word used when God speaks at the baptism of Jesus. Just as God is well pleased with Jesus, so God delights in giving us the kingdom. Just when we thought God had forgotten us, or was too busy navigating universes to notice us, it turns out God delights in giving us the kingdom.

It's interesting that the response to God's delight involves releasing actual possessions and wealth. After all, possessions bring us comfort. Wealth brings us security. But wealth can run out or be stolen or destroyed. When we are wealthy, the temptation is to forget God because we have all we need. When we lose everything, the temptation is to curse God for abandoning us. Jesus invites us to the possibility that the joy of God's kingdom is richer than wealth. But that kind of faith requires action, in this case, divestment. If we fear letting go of our earthly treasures, the delight of the kingdom will remain just out of reach.

Delightful God, set me free from the power of things. Open my heart to generosity. Put my faith into action for the sake of the poor. Amen.

If you're going on a lengthy road trip, you have to have your basics covered. Are the tires full and aligned? Did you check the oil and fill up the gas tank? There's much to focus on as the journey begins. But anyone who's driven on a long drive knows how easy it is to experience highway hypnosis, a sort of trance state where your mind switches to autopilot and you suddenly don't know how you got this far without crashing.

Jesus reminds the disciples about the importance of remaining alert and ready as the monotony of life drags on. He tells the story of a long-gone master returning home and a thief who breaks in during the middle of the night. In the first story, the master is so pleased to find the servants ready for him that he turns the tables and waits on them. This is a positive and informed alertness. The servants know the master is returning; they just don't know when it will happen.

In the next story, a regretful homeowner wishes they had been ready to prevent the thief from breaking in. This is a different kind of alertness, an awareness that harm can come unexpectedly. But who wants to live like this, constantly vigilant to the possibility of home invasion? Or constantly afraid that today could be your last day on earth?

I don't think Jesus is hoping to create fearful, survivalist disciples here. These warnings continue the theme of aligning action with our faith. If drivers want to prevent highway hypnosis, they open the windows, crank up the tunes, sip some caffeine, or chew on some sunflower seeds. If disciples wish to remain alert and ready, they pay attention to their spiritual disciplines, they open their eyes to opportunities to serve. This is not a call to live on edge in fear that God is waiting to trip us up. It is a call to participate in the beauty and goodness of God around every corner.

Surprising God, we never know when you will call us to action. Ready our souls to love as you have loved. Amen.

God Makes a Way

AUGUST 11–17, 2025 • STANLEY R. COPELAND

SCRIPTURE OVERVIEW: The scripture readings for the week have a common theme of God's making a way, and God's way always leads to restoration, forgiveness, justice, mercy, and love. We can stray from God's way or reject it altogether, but God never strays from us, will not forsake us, and always beckons us to pursue God's way leading ultimately to peace and a real experience of God's presence. The scripture readings conclude with acknowledgment that on God's way we are surrounded by a "cloud of witnesses"—saints of the faith are also our companions. Standing beside us along the way is Jesus accompanying us.

QUESTIONS AND SUGGESTIONS FOR REFLECTIONS

- Read Isaiah 5:1-7. How do we take the way of justice and mercy that God has provided for us and reject the way that leads to bloodshed?

- Read Psalm 80:1-2, 8-19. What do we need rescue from in the present day? Why do we need restoration and revival, and what purpose would it serve?

- Read Hebrews 11:29–12:2. Who do you see as a person or persons of faith who have shined a light on the path of God's way?

- Read Luke 12:49-56. How do we address divisions when they come upon us in our families, friendship circles, and communities of faith?

The Rev. Dr. Stanley R. Copeland is the pastor of Lovers Lane United Methodist Church, a multi-cultural congregation in Dallas, TX. Stan is the author of *Lord, He Went: Remembering William H. Hinson* (Abingdon Press, 2006) and the *Picklin' Parson Cookbook* series (Colinasway Publications, 2020, 2021, 2022: picklinparson.com).

In these verses from Isaiah, God is portrayed as a farmer who prepares the ground for a vineyard and plants grapes in hopes of yielding sweet fruit. Instead, God gets wild, sour grapes. The vineyard represents God's people. Isaiah says, "He expected justice but saw bloodshed; righteousness but heard a cry!"

Isaiah's words are reminiscent of the way the story of humanity begins in Genesis. God plants a perfect garden full of provisions with only one prohibition. The "do not" came with no explanation and an assumption that faith and trust would be enough. Disobedience was the result, and soon thereafter, bloodshed followed with brother killing brother. It was not God's way.

The story of Noah is a do-over based on filling an ark with the best of God-honoring people and all the animals to refill the earth after the flood. When the rain ceased and dry land appeared, God's way was draped with a rainbow of hope for a new day in pursuit of God's justice and mercy. Yet soon the inhabitants of the earth are on a quest to build a great city with a tower reaching to the skies. The builders constructed the tower and stated that it was built "to our own greatness."

Our faith story is one of God's never giving up on us though we fail to do what is right and good. All the while, right before us is God's way of justice, which is right, and mercy, which is good. It appears to be an easy choice, but our seeking our own way, on our own terms, to our own greatness is too enticing and too often our choice. Can we be a people of faith and trust God's way to lead us to that perfect love of God and neighbor?

O God of dirty hands, all for my good and well-being, lead me in your paths that lead to your righteousness, full of justice and mercy. Replant your vine in my heart that I may bear the fruit of your heart and your way. Amen.

Before reading the entire psalm, we must focus on its beginning, "Stir up your might, and come to save us!" It is hard to read this lamenting psalm without mourning the state of the church—as a being like the vineyard planted by God, full of hope but with sour grapes of conflict growing instead. Few Christian denominations have not suffered some form of schism or division. Why would God allow the walls of protection to be destroyed and the vineyard to be ravaged, burned, and cut back all the way to the ground?

I preached my first sermon in my rural East Texas home church from the pulpit behind the altar rail where I accepted Christ as my Lord and Savior. There, I had been confirmed in the faith and took the vows of membership in The United Methodist Church. My sweetest memories of faith from my youth happened amid that dear community.

The word *disaffiliation* changed my association, my relationship, my closeness with the church I call home. That church decided to leave—to disaffiliate from—the denomination of which I am a pastor. The United Methodist Church is only the most recent denomination to experience schism. We all are responsible for the sour grapes of conflict spoiling the hope for a thriving vineyard. Disdain for the ones thought to have lit the match that burned the vineyard down gets us nowhere fast.

Sometimes darkness must come for us to see the shining face of God. Death must happen for resurrection to break through the dreary morn, in the shadow of an empty tomb. There is but one way to restoration and that is the way that God makes to come and save us. God's way always starts with confession, before forgiveness can be fully experienced.

God of might and forgiveness, I want to feel your hand on my shoulder, for you alone can save us. Let me never turn from you; give me life as I call on your name. Amen.

The psalmist shares his heartfelt cry as one who believed God's way was one of restoration: "Restore us, O God; let your face shine, that we may be saved!"

A few years ago, my parents, in their eighties, lost their home and everything in it to a fire. We were at a wedding celebration in Dallas, and family had gathered from far and wide the night that lightning struck their home. My mother, who at the time was severely compromised by Parkinson's Disease, would not miss the party, and Dad was so happy that they were able to make the trip.

Being together with family in a hotel on that fateful night saved their lives. However, they lost every material thing of value that could never be replaced. Mom had collected newspaper clippings, funeral bulletins, photos, home movies, and more in large plastic containers with the year prominently displayed. Rarely would you go to their house that Mom did not have one of the plastic tubs out on the guest bed sorting and examining her treasures.

The day after the fire, we drove home to see the once beautiful farmhouse reduced to a pile of smoldering rubble. I made my way close to the space that once held the keepsakes, and literally rising from the heat of ashes was a piece of a newsletter from my church that had a photo of an open Bible on the front. The charred piece floated to the safety of grass in the yard. I picked it up and read these words, "The LORD is my Shepherd; I shall not want . . . . He restores my soul." God makes a way toward the gift of restoration.

God of the way of restoration, pick me up when I am down.
Lift your message above the ash heaps of my lowest season, and
open my soul to hear your song of hope. Amen.

All those who are named in the passage today—Gideon, Barak, Samson, Jephthah, David, Samuel—did great things. All also stood in need of forgiveness. Perhaps chief among the sinners was great King David, who was an adulterer and a murderer.

On June 17, 2015, in Charleston, South Carolina, a 21-year-old white supremacist wandered into a Bible study at the Mother Emanuel AME Church and killed nine African American Christians, injuring a tenth. The shooting happened after spending an hour with them in study and fellowship. He didn't know a person whom he murdered; each of them had welcomed him to be in their study.

Among these nine martyrs was the pastor of the church and a state senator—a young, gifted man named Clementa Pinckney. Three other pastors were killed that day, among them a 74-year-old retired pastor named Daniel Simmons. Alanna Simmons, his granddaughter, said, "Although my grandfather and the other victims died at the hands of hate, this is proof that they lived and loved. Hate won't win."

Nadine Collier offered these words to the man who killed her mother, Ethel Lance. She said to the shooter and for all the world to hear, "You took someone very precious away from me. I will never get to talk to her ever again. I will never be able to hold her again, but I forgive you and have mercy on your soul. You hurt me. You hurt a lot of people. But if God forgives you, I forgive you."

A "better resurrection" is about forgiveness. Forgiveness brings life to death. It lifts love above hate. It's how God makes a way. Whom do you need to forgive?

God of the way of forgiveness, I confess to be part of a people perpetuating warring madness. Heal us, we pray. Let me not be dissuaded from opening doors to others without counting the cost. Amen.

Martyrdom is not a comfortable contemplation. The passage for the day needs to come with the familiar warning that some of this content may be disturbing—*stoned to death, sawn in two, killed by the sword.*

The Salvadoran Civil War started a few months before my first seminary class. In the early days of this war that lasted twelve years, there was unprecedented death-squad activity, eventually claiming the lives of 75,000 people, mainly civilians. Also, in those early days of the war, Archbishop Oscar Romero was assassinated. This great man of peace was shot to death with a single shot from a U.S. military assault rifle while offering mass in the chapel of the Hospital of Divine Providence.

On a mission trip to El Salvador, I stood in that place where the archbishop's blood was spilt as he shared the sacrament of the spilt blood of his Lord. It was a powerful experience for me to be there. It raised me up to glimpse a "better resurrection"—God's better way.

On the day before his martyrdom, Saint Oscar Romero said, "Easter is itself now the cry of victory. No one can quench that life that Christ has resurrected. Neither death nor all the banners of death and hatred raised against him and against his church can prevail. He is the victorious one!"

This seems to me to be a better resurrection: Saint Romero inspires us *still* today and raises us up to acts of justice, mercy, and love, all wrapped up in a forgiveness beyond our own ability.

God of peace, Lord of love, as we reflect on those who have literally given their lives as a sacrifice in keeping with the way of the cross, lift us to see the better resurrection where your way of peace and love are never defeated. Amen.

The church I serve is eight decades old, and I am the fourth Senior Pastor. The cloud of witnesses here, like in most churches, are the shoulders on which we figuratively stand. It is not uncommon for people of faith to have a list of women and men who made a difference in their faith journey. Perhaps it is a bit unusual to have on one's list someone whom you have never known personally. I, however, have one on my list whom I never met, yet I live in the light of his legacy.

For thirty-one years, the church I serve presently was led by a pastor named Thomas Joel Shipp. As only the fourth pastor of this church, I am keenly aware that I stand on the shoulders of lay and clergy saints who served before me. At the age of 27 years old, the Reverend Tom Shipp became the pastor of the newly formed Lovers Lane Methodist Church. On the day the first building was dedicated in 1946, Rev. Shipp said, "Churches, like persons, have certain characteristics, traits, distinguishing features. Let us make this church an institution that stands, as we say, 'four-square,' for what is right, what is just, what is fair, what is of good report; an institution in which there are no shams, no make-believe, no halfway measures; where thoroughness and straight-forwardness are taught and practiced. May those within this church have high integrity, be faithful to ideals, dependable, true friends of others, and loyal to Jesus."

What a vision the pastor cast that day and then proceeded to live into, melting, molding, making, and leading such a church by God's grace. I am keenly aware that I am part of a legacy. To be part of this legacy means we live and love considering our faith in a God who wants the very best for us and desires a relationship with us that is perfected in love.

God of vision and legacy, melt and mold us into the people you would have us be, making us part of a church you desire, one that reflects your Son, our Savior, in how we love. Amen.

Is there any doubt about the fact that Jesus came to shake things up? He called people who heard this word for the first time and those of us who read it today to have our eyes opened to see that the track we are on is far from the path to God. Jesus came to shake things up and open our eyes to truly see.

Division is all around us, in our country and throughout our world. We do not escape divisions in our families, friendship circles, and communities of faith. Do we not see where this is taking us?

The "Jesus-shake-up" challenges us to the very bones about what we thought we could be sure of—namely, who is wrong and who is right. Our prayer is to have the eyes of the Spirit, to see the places in our lives into which God comes to "mess us up" and challenge our narrow beliefs and hypocrisies. The Spirit would have us see not our own agendas and desires but God's path leading us into new directions and convictions.

God's mission is always about love. Love does not keep us from divisions. But if our convictions are to love as Jesus loved, we cannot settle for living divided. Not everyone wants to love like Jesus, who called us to love our enemies, especially those who do not look like us and those who may believe differently than we do. Do we see clearly that God's signs are always pointing us to the life, lessons, and love of Jesus that shake everything up, ultimately for the good?

All-seeing and loving God, shake me up. "Open my eyes that I may see glimpses of truth thou hast for me. Place in my hands the wonderful key that shall unclasp and set me free. Silently now I wait for thee, ready, my God, thy will to see" (Clara H. Scott, 1895). Amen.

Unshakable Essentials

AUGUST 18–24, 2025 • LESLEE WRAY

SCRIPTURE OVERVIEW: This week's readings offer gracious underpinnings to our faith. They name God's essential gifts for sustaining and nurturing our life with God. These unshakable gifts cannot be obliterated by the world's great need or devastating circumstances. The readings from Jeremiah and Psalms are repeated in a pair from earlier in the year (Jan. 27–Feb. 2). God's plans for the authors' lives and our own are essential gifts, if only we can accept them. The kingdom given in the Hebrews passage "cannot be shaken," indicating the permanency of God's faithfulness to us. Jesus' teaching and encounter on the sabbath exemplifies the most unshakable gift given—mercy. These scriptural witnesses offer encouragement and direction for meeting the challenging circumstances in our time. With these essential gifts we, like those before us, may build an unshakable faith.

QUESTIONS AND SUGGESTIONS FOR REFLECTION

- Read Jeremiah 1:4-10. How can you trust God to empower you to follow God's call? How can you encourage others to live into their calling?
- Read Psalm 71:1-6. How can you continually praise God as your refuge?
- Read Hebrews 12:18-29. How do you discern what is required of you in praising God in the new covenant?
- Read Luke 13:10-17. How do you observe the sabbath now? What sabbath practice might you start that puts God's reign into action?

The Rev. Leslee Wray is a retired United Methodist minister, spiritual director, and founder of Serving Tree, a small business that supports and funds those "doing good: well" in their communities and the world. Leslee lives with her husband, Dan, on a pretty piece of woods in Mount Gilead, NC.

While a life with God welcomes free choice, once a commitment is made, some essentials cannot be refused, ignored, or misplaced. We must accept them as God's gifts, whether welcomed or not. They're unshakable pillars relegating us to the back seat, imploring us to trust that God's driving care knows what's best for us. They're reliable truths revealing that God alone knows what is absolutely necessary for our lives to be whole and good, which isn't a bad thing. It can be a hard thing but not bad. Just ask the prophet Jeremiah.

Called at an early age to prophesy during some of Israel's most horrific history, Jeremiah offers a brave and faithful witness to the unshakable essentials that surface when we say "yes" to a life with God. Jeremiah speaks of God's eternal hold on his life from an early point: "Before I formed you in the womb I knew you, and before you were born, I consecrated you." Jeremiah has the choice to welcome God's sovereign love and care or not. He has no choice, however, over God's choice of him. He cannot manipulate or control God's choices any more than we can.

When we think "essential," we think mandatory, and understand that what is deemed essential is necessary to the intended outcome, whatever it may be. Gracefully, God's gifts are given to us, and while they are essential for our success in following God faithfully, they are not mandatory should we choose a different path. Mercifully, God eternally holds us all, whether we welcome it or not. This unshakable, essential choice of God makes the hard things we're called to do wondrously possible.

Loving God, may we welcome your eternal hold upon our lives as the essential, driving care that loves and leads us to abundant life. Amen.

It's not hard to turn away from something we don't deem essential for our lives. It's hard to welcome this "unshakable essential" when we're taking care of things just fine. After all, why is such a reckoning needed for those of us who are working hard to do everything right? And it's not like God's judgment consists of a little "time out." How can we welcome something that appears so devastatingly harsh? Consequences that come from poor decisions, we get. What's difficult to comprehend is God's catastrophic response to a stubborn Israel who has finally gone one step too far. Sure, we understand God's anger with people abusing the gifts in front of them, but demise and exile seem a disproportionate response to some people behaving badly. Fortunately, the prophet Jeremiah corrects our grave misunderstanding.

The book of Jeremiah illuminates God's judgment as good through confronting Israel about what is not life-giving and good—namely, her negligible arrogance and self-deceit. Yet the prophet accentuates God's undying commitment by walking with these wayward people into the devastating consequences of their erroneous sins. It's one thing to drop the bad news at the door and quite something else to move into the house and live with those who are responsible for the bad news that has come. Such is the faithful witness of Jeremiah. From a young age, he follows God's will and allows God to speak through him. His witness is still crying out to those of us who believe we are above and beyond the need for God's essential judgment. Jeremiah's prophecy still implores us not to turn away from God's best.

Holy God, speak good judgment into our lives so that we may leave behind what is not life-giving and turn toward what is. Amen.

In the woods near our home, some wild lilies make an appearance each spring. They don't send out engraved invitations, notify their fans by email or Facebook, or send a text message to let anyone know they've arrived. Instead, they come quietly, bringing to life a brilliant white surprise in the middle of dirt and mud. So faithful is their coming we've come to trust and expect their arrival. While they come yearly, we still have to hunt them out. And we're always surprised by what we find. It's startling to find vibrant life in woods that are clinging to winter. Such is the way of hope and trust. They are our faith's "essential companions," ever with us, more than we realize. We just have to keep hunting them out, celebrating with wonder the surprise of their faithful presence.

A believer since youth, the psalmist here reflects such hunting and celebrating. A long relationship with God has led to trusting and expecting gifts of refuge, strength, and rescue. And yet the psalmist struggles with doubt and suffering. Hope and trust have slipped from view, prompting desperate praying: "Rescue me, O my God." The psalmist can't see hope and trust anywhere. Dire circumstances are clouding any expression of faith.

That is until what was true in the past is remembered. By faithful hunting, the psalmist discovers again that hope and trust have not left. The cold ground of fear and trouble buried them for a time, but they always come, surprising those looking by being present all along. They are as steadfast as God. It's why the psalmist can see them once again. Remembering God's eternal faithfulness raises hope and trust up, out of the ground. It's still a wonder, startling believers everywhere to find vibrant life in a world clinging to suffering. But such is the way of hope and trust. They are forever with us.

Thank you, God, for the faithfulness of hope and trust pushing their way to life amid the dirt. Amen.

If "the best defense is a good offense," then gratitude should be in ready supply. There's no better way to confront adversity than to shine gratitude in its face. It's the last thing adversity expects to see coming. It's why it's such a great defense against all that robs us of life. The great offensive play about gratitude is that it knows what it's up against and refuses to back down. Living lives of thanksgiving, especially when it's hard, will defend us well when adversity comes knocking. It won't stand a chance.

Today's psalmist seems to agree. Though in need of rescue from cruel enemies, the psalmist offers to God a promise: "My praise is continually of you." Instead of admitting defeat to present circumstances, this psalmist holds up gratitude as the essential defense against adversity.

Such defiant gratitude lives in my bedridden father. Instead of giving in to his immobility, he remains inquisitive and fully engaged in the lives of those around him. At 91, his memory remains keen, he's in control of his financial affairs, and he enjoys conversation with every visitor. With the means he has, he listens for ways he might help another. He has made every preparation in the event of his death. And yet what is most apparent is his kinship with gratitude. He cannot say "thank you" enough to his loved ones and to God.

None of this is easy. Lying in bed, he quietly wonders about death. He is losing his appetite, struggles for comfort, continues to fight off infection, and wrestles with feelings of being a burden. Yet in the midst of all that is so hard he remains committed to life. He is choosing gratitude as his essential defense against anything that dares to rob him of life. Adversity will never win as long as there is gratitude.

Loving God, help us live lives of gratitude, especially when adversity makes it hard to do so. Make gratitude our best defense. Amen.

In Ann Patchett's novel *Bel Canto,* a multicultural group of dignitaries is invited to hear a famous opera singer perform at a dinner party in a third-world country. While they are mesmerized by her singing, a band of rebels raids the party and takes everyone hostage for four months. Throughout their captivity, the opera singer performs each day, and the power of her music draws them all together—captors and captives, poor and rich, male and female. The power of beauty and song transforms all. Evil and brokenness are outdone by something unshakably good.

The writer of Hebrews names this good as the "kingdom that cannot be shaken." It's unshakable because it's not made of brick and mortar but of grace, mercy, and love. It's the place where Christ lives and reigns. Sin obliterates much in life, but nothing can kill the power of Christ's transforming beauty and song. Nothing can destroy the power of his saving love. When such power and love live in us, his song becomes our own. We then become a part of the unshakable kingdom defying the circumstances of a broken world and all that's wrong. This transformation is what makes a life with Jesus essential.

With the world's needs being dire, the temptation for despair is great. When we are confronted with life's overwhelming and shaky circumstances, we don't know how to help or respond. History is continually being shaped by people who refuse to let the atrocious circumstances they're living in define who they will be or how they will respond. We need a steadfast power that can hold us and not be moved, a gracious force that can guide our timid faith, and a love that will not let us go. We need Jesus and all that his unshakable kingdom offers. We need his song to become our own.

Jesus, we give you eternal thanks for the transforming power of the unshakable kingdom you make available to us. Amen.

Our oldest daughter has found adulthood difficult. Traditional college was not a good fit, and she struggled to discern the right path for her life. Ever tenacious, she enrolled in an online college program and has held fast to her conscientious work ethic. While her many jobs have made paying rent possible, they also left her feeling frustrated, discouraged, and beaten down from any hope of finding her place in the world. Emotionally, she has been "bent over" by the weight of trying to find her way.

Then, she became a teacher's assistant at a local elementary school. Instantaneously, the principal, teachers, staff, and children "saw her," embracing her as one of their own. They touched her soul with their affirmation, support, love, and encouragement. Their radical grace "set [her] free" enabling her to stand tall, to see her beauty and gifts in ways her struggle prevented her from seeing, and to unleash her sense of potential and joy for how she might share her life with the world. It's been a wondrous healing that has restored her life. It's been a wondrous reminder of how essential and transforming radical grace can be.

It's the same radical grace we see Jesus extend to the bent-over woman in Luke's Gospel. It's radical because the woman doesn't initiate her healing. She doesn't approach Jesus, ask for his help, ask another to intervene on her behalf, or offer any expression of faith. Instead, Jesus initiates everything, lifting her up, and setting her free from a life of despair and bondage. It's one thing to ask for help and receive it; it's quite another to have help come when we've lost all hope of its coming. Such grace has the power to transform us, unleashing our own sense of potential and joy so that we can share radical grace with others.

Loving God, may we continue to offer you eternal thanks and praise for your essential gift of radical grace. Amen.

Perhaps we should be grateful for the synagogue leader's messy faith in Luke's Gospel. So messy and trying is his response to Jesus' healing on the sabbath that it's not hard to say, "At least we're not *that* bad." After all, nothing helps us feel better about our own faith struggles than finding someone who's messing it up worse than we are. How good of this hypocrite to take the heat off our hypocrisy and highlight his own! If only we could stop here and let Jesus confront this church leader all on his own.

And yet the unshakable essential gift of mercy will not let us. Why we've not been banished for all the times we have judged another unjustly, allowed our self-righteousness to trample someone, or made sure there was no room for anything but our certainty, we may never know. But what we can know, if we don't already, is that Christ's mercy saves us every time. Maybe this is why Luke shares the synagogue leader's side of things. The author wants to make sure we stay in touch with our own missteps and vulnerabilities. He wants to impress the essential need for Christ's mercy in each of us.

Christ's mercy, however, is sometimes hard to see. Jesus' confrontational response to the synagogue leader is easy to interpret as unforgiving and harsh. Perhaps Luke wants us to see Jesus' response as a vivid sign of his merciful love for this man of faith. Like a loving parent passionately confronting a child about to touch a hot stove, Jesus wants to stop the grave misstep of this leader who, he knows, has a heart for God. Christ's mercy loves us like this as well. So much so that in place of judging others, we can embrace our messy faith, trusting Christ's mercy to show us the way.

Loving God, shower us with the essential gift of your mercy. Amen.

Called to a New Way of Life

AUGUST 25–31, 2025 • BONFACE GHERO WANYAMA

SCRIPTURE OVERVIEW: The four texts this week bring out a common theme of a new way of life. In Jeremiah and the psalm God warns about the consequences that come with the decisions the people have made. God then extends an invitation of grace and expresses readiness to welcome them back, assuring them safety and security. God is willing to walk with them again in a renewed relationship. The scripture from Hebrews opens with an invitation to a new way of relating to people who are unfamiliar to us, which is a way in which we welcome God. Luke's Gospel is a story of Jesus' challenge of the status quo and an invitation to a transformed way of hospitality.

QUESTIONS AND SUGGESTIONS FOR REFLECTION

- Read Luke 14:1, 7-14. When have you extended an invitation to others? What kind of invitations do you send out? What considerations do you have when extending the invitation?
- Read Jeremiah 2:4-13. What has God done in your life that you have forgotten and taken for granted? What is it that has taken the place of God in our lives?
- Read Hebrews 13:1-8, 15-16. Where have you seen people go out of their way to show compassion for others? When have you demonstrated love for other people?
- Read Psalm 81:1, 10-16. What do you think you can hold on to in place of God?

_____

The Rev. Bonface Ghero Wanyama is an elder in the Kenya/Ethiopia Annual Conference of The United Methodist Church.

Jesus used parables to connect with his audience. By telling stories that taught his message, Jesus could make connections to the real experiences his listeners would have had. The parable Jesus uses in today's passage is inspired by the events Jesus watches unfold. The people of the first-century world had a clear understanding of social status, and they paid attention to the ways seating arrangements and guest lists signified status.

This is not just a description appropriate to the first-century world. Problems in our societies mirror the same focus on status. In my home country of Kenya, wealth and possessions determine the social privileges one receives.

For Jesus, the meal setting becomes a strategic platform to share his gospel of transformation. He presents a new way of looking at social status. Jesus discourages his listeners from seeking the most prestigious positions at the table. He gives simple advice about avoiding the public humiliation of being moved down in status. Seeking a lower seat avoids the humiliation. Taking the lowest place results in being elevated to a more distinguished position. Jesus' exhortation is to pursue humility, a concept with significant status connotations. Humility was very rarely considered a virtue in moral discourse. Yet humility is a mark of followers of Jesus.

Jesus responds with wisdom to this situation in a way that might have left many surprised. His advice challenges normal practices. But by following his advice, we are freed from the constraints of our culture's power struggles and freed to create the welcoming community God envisions for the world.

God, as we minister with others, cause a change of heart in us so that we focus more on your glory than our own. Amen.

Jeremiah is singled out for service before birth. This brings a serious conviction of the prophet's heart. He knows he has been chosen and set apart for the immensely difficult task of upsetting the established systems—"to pluck up and to pull down, to destroy and to overthrow" (Jer. 1:10). The task clearly points to a preordained rejection of the prophet, but the situation in Israel calls for a hardened prophetic message rather than feel-good words. And these words start strong in Jeremiah's book. By verse 9 of the second chapter, Jeremiah is conveying to the people a lawsuit brought by God for their breaking of the covenant.

God's question reported by Jeremiah in verse five is rhetorical. Of course the ancestors found no wrong in God. But what else could have caused them to turn from the one who brought them out of slavery into the Promised Land—to break this covenant? Through Jeremiah's polemic, God reminds the people of the love, generosity, and warmth in the early days, how all that God did has been ignored by the people as they have followed worthless things.

Reading Jeremiah today, we are invited to consider how often things that do not matter occupy our attention. We do not take the opportunities to cultivate a relationship with God. Like the religious leaders of Israel too many of our pulpits are not used to proclaim the greatness and glory of God. Our once passionate love for God continues to decrease, and our focus shifts to other gods. Through Jeremiah's words, we are invited to a new way of faith that recognizes God's faithfulness even in our faithlessness.

Redeemer God, many times the things that do not matter occupy my focus. Fill me with the Spirit to discern the things that matter and help move me closer to you. Amen.

Jeremiah uses the metaphor of water to show that the people have turned away from God. Water symbolizes salvation, life, and blessings. The people are misguided not only by turning from God, the source of living water, but by turning toward other gods that will not provide the care they so desperately need. They have built for themselves sources of water that are not sustainable. They will find no water in broken cisterns.

By naming two evils, or "sins," Jeremiah highlights that leaving God and the subsequent attachment to other gods are separate sins, just as the first two commandments—to have no other gods and to not make idols—are two separate transgressions against God (see Exod. 20:3-4). The metaphor of the water is apt in describing the Israelites' covenant-breaking actions. Not only have they turned away from a constantly renewed source of fresh water, they have also turned toward vessels of water that can only hold existing water, indicating the water will become stagnant and undrinkable. Furthermore, these cisterns are broken, meaning they will not even effectively hold the stagnant water they contain, as what water does exist will seep through the cracks and disappear into the ground.

Our choice to ignore the ways of God, who is the source of all our needs, leaves us vulnerable. Our efforts are fruitless if we do not involve God. And when we stop focusing on God, something else will fill the void. We will shift our focus to other gods that will not provide the provisions we seek. We will attempt to fashion a new way of life for ourselves apart from God. It is only a matter of time before we understand the limits of the broken cisterns we have built for ourselves, and the ways we are left thirsting for more.

I am vulnerable, O God, living in a dry land. Turn me back to you, the fountain of living water, that I may drink deeply and live fully. Amen.

The Hebrews had a terrible experience in Egypt, but in their suffering they called out to God for deliverance and were led to freedom. The journey to freedom was difficult, but God was present with them every step of the way. They were brought to a new land and sustained along the way. They discovered that they were not only being called to a new place but into a new way of life, a new beginning. They were called to join in the singing of praises to God, the source of all freedom.

God had warned the people that the pathway to blessings was faithfulness. God warned against idolatry. After reminding them how they were brought out of the land of Egypt, God made them an interesting promise—if they would open their mouth wide, God would fill it. If the people would come to God with a great petition and surrender, God would fulfill their petitions.

There is nothing good that God will not do for God's people who choose to be obedient. "I will do whatever you ask in my name, so that the Father may be glorified in the Son" (John 14:13). In return, God wants obedience, recognition, and yielding of the heart and will. This is a lot, but lives of faithfulness to God have shown that obedience and yielding lead to blessings and joy. Still Israel would not obey God. God allowed them to have their way and gave them over to the misery of following their own desires. Then God mourned their continued folly and stubbornness.

As God's people, we have a role to play in the emergence of our new identity. It's not enough to promise to follow; we must take the steps as well. When we do, we are assured of spiritual and physical nourishment.

Thank you, God, for giving new life, for putting a new song in the hearts of your people so that they may shout and live their praise of you. Amen.

The scriptures this week have consistently called God's people to a new way of living. It is the writer of Hebrews that gives some frame to this new life. The foundation for Christian faith is Christ. Believing in Christ should lead to a visible change in practical ways.

Belief in Jesus should first bring positive change in our practice beginning with the way we treat other people. Love for others is important. Because of the importance of love, believers are exhorted to love one another in the fellowship. Love should be the foundation and engine of Christian fellowship. But beyond the community, followers of Christ should also show hospitality to strangers. Normally we are comfortable with entertaining people we know, but here the author says we must show hospitality to people we don't know. This was, perhaps, a very practical instruction, as travelers in the first century relied on the kindness of strangers to survive. The story of the good Samaritan comes to mind (see Luke 10:25-37). We are called to help those who need us without expecting anything back.

The rest of this passage explores how the audience was to relate to those in prison, behave in marriage, and consider money. These exhortations may be specific to situations the community was facing; for example, the call to care for those in prison was an acute plea because practicing Christianity was illegal and led to imprisonment. Those reading could just as easily find themselves in the same situation.

The specifics may be different, but the message is clear: Belief in Jesus should bring change to the ways we treat other people.

Dear God, give me the eyes to see differently and ears to hear the cries and struggles of others, especially those around me who are hurting and in need. Amen.

Here we see an invitation to sacrificial life. The author begins by describing the believer's position before God. This believer is now done with all earthly ordinances and has no interest in the ceremonies of the law. As a believer in Jesus, who is the substance of all, the believer has nothing to do with altars of gold or stone. The worship is spiritual, and the altar is spiritual. What then is next? Is there no need for any sacrifice?

The sacrifice has to continue. The believer is called to offer a transformed continual sacrifice. Instead of presenting a sacrifice of lambs, bulls, and sheep, the believer is to present to God continually the sacrifice of praise. Having done away with the outward and the physical, Christians now give themselves entirely to the inward and to the spiritual. They have the opportunity to offer the sacrifices of praise to God.

But these sacrifices of praise would mean nothing without the foundational sacrifice that Christ made. Christ is the foundation of the believer's faith, and all sacrifices must be offered through faith in Christ.

The author lists sacrifices that are pleasing to God—praise and doing good, especially sharing what we have with others. Giving thanks means to confess God's name. It is pleasing to God when we openly and willingly proclaim our faith. Hebrews tells us to "hold fast to the confession of our hope without wavering, for [God] who has promised is faithful" (Heb. 10:23). The letter to Hebrews is a call to hold firm to the faith and finish well, enduring until the end. Faith that inspires works of love is a pleasing sacrifice to God.

May I remember that you, Christ, are the ultimate sacrifice. Increase my faith so that I may continually offer a sacrifice of praise in words and deeds. Amen.

We continue to hear a message that addresses the fabric of status structures in society. In today's passage, Jesus speaks directly to his host—the one who appears to control the system and holds a greater control over the rules of the game for this particular meal. Jesus' advice undermines the very system that upholds status difference at meals. Jesus advises the host not to invite friends, relatives, or rich neighbors to meals, since they are able to repay with a corresponding invitation. Such social reciprocity is the backbone of the patronage system endemic to most societies.

Don't we expect repayments for the things we do for others? "You scratch my back; I scratch yours" is mostly what informs our relationships. I'll do this for you, and you'll do something for me. Most relationships flourish under such arrangements and are not always bad. However, Jesus introduces us to a new game. He wants us to follow him into a more redemptive purpose in our relationships. He calls for a deliberate inclusion of "the poor, the crippled, the lame, and the blind"; those who cannot return the favor of invitation.

Jesus' message here resonates with what we find in Isaiah. In Isaiah, the poor and the blind are mentioned explicitly as the recipients of God's grace (see Isa. 29:18-19; 42:5-7; 58:6-8). Jesus again challenges the status quo by subverting the payment and repayment structure that governed social engagements in the community. Jesus promises that God will repay such hospitality at the "resurrection of the righteous"—God promises to remember! It is, as well, another facet of the new way of life.

God, open my eyes to the opportunities you provide me to bless those who are not like me, those from whom I can expect nothing back. Forgive me for spending a lot of my time investing in the wrong place. Amen.

The Difficult Words of God

SEPTEMBER 1–7, 2025 • DERRICK SCOTT III

SCRIPTURE OVERVIEW: While God's words may sometimes be difficult to hear, God speaks with deep honesty that is important for God's followers to hear if they seek to grow. Jeremiah brings another warning of impending judgment. If the people will not turn to the Lord, God will break the nation and reshape it, just as a potter breaks down and reshapes clay on a wheel. The psalmist praises God for God's intimate knowledge of each one of us. Even from the moment of conception, God knows us and has a plan for our lives. Philemon is often overlooked, but it packs a punch. A text that some have used in the past to justify slavery teaches a very different message. Paul warns Philemon not to enslave Onesimus again but to receive him back as a brother. Secular power structures have no place in God's kingdom. In Luke, Jesus uses striking examples to teach us that the life of faith cannot be lived well with half-hearted commitment.

QUESTIONS AND SUGGESTIONS FOR REFLECTION

- Read Jeremiah 18:1-11. How does the image of the potter point to the Creator's intentions of loving and shaping us?
- Read Psalm 139:1-6, 13-18. God knows you better than you know yourself, yet God has given you the ability to make your own decisions. How do you respond to God?
- Read Philemon 1:1-21. Holy pressure can encourage someone to do the right thing, but where is the balance between not enough and too much holy pressure? What examples of holy pressure do you see in the world today?
- Read Luke 14:25-33. What cost have you paid to follow Jesus? How has God uniquely moved in you to produce radical change?

Derrick Scott III is a campus minister and lay leader in the Florida Conference of The United Methodist Church.

The prophet Jeremiah received a word from God. But the word Jeremiah received was not so much for him as for God's people, both those in Israel at the time and for all of us who come after. Jeremiah is not only responsible for hearing God's word but for conveying it in a way that the people can understand so that it will challenge and nurture them for generations. To do this, prophets like Jeremiah are tasked with acting out what they have heard. These enactment prophecies bring the prophetic words to life in physical, active symbolism. Jeremiah must go to the place he is sent to see the potter and physically bring that image to the people.

Years ago, while serving in campus ministry, I had a student who always had a word of wisdom for our community. She often arrived with a deep sense of God's heart for her fellow students and could somehow translate that heart into words that were consistently helpful for them. After a year or so, I pulled her aside and said, "You know, you really are a prophet among us." And then she cried. She wiped her tears and asserted: "I'm not interested in being a prophet—their whole lives are consumed with words from God for everyone else. That's not the life I want."

We have evidence that Jeremiah didn't want that life either. But his people were all the better for his obedience to hear and interpret, to see and embody the word from the Lord. If there was ever a time that we needed the voice of the prophets, it is now. Where are the prophets among us? Is it you?

Holy Spirit, give us the courage to hear and translate, to see and embody the word of the Lord for the sake of others. Amen.

Some of Jesus' most challenging words are often said when he encounters large crowds. We know that Jesus loves all people, whether it is the one, the ninety-nine, or the multitudes. But even in today's passage, there's a bluntness to his homily that makes his words difficult to accept. We miss Christ's intention if we think about it too broadly. It has to become specific, personal to us as individuals.

I wonder if someone in the crowd struggled when the words of Jesus caused them to make different choices than their family of origin. How many had enough experience building towers to know how much planning was involved? Were there military members in the crowd who had lost people precious to them because their commander hadn't sought a peaceful solution?

We know some have heard these words and walked away from Jesus. The price was too high. Yet multitudes have heard and read these words and have taken up their own crosses to follow Jesus. It is, after all, the most challenging words that call us to consider who we truly want to be in this world and that inspire us to do great things in response. The direct words of a coach on the basketball court can lead a team to a state championship. The frightening words of a physician can cause a patient to make lifestyle changes that lead to better health outcomes. The sharp tone of an activist can wake up an electorate to use their power for good in the community.

Scripture is clear that the life of true discipleship may not be for everyone. Jesus' words are meant to challenge his hearers, to call them to action, and to help them understand the full cost of what they are committing to. We too must consider the cost of discipleship as we commit today to following Christ.

Holy Spirit, give me courage to receive Christ's words that are hard to hear but are ultimately for my good. Amen.

God's knowledge of each of us is vast. Psalm 139 confirms that the Lord knows us intimately—even better than we know ourselves. God pays attention to us on the good days and the bad. God sees the hidden desires and the authentic motivations. God is mindful of us when we take action and when we rest. As the psalmist says in verse 4, "There isn't a word on my tongue, LORD, that you don't already know completely" (CEB). We are truly seen by a loving God.

But as I read today's passage, I got to verse 5 and wondered if the psalmist ever wanted to know everything that God saw in them. Initially, I was eager to hear God's assessment of me. But after a few moments of consideration, I began to have second thoughts. Am I ready to hear the God's-honest truth about my life? Do I have the courage to face the parts of my life that from God's perspective still need work? Will I take responsibility for the growth areas that God reveals to me? Am I brave enough to acknowledge the good that God sees in me? Am I prepared to steward the gifts God has given me for the sake of the poor and downtrodden instead of for myself? God knows all about me. How might God's perspective change the story I tell to myself?

A mark of maturity is the capacity to receive the truth about ourselves as a gift to treasure, not a conversation to dread. As we make ourselves more open to the truth of God's word, may we be "all ears" to the One who has intimate knowledge of us and calls each one of us beloved.

God who is near enough to know me, give me openness to hear your truth about who I am. Grant me the courage to face my true self, and, with your grace, overcome my shortcomings. Amen.

My third grade teacher was Mrs. Hamilton. She was the first teacher who did not go easy on me. She was intimidating and commanded the full attention of her classroom. I was often afraid to speak in class and doubly afraid not to do my best work. She had one goal: to stir the fear of God in us if we were not the best students in the school.

Some context: Mrs. Hamilton was a Black educator who taught in an inner city public school where the majority of students came from lower income families. She knew that if her students did not get a strong foundation in elementary school, they would not have a fighting chance in the years to come. Mrs. Hamilton didn't have time to be nice. She wanted us to succeed, and that was more important than whether or not we thought she was a nice teacher.

It would be years before I realized that Mrs. Hamilton really loved her job and was one of the most committed teachers I would ever have. I made my best grades and did my most honest work in Mrs. Hamilton's class. Her words and teaching style made me a better student. And to this day, I am glad she didn't go easy on me.

In today's Gospel passage, Jesus, like Mrs. Hamilton, is blunt and sharp. But we must listen and read his words with this assumption in mind: Jesus absolutely wants us to be his disciples. The call to consider the cost of following comes from the One who delights in making room for us. But the road ahead will not be easy. At times, the word of the Lord will delay niceties so that we get a dose of reality. May we not miss the goal of this word from the Gospel.

God, do not go easy on me. I want to become the best disciple I can be. Show me my flaws so that I can be like you. Amen.

Today's psalm echoes the words spoken in Jeremiah 1:4-10. The psalmist speaks of a God who creates our "innermost parts" and weaves us together in the deep parts of the earth. God sees us and loves us before we do anything. God has been hands-on in creating us. The word of the Lord comes to us with an understanding of how we got here and how delicate we are. The God who speaks is the God who knit us together. This Creator who knows we are fragile is the one who calls us to be disciples.

More than twenty years serving in campus ministry has given me the joy of watching college students grow into their vocational calling. I have been particularly proud of those who have found themselves in some kind of Christian ministry. At this point, my former students are now staff members in congregations and ordained clergy in the denomination. I remember a young man who had to be almost forced into an intern position but is now the head of communications for a large church. And I recall a young woman who would barely talk in Bible study, but who is now coming into her own as a communicator of the gospel. They all had moments of "I don't think I can do this." Their fears, hesitations, mistakes, and detours did not change the potential for ministry that was always there. God knew them, and God called them.

The God who knows our fragility is the same God who calls us to be disciples. The God who saw our vulnerability from the very beginning also calls each of us into ministry. May we be willing to receive words of guidance from the One who has formed us, knows us, and calls us.

God, remind me that your words are not detached from your knowledge and love of me. Amen.

The power of the word of the Lord is that it speaks to us with enough room to speak beyond us into the world we live in. This passage, a short letter attributed to the apostle Paul, is a message that is, all at once, about Paul, Philemon, Onesimus, and also you, me, and all of us together.

In many ways, this letter is Paul's attempt to call Philemon to deepen his commitment to be a disciple of Christ. And in this moment, that looks like receiving Onesimus as a brother whose sins have been forgiven. In delivering this call, Paul is not only the messenger: His life embodies the message. Paul is himself a prisoner, yet called to shepherd the flock of God by delivering the words of God, even to individuals. Paul invites Philemon to consider a similar vocation, though from a different place in the world. The word to welcome Onesimus as he would welcome Paul may come as a blunt and sharp word. But Paul knows Philemon, believes in him, and anticipates seeing first hand the ways that this disciple will receive a hard word and do a hard thing.

This letter is specific to Paul's ministry in his world and Philemon's ministry with Onesimus as a sibling in Christ, but it is also a word for us today. It points to much larger societal and systemic realities of the Roman world, but it also invites us to consider the systems of oppression that limit the work of the gospel in our day. It's a word from the Lord by disciples, for disciples, and to disciples. May we be willing to receive it.

Holy Spirit, give me a heart to receive the word of the Lord that calls me to do hard things. Amen.

But the piece he was making was flawed while still in his hands."

Over the last few days, we have focused on the difficult words of the Lord. We have been reminded that these words have weight and are challenging, but they are also grounded in God's knowledge of and love for us.

In Jeremiah's prophecy, verse four is the most striking to me. Even as the clay is being formed, it has the potential to be malformed. The flaws are not an indication that something is wrong with the clay; rather, they are a part of the process that comes with being shaped by the hands of the potter. The flaws are not surprising to the potter, and the potter is still committed to finishing what was started.

Maybe the most powerful word we can receive in our day is that our flaws are not a problem. That is not to say that there isn't work to do. We are people prone to sin and still fearfully and wonderfully made. We may need a pep talk or a strong encouraging message, but that is not evidence that we are off course or doomed to failure. If you read Psalm 139 or Luke 14 thinking, "something must be wrong with me," you will miss all the ways that God sees so much good in us and believes in us.

The word that brings us to life and into ministry is the word that declares, "your flaws are not a problem because you are in my hands." The God who speaks is the God who knows us and believes in us. That word can lead us to do hard things and to be people of profound grace. So may we hear the difficult words of deep affirmation that come from the heart of a loving Creator.

Holy Spirit, help me receive the word that my flaws are not a problem for the One who loves me. Amen.

There Is More Than This

SEPTEMBER 8–14, 2025 • FELICIA HOWELL LABOY

SCRIPTURE OVERVIEW: Jeremiah's warning of coming judgment continues. The children of Israel have become foolish, have ignored God, and have become good mainly at doing evil. God is going to respond to this situation. The psalmist describes the state of all who are foolish: They deny God and follow their own corrupt desires, including oppressing the poor. The author of First Timothy, traditionally Paul, says that this was also his former way of life. He has been foolish and ignorant, a persecutor of the followers of Christ. In fact, he had been the worst of all sinners; yet Christ has shown him mercy, not judgment. Jesus tells two parables to reveal God's heart. Rather than neglecting the ignorant, the foolish, and the lost, God searches to find each one of us.

QUESTIONS AND SUGGESTIONS FOR REFLECTION

- Read Jeremiah 4:11-12, 22-28. How do your actions show others that you know God?
- Read Psalm 14. When have you, like the psalmist, felt that no one knows God? How did you have faith that God would restore God's people?
- Read 1 Timothy 1:12-17. Recall a time when you felt unworthy of Christ's full acceptance. How has that experience made you more grateful for Christ's mercy?
- Read Luke 15:1-10. In a world full of death and violence, how do you rejoice when God finds one lost person?

The Rev. Dr. Felicia Howell LaBoy is a pastor, leader, certified transformation coach, and author. She is the Lead Pastor/Life Coach at First United Methodist Church in Elgin, IL, and the author of *Table Matters: The Sacraments, Evangelism, and Social Justice* (Cascade Books, 2017).

Destabilization. Destruction. Desolation. These words clearly describe the context that is forthcoming for Jerusalem and Judah, but they also describe the state of many Christian faith communities in the U.S. Few of us could have foreseen that once we had survived the COVID-19 pandemic, we would still be faced with largely empty buildings and aging congregations. Even with our shifts online, many of us are left wondering if this is all there is. Have we finally come to the end of our beloved churches or even the end of the church—where we found hope, comfort, love, friendship, and meaning?

Even for those not concerned about the status of churches, signs of destabilization, desolation, and destruction abound. Increasing homelessness, especially of the elderly and our veterans; the widening socio-economic gap; and the growing division in our communities that turns neighbors into enemies challenge our society. We relate to Jeremiah's growing concern for the destruction to come that finally materialized.

While it is easy and, in many ways, necessary to focus on the challenges—first to attend to those who are suffering and second to discern and learn from what caused it—these verses from Jeremiah offer us a glimmer of hope. Not hope that the destruction isn't imminent, but an assurance that God has not left us alone. Somehow, despite our foolish attempts to live on our own terms with no concern for the well-being or justice of others, we are still God's people.

Whereas God may make a full end of the world as we know it, God will not make a full end of us. God's judgment ultimately allows for a clean break, a new beginning. Something more than this exists on the other side.

God, remind us that even in the midst of destabilization, you are still our God and we are still your people. Help us to hold on to the hope that there is something more. Amen.

My promising career as a rising manager in a Fortune 100 tech company with access to the most senior executives was gone in a matter of months. I hadn't done anything wrong. In fact, several of those same executives supposedly were looking for a place to put me until the "right" job opened—it never did. I was thirty-five and about to lose my home. I had a fledgling startup business, few friends, and a call to ministry I was trying desperately not to hear or answer. Driving home from a trip to Chicago, I happened upon what had been a cornfield but was now a barren section of charred land. The corn had been harvested and the remaining stubble had been burned. As I drove past with tears streaming down my face, I heard God say to me, "This is how your life looks right now." And I remember shouting back, "Thanks—I thought you loved me."

After harvesting, some farmers burn what's left over to clear land, fertilize soil, and prepare it for new plantings. Even though I understood this intellectually, it took years for me to understand that the destruction of my old life is what made walking into my call and my new life in ministry reasonable.

In this passage, we note first that the hot wind that is sent is not helpful but will destroy almost everything in its path. Both the just and the unjust will be painfully affected. Second, even though the people have refused to acknowledge God as God and abide by the covenant between them, God still calls them God's people. And because they are God's people, God offers a new covenant, a new way of being God's people even in a foreign land (see Jer. 31:38). God does not stop the devastation to come or rebuild what was, but instead builds something new from the ashes.

God of new beginnings, help me release what you are done with. Remind us that you are our God and we are your people. Amen.

As we look at our near-empty churches and note how it seems no one is interested in going to church anymore, we can read Psalm 14 with an air of superiority thinking of these folks as foolish. However, to do so would be to miss the original lesson of the text and a critical lesson for our time.

The author is addressing God's people and pointing not to philosophical atheism (i.e., no belief in God) but rather practical atheism, acting toward others as if God does not exist. As I write this devotion, we see signs of corruption, injustice, and oppression—soaring housing prices and inflation, increasing child poverty, racism, migration issues, and an increasing political division that is tearing our nation apart.

While it would be easy to point the finger at others, researchers tell us that many people want nothing to do with our churches because we are practical atheists. Those who claim to be Christians have become caught up in cultural wars or are so inwardly focused that they've neglected the call to fully live like Jesus, healing the sick, feeding the hungry, and loving unconditionally.

But there is more! As Psalm 14 promises, deliverance can come from Zion—from God's people when we remember who we are and whose we are and stop acting like fools. We can act like we know and belong to the God made known in Jesus Christ. We can live in covenant with one another and our world to do good and bring about deliverance, restoration, and joy—the kin-dom of God on earth.

God, forgive us for refusing to do all the good we can, by all the means we can, in all the ways we can, in all the places we can, at all the times we can, to all the people we can, as long as ever we can. Embolden and empower us to be agents of deliverance, healing, and restoration so that we may point others toward you. Amen.

A once-popular practice in some Black churches was "testimony time." Before the worship service began, the deacons would lead a time for prayer and praise to be offered, followed by testimonies from the congregation of where they had seen God at work. Testimony time prepared our hearts for worship, opening us to the "more" that God wanted to do with and through us during the ministry of music and preaching.

A contemporary, non-church practice of testimony time has been made famous by self-help gurus as a way to help persons battling anxiety, burnout, and depression—a daily gratitude journal. Each day before going to bed, people are encouraged to write three things for which they are grateful, whether they are new things from the day or ongoing good things they continue to experience.

In his letter to Timothy, Paul writes his own testimony time, highlighting the good God is doing in his life even in the face of struggle. This tradition of sharing our testimony goes back to the very beginning of the Christian faith.

Even before COVID-19 caused us to shorten our service times, many congregations had stopped testimony time. Furthermore, few of us create weekly, much less daily gratitude journals of what we're grateful for "even though." A return to some practice of testimony time would do wonders in helping us see beyond where our churches are now to where God is leading us.

God of the "even though," thank you for doing in and through us far more than we ever dared to think or even imagine. Revive in us a spirit to share our testimonies about what you have done so that we may be encouraged and prepared for the journey ahead. Amen.

Often, we think of individual spiritual practices as something we do just for ourselves, practices that fortify and prepare us for the day ahead. This is only partially true. Our faith is personal but is never meant to be private. There should be some outflow during the day of what happens during our quiet time.

As this text demonstrates, there is something life-giving when we reflect on our spiritual growth. We may not be all that we can be, but we are certainly more than we would be without grace. Paul knows that without God's intervention, he would have been stuck, unable to move beyond his ignorance. And I believe part of his reflection in this passage is to encourage Timothy that God could do this and much more for him.

The church is often accused of hypocrisy, of being unwilling or unable to acknowledge the ways we have missed the mark we preach. It should not be that way. The Bible has no problem telling the stories of God's grace for flawed human beings, and neither should we. I wonder what would happen if we, as individuals and as churches, collectively told the truth about our struggles—about who and what we were before God in God's grace and mercy "got a hold" of us and about the ways God still works through us even as we continue to miss the mark. Sharing our stories might make us more merciful, less judgmental, and a little more human.

Merciful and gracious God, embolden us to share our stories of your faithfulness to us, even though we are not always faithful to you. Help us give witness to an authentic faith that encourages others to practice patience, kindness, and acceptance toward themselves and others. Amen.

In an era in which we're told that we should not pursue perfection but progress, it seems like overkill to risk ninety-nine sheep for just one. I mean, the rest could wander off while the shepherd is searching. Worse still, this passage tells us that the shepherd has left them in the wilderness! What about their care? All over just one sheep—ugh!

As a clergy person with more than twenty-four years of ministry, I have found that the single largest hindrance to evangelism is that current members (i.e., the ninety-nine) are often quite concerned about the amount of time a shepherd should dedicate to locate and carry lost sheep home. We expect that "lost sheep" should be able to find their way to church whenever the church gathers. If the ninety-nine know what to do, one should be able to do so as well.

But Jesus and his audience understood sheep better than we do. Instead of crying out, a lost sheep curls up and lies down. It becomes immobilized by fear. For a lost sheep to get back to the fold, it has to be carried. In a similar way, those new to the faith, those who haven't been to church in a while, and those who have been wounded by the church need to be "carried" back into our congregations, usually with more time and attention from not only the pastor (shepherd) but also from those in the church community (the ninety-nine). Adjustments have to be made for the one that haven't been made for the majority because the needs are different.

Jesus is clear. When our righteousness becomes more important than making room for one more to enter the kin-dom of God, our priorities are not in alignment with God's. Further, we are missing out on joy that this world can't give or take away.

God, make us secure enough to join you in seeking and ministering to those who can't cry out and who need just a bit more. Amen.

One of the themes suggested by *Feasting on the Word: Preaching the Revised Common Lectionary* for this passage is the difference between *saving* and *welcoming*. Specifically, the author suggests that the entire passage is more about welcoming—one might even say "radical welcome."

Just look at the text. Jesus tells the parable because the religious leaders think he's too welcoming of tax collectors and sinners. Not only does Jesus welcome sinners and tax collectors, he eats with them—often. Once the lost sheep and the lost coin are found, both the shepherd and the woman welcome friends and neighbors for a celebration that mimics the celebration in heaven of those whom God is welcoming to God's kin-dom.

Welcome. Save. As the commentator suggests, "Saving is about power, whereas welcoming is about intimacy." Saving says *we did our duty; now God, and perhaps the pastor, can do the rest.* Welcoming says *something was missing from our community before you came; we're glad you're here.*

All the current research says that folks are looking for a place to belong before they are ready to believe. The first church understood this. At Pentecost, people were welcomed into the community, new leaders called, doctrine and polity changed, and things were sold so the faith community could accommodate more.

Many churches no longer do altar calls that focus on saving people's souls. As that practice has waned, are we picking up practices of radical welcome? If we take welcome as seriously as this text does, we'll have to find more concrete ways to call people near, especially those who currently are not of the household of faith. Offering such welcome is truly living as Christ lived.

Welcoming God, embolden and empower us to be as radically welcoming as Jesus was to everyone—especially those who are the so-called least, last, lost, and left-out. Amen.

All-Consuming

SEPTEMBER 15–21, 2025 • MICHELLE STIFFLER

SCRIPTURE OVERVIEW: "Consumed" is a common theme of the human experience. We consume, we are consumed—this is the perpetual cycle. Both Jeremiah and the psalmist are consumed by grief and despair yet cry out to God for redemption. Instruction to Timothy reminds us that prayer can be an all-consuming force in our life. In Luke, Jesus uses a strange parable to warn about the all-consuming powers of seeking financial gain. In all circumstances we can choose to be consumed by God's faithfulness, running to God in prayer and lament, reaching for God as our only lasting goodness. Pain, devastation, and temptation have the power to pull our gaze from God, quickly pulling our hearts from full devotion. But there is always a way back. In complete dependence, we lift our eyes and hands and ask for God's mercy.

QUESTIONS AND SUGGESTIONS FOR REFLECTION

- Read Jeremiah 8:18–9:1. When have you experienced suffering so extreme you wished for more tears?
- Read Psalm 79:1-9. Recount a time when you were desperate for God's deliverance. How did you balance your dual desire for God's gentleness and God's fiery anger?
- Read 1 Timothy 2:1-7. Name several people you know, or knew, who were people of prayer. What markers of peace, godliness, and dignity did they carry that exhibited their commitment to intercession for others?
- Read Luke 16:1-13. In what particular instances has God honored your small faithfulness by blessing you with more responsibilities and opportunities?

Michelle Stiffler is a trauma-informed trainer, somatic coach, and freelancer who writes about faith and movement from her home in the Arizona desert.

There is perhaps no experience as insular and disorienting as grief. It absorbs the whole person, clouding the mind, narrowing the senses so that agony is all one sees, hears, feels, smells, and tastes. Grief drowns the soul's capacity for wonder, hope, and delight, reducing the spiritual relationship to two questions: "Why?" and "God, where are you?" God permits these questions.

This statement is part of the larger message God has been revealing to Jeremiah throughout the previous seven chapters. In today's passage, the answer is plain: The people of Jerusalem abandoned God for idols; now God has abandoned the people. God's case against the people of Jerusalem is their shameless idolatry, and the warning is simple—destruction is coming. But just as we see throughout scripture, God gives warning along- side an offer toward hope. The people can acknowledge their idolatry, throw out their idols, confess their sin, and return to God. Or the people can dismiss God's message, continue in their idolatry, and ultimately reject hope. Jeremiah knows that if the people remain unmoved and unrepentant, they will experience devastation. Their imminent suffering is the source of Jeremiah's inescapable grief.

Repentance brings salvation. That is the message for the people of Jerusalem millennia ago, and it is the message for us today. God invites us into relationship, but it requires full obe- dience. There is no such thing as partial commitment, no neutral worship of anything other than God, no passive turning of the heart and eyes from God. The focus of our gaze will consume us. Will we choose to be consumed by life, or will we allow other attractions to consume us and eventually lead us to destruction?

God, when we turn our hearts away from you, please call us back. Help us listen and follow. Amen.

Throughout nine years of nonprofit work, I've met hundreds of women suffering abuse and trauma. Their heartbreaking stories of generational dysfunction, extreme adversity, and unfathomable injustice have transformed my perspective on privilege and lack, pain and resilience. Encountering these stories expanded my compassion, and for a time, I secretly considered myself quite high in the tiers of compassionate folks. But God called me out one day, making me aware that I loved those in poverty, but I didn't love those with plenty. I didn't see the problem, but God did—half of my role was communicating with the funders of our programs! My insecurities surrounding money and apprehensions toward people with larger amounts of it would restrict my efficacy with donors, potentially leaving our programs unfunded. Interestingly, the Lord's method for increasing my love was forcing me to confront and release my fears.

At the beginning of the book of Jeremiah, God calls Jeremiah to be a prophet. Jeremiah is young and intimidated by this massive calling. God's command is gentle but direct: "Do not be afraid of the people." No matter the individual call on our lives, we must remember that fear is natural. But in matters of faith, it is not helpful. It tamps our capacity for compassion, humility, and empathy—vital characteristics for reflecting God's love and delivering the message of salvation. By today's passage, Jeremiah has surrendered his fear. Free from the burden of unnecessary worry, Jeremiah is free both to love the people and to mourn their fractured relationship with God. This vulnerable display of compassion communicates a merciful truth to the people: You matter. Those transformative words cannot be spoken in fear. They can only be translated in the language of love.

Lord, clear our hearts of fear and give us compassion for all people. May we see each person with your eyes of mercy, lifting them to you in prayer. Amen.

Once again, grief reduces the spiritual relationship to a question: "How long?" In my own despair, I've certainly asked this question, finding it to be both natural and utterly bizarre. How often are we given the exact timeline for our suffering, a guaranteed date and time when normalcy and happiness will be restored? Tolerance of ambiguity is no small thing. It requires the relinquishment of so much we hold tightly—control, reasoning, autonomy, fairness, and maybe even a sense of dignity. Yet we do have a choice: We can come to God with "How long?" and a closed fist; or we can come to God with "How long?" and open hands.

The psalmist writes from the latter position, and our clue is the narrative preceding his question, "How long?" Throughout the first four verses of Psalm 79, the author releases profound pain by verbally processing through the horror and injustice that seems all-encompassing. This is not a rant or act of complaint; it is a posture of honesty and humility. We are generally hesitant to share the deep truths of our situation with one another, especially when those deep truths are difficult because such honest sharing makes us vulnerable. But such openness moves us toward protection and wholeness, whether with other people or with God. Some days, openness is an overflow of praise, but in times of suffering, openness is uninhibited lament. They sound different, but both are necessary and healthy; both are an act of trust and hopeful dependence. Prayer is where we inhale and exhale fully, aware of God's grace in both.

Dear God, it is easy to close ourselves off and shut down, but it is not your desire that we live that way. Help us open ourselves to you with trust and hope. Amen.

Yesterday's reflection examined prayer as release. Today, we observe prayer as request. The psalmist and their exiled people have specific needs: mercy and rescue. In my own places of oppression and powerlessness, I've also pleaded for these things. Maybe you have too. Prayers from "the brink of despair" (NLT) are prayers of boldness, not weakness. To move through life's tragedies with faithfulness, we must reckon with realities that can either fracture or fortify our faith.

First, there are inherited patterns of sin that we did not choose, generational or systemic tendencies that turn us from God. Yes, we can exercise free will and choose the way toward God, but some spiritual struggles are bigger and deeper than our control. The way through is beyond us, and our only resolve is asking God to forgive our collective sin and to help our bodies and minds forget the paths that instinctually lead us away.

Second, witnessing evil brings both sorrow and anger. These appropriate responses can render us inactive, or they can fuel our forward progress, pushing us toward God with purpose and prayer. Prayer is where powerlessness becomes powerful and hopelessness becomes hopeful.

Finally, we must rely on God's presence as urgently as we depend on God's provision. If our encounters with God are largely transactional, we not only miss the gift of relationship but neglect our capacity for resilience. We cannot predict the afflictions to come—safe places destroyed, loved ones lost, innocence trampled, pain endured, injustice heaped on us without relief. In this broken world, emotional and physical needs sometimes go unmet, but our souls can be fully comforted by God's compassion alone.

Lord, in our weakness and hopelessness, give us the strength to pray with boldness, to depend on you without shame, and to trust that your compassion is provision and power. Amen.

My maternal grandparents lived on a lush, green acre in central Ohio. My younger sisters and I spent many a childhood summer there, playing board games from our mom's childhood, eating lunches on the screened porch, creating imaginary worlds in the massive trees on their property. Grandpa and Grandma were a people of routine, and nearly everything that happened in their home was expected, including their morning prayer time at the breakfast table. Their prayers were long. For a child attempting to stay quiet, their prayers were forever long, guided by a forever-long list of people for whom my grandparents diligently prayed daily.

Even as a kid, I knew I was on that list, alongside missionaries, family, the sick or bereaved, and those who did not yet believe. I was less familiar with the routines of my paternal grandparents, but I knew a powerful legacy of prayer was happening in their home too. Their list was also long, with acquaintances from airplanes, beaches, and parks being added to the list weekly.

Prayer was a constant in my home also. During periods of my life when I didn't know how to pray (or if I even wanted to), I recalled those prayers and took comfort knowing my grandparents and parents were interceding on my behalf. Decades later, my parents faithfully continue the family legacy of prayer, and by God's grace, so do I. It's quiet work, a simple practice that lends clarity and truth to my words and actions. I read Paul's words in 1 Timothy 2:1, 3, and I'm grateful: "Pray every way you know how, for everyone you know . . . this is the way our Savior God wants us to live" (MSG).

God, may our prayers be never-ceasing. Amen.

Today's parable is not so different from the parable before it—the story of the prodigal son. Both stories use the same word to describe the main character's wastefulness. Both stories reveal the sin of misusing the resources given to us—notice that the manager is not being fired for lying, cheating, or stealing, but for wasting. And both stories present redemption from a life of squander.

Scripture contains other instructions for management of resources. God gives the Israelites clear guidelines for managing the gift of manna in the wilderness (see Exod. 16). Proverbs 8:33 warns, "Mark a life of discipline and live wisely; don't squander your precious life" (MSG). In Luke 19, the parable of the talents exposes God's disappointment at passively wasting what we have been given by hiding, hoarding, and protecting.

Though a prominent virtue in the Christian faith, we often miss the importance of stewardship. Stewardship means using well what we've been given and ensuring the good gifts given don't go to waste. Everything we have is God's—before it was given and after it is given. Each of us has been generously entrusted with a portion of God's abundance. Our literal breath is the Spirit in us—power on loan to accomplish God's good purposes and express the Divine Mystery as we have experienced it.

There's risk involved in living this way, as it is not the way of the world. Seeing beyond the measures and values of this world requires foresight. Reaching for what is eternal requires discipline. But there is risk in wasteful living as well. When we are wasteful with our portion of resources and when we withhold our skills and abilities, we miss out on experiencing God's kingdom here and now.

God, empower us to use the gifts you've given wisely. Help us to be faithful stewards of your world. Amen.

In Genesis, Adam and Eve were tempted with a deceptive invitation: "Look! This one thing can change your lack, your dependence, and your power. It could change everything!" The enemy is an expert in turning our gaze and knows the truth better than we do—that our hearts will follow our eyes.

Surrounded by the flashy lights of the world, it is easy to become caught up in the temporal, believing our life could be perfect if only we had more . . . fill in the blank. We eventually realize we can't add hours to the day or take age from our bodies. We chase new positions and places, and finally acknowledge "perfect" is an evaporating ideal.

But money appears to solve so many problems, and gathering more of it is often within our control. If we work more, we acquire more. If we have more, we can do more, take more, store it all up. With effort, we could be so much more. Accomplishment whispers our worth, tells us we earned what we have, that it is ours to keep. We forget we are not here forever, that our time on earth is brief. Eventually, our hands will be empty.

Will our souls be empty too? Will we find we wasted a lifetime protecting possessions that fade as quickly as the body? The writer of First Timothy echoes Jesus' message from Luke when telling Timothy, "The love of money is a root of all kinds of evil" (6:10)—a passage we will explore next week. Money is not the problem; the love and worship of money is. Jesus tells us we cannot be beholden to both money and to God. We must choose. The record of our lives can read as an account of obtaining and consuming, feverish striving and tight-fisted fear. Or the story of our days can be the story of trust, faithfulness, and dependence on God.

Lord, the measures and values of this world will never be enough. Calm me from the frenzy of consuming. Teach me to trust you more. Amen.

With God and with One Another

SEPTEMBER 22–28, 2025 • CEDRICK BRIDGEFORTH

SCRIPTURE OVERVIEW: While Jeremiah is in prison, God tells him to buy a field. This transaction shows that in the future, life will return to normal. It is another enactment prophecy, where a prophecy is given through actions instead of just words. The psalmist rejoices in the protection that God provides to the faithful. God is a fortress, a covering, and a shield. Paul admonishes his readers not to fall into materialism. The love of money, not money itself, is the root of all kinds of evil, and those obsessed with it build their hopes on shifting sands. Jesus tells a parable about a rich man who has fallen into that very trap. Only after death, when it is too late, does he realize his mistake.

QUESTIONS AND SUGGESTIONS FOR REFLECTION

* Read Jeremiah 32:1-3a, 6-15. How do you live as if God's promises were already true?
* Read Psalm 91:1-6, 14-16. How do you turn toward God with hope in times of darkness?
* Read 1 Timothy 6:6-19. Whether you have few or many possessions, how do they get in the way of your following Jesus?
* Read Luke 16:19-31. God knows each of us by name. Do you know the names of the persons in your community who have obvious or internal unmet needs?

The Rev. Cedrick Bridgeforth is the resident bishop of the Greater Northwest Episcopal Area (Alaska, Oregon-Idaho, and Pacific Northwest Conferences) of The United Methodist Church. Cedrick enjoys cycling, writing, and doing life with his spouse, Christopher.

Jeremiah's discernment about purchasing property shines a light on the historic denial of property rights to people of color and indigenous people. It also beckons us to admit that the current plight of those living without secure housing is a global crisis. The economic elites and political scavengers hold the riches and access to them. It is a privilege to be in a position, by birth or by economic status, to be able to purchase or own property.

When I purchased my first home in 2008, it was a dream come true. Although I had served my country, completed my education, and excelled in my vocation, the possibility of home ownership seemed impossible. I met a person who told me about a first-time buyers program. I met his offer of information with skepticism. I discounted his words until he gave me a tour of the property he purchased through the same program. Within months of learning of the program, I was moving into my new home. Within weeks of completing my purchase and hosting a housewarming party, the world's economic systems collapsed. The housing market went from a glorious opportunity to a ticket to ruin for many.

The housing bust and economic downturn of 2008 were not the origins of the housing crisis. They shed light on the vulnerability of millions living on the edge, even when they do live in a secure structure. The systems that allow persons to live inside a home are not structured for times when the economy fails entire segments of the population. What we now know is that most people are only one or two decisions away from being unhoused.

God of the housed and the unhoused, may we find shelter in you and safety with one another. Amen.

An early experience I had with my mother's care and concern came when I was four years old. My sister was four years younger than me and I wondered if I could hold her without dropping her. I recognized a moment for me to test that curiosity one afternoon when I heard her crying. My mom was on the porch talking with a neighbor. I went into the room, lifted my sister from the bed, and took her to my mom. As I approached my mom and our neighbor, my mom exclaimed, "You're going to drop that baby!" Her assertion startled me. Why would I drop the baby? I only wanted to know if I was strong enough to lift her. My mother, however, demonstrated her protective nature, a nature that sustained both my sister and me as we grew.

Throughout childhood, adolescence, and adulthood, I have witnessed a consistency in my mom. She has a way of making her presence, her opinion, and her love known without always needing to use words. It is in a tilt of her head when someone says something offensive, a hand on her hip while observing absurd behavior, or a random early morning text message inquiring about my location. All demonstrate a watchful, protective, and corrective presence, based on a welcomed responsibility to love.

The psalmist points to faithfulness and protection that is present in the Most High's shelter. When we know love is present and true, the burden of proving our self-worth is lifted and we become more open to that love. When we are connected to people who take on the responsibility of loving us with utmost seriousness and consistency, we better understand the protection God promises, and we are free to become all God creates and calls us to be.

God of the parented and the orphaned, may we find identity in you and belonging with one another. Amen.

I once toured the Killing Fields near Phnom Phen, Cambodia. As we moved throughout the mass graves that hold the bodies of more than one million people who were killed between 1975 and 1979, there was a juxtaposition of sounds: birds chirping in the trees, roosters crowing in the foreground, and children's glee and laughter breaking through tourists questioning the legitimacy and horror of what they were seeing.

Estimates suggest the Khmer Rouge policies and practices caused the deaths of almost three million people in Cambodia. And it is only one of a multitude of genocides and injustices committed in our world's history, many of which still continue to occur today. Atrocities as large as genocide and as small as voter suppression strip persons of their human dignity and right to life, liberty, and any semblance of happiness.

Assurance of "rescue" and "protection" is a salve for those in distress. "Whenever you cry out to me, I'll answer," (CEB). The psalmist puts definitive and compassionate proclamations in the mouth of God. Those facing death, war, and sickness can rely on a God who will be present with them in their plight and in the plight of all people in all places.

This promise doesn't provide answers to all our questions. Genocides still unjustly and horrifically end the lives of millions. But God promises to be present with those suffering. And hearing God's call for justice throughout scripture empowers those of us with earthly power and privilege to stand up against tyranny and oppression.

What do we say in the face of tyranny, apathy, and privilege that denigrate and annihilate? What do we cry out to God for the sake of humanity and all of creation?

God of the sinners and the sinned against, may we find salvation in you and reconciliation with one another. Amen.

One of my college professors irritated students who held theological, political, or ideological views that differed from his. Because of his studies and lived experience, he took great pride in exposing students to information that was not always included in our textbooks, discussed on the nightly news, or preached about in sermons. One student in my year was determined to set a trap for the professor to create a situation that would lead to his termination or some semblance of censure.

My classmate went to great lengths in every class session to rile the professor by challenging his perspectives and demanding he recant some of his assertions. The professor continued on his rants and shared to his own heart's delight. One day the student came into class ready for an all-out war with the professor. As soon as the professor began his lecture, he was met with a verbal challenge from the student. There were several exchanges between the two of them while the rest of the class sat in awe of the verbal sparring.

The professor finally asked, "What do you want from me?" The student responded, "Tell me I'm right! Just tell me I'm right!" The professor looked directly at her and said, "You're right." The student responded with glee, "I knew it. I knew I was right!" As the professor began to return to his lecture, he mumbled, "It is such a small thing to be right, when what God requires is righteousness."

Our desire to be right can easily supersede our godly desire to be righteous. As we "fight the good fight," we must invite opportunities to "pursue righteousness, godliness, faith, love, endurance, gentleness" in our lives.

God of the faithful and the searching, may we find righteousness in you and mercy with one another. Amen.

There is a difference between being rich and having everything you want. There is also a difference between poverty and living within one's means. The systems and ideologies that differentiate the "haves" from the "have-nots" are at work at all times.

While on a mission immersion experience, I was introduced to the concept of a floating village with homes, stores, schools, churches, temples, and clinics. The sturdiest structures were supported by barrels, while others were more rudimentary and included plastic bottles and used tires. As our tour boat careened through the village, those resting in their hammocks, fishing, or caring for their daily tasks were not phased by our presence. Their focus was on what they were doing. Our gaze was upon their artistry, ingenuity, tenacity, and ability to do life and make a living upon the waters.

The call for disciples to "be rich in good works" is a must for those making life out of others' discarded goods. Those living in the shadows and out of sight rely on others within the same reality to survive. What they do or possess comes from those around them. The author of First Timothy is speaking to those who find themselves in positions of wealth and calls on them to place their trust in God and put their resources to use building up the lives of those around them.

We saw people relegated to the waters because of their station in life, national origin, or access to education and other services. It was not their lack of money or wealth that dictated their living situation. It was the wealth and riches of others in local and distant lands and the desire for more that relegated them to life on the water.

God of the haves and the have-nots, may we find grace in you and compassion with one another. Amen.

My maternal grandparents lived in a small town in Alabama. Everyone knew everyone and everyone knew everyone's business. People were known or identified by their legal names as easily as they were by a nickname based on a physical characteristic or trait that may or may not have been endearing or flattering.

My grandparents spent most of their time on the swing-donned front porch in their small front yard. As individuals and families would pass along the street, my grandparents would say hello and exchange pleasantries. Almost all of those who passed by called my grandparents by name: "Mr. and Mrs. Griffin." Even when one of them was not present in the yard or on the porch, the greeting was the same. It was true in response as well: My grandparents, singularly or in unison, would respond by calling the person's name. If the person was someone with whom they had greater intimacy, they would add more inquiry about an ill family member, scholastic or athletic achievement, a job prospect, or a new baby.

Those who passed by my grandparents' house were seen and included as members of their larger community. I was not aware of who lived in a brick home, a shanty, or a tent in the backyard. The particulars of the home status of those passing by did not determine if they were greeted. It didn't factor into the depth of engagement in the fifteen or twenty seconds of the exchange.

Lazarus had a name. We do not know if the rich man knew Lazarus' name in life; he certainly relied upon the name in the place of his death. Every person has a name and longs to be seen for who they are, not for what can be gained from them.

God of the seen and the unsettled, may we find dignity in you and peace with one another. Amen.

The morning headline read "Widow Donates Millions!" As I read the article and learned of the woman who had donated a large sum of money to a nearby university, it was clear this woman and her deceased husband lived modest lives and never beyond their means.

Later in the day, I had lunch with two colleagues, and the subject of the morning news centered our conversation. One of my lunch mates was in deep anguish as he told of his encounters with this widow. He had officiated the funeral for her husband and had counseled the woman upon her husband's death because they were members of his congregation. He said, "We asked her to participate in our annual stewardship campaign by increasing her giving by one percent over what she gave the prior year. She did what we asked. We asked her to consider donating to our debt relief fund. She agreed to consider it."

He recounted the missed opportunities to ask her to give a larger, specific amount or to give according to her abundance. The university, in contrast, positioned itself to benefit from her generosity by asking her to include the university in her estate planning and to donate at least two million dollars from her existing portfolio. She did what they asked of her without hesitation.

My colleague and the university each had an opportunity to bless someone else with clear and direct solicitation. My colleague based his inquiry on assumptions of scarcity. The university engaged from a position of abundance.

The rich man lived well. He held perspectives of others that did not serve him well. Much like the rich man ignoring Lazarus, my colleague made assumptions about the widow and the perspective he should have had. Both missed opportunities to discover something new or to change their perspective.

God of the bold and the timid, may we find answers in you and commonality with one another. Amen.

Did you know that you can enjoy
The Upper Room Disciplines
in multiple formats—digital or print?

The Upper Room Disciplines is available in both regular and enlarged print, but are you aware that it is also available in digital formats? Read *Disciplines* on your phone, computer, or e-reader. Whatever your preference, we have it for you today.

The Upper Room Disciplines is available in a variety of formats:
- Print (regular-print and enlarged-print versions)
- eBook
- Digital subscriptions (website, email, and app)

For more information, visit Store.UpperRoom.org or call 800.972.0433.

Need to make changes to your account?
Call Customer Service at 800.972.0433 or email us at customerassistance@upperroom.org. Customer service representatives are available to help you with any updates.

God Who Lives in Us

SEPTEMBER 29–OCTOBER 5, 2025 • NADIYKA GERBISH

SCRIPTURE OVERVIEW: Lamentations opens with a description of the plight of the people of Judah, the southern kingdom. The people have been taken into exile as part of God's judgment for their idolatry. The psalmist struggles to sing the songs of the Lord. In fact, those who overthrew Jerusalem have forced them to sing for their amusement, so the joy is gone. The psalmist prays that one day God will repay the invaders. In Second Timothy, Paul praises God for Timothy's faith and for the legacy of faith that comes through his family. He charges him to preach boldly and without hesitation the gospel of Christ. In the Gospel reading, Jesus challenges the disciples to show greater faith and to understand that we are all servants in God's kingdom.

QUESTIONS AND SUGGESTIONS FOR REFLECTION

- Read Lamentations 1:1-6 and 3:19-26. Where do you find hope in the midst of pain and suffering?
- Read Psalm 137. How do you remember your spiritual traditions and sacred places? How do you look for God's work in new and challenging circumstances?
- Read 2 Timothy 1:1-14. What spiritual practices help you to "guard the good treasure entrusted to you"?
- Read Luke 17:5-10. How might a posture of cyclical servanthood to and with all creation transform or increase your faith?

Nadiyka Gerbish is a Ukrainian writer, translator, podcaster, and European rights director for Riggins Rights Management. Nadiyka is a member of Calvary Chapel in Ternopil, Ukraine.

Death, destruction, violence, and suffering are not something constrained to the history books for us to read by the fireplace with a mug of hot chocolate in hand, the wind howling to enhance the aesthetics of our experience. The invasion of Ukraine has brought history to my doorstep. The wars, famines, captivity, and plagues have a place in our present. The pain is real.

I remember walking through towns in the eastern parts of Ukraine, full of festivals and ambitious startups. These towns are there no more. They have been flattened by the enemy, their inhabitants killed or scattered. I remember my numb crying of God's name the day I learned that the war had broken out, as if the whole infinity of confusion and ache could somehow be contained in God's name alone.

I am writing this on a crisply warm day, glorious in its autumn beauty, with the summer aftertaste just melting away, seeping through our fingers. With its misty mornings and burning meteor tails by night, this should be the perfect season for bonfires, family hikes, and those last swims before the water gets too cold. Yet the reality of living in a country at war comes with jarring corrections of reality. Parents check school basements instead of curricula. Children donate their allowances to the army. Anxiety about the coming winter is creeping in.

In Lamentations, Jeremiah articulates the anguish of his people. But right there, in his pain, I also feel his hope flickering. For as Judah goes into exile, her "portable homeland," as Heinrich Heine described the Torah, goes there with her. Her sacred rituals are still observed in the places of her temporary residence, and the everlasting God still listens to her mournful prayers, even while dealing with her sins.

Dear Lord, help us remember that you are with us in every season of our life, every struggle, uncertainty, and sorrow; never forsaking us, even for a moment. Amen.

Certain events described in the Bible were so disruptive to the inherent theology of the Jews that they questioned their whole faith foundation. The Messiah crucified was definitely one of those events. But in Jeremiah's time, what appeared totally beyond God's will was the destruction of the Temple. These events were incomprehensible and required no explanation because none could be provided. And yet these theological crises were the turning points that unsealed the working of God's plan in God's nation and in the world.

When the war in Ukraine began, my friend Paul, a Dutch publisher, asked what he could send, not just to the humanitarian stocks we keep filled for any war-afflicted person who needs help but to me, personally. I told him that a small, old pre-World War II candlestick from a flea market of his country would cheer me up: It would remind me the wars were finite. Paul sent me two. The candlesticks stand in my home office, topped with handmade beeswax candles. They became quite handy during blackouts when the Ukrainian critical infrastructure was methodically shelled by the enemy to bring not just destruction but discouragement and exhaustion. The candlesticks are beautiful and bring me good cheer indeed.

But in addition to knowing that wars are finite, as my candlesticks remind me, I now know something else. Even if the wars are finite and the evil is defeatable, still there is pain that will stay with us as long as we live. To hope, to wait quietly upon the Lord, our emotions and natural response would never suffice. There must be something else: a will, a decision to trust—something also known as a leap of faith.

Dear Lord, help us remember that you have great love toward us and your compassions never fail. Help us put our hope in you, in good times and times of trouble. May we wait quietly for your salvation and know we are safe in your hands. Amen.

I so love the passion in Paul's letters: the honesty, the vulnerability, the anger at times, the longing. I am always intensely moved by reading the lines in which one seasoned man is writing to another—younger but already well-experienced—about his tears. Paul envisions how satisfied he will be to see Timothy in person again, but also how delighted he will be to observe the fruit of the Spirit in him, shaped and ripened by the turbulent times Timothy has experienced on his own while his older friend and mentor was away. Until then, Paul encourages him to keep going.

This "keep going" thing is often something that challenges us the most. There are seasons when the unavoidable continuity of our daily journey seems almost unbearable, mostly in times of trouble—but not only then. Even at our happiest, we tend to recognize the passage of days, the tectonic shifts occurring all the time, even when quiet and invisible. We know that life is never a curated scene with lines, characters, and transitions carefully picked (and then edited, double-checked, and proofed) by us, the playwrights; it's a complicated combination of dreadfully real people and situations consistently changing. So, even at our most content, we are so afraid to lose what we have in the present moment that sometimes we lose that precious moment itself. The "keep going" becomes challenging because fear immobilizes us. And so do pain, weariness, and disappointment. More often than not, this stubborn "keep going" mode has to be switched on by our decision—the decision to let the Spirit equip us with God's power, love, and self-discipline, no matter how the current landscape of it all looks to us.

Dear God, thank you for caring for us, for noticing our tears and fears, and for filling us with your peace. As your Holy Spirit urges us to keep going, help us always to trust you and your love for us. Amen.

Writing to Timothy, Paul mentions the two-fold essence of ministry, reminding him of the gift he received and the responsibility accompanying it. Timothy is to develop a spark into a flame, becoming God's partner in the co-creation process.

It always amazed me that the divine approach to creation is invariably rooted in love. There was already a perfect communion in the Trinity, and definitely no need for God to create a human. It was the overflow of the ever-existing love that resulted in the creation of a person. And to this kind of love, Paul encourages Timothy to aspire.

Later in the epistle, Paul also forewarns Timothy about spiritual and moral decline among Christians who love themselves rather than God (see 3:1-5). Augustine describes such depravity as being turned in on the self; the people's tendency to act with reference only to themselves, pursuing selfish desires, somehow ignoring the quiet inner yearning to belong and care for others.

This inerasable desire to be a part of a community certainly bears the divine imprint of the ultimate blessing of communion. The grace of God is on the opposite side of selfishness, detachment, and isolation. It uplifts us to the openness and readiness to embrace the other—and with this, to be embraced back.

Love aimed outward means an irrepressible drive toward God, the universe, and one's neighbor that liberates us from spiritual blindness and transforms us from individuals into a community. It's also the kind of love that focuses on the divine but is yet bound in the body. This love nudges us to get up and move, to answer the longing, and to accept the calling of the sacred spark inside us.

Dear Lord, please help us to rekindle the love you placed in our hearts, ministering to others and accepting their ministry to us so we can grow into a community of people who honor you. Amen.

As I write, the critical power infrastructure of my country has just endured the first enemy shelling of the fall season. The winter is coming, and the war of attrition is grinding on. Even though millions of our people have become refugees overseas, there are still many others coming from the burned eastern towns and settling in remote villages in the west where it is believed to be safer, at least for now. Yesterday, on my way to visit a displaced family, I drove a narrow gravel road among vast fields, occasionally passing a lone tractor or a postal service pickup. The trip felt rewarding, for I knew I was acting in the name of the caring Savior.

This kind of ministry might not look efficient. It's not like having several thousand people listen to you speak of Christ's love in a comfortable hall. With modern Christian communities often having their eyes set on visible success, such humble deeds of divine love ultimately simplified might not be a priority. But these are the acts of those who follow Christ—the constant, steady workings of those who suffer for the gospel.

Psalm 137 captures the conflict Israel's exiles experienced. How could they be expected to go on, day in and day out, in the face of such despair and loss? The decision to move forward during a time of crisis is fraught with fear: Does moving on mean we forget the atrocities we have experienced? Does it mean we let go of the good days that are past?

Yet as the psalm concludes, it is the memory that empowers us to move forward. In the midst of the Babylonian exile, life for the Jewish people went on. Even in their grief, they placed their hope in God and took the next step.

Dear Lord, help us always be the eager workers in your field, moving forward in our continued work for the kingdom. Amen.

Our faith is not a miracle-providing force. Our faith is a declaration of our dependence on God. God requires our faith not for the sake of some supernatural performance but to make us able to care for the souls that God loves and is willing to save.

There is nothing grand in uprooting a tree and planting it in the sea. Actually, mere science, enacted by the faith in the majesty of God's creation, is performing miracles at an ever-increasing speed. Genuine greatness starts at a kneeling position and one's readiness to wash others' feet. This attitude of heart requires a different kind of faith, faith in the ultimate love of God and the divine dignity of every person.

Simone Weil, a 20th-century French philosopher, political activist, and mystic, elaborated on the story of Jesus telling his followers, "I was naked, and you clothed me" (see Matt. 25:31-46) in her book *Gravity and Grace*. She observed that the people who cared for the poor were "in a state which made it impossible for them not to feed the hungry and to clothe the naked; they did not in any way do it for Christ, they could not help doing it because the compassion of Christ was in them." They were not helping their neighbor for Jesus but helping Jesus himself. The joy of serving the Lord doesn't come from having our deeds recognized. It overflows when we're simply doing what we are called to do and doing it with, through, and because of the Lord.

There is no remedy for the world's future at our hands. It is only through our faith in God that lives in us and flows through us that God will work in the world. We are responsible for living our best, making weighed decisions, caring for others without ceasing, loving others the way God loves us, and exercising joy inside the ultimate unsafe world of today.

Jesus, we want to be your faithful ambassadors on this earth. Live in us, dear Lord, and love through us. Amen.

The other day, I found aphids on our dracaena. As I was washing its leaves and sprinkling them with some special chemical solution, I thought about how some species, some crops—and some people too, like the disciples—require special treatment. They desperately ask Jesus to give them more faith. Jesus tells them it is not more faith that they need; they instead need to act on the faith that they already have. Like deep roots unseen underground, the support they need to follow is already there. They just need to turn their attention to growing.

Some seeds take more time and care than others to grow. Likewise, in our spiritual life, there are many invisible, unrecognized efforts that lead to the most deep-rooted results. The footnote characters often change the whole direction of a plot. The small, everyday acts of kindness change the world in a more profound way than the well-articulated and famed shifts in governmental policies. The truth of the gospel is enacted in the most humble, unpretentious ways. It depends on the daily individual decision of every single person in the community of believers.

The parable of the servant that Jesus tells following this admonition reinforces the demands of faith Jesus has just explained. More faith is not their problem: Responding to God's work in their lives is what Jesus is calling them to. And they should not expect reward for their efforts, as it is simply what is expected.

There is a simplicity and clearness to the narrow path that defines the life of the one who follows Jesus. There, the echoing sounds of the road left behind eventually get lost in the wind. Instead come the peace and joy of doing little and leaving God room to do much more.

Dear Jesus, may we follow you on the path you prepared for us, never losing the peace that comes from trusting your holy will. Amen.

A Practice for Spiritual Growth

OCTOBER 6–12, 2025 • MARK W. WETHINGTON

SCRIPTURE OVERVIEW: The scriptures this week can be set within the context of the Examen of Ignatius of Loyola, a daily practice that invites us to review our day in light of God's presence, mercy, and empowerment. In the passage from Luke, some men with a skin disease request that Jesus help them, but after all ten of them are healed only one returns to give gratitude to Jesus. The psalmist reviews some of the history of the Hebrew people and recollects times of fire and water. The letter to Timothy reminds the church of the importance of repentance and the approval (forgiveness) of God. The prophet Jeremiah speaks to the Hebrew people while in exile in Babylon and encourages them to cooperate with God in living into a new day in God's plan of salvation.

QUESTIONS AND SUGGESTIONS FOR REFLECTION

- Read Jeremiah 29:1, 4-7. When was the last time you looked upon tomorrow as a new day filled with new possibilities?
- Read Psalm 66:1-12. When have you taken the time to think back upon the last 24 hours and recognized sins in your life, or when you failed to notice God?
- Read 2 Timothy 2:8-15. Have there been times when, in the midst of a hardship or after a time of falling into sin, you have felt "approved" by God?
- Read Luke 17:11-19. Are there times when you have received a gift from God but failed to give God thanks?

The Rev. Dr. Mark W. Wethington served as a United Methodist pastor in North Carolina for 29 years, taught at Duke Divinity School, and served for 15 years as president of the Wesley Heritage Foundation. The Foundation produced *Obras de Wesley*, the translation of John Wesley's works into Spanish. He and his wife, Beth, share six children, four grandchildren, and a black lab.

Psalm 66 opens with exuberant praise to God. This hymn stands as one of many in the tradition of putting words to the thoughts and emotions of the author's relationship to praise of God. Many children of God have lived lives of holy example and passed on their faith experiences and wisdom through writings. Some of these persons are known only to us personally, while others have been well known by many through the ages. One of the latter is Ignatius of Loyola, a cherished saint of the church.

Ignatius was a Spanish Catholic priest who was one of the founders of the Order of the Jesuits. Born in 1491, he served in the military and was critically injured. During a long period of recovery, he read books about the saints of the early church. In response, he committed his life to being a faithful follower of Jesus Christ.

Growing in faith, he began to pen what became known as *The Spiritual Exercises*, now a time-tested means of growing in relationship with Christ. These exercises, divided into four "weeks," have had a radical impact upon the church and upon the lives of those who have entered into it.

As part of *The Spiritual Exercises*, Ignatius offered the Examen, a spiritual discipline of five parts which he encouraged Christians to practice once a day. The Examen has been passed on through the generations and is used regularly by Christians around the world. The Examen has made a tremendous impact on my life. This week's meditations will lead you through the five movements of the Examen.

Take Lord, and receive all my liberty, my memory, my understanding, and my entire will . . . Thou hast given all to me. To Thee, O Lord, I return it. Amen. *

*Prayers this week are from St. Ignatius and the Ignatian tradition, found at https://www.ignatianspirituality.com.

In today's reading from Luke 17, when the men who suffer from a skin disease recognize who is walking near them, they cry out, "Jesus, Master, have mercy on us!" In other words, they *request* that Jesus stop and come to where they are, for they desire his healing presence and power. Jesus accepts the request of these men to come to them, and he heals all ten of them.

The practice of the Examen as outlined by St. Ignatius of Loyola is made up of five sections or movements that encourage one to look back over a past period of time, generally one day. Mark Thibodeaux, a contemporary spiritual director who guides persons through the spiritual exercises of Ignatius and the practice of the Examen, offers an "R" pattern for moving through the Examen: request, relish, review, repent, and resolve. The story of the ten men calling out to Christ provides an example of the first movement—request.

Our requests to God are heard, but we must ask. In fact, God wants to hear our requests (see Matt. 7:7). The first movement of the Examen is to request God's presence during a time of self-examination. Welcome God and recognize that God is present with you to guide and inspire your time.

Today, practice requesting God to come be with you. Ignatius emphasizes that we should welcome God's presence as we would the presence of a friend. Take about three minutes at the close of this devotion to either close your eyes or look out on the world and ask God to come into your presence in a way in which you can recognize and rejoice in that presence. Remain in God's presence for as long as you like.

Come, Lord Jesus, come and dwell deeply within and around me. You are a dear friend with whom I seek to be in conversation. Amen.

*R*elish is the word which helps us to remember the second movement in the Ignatian Examen. To relish something is to be exceptionally grateful for it. After requesting God's presence, we offer gratitude (relish) for experiences of the past day for which we are exceptionally grateful, perhaps something for which we have not taken time to be grateful.

Today's scripture shares the rest of the experience Jesus had with ten men who cried out for his mercy in light of their suffering. Jesus went to them, responding to their request, and out of mercy and love he healed them. The men went away, but one of the ten returned to give thanks to Jesus. Only one of the ten expressed relish for what Jesus had done for him.

So often things happen in our lives for which we should be grateful. As we encounter times of struggle and wilderness, we also encounter times when we are fully aware that God's grace has been active. But we fail to express our gratitude for the gift of God's love and mercy. Sometimes these gifts of God are given through the lives of others, through an experience in God's creation, or directly from God.

Today, take a few minutes to request and welcome God's presence, then reflect on the last 24 hours of your life. Are there events, people, or an aspect of nature which especially graced your life? Take a moment to dwell on these things and relish them in a way that acknowledges the deep gratitude within you.

The man who came back to relish what Jesus had done for him was a Samaritan. We never know from where our blessings come. The Examen encourages us to take time to look back and notice how God has been active in our life. If we move forward too fast we are likely to miss where God has been present.

What am I especially grateful for in the past day? When did I feel joy? When did I feel troubled? Where have I noticed God's presence?

THURSDAY, OCTOBER 9 ～ *Read Psalm 66:5-12*

The psalmist reviews a long history of both goodness and failure in the life of the chosen children of God. There is wondrous gratitude expressed (relished) because of the covenant love which God has shown to his children. The psalmist recalls how God saved the Hebrew people from their suffering in slavery; guided them out of Egypt, enabling them to pass through the waters by "turning the sea into dry land"; defeated their enemies; tested them as "silver is tried," abiding with them through "fire and water"; and finally brought them "to a spacious place," the Promised Land. This kind of recollection (review) is very important in our lives of faith.

The Sankofa bird is a symbol which originates out of Ghana. The bird has its head turned backward, remembering where it came from, but in its beak it is holding an egg. The Sankofa bird reviews its past while holding hope for the future. The review movement of the Examen encourages the same.

The "review" movement of the Examen encourages prayerful looking back at the past day. What did I do? Where did I go? Whom did I encounter? In what ways was I blessed? Did I do something which hurt someone? Did I think thoughts which were harmful to me or others? Did I sin, and in what way? Was it by word or by action, or by something I neglected to say or do? Where was God present in the past hours? Where was God present and I missed that presence, and only now am realizing that God was there?

Take several minutes first to request God's presence, to relish the grace you have received, and then to review your actions throughout the past day. When or how did you experience fire or water?

God, as I review my day, give me the light to know you and to know myself as you see me. Amen.

A Practice for Spiritual Growth   337

Repentance is the fourth movement in the Examen of Ignatius. Having spent time reviewing the past day, there will certainly be things which transpired for which we feel remorse and for which we need to repent. It is often appropriate, and an important part of our spiritual life, to experience regret for something sinful which we have done or said. Feeling and expressing sorrow to God and asking for forgiveness is the right response to one's review of the past day.

If there is a sin which is grave, we can also pray about seeking forgiveness from the person that we have offended. The Society of Jesus often spoke about being a contemplative in action. This means that our Examen should not only be an act of the mind and heart but should also evolve into actions which are transformative.

In today's reading from Second Timothy, the writer appeals to his audience to "die with Christ." We die to Christ when we "die" to those sins, both words and actions, which keep us from giving testimony to the living and loving Christ in our lives. When we die to those things which harm and deny the Christ within us, then we are raised to new life in Christ. Through repentance we present ourselves to God as one approved by God, for we have received God's forgiveness.

Today, take time to move through the first three movements of the Examen, then center on one thing during the past hours which you either did or said to someone which was offensive or sinful. Ask God for forgiveness of this and explore some way in which you can seek amends from the one whom you offended or sinned against.

Soul of Christ, sanctify me. Body of Christ, save me. Blood of Christ, inebriate me. Water from the side of Christ, wash me. Amen.

The prophet Jeremiah is a perfect example of how to resolve in one's heart and mind that tomorrow will be different, that it will be a new day. At the time of Jeremiah's ministry, the people of God are in exile in Babylon. Jeremiah shares with them God's word, namely, that they should "build houses and lie in them; plant gardens and eat what they produce. Take wives and have sons and daughters . . . multiply there, and do not decrease." In other words, do not give up! God is preparing for you a new day! In the beginning days of his prophecy in Judah, Jeremiah weeped over the disobedience of God's children. In time, Jeremiah's weeping changed to words of comfort and promise.

The fifth and final movement of the Ignatian Examen is to resolve: Resolve that tomorrow will be different because God has worked in your life to foster your gratitude, to encourage you to examine your life, to repent of any sins, and to offer forgiveness. Because of this you can resolve that God is creating a new day for you. The final movement of the Examen is one of undeniable hope in a new day as you resolve not to repeat sins of the past but to welcome God's transforming Spirit such that you can live more faithfully as a follower of Jesus Christ.

The Examen is a daily spiritual discipline which, when practiced faithfully, provides a way of growing in relationship with Christ. At the close of today's devotional, take time to consider how you will resolve to be different tomorrow, different in a way that you do not repeat the sins of the past day. Resolve to live a life more faithful to the way of Christ.

May it please the supreme and divine Goodness to give us all abundant grace ever to know his most holy will and perfectly to fulfill it. Amen.

The hymn by Brian Wren entitled "This Is the Day of New Beginnings" reminds us that each new day is an opportunity to hope for the future God makes available to us and to put aside the struggles and sins of yesterday. We *request* God's presence with us during the Examen; we *relish* the past day of life and give gratitude for the blessings received; we take time to *review* the past day and recall its blessings but also recall any thoughts, words, or actions which were sinful; we *repent* of any of these things from the past day, seeking God's forgiving grace; and we *resolve* that, by the grace of God, we will live more faithfully tomorrow.

Since Ignatius introduced this spiritual practice in the 16th century, Christians through the ages have been practicing this discipline daily, discovering it to be an efficacious way of growing in relationship with Christ. Through the Examen we can better see God's presence and work in our lives each day. When we become aware of God's presence, we have clear and specific reason to "make a joyful noise to God" and to "sing glory to his name" as the psalmist calls us to do. We are better equipped to name the awesome deeds of God.

At the close of today's devotional, take fifteen minutes to practice the Examen in its entirety. Perhaps the Examen will become an essential part of your life every day, drawing you closer to the living Christ, who desires to be closer to you than any friend could ever be.

More than ever, I find myself in the hands of God. Christ began the relationship with me, and Christ invites me to be his lasting friend. It is a profoundly deep experience to feel myself so totally in the hands of the living Christ. Amen.

Thankfulness in All Things

OCTOBER 13–19, 2025 • SHONDA NICOLE GLADDEN

SCRIPTURE OVERVIEW: We start this week by reading several of the scripture passages associated with the Canadian day of Thanksgiving. Then we turn to the lectionary readings for the nineteenth Sunday after Pentecost. At last Jeremiah is able to bring a message of restoration and hope. God promises a new covenant with the people, and they will internalize the law in their hearts so that they will keep it. The psalmist rejoices in such a reality—meditating on God's law allows faithful walking in God's paths. The reading from Second Timothy confirms the ongoing power of God's law in scripture, which is given by God for our good. Luke hits on a different theme through the parable of a persistent widow, reminding us to be similarly tenacious with our prayers to God.

QUESTIONS AND SUGGESTIONS FOR REFLECTION

- Read Jeremiah 31:27-34. How have you broken your covenant with God? How has God responded?
- Read Psalm 119:97-104. The Jewish laws of the Hebrew scriptures are part of our Christian heritage. How can you delight in the law?
- Read 2 Timothy 3:14–4:5. How can you learn or teach from scriptures you do not normally read?
- Read Luke 18:1-8. Through the familiar call to pray always, the author reminds us that we are called to pray for what God wants. What is at stake when you pray for justice and mercy?

The Rev. Dr. Shonda Nicole Gladden is a faith and justice professional working tri-vocationally at Indiana University Indianapolis, Broadway United Methodist Church, and as the CEO of her own social enterprise, Good to the SOUL, LLC. Shonda is an ordained elder in the African Methodist Episcopal Church. She is the mother of a Generation Z high school scholar and a proud member of Alpha Kappa Alpha Sorority, Inc.

Thanksgiving Day (Canada)

I've generally never been one for tolerating a lot of noise. While my son seems to find refuge in playing his guitar and singing boisterously at any given moment, I generally prefer the sound of silence, the tranquility of a rustling breeze at sunrise, or even the sound of light rainfall on a calm spring afternoon. Accordingly, the scriptural admonition in Psalm 100, and quite a few other places throughout the Christian canon, for "all the earth" to "make a joyful noise" has always sounded rather dreadful to me. Must we really be noisy for God?

Yet as a daughter of charismatic, historic Black Church upbringing, I fondly recall the ways noisy worship has accompanied moments of necessary spiritual breakthrough for me and many others. I recall the sounds of the Hammond organ, evoking an ecstasy of praise and dancing with jubilant shouts. This was the soundtrack of liberation, freedom, and overwhelming joy. As I reflect on these memories, I recall God's faithfulness and the power of the sounds of music not only to be a source of excitement but also to serve as a vehicle of overpowering the noise of the world.

We live in a noisy world that can be anything but joyful. News stories of wars and despair abound. They can discourage us if they are all we are hearing. When we make a joyful noise to the Lord, even if only for a moment, we offer a counter sound to the cacophony of worldly chatter that says, "I am choosing resistance to being like the world." "I am courageously voicing something different so that my spirit may not be downtrodden." When we make a joyful noise to the Lord, we begin to see ways forward that give rise to thanksgiving in all things.

God of silence, noise, and the sounds in between, cultivate in me a deep appreciation for the vast ways you desire to be known, and help me to revel in the beauty of joyful noise. Amen.

Have you ever tried to put together a piece of furniture that comes in many precut pieces with tiny bags of hardware and an instruction guide full of graphics with minimal assembly guidelines? When you're in the store, it's easy to envision the piece assembled well and adorning some part of your home. Yet once you are face to face with the unassembled pieces, the process of realizing that completed project seems daunting. Like assembling furniture from precut pieces, sometimes the simplest activities become inordinately complex when we have preconceived notions of how things should go.

In the Gospel lesson for today's reflection, a crowd has followed Jesus to the other side of the sea in search of some answers. They want to know, "What must [they] do to perform the works of God?" Heretofore, religious systems have given followers instructions for how to reach the pinnacle of the faith. This crowd seems to want nothing more than to use their faith to perform accordingly. In a culture of doers, it's counter-cultural to be a believer. Yet this is the lesson Jesus shares: Believing in Jesus is the work of God. There is no complex set of instructions or special tools required. Belief is enough.

Of course, we sometimes prefer lists and boxes to check to prove that we are aligning ourselves with God's expectations. It's easier to know we are going in the right direction if we have a clear-cut pathway to what we should do. Sometimes though, God doesn't give us that. Belief is enough. When it feels too difficult to get to belief, we can pray to God that our faith will be rekindled. After all, this is the work of God.

Holy One, thank you for your presence in my life. Help me remember that there are things I cannot control. Help me to rest in the realities that you are God, and I am not, and that there are works that you are performing on my behalf even now. Amen.

Recently I was in my university office when a student frantically came in asking if I had a moment to listen. It is not out of the ordinary for students to drop in for counsel. I generally have snacks and a box of tissues ready for such occasions. This interaction caught me a little off guard because this student's generally calm disposition seemed frazzled. Their face was flush, their hair a little disheveled, and their voice expressed that something was amiss. In that moment, I did not know what to expect; I was simply grateful that I was a trusted confidante.

There are times in our lives when anxiety and uncertainty are unavoidable. We may receive unsettling news at the doctor's office, a spouse may decide the marriage is not what they expected, our children may choose paths of which we don't approve. Life is filled with legitimate reasons to be anxious. I do not believe this Philippians passage is giving readers a stern mandate to avoid anxiety, but rather a prescription for how to recover when anxiety arises. Perhaps we can understand Paul to be saying "We *do not have* to be anxious about anything."

I am reminded of the lyrics of the beloved hymn by Joseph M. Scriven, "What a Friend We Have in Jesus" (UMH #526): "O what peace we often forfeit, O what needless pain we bear, all because we do not carry everything to God in prayer." We are connected to a God whose compassion for us has no bounds. We will still face anxieties and stress, but we need not face them alone.

Creator God, loving Savior, create in me a spirit that casts all my cares upon you. When doubts or anxieties overwhelm me, help me return to a space of calm and rest in your peace— whether I understand things or not. Amen.

I have a friend who has sojourned with alcoholism for roughly sixty years; thirty of those years my friend has celebrated being sober. This sense of sobriety has consumed our global consciousness for more than a century, so much so that many of the modern dictionaries focus on the definition of sober as being "not intoxicated" or "abstaining from the consumption of alcoholic beverages." The myopic view carried from the Prohibition era very likely resonates for many because each of us knows someone, or knows of someone, perhaps we even are someone, who has struggled with addiction in one form or another. The Second Timothy passage could rightly encourage us to "endure suffering" as a means of getting us to sobriety in this sense. If this helps you, we give God thanks.

Yet it's the second definition of *sober* in the Oxford Language Dictionary that has captivated me in relation to this text. This second definition defines sober as "serious, sensible, or solemn." After reflecting on the many ways ministry for young Timothy would be challenging, filled with people uninterested in hearing the message of the gospel and forgoing "sound teaching," Paul encourages a young Timothy to be sober in everything.

We live in an era where divisiveness exists even among believers. Political machinations have compelled people to see one another as enemies, and issues of grave concern have split denominations, families, and friend groups. Now is certainly a good time to lean into sensibilities like compassion, generosity, and understanding. May we be intentional in seeing the humanity in those who have a different opinion. May solemnity and seriousness guide us toward the greatest good.

> *God of the addict, the lost, and the confused, be present with us today wherever we are. When sobriety evades us—whether in disposition or reliance on things other than you—bring us back to a place of solace. Amen.*

On a cold winter day, I awakened to a house that was as cold inside as it was outside. When I went to check the thermostat, it did not register any temperature. I didn't hear the blowing of our furnace fan. I deduced that the thermostat battery needed to be replaced. Not a difficult fix—but because I only checked the battery when I needed it to be working, I was temporarily subject to some uncomfortably frigid temperatures.

Do you have a favorite wardrobe accessory that has been a staple in your closet for years? Maybe you have a favorite tool in your toolbox that you rely on when it comes time to go to work on an important project. Or maybe you have a tried-and-true friend who has seen you through tough times through the years. From clothes to tools and even friends, life is better when we know we can rely on them to be there when we need them.

More than material goods or even earthly friends, we have a God who has been faithful through the ages. But if we check in with God only when we need something—perhaps like the battery in my thermostat—we experience times of needless discomfort.

The prophecy of Jeremiah declares that God will make a new covenant, one written on our hearts and not just on a piece of paper or a tablet. This new covenant is one that the people of God will live and breathe, day in and day out. It binds God's people with God in a way that means we never cease to be in contact with God, to be aware of living within God's love. We will not need to "check in" with God because we will be walking with God each moment. God's faithfulness will be experienced by each person continually and forever.

Dear God, may I be attentive to you and your presence in all things. Write your law and your love on my heart. Amen.

SATURDAY, OCTOBER 18 ～ *Read Psalm 119:97-104*

My dear friend and their spouse tend to a colony of bees on their Indiana farmland and annually they harvest honey from their bees. While they sell many jars of honey in various markets across the state, my friend almost always has a special jar of honey for me when we see one another after the first harvest. The honey has the sweetest, most delectable taste, and I am always sad when the bottle is emptied. I don't know what makes my friend's honey so wonderful, but I cannot imagine anything sweeter.

In today's scripture reading, the psalmist declares that the words of God are "sweeter than honey to my mouth!" I cannot even fathom such a thing. What would it be like to encounter the scriptures as something that not only edifies the spirit but also satiates a natural desire for sweetness?

Of course, this is lyrical hyperbole since we cannot actually taste the words of scripture—not in a physical sense. But what a beautiful image to reflect on today. May your time of reflection awaken in you new passions, and may you be energized with pleasant sensory experiences. In a world that is bitter, it's good to experience sweetness. Consider this as you pray for yourself and those around the world.

Loving and faithful God, allow me to taste the sweetness of your presence as I walk throughout this day. May I not be overcome with bitterness, and may I taste and see how your goodness can help me be thankful in all things. Amen.

Parables always present us with interesting opportunities to find spiritual sustenance in historical and sometimes archaic renderings of stories. Sometimes there seems to be little logical resolution to the story. At other times, the message is only made plain with Jesus' explanation. And even then, the cultural distance between the textual context and our own makes it hard for us to truly glean what is being said. The Gospel lesson with which we close out this week of thankfulness is no different. In the text, we encounter a story of a persistent widow who pursues a judge, begging to have her accuser brought to justice. It would seem that the widow's plight was without hope. Yet she persisted.

Can you imagine how people who knew that she was begging looked upon her situation? I wonder if her friends tried to convince her that she was pursuing a lost cause. The judge seems not to believe she deserves justice. But to avoid her "wearing him out," he grants her what she has desired all along. Oh, that justice would be awarded that simply—that carceral states were things of the past and abolitionist sanctuaries would be found globally, where people would not have to be shamed for pursuing what is rightfully theirs. As believers, we ought to be the kind of faithful people that will be found at the eschatological end of all things.

May we advocate for those who are in need of justice. May we withhold judgment from those who seem to be fighting lost causes. And should we be in positions of power to grant people grace, may we recall this parable and dispense that grace in abundance.

Holy God, you know my rising and my falling. You are a God of vengeance and justice as well as a God of mercy and grace. Help me discern how to reflect your character in everything I do this day. Amen.

Experiencing God's Accompaniment

OCTOBER 20–26, 2025 • CRISTIAN DE LA ROSA

SCRIPTURE OVERVIEW: God's redemption and accompaniment of people are the common themes in the texts from the Hebrew scripture. People can rejoice and give thanks to God for the gifts that nurture life. There is a clear presence of God walking with the people. Expressions of hope, satisfaction, and praise communicate the presence and experience of God as the one that will bridge the human and the divine. The readings from the New Testament have a very different emphasis. God continues to accompany the people but is now the one who holds the people accountable for faith practices, ways of life, and faithfulness.

QUESTIONS AND SUGGESTIONS FOR REFLECTION

- Read Joel 2:23-32. How do you experience the presence of God in your life? How have natural events been a sign to you of God's presence?
- Read Psalm 65. What does it mean to be accompanied by God today? How do you find joy and happiness in your closeness to God?
- Read 2 Timothy 4:6-8, 16-18. When has God strengthened you in the face of evil?
- Read Luke 18:9-14. What aspect of your life do you need to approach with renewed humility?

The Rev. Dr. Cristian de la Rosa is originally from Mexico, now serving as Dean of Students and on the faculty for contextual theology and practice at Boston University School of Theology. Cristian is an ordained elder in the New England Annual Conference of The United Methodist Church.

Experiencing the presence of God during good times is a celebration, a *fiesta*. When we have and enjoy more than we need, particularly after difficult times, it is easier to sense the accompaniment of God. Prosperous times make it possible to identify and create spaces where we can give thanks and praise God for being faithful. It is clear that the overflowing of resources and the promise for a better future bring hope and a desire to praise God, give thanks, and celebrate.

In this text there is a promise of restoration from the difficult times that may have been similar to the global COVID-19 pandemic we recently experienced. The promise of Joel is that the suffering, struggles, and devastation of life will be no more. Instead, there is the assurance of food security and God's promise that all that was lost will be restored until we are satisfied.

An interesting promise within this prophecy is that the "people shall never again be put to shame." In some cultures, there is no return from being shamed as an individual or as a family. Being shamed has moral and ethical implications that impact individuals as well as the community—in this case, the whole family of God. The shame experienced may relate to dehumanizing practices and devaluing the image of the Creator in each person. We not only give thanks and celebrate the accompaniment of God as our life is saved through food security but also as our dignity is restored and we are freed from processes of dehumanization.

God, accompany me in my everyday experiences. May I be able to feel your presence as I gain new insight into the need for restoration and dignity. Amen.

Joel communicates the promise that God makes for a new multi-generational and inclusive family of faith. Sons, daughters, the elderly, the youth, and those who have been enslaved will be filled with the Spirit of God. Everyone is called, challenged, and equipped with gifts to build across differences in a word where restoration and salvation are urgently needed.

An inclusive vision of a new reality is made clear in the promise of the pouring of the Spirit on all humanity. People will not only listen to the prophets but will prophesy themselves. People will not only talk about possibilities but will have dreams of something new. Young people will not only survive in a world of violence but will cast visions of new life. Those who are not considered part of the community will become part of a new inclusive family of God.

The systems and structures of oppression in our world become more complicated with each passing day. And each new headline shines a light on the ways power imbalances in our society produce violence. Armed conflicts and economic systems take life and create a wider gap between those who have much more than they need and those who don't have enough to survive. However, it is in this complexity that the accompaniment of God urges us to find hope and participate in the work of restoration and salvation. God's accompaniment is turned into the pouring out of the Spirit on all flesh. This Spirit can indeed empower and facilitate transformation, bringing about a new way for humans to relate to one another as brothers and sisters, sons and daughters, old and young, oppressed and free.

Creative God, help me see the possibilities of building the family you call us to be in these complex times. Provide the wisdom to discern my calling and sense your accompaniment in my struggle for life. Amen.

This psalm extols the beauty of creation and praises the One who creates us, delivers us from our destructive practices, and invites us into a new relationship with the rest of creation. Humanity as well as all of creation gives thanks and sings about the intricate designs of life found in the seas, the mountains, the wilderness, the meadows, and the valleys.

Our perspective on the beauty of creation affects our relationship with God. Places like Machu Picchu and the Sacred Valley in Peru are evidence of divine power and inspire human wonder. Such places are regarded by indigenous people from the Andes as places where the divine dwells. To these indigenous peoples, the earth is known as *Pachamama* and is considered a type of divinity, a mother that provides, nurtures, and houses us as children of the Divine. In our Christian faith, we extol God as creator and protector, and psalms like this one praise the God who is in control of the created earth. But in practice we easily forget that it is truly God who holds the authority.

We also forget our call within God's authority to be caretakers of creation. We overlook the fact that our existence depends on the well-being of our planet. We exploit the seas, tear down the mountains, hunt in the wilderness, turn meadows into fields for agriculture, and turn valleys into industrial towns and cities. Through these destructive practices, we upset the balance of creation and disrupt intricate living designs that protect us, renew the planet, and provide for our existence. Only when we return to a focus on God as the true authority of creation and retake our place as caretakers under God's guidance will we be able to work with God to restore creation and all humanity with it.

Creator, inspire me to find ways to protect the beauty of your creation that nurtures humanity in your world. Amen.

In today's passage, Paul reflects on the work of his life. He sees that God accompanied him, and he shows that God will accompany us too. By keeping the faith we overcome the struggles, finish the race, and recognize the fullness of our own engagement when we believe.

Our life project is a journey of faith in which we constantly encounter the unexpected and face challenges we never imagined. Along the way we also encounter formative experiences, great opportunities for service, and spaces for reflection where faith becomes a key resource.

Formation, faith, and gathered knowledge through experiences guide our practices and engagements in relationship with God and one another. This text from Second Timothy notes how we become like a libation as we keep our faith and do what is right with God, one another, and the rest of creation. The accompaniment of God is the vital element as we do our best to fulfill what God is calling us to be and do. We long to say with certainty at the end of our journey that we "fought the good fight," "finished the race," and "kept the faith." Our work to build community and the family of faith is noted by God as we finish our life journey in harmonious relationships.

God, I recognize the need for your accompaniment as I journey in the world. Help me recognize you in my own struggles and service opportunities. I pray my practices reflect your righteousness. Amen.

In the struggle to figure out who we are or who we are becoming, we will encounter times in our lives when we feel that no one understands us. Even though we are surrounded physically by people we know and love, they feel so far away that it is as if we have been abandoned. As we gain awareness about our own self-transformation, we may struggle to communicate this newness to others, or they may struggle to see us in a different way than they always have. When changes involve shifting ways of life, like needing to find a new job or terminating relationships, it can seem that there is no one we can count on for support.

Change is a sign of life and growth. Ongoing change is a sign of engagement with the living God. Through an openness to the newness of God, we experience new life with all its risks and uncertainty. What gives us hope in such times of change is to remember that God stands by our side as we leave the past and walk into the future, even when we are unsure of what that future holds. God walking by our side is the divine accompaniment we need to bridge our old identity to our new. Saint Teresa of Avila wrote about the accompaniment of God that moves within us. She writes, "May today there be peace within. May you trust God that you are exactly where you are meant to be. May you not forget the infinite possibilities that are born of faith. May you use those gifts that you have received, and pass on the love that has been given to you. May you be content knowing you are a child of God. Let this presence settle into your bones and allow your soul the freedom to sing, dance, praise and love. It is there for each and every one of us."

O God, help me recognize your presence with me when others feel far away. I want to receive your peace within. Amen.

This second part of the psalm witnesses to the bounty of the earth and the ways God accompanies the processes of life designed to provide water, grain, and flocks in abundance. There is a note of joy in the singing of the furrows, grasslands, hills, meadows, and valleys expressing gratefulness for God's care. It is a celebration of abundant life singing with joy about the relationship of nature and God.

As we reflect on the designs of life producing the bounty of this earth, we cannot avoid considering global warming. Unfortunately, it is a problem of our own making. Climate changes around the world point to the ways we have failed to care for the earth. Civilization and industrialization have supported the development of nations to the detriment of the land on which they are built. Contamination from coal, oil, and natural gas, alongside the devastation of forests, is accelerating the negative impact we have on the environment.

Our practices, ways of life, and consumption habits continue to ignore the sacredness of God's creation and the need for a good relationship with one another and the rest of creation. Native American traditions include the understanding that what we do will impact at least seven generations after us. Events like world wars, colonization, globalization, and industrialization will impact humanity for centuries after us. It is important to address the challenges we face today and find hope in the accompaniment of God.

God, help me understand the sacredness of life. Forgive my own practices that contribute to the breaking down of creation. Help me respect all that nurtures life on this earth, and help me be an advocate for your justice throughout the world. Amen.

In the Gospel reading for today, Jesus teaches about the different postures we might have before God. The first example is that of the Pharisee. Because of his social location, he boldly declares that he is righteous and gives thanks to God for his place in the world that allows him not to be identified as a sinner.

The other person is a tax collector, and he also knows his place in society. Tax collectors were clearly known as sinners by occupation. The economic system likely forced some to be tax collectors, but the necessary resulting relationship with the community afforded little grace.

In the parable, the identities of these two individuals are reduced to their occupations. Yet the identities and perspectives of individuals in these roles must involve more than their occupations. We are each multi-dimensional beings, and our perspectives are multi-faceted, made up of the awareness, attitude, relationships, and particular environments in which we find ourselves. Who we are and who we say or pretend to be, particularly before God, can indeed be so complex that we struggle to understand the nuances ourselves. Such struggles affect our relationship with God and with those around us.

The tax collector is aware of the social and religious limitations on him. He is clear about the condemnation by his own community due to his occupation. However, he is also aware of something more. In his cry for mercy—from a distance—he claims the accompaniment of a God that forgives, redeems, and saves. In humbling himself, he is recognized, justified, and exalted. Indeed, God continues to accompany us in our search for identity and new relationships.

Sustaining God, I ask for awareness about my own identity in relationship to you, my family, my community, and the rest of creation. Amen.

The Faith of the Saints

OCTOBER 27–NOVEMBER 2, 2025 • ERIN RACINE

SCRIPTURE OVERVIEW: Habakkuk stands aghast at the destruction and violence all around and wonders why justice never seems to conquer. At the end of the reading, God contrasts the proud with the righteous who live by faith. The psalmist delights in God's righteousness and in the commandments of God; however, he acknowledges his small place. Adversity appears in Second Thessalonians also, but here the struggles endured by the faithful serve a particular end: They stand as signs of the imminent return of Jesus Christ. In the Gospel reading, Jesus tells Zacchaeus, "Today salvation has come to this house," which reminds us that the righteous who live by faith are not necessarily socially or religiously acceptable.

QUESTIONS AND SUGGESTIONS FOR REFLECTION

- Read Habakkuk 1:1-4 and 2:1-4. How can you wait actively for God's response to your prayers and complaints? How will you enact God's response when it comes?
- Read Psalm 119:137-144. How do you follow God's commandments in the face of injustice and corruption?
- Read 2 Thessalonians 1:1-4, 11-12. The work of the church has never been easy. How does your faith community work to exude God's love in a time when many reject or feel rejected by church institutions?
- Read Luke 19:1-10. When have you run to Jesus? How can you share your experience so others pursue Jesus as well?

The Rev. Erin Racine is an ordained elder in the Tennessee-Western Kentucky Conference of The United Methodist Church and pastor at Calvary United Methodist Church in Nashville, TN.

That's not fair!" As a child, I spoke these words frequently. Whose turn was it to pick the movie? Whose chore list was longer? Who got the largest brownie? With any real or perceived inequality in my family, I was quick to speak up, "That's not fair!"

Now, as an adult, I can recognize that those experiences of perceived injustice didn't cause me any real harm. But we don't have to look far to see true inequality in the world. There are injustices all around us that cause real harm to God's beloved people. Some children grow up in safe environments with access to healthy food and quality education, while other children grow up in economically depressed areas or war zones where safety and basic necessities are scarce. Some people can move through the world with relative ease simply because of how they look, while others face a more difficult time accessing resources and power. If we haven't experienced such injustices ourselves, we have only to spend a few minutes scanning the news, and all of us can join in crying out, "That's not fair!"

The prophet Habakkuk has also witnessed and experienced injustice. Conflict, violence, and destruction are all around him. The law has grown weak, causing harm to God's people. Habakkuk's response to it all is to cry out to God. None of it is fair; none of it is acceptable. For the prophet, faithfulness means making some noise and getting God's attention so that God can do something about the injustice. Habakkuk reminds us that we too can cry out and make some noise when harm is being done. Through both prayer and peaceful protest, we can join the company of saints who have faced injustice and said, "That's not fair!"

Loving God, hear the cries of our hearts for the needs of your people. We lift them up to you this day. Amen.

Recently, I sent several emails to my state lawmakers. A tragic event happened in my community, and I want them to create safeguards so that it will never happen again. After I sent off my first round of emails, I awaited their responses. When I heard back from one lawmaker, I became frustrated by the reply. It seemed as if the lawmaker had not read my email at all; the response simply defended the status quo. But another lawmaker's reply gave me hope. This person agreed with me that something needed to change. They assured me that they were working to propose laws that would accomplish the outcomes many seek. I believe they have a vision for a better future.

The prophet Habakkuk has cried out to God about injustices all around him, and now he awaits a response. He faithfully keeps watch, expecting God to respond to him. And God does. God tells Habakkuk to write down a vision and share it with the people: God will indeed act to restore justice. It may seem to take a long time, but the people can rest assured that God's vision will eventually come to pass. In the meantime, they should remain faithful.

Habakkuk reminds us that while we can expect God to hear our heartfelt cries, we should also faithfully watch for God to respond. What will God say to us? How will God answer our cries? When injustice seems never-ending, we are called to trust in God's vision of a world in which justice is restored. Can we catch glimpses of this better future here and now? Can we share God's vision with others, so that they too can keep watch? How can we help this vision become reality? Let us remain faithful as we watch and wait.

God of justice, thank you for hearing our heartfelt cries. Help us to remain faithful as we watch and wait for your response. Amen.

To what do you cling when you are struggling? Perhaps you grab a sweet treat or lose yourself in a good book or movie. Maybe you pray, exercise, or practice mindfulness as a way to lower your stress level. Or maybe you call upon trusted friends, family members, or a therapist to share about your troubles. Whether we turn to these particular coping strategies or others, all of us cling to something in seasons that seem unbearable.

In this passage from Psalm 119, the psalmist is struggling. Enemies who have disregarded God's laws despise the psalmist. The psalmist's back is against the wall, and the circumstances seem unbearable. In the midst of these struggles, the people's coping strategy is to cling to the word of God. The psalmist understands that God's righteousness will stand long after these troubles are over. Despite everything, the psalmist is able to find joy in God's commandments. How is this possible? The psalmist's hope is rooted in belief that God's word is the true path to life. In faith, the psalmist affirms God's abiding faithfulness and in so doing finds joy.

The psalmist's witness invites us to cling to God's word when we are struggling, to root our hope in God's promises and affirm God's faithfulness no matter what our circumstances. While this coping strategy may not right all wrongs or take away our struggles, it helps us remember that God is with us, giving us courage to face the challenges ahead. It might even help us find joy in the midst of the unbearable.

Faithful God, we give you thanks that we can cling to your word in seasons of struggle. Help us to root our hope in your promises, that, with the psalmist, we may affirm your enduring faithfulness and find joy. Amen.

Paul, Silvanus, and Timothy believe that the Thessalonian church is a model Christian community. They begin their letter to the church by celebrating that the congregation's faith and love for one another are increasing. The authors also acknowledge that the congregation is experiencing hardship and persecution. Though the church's neighbors harbor hostility toward them, the congregation perseveres in faithfulness.

It is no secret that the Christian church is losing its majority status in the United States. The number of people with no religious affiliation or who no longer attend church is on the rise, hastened further by the COVID-19 pandemic. Much has been written about the reasons for this decline in the church and how to remedy the situation, yet the trend continues.

While the decline in numbers is certainly worth examining, it strikes me that today's passage contains no mention of how many people attend the Thessalonians' worship services. We don't know how much money they've raised or how many new members have joined. This model church is praised for its growth in faith and love and its steadfastness in the face of persecution.

Many churches seem to suffer from a toxic nostalgia for "the good old days," when pews were filled every Sunday and budgets were easily met. While it is certainly appropriate to grieve what has been lost, I wonder if too much focus on what was prevents us from recognizing and celebrating what is. From a church that rallies around a beloved member who is sick, to an elderly saint who sits with a child in worship, to a congregation that provides showers for their unhoused neighbors, signs of faithfulness are all around. How might you celebrate the ways your community of faith is growing in faith and love?

Spirit of God, awaken us to the ways your church is growing in faith and love. May we remain steadfast in our faithfulness. Amen.

Many years ago, I worked in a church that had a large statue of Jesus. One day, as young children were gathering for a time of worship, a little girl came running in. She shouted excitedly, "I found Jesus!" The adults in the room chuckled. We knew she was talking about the statue, but her words had the zeal of an evangelist. She had found Jesus, and she wanted everyone to know about it.

Years later, I happened to be at the same church on a Sunday when graduating high school seniors were leading worship. That little girl was now a young adult, ready for college. As she spoke about her faith, I thought about her many gifts and how she was using them to honor Jesus, whom she had found so many years ago. But I also thought about the faithful community of saints who had honored Jesus by caring for her as she grew, praying for her, teaching her, and eventually empowering her for ministry. As God worked in and through all of them, Jesus was glorified.

This letter to the church of the Thessalonians, which began with a prayer of thanksgiving, continues with a prayer that God would accomplish good and faithful work through them. The gifted people of God in this model church are worthy of their call only by the grace of God; their faithful hopes and intentions will be fulfilled only by God's power. While the work of faith is theirs to do, the outcome is up to God. Yet when they faithfully seek to honor Jesus, Jesus honors them.

Though we may not always witness the outcome of our faithful hopes and intentions, let us pray that God will accomplish good and faithful work through us. May Jesus be glorified!

O God who calls us, work in and through us that our faithful hopes and intentions may glorify Jesus, in whose name we pray. Amen.

ALL SAINTS DAY

Jack sang his faith, teaching me that Jesus leads us like a shepherd. Alice prayed for me every day. Mildred made me root beer floats and encouraged me to use my gifts. Michael was a steadfast presence in a season of grief, a sign of God's abiding care. These are just some of the saints I remember with gratitude on this All Saints Day. Whom do you remember with thanksgiving?

These saints no doubt were born in different times and places. They expressed their faith in diverse ways: some with reserve, others with passion; some with their words, others through action. None of them was perfect. Yet each, in their own ways, helped make God known to us. They contributed to our inheritance of faith.

In his letter to the Ephesians, Paul celebrates the inheritance of faith that the church has received through Jesus Christ. He prays that they will gain understanding about their call and the hope of this inheritance which is made possible through the power of God in Christ. To that end, Paul recounts the authority given to Jesus: He is above all things, now and forever, and the head of the church, the body of Christ.

To a minority community of faith in the first century, this would have been a much-needed word of encouragement. For us, nearly two thousand years later, this word is also empowering. Our inheritance, made possible by the grace of Jesus Christ, has been passed down through generations of faithful saints. However, we are not simply the inheritors of this faith but also the legacy-bearers for the next generation of saints. How will we, as the body of Christ, pass our inheritance of faith on to others? How will we make God known to them?

Christ our hope, thank you for this inheritance of faith and the generations of saints who passed it on to us. May we faithfully share it with others. Amen.

Lately, I have been learning about the incredible power of repair. When we lose our temper with others, our relationships can suffer. But if we can return to challenging conversations once we're calm, we can work to repair our relationships. By acknowledging our feelings, admitting that we have messed up, and apologizing for our behavior, we take responsibility for our actions. And then we can take steps to do better, such as taking deep breaths the next time our tempers flare. I still don't always get this right, but the work of repair has helped to foster reconciliation in some of my most important relationships.

In today's passage, Zacchaeus has messed up. He has exploited the tax system and defrauded people for his own personal gain. He's made himself wealthy on the backs of the poor. But then he meets Jesus, who invites himself over. While Zacchaeus is happy to welcome Jesus into his home, the people who see this happening begin to grumble. They resent Jesus spending time with such a person. So Zacchaeus begins the work of repair. He acknowledges that his behavior has hurt others and he takes steps to do better, promising to give half of his possessions to the poor and pay back those he has cheated by giving them four times as much. Zacchaeus' encounter with Jesus has called him to the work of repair and has fostered reconciliation with God and with those he has harmed. Sometimes repair is the work of faith.

In what areas of your life might Jesus be calling you to begin the work of repair? How might you acknowledge your behavior and apologize? What steps could you take to do better?

Jesus, we give you thanks that even when we mess up, you still seek relationship with us. Help us to do the hard work of repair so that we can be reconciled with you and with others. Amen.

Focus

NOVEMBER 3–9, 2025 • HEATHER NEAL BENNETT

SCRIPTURE OVERVIEW: The passages for this week remind us to stay focused. Without focusing, we become distracted and disoriented like the community in Second Thessalonians. In Haggai, the remnant have to be reminded that God has, is, and will be with them. In Luke, the Sadducees are refocused to see that God does not operate as humans understand. The psalmist reminds us what it looks like to be focused on God. The passages are reminders that God is always with us. God has given scripture, one another, and creation to learn from and experience God if we focus.

QUESTIONS AND SUGGESTIONS FOR REFLECTION

- Read 2 Thessalonians 2:1-5, 13-17. Spend a few minutes in silence, focusing on your inhalations and exhalations. Allow any distractions to enter one ear and exit the other; do not give them more awareness than that.
- Read Haggai 1:15b–2:9. Create a one-line drawing of what captures your attention. Begin at one point and do not lift your pencil until finished.
- Write down a list of questions you have for Jesus. Read Luke 20:27-38. How do you feel about your questions after reading Jesus' response to the Sadducees?
- Read Psalm 98. Study creation this week from your window or in nature. How does creation praise God?

Heather Bennett has a passion for helping Christians understand their biblical call to care for creation. Heather has an MS in Sustainability and MA in Practical Theology focusing on biomimicry and theology. She is a member of Lebanon First United Methodist Church in Lebanon, TN.

Over the course of a twenty-five-year marriage, I can't count the number of times I have started sharing details with my husband only to pause and say, "Wait, I have already told you this. Don't you remember?" To be fair, my husband has also had to do this with me. The author of this passage does the same with his community, giving details, then saying, "Don't you remember I have already told you this?" Oops.

The author doesn't dwell on their forgetfulness but rather refocuses them. The community has become anxious regarding rumors about Jesus' return. Some are claiming the same teachings the community received but are falsely claiming revelations and new teachings as well. It is confusing to the Thessalonians. The community has forgotten Paul's previous warnings that rumors would abound and there would be false teachers who would try to grab their attention. The community is focused on what the detractors are saying instead of what they have been taught. They need to refocus. Paul leads them away from the distraction. He refocuses their attention on their beliefs and their experiences with Jesus.

Today, there are people who claim to speak on behalf of Christianity, but we are to beware. Some portrayals of Christianity are not in line with what we know of Christ through the Bible, traditions, our experiences, and reasonings. This passage reminds us to take a deep breath when we hear or see these false leaders. On exhalation, we refocus on Jesus in order to continue our journey of learning and experiencing Christ as individuals and with other believers. We are to share with others through word and action. We must be intent and focused on learning and experiencing Jesus in order to be witnesses to Jesus in the world.

God, help us to focus on you. Amen.

My middle school years were spent on a basketball court. I loved being on a team, and when I read this passage from Second Thessalonians it reminded me of a coach in a huddle, motivating their team.

"Huddle up, friends," the coach says. Arms wrap tightly around the nearest shoulder forming a tight circle. "The noise around us is loud and confusing. Sometimes the people who cause the noise and confusion claim to believe what we believe, but we know their game plan. Don't let them distract you. " The coach, making eye contact with each player, is intent on conveying the seriousness of the situation. "You know them," the coach yells, tilting their head to indicate the crowd, "but do you know you? You are loved. You have been chosen, and you, you have chosen Jesus Christ." The coach gazes lovingly at each face. "Friends, hold on to each other. Stay firm in what you have been taught and pay no mind to the noise." The coach puts one arm into the huddle and others follow. "Beloved community of Christ-followers, look at our group. Feel the comfort and strength of God to go out and live as followers of Christ, above the noise." Together, arms drop then fly to the sky with a unified "break!"

What a motivational speech! It is a reminder that we are to stay focused on God and Christ's teachings, even when surrounded by noise. As a community of believers we learn from one another, pray with and for one another, worship together, engage interpretations of scripture, support one another, love and are loved by one another, and encourage one another. And together, we make a great team.

"Now may our Lord Jesus Christ himself and God our Father, who loved us and through grace gave us eternal comfort and a good hope, comfort your hearts and strengthen them in every good work and word." Break! Amen.

Years ago, I pulled into my driveway behind a police car. A member of our church was a police officer and nothing looked amiss, so I was unconcerned. Then my husband, with my leashed dog, came out of the house and said in a serious tone, "Everything is okay." I looked at my husband, then my dog, and then the house; all looked the same as when I left. But the way my husband kept insisting all was okay made me realize not everything actually was. Our house had been broken into, and several items had been stolen.

In our privileged lives, we experience "everything is okay" days without much thought to the alternative. When I read verse 5 instructing the Israelites, "Do not fear," I was reminded of this experience. "Everything is okay" actually meant something was not okay. In the same vein, I interpret "do not fear" to mean there is a reason to fear.

Haggai is speaking to the remnant Israelites who have been conquered and exiled from Judah. These people have experienced terror, oppression, and upheaval and are still living with trauma. They are well aware there is something to fear. For them to hear the words "do not fear" from a prophet of God must have evoked a collective exhalation of relief. "I am with you," the Lord says through Haggai. "My Spirit abides among you." There is a structure to these words that relates to the remnant's present, past, and future with God. A reminder of God's presence and covenant in the past when they left Egypt is bookended with these two commitments of God's current presence. A promise of God's presence and action in the future assures them this presence will not go away. God promises to be with the Israelites and with us. Whether everything is okay or some things are not okay, God will be with us no matter what.

God, you are always present in my life. Help me to be present in your presence. Amen.

I will again shake the heavens and earth, the oceans and the dry land. I will shake all the nations, and the treasures of all the nations will be brought to this Temple . . . . The silver is mine, and the gold is mine" (NLT). The phrasing of "the heavens and the earth" is used throughout scripture in regard to God's cosmic action. Because of this familiarity, it's easy to overlook the specific natural elements of the language.

Yet it is the nature imagery that draws me in. The imagery used here is the same as the habitats of Genesis 1—the heavens and earth, the oceans and dry land. And then God shakes the nations so that "the treasures of all the nations will be brought to this Temple." God's action will restore the Temple beyond its former glory. If we understand the natural habitats to be equivalent to the nations that shake, the treasures of such natural habitats must be nature's inhabitants—sun, stars, moon, birds, fish, animals, humans. Even silver and gold come from the earth. The earth and all that is in it is God's Temple.

I have been in beautiful churches and cathedrals with stained-glass windows, silver candelabras, and gilded altars handcrafted by talented artists. But the most beautiful cathedral I have been in is Muir Woods, surrounded by redwoods, horsetails, sorrels, chipmunks, and banana slugs. God "will fill this place with glory." I experienced that glory in Muir Woods.

We often overlook scripture referring to nature as if it were nothing but a setting, a background for the interaction of humans and God. God gave us two sources to learn from and through which to experience God: the Bible and creation. I believe we ignore God's more-than-human creation throughout the Bible and in our world at our and creation's peril.

God, help us to be open to your word through the Bible and your creation. Amen.

Do you remember the camp song "I Just Wanna Be a Sheep (Baa Baa Baa Baa)"? This song was my introduction to Pharisees and Sadducees, and Sadducees were "sad, you see." Perhaps camp songs have contributed to the negative images we sometimes have of the Hebrew leaders!

In today's passage, we read of the ancient Hebrew custom of levirate marriage. According to this custom, when a man died before having a (male) child, his wife was required to marry the man's brother. The Sadducees who bring this question to Jesus have taken this custom to theoretical extremes. Perhaps there actually was a man who was husband number seven to a woman and was concerned to think he would not be the husband reunited with his wife in death or that he may have to share her with six others. More likely, the Sadducees are adept at interpreting scriptural law and want to challenge Jesus in debate, as they are used to doing with one another.

Committed to literal interpretations of laws and life, the Sadducees are having trouble understanding resurrection. They understand the levirate law, but in the context of resurrection, they are asking Jesus for clarification. Jesus' response moves these Sadducees from how marriage is practiced in Hebrew culture to how things will be done in God's kingdom. For people who think literally, the examples Jesus gives of how God's kingdom operates are beyond their ability to imagine. Jesus' response challenges not only levirate marriage but also the idea that God operates according to human standards.

Today, we often have an awareness of when to read scripture literally or when we are to glean intention from scripture. But we can all relate to these Sadducees too. We often believe that scripture and God conform to our beliefs rather than us to God's.

God, when I am expecting your ways to be my ways, remind me that I just wanna be a sheep. Amen.

The juxtaposition of the songs of praise and the songs of lament can sometimes be jarring. On first reading, the psalms do not seem to offer unified voice, but rather a back and forth of "Thank you, God!" and "God, where are you?" And yet we can see unification in the praise for God's reign. Even in the depths of despair the overarching voice of the psalms proclaims God's power. While the psalms of lament help us not to feel alone, we can also experience the psalms of praise as a breath of fresh air, a moment to rest in the assurance of God's presence and love.

Psalm 98 exudes from a soul that knows without any doubt that God reigns. It reminds me of childhood—playing outside, running free, feeling the soft grass beneath my feet, and skipping with arms flung wide down a hill. Pure joy exudes from my body. The depth of praise makes this psalm personal: The psalmist has experienced firsthand the victory of God and cannot keep silent. This embodied experience cannot be contained. And the psalmist is so confident, so sure.

As an adult, I am often not so sure. Reading this psalm, I felt a bit envious of the psalmist and found myself praying, "Why can't I be as sure as this?" I felt God kindly respond, "How much time do we spend together?" I thought of the life of David, the traditional author of many of the psalms. David learned at the feet of his elders and spent a lot of time alone in the pastures with God's creation. David engaged in both formal learning and informal time experiencing and conversing with God. I felt God's response to my question not as a rebuke but an invitation to spend time with God. If I want to experience the psalmist's surety with God, I need to spend meaningful time with God throughout the day. Is this not what we do for our most important relationships?

God, I am happy to be here with you right now. Amen.

The psalmist's joy is so unconstrained that the universe is invited to join in. The psalmist moves from soloist to conductor of a symphony, inviting all to participate. As they sing, they move the baton toward the harpists and sopranos inviting them to join. Next come the trumpets, ram's horn, altos, and basses. The raised arms and baton of the conductor has the music crescendoing and the vocalists shouting for joy! Then the tempo slows under the conductor's direction as the sea and all that is in it resound; the rivers clap. The mountains join their voices with the vocalists, joyfully singing, reaching another crescendo. The earth is filled with the sounds of praise.

This psalm reminds us that it is not only humans who praise God but all of creation. Humans choose whether they praise God, but the rest of creation is constantly responding in praise. The invitation is not just for the seas, rivers, mountains, and inhabitants to praise God; the invitation is for *all* to praise God—*as one*. To praise God as one alongside creation, we have to recognize that we are connected with all of God's creation.

When I was a child playing in the woods, I could feel this praise. I could not cognitively understand it, but I recognized that I was surrounded by the God-created world, and this creation was pointing me to the Creator and beckoning me to join in praise. This foundational experience paired with the biblical mandate to care for creation weighs heavily on me. Our poor care-taking has silenced the praises of some of God's creation. This psalm not only reminds us to be in relationship with God so we can exude praises to God, but to be in relationship with all creation so that it too can continue to praise God.

God, may our relationship with you overflow to your creation, and may we be reminded of our connection with one another. May our conjoined praises please you. Amen.

For the Transformation of the World

NOVEMBER 10–16, 2025 • MARA RICHARDS BIM

SCRIPTURE OVERVIEW: The two readings from the book of Isaiah come from different eras in the lives of the Israelites: before the Babylonian exile and after. Both passages convey God's vision for the new creation. The reading from Second Thessalonians addresses those in the church community at Thessalonica who are not abiding by the group's covenantal agreement. The Gospel reading from Luke recounts a scene at the reconstructed Temple in Jerusalem toward the end of Jesus' public ministry. Jesus prophetically announces that the Temple will once again be destroyed and that his followers will face persecution. Collectively, the four readings speak of God's continued transformation of the world and the ways Christians are to participate in it.

QUESTIONS AND SUGGESTIONS FOR REFLECTION

- Read Isaiah 12. How are you being made whole by God's love today?
- Read Isaiah 65:17-25. Where is God calling you to share your gifts and talents in the world today?
- Read 2 Thessalonians 3:6-13. Communities are made up of individuals, each with a responsibility to themselves and to the group. How is your spirit being formed privately and how is it being formed in community?
- Read Luke 21:5-19. Where do you experience the Divine's presence in your life today? How are you being called to act in the world?

Mara Richards Bim is a candidate for ministry in The United Methodist Church. Mara is a member of Arapaho UMC in Richardson, TX, where she joyfully attends with her husband and young daughter.

In the first ten chapters of the book of Isaiah, the prophet pro-claims God's judgment on the people of Judah and Israel for their defilement of God's dwelling place in Jerusalem. God's judgment will culminate in divine wrath, and God will send invading armies to burn Jerusalem to a stump. But the flames of destruction will be more than wrathful punishment—they will purify the city and its inhabitants of their sins. From the stump will sprout a new shoot: a child to lead and to usher in an age of peace in which the wolf and the lamb will live side-by-side. On that day, God will bring together the purified remnants of the people of Israel who, in turn, will invite other nations to join them in praising God. All the people will celebrate their redemption by singing together the hymn of praise found in Isaiah 12.

Martin Luther King, Jr. famously said, "The arc of the moral universe is long, but it bends toward justice." One might also say that God bends the fabric of the universe toward wholeness. The biblical narrative reminds us time and again that God is con-stantly creating and redeeming all of creation. The rich imagery and poetry of the hymn point to this and are worth meditating upon. God is a parent who, having taught her remorseful chil-dren a painful lesson, now offers a comforting embrace. God is a source of strength in moments of fright. God's saving grace is a drink of cool well water on a hot summer's day. God comforts. God strengthens. God preserves.

Creator of all that is and all that will ever be, I come before you humbled and full of love. Thank you for your love and patience. Forgive me when I fall short in your sight. I pray that you transform me as you continue bending the universe toward wholeness. Amen.

Today's reading comes from a climactic moment in the later writings of Isaiah, believed to have been written after the Israelites returned from Babylonian exile in 538 BCE. Upon returning to Jerusalem, the Israelites were tasked with rebuilding their lives and the Temple. As we all know, building or rebuilding anything is hard work. The Israelites, instead of doing the hard work of rebuilding, turned their backs on God. They profaned the sabbath, participated in unholy worship practices, and harmed one another through words and deeds. Of course, none of this brought them peace or comfort. Now, Isaiah calls them to return to God's work and offers them a vision of hope for the future.

Our God is the great Creator who called forth light, brought order to chaos, and planted humankind upon the earth. Now, the Creator is at work again creating new things. Note that the text says that while the trials and tribulations of the past will not be remembered, it does not say that all will be destroyed. Instead, new heavens and the new earth will be created from what exists. In these three verses, the Hebrew word for "create" is used three times; the word for "joy" or "delight" is used six. God is creating something new and joyful and invites the Israelites (and us) to join in.

How are we, as people of God, to participate in God's work in the world today? We, like the Israelites, are called to repent, to love God, to seek justice for the oppressed, and to cease harming one another. We are to do the work of building a better world while looking with joyful expectation to the coming new creation.

Great Creator, show me where I am to do your work in the world today. Give me hope and strength so that I may be a light to all I encounter. Amen.

Isaiah has delivered God's promise to the Israelites: No matter how desperate things seem, God is at work creating something new. The Israelites must not lose hope. They must repent and continue the work of rebuilding Jerusalem and God's Temple on the mountaintop. Why was rebuilding so important? For the Israelites, God's presence was to come and dwell in the Temple. They were invited to rebuild a home for God.

What does the promise of God's new creation look like? The vision is filled with hope, joy, and peace. Infants will live to see old age. People will enjoy the fruits of their labors. They will rebuild God's home as well as their own homes, and they will plant their own food, building a community. Calling back to verses earlier in Isaiah (11:6-9), this new vision is one of total restoration of creation. The reference to the serpent in verse 25 brings to mind the garden of Eden (see Gen. 2–3) and indicates a return to the status of creation before the serpent tempted Adam and Eve—God's original perfect design.

Our world today is a far cry from Isaiah's vision. Racial and socio-economic disparities create far too high infant and maternal mortality rates, especially for persons of color. Exploitative employment and housing practices mean too many families never get the chance to build a life rooted in a peaceful community. Like the Israelites before us, we are called to rebuild. We are "to do justice and to love kindness and to walk humbly with [our] God" (Mic. 6:8). We are to do the necessary work of building and planting thriving communities so that we all may look with joy toward God's new creation.

God of peace, open my heart to building your community— one with deep roots where all children and all of creation can flourish. Amen.

2

THURSDAY, NOVEMBER 13 ~ *Read 2 Thessalonians 3:6-13*

Today's reading addresses those in the church at Thessalonica who are "living irresponsibly, mere busybodies, not doing any work." Some folks in this budding church aren't pulling their weight.

Community is built on a shared commitment. For the early churches, community was an essential element in the new faith. Those who followed the risen Christ kept sabbath together and then worshiped together the next day (the first day of the week) before going about their labors. They ate meals together, they prayed together, and they pooled their resources together. Those who are disrupting the flow are not only rejecting the shared commitment of the community; they are making it harder for others. It isn't that these disruptive busybodies can't work. Rather, it's that they refuse to fully participate in the community. They show up to all of the shared meals, but they never bring a covered dish and they never stick around to help clean up.

Today, community is just as important in Christian formation as it was two thousand years ago. Our shared commitment to living as Christ taught us binds us together. Together we wrestle with scripture and listen for what the Spirit is revealing through it today. Together we live our lives based on the model of Jesus. Together we do God's work of building and repairing the world around us. Together we witness to the Spirit's living, breathing work in the world.

Holy Spirit, breathe renewed life into me so that I may root down deeper in my community. Strengthen my community and pour out your presence upon us so that we may branch out and blossom within the world. Amen.

For the Transformation of the World 377

In Second Thessalonians, the author emphasizes the importance of community both to the early church as a whole and to the spiritual lives of the individuals within it. In fact, the letter goes so far as to say that the "busybodies" who are deliberately disrupting the life of the community should not be allowed to share in the communal meals.

Some present-day politicians misuse this passage to justify tying work requirements to poor people being able to feed themselves and their families. The letter to the Thessalonians is not addressing those who cannot participate in the work of the community because of physical differences, mental illness, or lack of available work. Nor is the author's assertion simply about sending some of the community members to bed hungry. Such a command would be contrary to Jesus' own example of feeding the masses who hungered for both spiritual and material sustenance. To be prohibited from the communal meals in the context of Second Thessalonians is to be made aware of one's own responsibility for one's spiritual nourishment.

Those of us committed to following Christ Jesus are responsible for nourishing our own souls and for providing spiritual sustenance to those with whom we are in community. It is not enough to show up to church and be spoon-fed a sermon (even a really good one!). We must read scripture for ourselves and wrestle with it in community. We must participate in time-honored spiritual practices like prayer, fasting, *lectio divina*, and the Ignatian Examen. We must tend to our spiritual lives just as we might tend a garden. Our spiritual lives require careful attention and effort in order to produce fruit. If we do not put in the work, we will go hungry.

Holy Spirit, sometimes I forget to show up and greet you. Forgive my distractions. I am here now. Touch my soul and rekindle the flame of connection. Amen.

L uke, writing roughly fifteen years after the Romans bru-
tally slaughtered Jewish rebels and destroyed Jerusalem, is
recalling Jesus' prophetic words to his followers. Jesus knew his
followers were facing immanent peril. His words were intended
to embolden them to stay true to the way he had taught them
while sharing their testimony with the broken world.

The disciples do not yet understand that God's holy presence
is not contained in the Temple. They do not yet fully realize that
they have experienced God's presence in the life and ministry of
Jesus. They cannot yet imagine Jesus' upcoming death and resurrection and the meaning it will hold for their lives. And they
certainly cannot fathom the coming events of Pentecost when
the Holy Spirit will pour over them. However, those of us living
today have the gift of knowing their stories and our own. We
know that God's presence cannot be contained by stones, could
not be destroyed in death, and is still at work in our world.

In an increasingly militarized and polarized world consumed by war and violence, Christ still needs prophetic disciples willing to speak truth to power and to witness to God's
ongoing, living presence in the broken world. We can live into
this calling. We need not be terrified. Christ Jesus will give us
the words and the wisdom.

*Christ Jesus, open my eyes to the divine presence still pulsing
through the world today. Fill my heart with wisdom and my
mouth with words so that I may do the work of serving as a
faithful witness to your justice, mercy, and redeeming love.
Amen.*

For many years I lived in Brooklyn, New York, and took the subway into Manhattan each day. It became second nature to step onto the train and mentally close off from everyone around me. I could easily spend thirty minutes absorbed in a magazine or in my own thoughts before realizing I was literally standing shoulder-to-shoulder with someone else.

All that changed on September 11, 2001. I was living in New York when hijackers flew planes into the Twin Towers of the World Trade Center. In the days following, the city, like the nation, shut down and went into total mourning. Days later, when I finally reemerged from my home and stepped back onto the train, I looked into the faces of those traveling with me. We all did. New Yorkers still talk about their first subway ride after 9/11. For many it was their first time speaking with fellow travelers. We found solace in journeying together.

The biblical narrative tells us repeatedly that life will be very painful, but that we do not travel alone. The Divine is always by our side. Of course, we humans can become so distracted and self-absorbed that we neglect the daily practice of connecting with the Divine. Then, when a crisis disrupts our lives, we panic and fear that we are alone. Or worse, we forget that we are God's beloved and reject the Divine's comforting embrace altogether. God does not cause evil and suffering, and Jesus did not promise a life free from pain. Instead we are promised that as we journey through this earthly reality toward the new creation, the great Creator will answer before we call, Jesus will fill us with wisdom, and the Spirit will intercede on our behalf "with groanings too deep for words" (Rom. 8:26).

Divine One, I know you are traveling alongside me today and always. Remind me. Open my eyes to your presence and my ears to your whispers. Amen.

A New Kind of Power

NOVEMBER 17–23, 2025 • GARRETT JACOB

SCRIPTURE OVERVIEW: There is irony in attributing the title of "King" to Jesus. All our passages paint a picture of the Savior's reign, but they describe it in a way that does not exactly scream, "all-powerful king." Jeremiah prophesies about a future king who will bring security for all the people; Luke records the song of Zechariah, the father of John the Baptist, which promises a child who will bring mercy; the Gospel reading tells the story of Jesus' death as an act of mercy for our forgiveness; and in Colossians, Christ is placed above all earthly rulers and powers. Does this absence of physical might mean there has been a mistake somewhere along the way? Not necessarily. A large part of the work of Jesus was challenging the beliefs of his time, and kingly language regarding a man who practiced non-violence, participated in the forgiveness of sins, and preached the ultimate importance of love, is no exception.

QUESTIONS AND SUGGESTIONS FOR REFLECTION

- Read Jeremiah 23:1-6. What does hope for redemption look like in a world that can sometimes seem so far from it?
- Read Luke 1:68-79. How have you seen God fulfill promises in your life? What was the moment like when you realized God had a plan all along?
- Read Colossians 1:11-20. Where are you needing endurance and patience? How can your relationship with God positively affect the way you exist in those spaces?
- Read Luke 23:33-43. What are ways you expect God to show up in your life today? How might these expectations be keeping you from seeing God already at work?

Garrett Jacob is a Christian Leadership graduate from the College of Theology and Christian Ministry at Belmont University in Nashville, TN. He currently serves Belmont's Office of the President as a Presidential Fellow.

The Israelites journeyed through many cycles of intense oppression from neighboring nations. Israel's enslavement in Egypt, which lasted almost four hundred years, was only one experience of exile and oppression. Yet throughout their history, God also promised to deliver them from such abuse. Jeremiah's prophecy is but one instance of God's speaking through the prophets promising God's chosen people a savior. As they envisioned what this savior would be like, it's not outlandish to consider they may have expected their savior to be a great warrior king, someone who would save and protect their nation physically.

But in this text, we also find a hint that the Israelites might not receive a warrior king after all. While language indicating a king is used in Jeremiah's message, the author also uses language pertaining to shepherds. The Good Shepherd is a common theme throughout scripture, in both the Hebrew Bible and the New Testament. In opposition to kings, shepherds were relegated to one of the lowest rungs on the social ladder. The metaphor of a shepherd as protector would have been a reminder of the kind of king God intended to send. God sending a shepherd to protect Israel would not have met the expectations of those who looked for a Savior king who would rule with might. And yet we know now that a shepherd was exactly what Israel—and the world—needed.

God, thank you for sending not a king with might and force but a Good Shepherd with love and peace. Help me to trust that you will provide what I need even if it does not look like what I thought or hoped it would. Amen.

When reading scripture, I've learned to get curious when I pick up on a pattern. In this text from Luke, three different people say that if Jesus truly had the power he spoke of, then he ought to save himself. Groups of three should draw our attention as representing something important in scripture.

It should not surprise us that the people around Jesus are still missing the point of his work. Nonetheless I am shocked that even at this point in Jesus' life and ministry—after all the works he has performed, after his numerous teachings on the true kingdom of God, after the model he has lived of trading stereotypical "power" for healing and vulnerability—people still project their own definitions of power and strength onto him. After all they have witnessed from this man, they cannot see past their humanity enough to fully realize his mission.

Like Jeremiah's audience, the people around Jesus equate power with physical strength, control, and wealth. So how can someone claiming to be so powerful submit themselves to being hung on a cross? Let's be honest—we still equate power with these identifiers today, and Jesus' death is still mystifying. Even in dying, Jesus is teaching a new kind of power. Though he is mocked and tortured, Jesus does not fight back in actions or words. In fact, Luke notes that he petitions God to forgive his oppressors instead. He shows empathy; he offers himself vulnerably.

Perhaps the author of Luke wants us to agree with the bystanders even for just a moment, to root for Jesus like the underdog, waiting for him to reach his full potential. We wait for the moment of triumph, only to encounter Jesus forgiving one more time. This, I hear the author of Luke saying—this is power.

Almighty, your power is beyond all we may ever know. Fill your people with your heavenly power over our simple, sometimes selfish, earthly version. Amen.

A New Kind of Power   383

The third person to mock Jesus while on the cross is one of the criminals crucified beside him. To paraphrase, this criminal says, "Aren't you supposed to be one with God? Just get yourself down, and save us while you're at it too!" Before Jesus can respond, a voice from the other side of Jesus chimes in. But rather than join the chorus of mockery, this voice, the other criminal, scolds the first. He sees the situation for what it really is. He admits that the two of them have committed actions deserving of their punishment, while Jesus is guilty of nothing. He then asks Jesus to remember him, to bring him along wherever Jesus is going next. And although he confesses that he is being justly punished, Jesus tells him, "Today you will be with me in paradise."

Jesus is in the business of forgiving and redeeming. The only person he responds to in the entirety of this passage is the second criminal who comes to him honestly and vulnerably. I think this tells us a great deal about having a relationship with God. God is not looking for us to figure everything out, nor is God expecting us to be perfect, to do no wrong. Instead, God is looking for us to accept the reality of all that we are, the good and the bad, and bear it vulnerably. With this posture, we can see what is really happening in front of us, just like the second criminal. God's mission, and therefore Jesus' mission and purpose, is redemption.

Lord, I am in awe of your redeeming work. Thank you for drawing me close, for continuing to show me that you want me and care for me. Thank you for sending your son to model for us the vulnerability with which we can approach you, and the true power of your redeeming grace. Amen.

In this section of Colossians, Paul tells the believers at Colossae that Jesus was and is every bit as almighty as God; that he was there from the very beginning; and that all things, from the smallest leaf of an olive tree to the mightiest authority in their time, were brought into being through and for him. Paul says, "In him all the fullness of God was pleased to dwell." Jesus was one with God. Jesus was the physical embodiment of God on earth.

Among other things, this means that God, through Jesus, chose to experience the fullness of human life, including suffering. And God chose this not just to see what it was like. God chose to suffer in order "to reconcile to himself all things."

Before Jesus, suffering was not something that pertained to God. Suffering did not affect its creator in the same way it affected people. But God chose to experience what it was to be human—then ultimately, to know suffering intimately.

Through Jesus, God is able to laugh and cry with us, to dance and to weep with us. God surrendered to suffering and death, experiences that would otherwise never have been a part of God's essence, all for our sake.

This passage reminds us that we are actively chosen again and again by an almighty God who longs to be with us so much that God would become one of us and walk alongside us as we live out the life our Creator has given us.

Creator and Redeemer, thank you for reminding me that I am never far from you, even bringing suffering upon yourself to make sure of it. Amen.

So what is power for? So far this week we have explored the way Jesus turns our idea of power on its head. We have seen what this upside-down power looks like in Jesus' case, but what does it mean for us? In his letter to the Colossians, Paul hopes the believers in Colossae will be filled with power from God in order to endure, be patient, and be grateful. Personally, those are not qualities I would typically associate with strength. But when looking back at the history of Christianity, Paul's wishes seem more and more in line with those of Jesus.

Early believers were often targeted, oppressed, and ostracized. Surely it takes a lot of strength, patience, and endurance to withstand constant attacks because of your faith, especially when it is so new and is not based on something quite as tangible or historical as Jewish law. Responding to attacks with patience, gratefulness, and endurance was likely difficult, and historical records suggest that many did discontinue their work.

Today, Christianity as a movement finds itself more often the oppressor than the oppressed. Those who identify as Christians are accepted much more so than in the early days of Christianity. Even with this worldly power behind us, we still individually struggle to endure within the upside-down power of Jesus. Perhaps because of the worldly power of Christianity, the ideals of love, vulnerability, generosity, and forgiveness still seem a counterintuitive path forward. It takes a strong person to endure. It takes a strong person to continue to be vulnerable when shamed. It takes a strong person to continue to give when everything is taken from them. Being faithful is powerful.

God, grant me the power to endure, to be patient, and to give you joyful thanks. Amen.

Once on a spiritual retreat, our host tasked the group with an afternoon and evening of silence that would end after dinner. Following our meal I found myself more mindful of my words when the silence was broken. I was finally given the opportunity to speak with others again, and I did not want to blurt out just any old thought. I felt that words should not be taken lightly, so what I said once my voice was returned felt extremely important.

Prior to today's passage in Luke, Zechariah has been sentenced to nine months without speaking, the result of not believing the angel Gabriel's message that he was to have a son. His silence is finally broken after his son is born and named John, as Zechariah had been instructed. I experienced only a few hours of silence; I cannot imagine the relief or the reverence in being able to speak again after nine months.

As I did, though, Zechariah seems to choose those first words carefully. As his tongue begins to stir, regaining feeling for the first time in what must have seemed a lifetime, quiet mumblings turn to what seem like words, which slowly turn to earnest, overjoyed praise. Zechariah announces to all in attendance that God's promise spoken through Jeremiah (23:5-6) is finally being fulfilled; that God has redeemed them.

Out of all the things Zechariah could have said after so long, what he wants to say most is that God is acting on the covenant with Israel. Zechariah reminds us that God has not forgotten us, whether it has been a matter of months or a matter of centuries. If we trust in God, if we endure and have patience, God follows through.

Faithful God, you keep your promises perfectly. Forgive me when I forget that. Continue to show me how to trust your timing over mine. Amen.

REIGN OF CHRIST

In the second half of Zechariah's speech following the birth of John, Zechariah turns to speak directly to his new son. In a prophetic declaration, Zechariah speaks about who John will become in relation to God and the Messiah, how John will lead the way and prepare the world for the King. Through his words about John, Zechariah tells more about the mission of the coming Messiah as well.

The first half of his speech (vv. 68-75) portrays the Messiah in the more recognizable role of physical protector that we have seen in other passages this week. This second half of the speech narrows in on the spiritual salvation and light that the Messiah King will bring into the world. In contrast to a God who will intervene to rescue the Israelites from oppression by their enemies, now Zechariah speaks of the "tender mercy" of God, and the sun that will shine upon those in darkness to "guide [their] feet into the way of peace."

Zechariah affirms the Israelites will be sent a King to save them. He declares that this child, John, is to pave the way for the Messiah. But then goes on to say that there is more to this King than they traditionally think. Yes, Israel will be saved from their oppressors, but that is not the focus of the Messiah's work. While the enemy of Israel as a physical nation might be other nations, the enemy of Israel as God's people is sin. Therefore, the true heart of God's mission is reconciling the lost and dead to life with the Divine.

God, you transcend any good thing I could ever hope for myself. Thank you for loving me enough to walk alongside me and guide me toward life everlasting. Amen.

Giving to God the First

NOVEMBER 24–30, 2025 • NATHALIE NELSON PARKER

SCRIPTURE OVERVIEW: We start this week exploring the scriptures associated with Thanksgiving Day in the U.S. and then turn toward the beginning of Advent and the coming arrival of the Christ child. Isaiah looks forward to a future day when peace will reign in Jerusalem. All nations will come to hear the wisdom of the Lord. The psalmist rejoices in going up to Jerusalem in his own day. Jerusalem is a center of peace and a place for righteous judgment among the nations. Both readings inform Jewish expectations of a bright future with the arrival of the Messiah. Paul tells the Romans that part of receiving the reality of the Messiah is self-preparation. We should put aside immoral living and put on the Lord Jesus Christ. Matthew looks forward to the future return of the Son of God, which will happen at an unexpected time.

QUESTIONS AND SUGGESTIONS FOR REFLECTION

- Read Isaiah 2:1-5. How do you look to the Bible's stories, prayer, and the Holy Spirit to help you work toward God's reign?
- Read Psalm 122. What does it mean for you to pray for peace?
- Read Romans 13:11-14. How do you stay awake to salvation's nearness?
- Read Matthew 24:36-44. Who in your life lives as though they expect Christ's imminent return? What does it look like to be ready to meet Christ?

The Rev. Nathalie Nelson Parker is the Director of Recruitment, Retention, and Innovation at Gammon Theological Seminary and Principal Consultant of Civitas Consulting Group, Inc.

An African Proverb states, "If you want to know the end, look at the beginning." The start of something likely intimates what it will be like at the end. Deuteronomy 26:1-11 captures a pivotal moment in the Israelites' journey upon entering the Promised Land, a moment that captures a crucial transition from "what was" into the promise of "becoming." The Israelites are transitioning from the end of oppression and bondage under Egyptian domination into the freedom and liberty of God's grace. The entering of the Promised Land symbolizes not only the acknowledgment of God's faithfulness to fulfill God's promises but also God's consistent provision throughout tribulation. By presenting the first fruits of the land, the Israelites express gratitude for God's fulfilled promise while marking the inheritance of new abundant life in God.

So why the "first" fruit? Would not the last, most prominent, or most attractive fruit be a better offering of gratitude to God? "First" means *beginning*, *best*, and *chief*, offering a historical context of why giving the first illustrates a tangible act of giving one's best, particularly giving to God before anything else.

In the sacred act of offering the first fruits, the Israelites acknowledge God's faithful provision and celebrate their liberation from Egypt. This practice is more than a ritual; it embodies a profound connection to the power of giving as gratitude. Giving, whether of material wealth or the offering of our time and talents, transforms into a tangible expression of gratitude and dependence on God. As we reflect on the abundance in our lives, we cultivate hearts of generosity, recognizing that our offerings are declarations of trust in God's sustaining grace.

Gracious God, teach us the depth of giving as an expression of faith. May our offerings declare trust in your sustaining grace and transform our world through the light of Christ. Amen.

Joy is more than a fleeting moment of happiness. It is a state of being through God's Spirit. Joy is a transformative force. According to Psalm 100, joy is a power honed through the spiritual practice of worship and community that beckons us to experience God fully. Joyful worship can break barriers, uncertainty, and external pressures. It fosters a sense of belonging and connection while uniting God's people. Psalm 100 explores how our expressions of joy contribute to a just and inclusive kingdom.

Joy is a command in Psalm 100; it is not a selective gift but an open invitation. Exclamations like "shout," "celebrate," "praise," and "bless" offer an open invitation to all who are willing to partake in a state of joyful worship to foster unity and belonging. Inclusivity is the heartbeat of joyful worship, breaking down barriers that exist among God's people. Psalm 100:3 paints a beautiful illustration on an inclusive canvas: "Know that the LORD is God. It is he who made us, and we are his; we are his people and the sheep of his pasture."

Close your eyes and picture joy. Can you see the various shades, textures, and images? Do you notice diverse communities embracing the joy of worship? Psalm 100 is not just challenging us to praise God with joy but to ensure our spaces are inclusive and joy-filled for all who belong to God.

God of joy, guide our worship to be inclusive and joy-filled. May our praise contribute to a just and welcoming kingdom. Amen.

In the 1994 film *Forest Gump*, the lead character portrayed by Tom Hanks introduced the world to the now well-known phrase, "Life is like a box of chocolates; you never know what you're going to get." The simple observation depicts the duality of life's uncertainty and sweetness, a metaphor for the complexities of the human experience. Whether it be joy or pain, trials or triumphs, all experiences make up the intricacies of life. Although we cannot control what happens, we can control the perspective we embrace in light of what we endure.

The apostle Paul calls for the people of Philippi to rejoice always and embrace God's peace in times of difficulty. While being detained in a Roman prison, Paul thanks the community for their prayers and generosity while challenging them to pursue Christ as the source of true joy and peace in light of profound social and political discord. Paul's words emphasize how a disciplined mind, focused on truth and praise, leads to peace beyond understanding. Paul writes in prison, but his words and state of being exude spiritual liberation. Our scriptures are full of stories of individuals who faced severe challenges yet still found peace. These stories inspire us to examine our thoughts and actively nurture a mindset of peace.

Paul faced adversity with a Christ-centered mindset. In moments of uncertainty, he anchored his thoughts in God's truth, finding peace that surpassed his circumstances. He was able to use his testimony to witness and disciple others. Moreover, his words illustrate the transformative power of cultivating a disciplined mind rooted in Christ.

Gracious God, help us cultivate a Christ-centered mindset that transcends understanding. Amen.

Thanksgiving Day (USA)

Much of Jesus' ministry centers on the sustenance and symbolism of bread. From the multiplying of the loaves given to the five thousand gathered on the hill to the breaking of bread with the disciples during the Last Supper, bread holds practical and spiritual significance within the story of Jesus, significance that continues today.

What does Jesus mean by proclaiming himself "the bread of life"? Jesus' ministry is often engaged with people experiencing marginalization at various levels. While addressing hunger, thirst, oppression, and poverty, the illustration of bread signifies Jesus' humanity and divinity when addressing the needs of others. As bread provides a source of nourishment to those who are hungry, Jesus exclaims that he is the source of eternal life for the world.

Jesus, described as the Bread of Life, invites us to ponder the spiritual nourishment the Spirit provides to us individually and collectively. In a world where many yearn for meaning and purpose, this passage urges us to reflect on our role in receiving and sharing the providence of the Bread of Life with those in need. W. T. Purkiser states, "Not what we say about our blessings, but how we use them, is the true measure of our Thanksgiving."

Let us consider our lives as a big Thanksgiving feast. A table spread, loved ones and friends gathered, and we become whole with food and fellowship. When we receive and partake of the abundance of Christ, we spread joy and togetherness. Similarly, we must share the Bread of Life, like sharing the most extraordinary, life-changing meal with everyone around us.

Gracious Provider, help us share the Bread of Life with those hungry for meaning. May our actions reflect the Thanksgiving in our hearts. Amen.

During the bustle of the morning routine, in between brushing teeth, packing backpacks, and pouring milk into cereal, my six-year-old, in his wide-eye glee, will break the monotony of the morning habits and shriek, "You will not guess what I dreamed." With inner laughter and outward curiosity, I brace for bold tales of fighting dragons, flying above clouds, or simply a wish for swimming in pools of ice cream. I bask in the visions of his innocent and hopeful imagination. Although far-fetched, his stories remind me that dreams or visions are a hopeful peak at what is possible but does not yet exist.

Likewise, as we read the text of Isaiah, we hear of a vision from God to the prophet of turning swords into plowshares. It is a divine dream about turning from fighting and discord toward peace and justice. This text invites us to dive into the profound vision, urging us to be agents of transformation in a world marked by conflict.

When we choose to draw close to God and, through the Holy Spirit, practice the disciplines of prayer, worship, and scripture reading, we choose peace. Our spiritual practices reflect our external actions toward others, particularly in a world deeply divided on countless issues. The vision of the prophet is stirring, wildly hopeful in our current contexts of war: "Nation shall not lift up sword against nation; neither shall they learn war any more."

We who read these words must hold on to Isaiah's vision and consider how we can contribute to God's vision for a world of peace and justice.

God of Peace, guide us in transforming instruments of harm into tools of justice and growth. Empower us with your Spirit to contribute to your peaceful and just vision for our world. Amen.

This psalm of David is a pilgrimage song, most likely written for a transition or travel. As a custom, many Jews would make a pilgrimage to Jerusalem to visit the Temple, pay taxes, and celebrate holy days. The journey was often physically daunting and dangerous, involving travel on foot, horse, or donkey for miles from surrounding areas.

The psalmist's heartfelt plea for the peace of Jerusalem draws us into the profound power of praying for the well-being of communities everywhere. But the specificity of this verse naming the holy city of Jerusalem undoubtedly causes us to consider the violence that currently embroils the Middle East. This text invites us to explore the intricate weaving of God's grace with justice, peace, and prayer, urging us to recognize the interconnectedness of these elements. We are challenged to move beyond personal concerns in our intercession to incorporate a worldview of collective responsibility. We are offered an opportunity to examine our lives and the larger world through prayer, understanding the transformative impact of prayers driven by a commitment to justice.

Imagine a city where people fervently pray for peace, which leads to collective actions promoting justice. This vision of the God-filled possibility of peace captures the essence of this psalm's plea. Through this song, let us reflect on how our prayers can extend beyond ourselves, reaching into the heart of our communities and communities around the world.

Compassionate God, teach us to pray for the well-being of communities—ours and those around the world. May our intercession be a force for justice and peace, bringing transformative power. Amen.

FIRST SUNDAY OF ADVENT

I am often amazed by the vigilance of my six-pound toy cavapoo. He spends endless hours quietly and restfully lying around the house. And yet even in moments of deep sleep, he can become immediately awake and alert. The faintest sound of footsteps down the driveway or the distant crack of a car door down the street—sounds I don't even perceive—arouses the most visceral reaction of awareness from him. He is suddenly on guard and ready to attack to a degree out of proportion to his physical ability.

Romans 13:11-14 and Matthew 24:36-44 call us to rouse from slumber and adorn ourselves with the armor of God. It is a directive to stay vigilant and prepared. The Advent season commemorates the coming of Christ, and the call throughout these four weeks preceding the birth of the baby is for us to prepare—prepare for the coming of a Savior who will bring justice and love embedded within every thorn, tear, and nail endured for our gift of eternal life.

Jesus awakens us to the significance of our role in God's unfolding kingdom to actively pursue justice and love. Christ's life reflects the inseparable fabric of love and commitment to justice. Let us prepare to work for justice and love this season and all year long.

Gracious God, awaken us to the urgency of justice and love. May our spiritual readiness be a testament to our commitment to the work of revealing the full nature of your kingdom and what it means to live within it right here, right now. Amen.

Liberation and New Life in Christ

DECEMBER 1–7, 2025 • GIFT & MAZVITA MACHINGA

SCRIPTURE OVERVIEW: The scripture readings this week center on the anticipation for a righteous and just ruler, divinely appointed, who will bring prosperity, defend the afflicted, and crush oppression. The passages also touch upon the role of John the Baptist in heralding the coming of the kingdom of heaven, emphasizing repentance and the transformative power of the Holy Spirit. The broader context suggests a connection between the Hebrew Bible prophecies of a coming ruler and the arrival of John the Baptist. Additionally, there is an overarching call for repentance and the acknowledgment of God's glory and marvelous deeds.

QUESTIONS AND SUGGESTIONS FOR REFLECTION

- Read Isaiah 11:1-10. Reflect on a time in your life when God brought transformation to a seemingly hopeless situation.
- Read Psalm 72:1-7, 18-19. Consider the ways you lead in your church or community. How can you better lead toward God's righteousness, justice, and peace?
- Read Romans 15:4-13. Who needs to be welcomed and loved by you or your congregation? How have you closed doors to people seeking Jesus because of your judgment and unwelcoming environment?
- Read Matthew 3:1-12. What are you doing to make a clear pathway for Christ in your life?

The Rev. Dr. Gift Machinga is a pastor of Zimre Park United Methodist Church in Zimbabwe. In addition to being the Secretary of the Zimbabwe East Annual Conference, Gift serves as the Chair of the Board of Discipleship and leader of the Discipleship Resources International (DRI) Publishing Team in the Zimbabwe Episcopal Area.

The Rev. Dr. Mazvita Machinga is a registered psychotherapist and a deacon in The United Methodist Church. Mazvita previously served Africa University as lecturer, school mental health counselor, interim Dean of Students from 2016-2018, and James Walker Endowed Chair from 2019-2021.

Psalm 72 is a prayer for a leader who will judge with righteousness and will care for the poor with justice. Christians understand this psalm to point to the king who would come, rule, and reign that way—Jesus Christ. As Christians, we have always believed that only Jesus can do this. Unlike too many kingdoms we have on earth, which are self-centered, unjust, and have no fear of God, Jesus' reign is just, fair, and focused on God's glory.

A few years ago, thousands of residents poured onto the streets of my country's capital city, Harare, to celebrate the resignation of a presidential leader who had been in power for over thirty-eight years. People were dancing and singing up and down the streets in anticipation of a new leader who would respect human dignity and would be just. Like the psalmist, the citizens of Zimbabwe were concerned with how their leader governed the people. For years, people had been yearning and praying for new leadership.

Earthly leaders can be better or worse, but they can never be the king Jesus came to be. Jesus reigned through serving people in need, through eating with the outcasts, through judging in righteousness, and through justice. Jesus led people to live in harmony and to prosper in ways no earthly king has ever done. The psalm's conclusion reminds us that no one has ever or will ever surpass the bar set by Christ as ruler: "Blessed be the LORD, the God of Israel, who alone does wondrous things." Our celebration of Jesus Christ as King and Messiah means that when we place Jesus first in our lives, he restores our broken lives and systems.

What does it mean for Christ to be our only king?

In 735 BCE, Aram and Israel invaded Judah. Consequently, Judah became a state of Assyria but later revolted. The revolt was crushed, and King Hezekiah had to surrender. Just before Isaiah 11, God declares punishment on the people of Assyria: Assyria would be like a tree cut down at the height of its power, never to rise again. But then—"a shoot shall come out from the stump of Jesse, and a branch shall grow out of his roots."

Most often when a tree is cut, the base of the tree left behind quickly dies. On occasion, a new sprout will grow from that stump, bringing life back where it was once cut off. This is the metaphor used by Isaiah to look toward the hope in God to bring transformation and life to the exiled people of Israel. Their hope in God is not dead. From the stump would grow a shoot, a new hope of life and a way forward.

My father- and mother-in-law's story of hope and life is a similar testimony. The two had spent ten years failing to conceive in marriage. I am told my mother-in-law (Grace) was ridiculed and mocked, while my father-in-law was told to divorce Grace and send her back to her home. After years of pursuing traditional healers and other avenues toward conception, Grace encountered Jesus through the women of The United Methodist Church. When she gave her life to Christ, Grace's spiritual life was transformed. A year later, Grace conceived and the couple welcomed their first son, eventually followed by three more children. After many years of facing a stump, a new shoot grew in this couple's life.

The new shoots of life don't always look like we want or expect them to, but they come nonetheless. No matter how hopeless our life or situation looks, the words of Isaiah promise that new life will spring forth from the stump we currently see.

Thank you, Lord, for creating something new from the stumps in my life. Help me to rest and be strengthened in you. Amen.

A few years ago, my husband faced a life-threatening situation when he was stopped by individuals posing as police traffic officers. They coerced him to drive into a remote area where they demanded money under the threat of harm. Terrified for his life, he began to pray silently, seeking divine intervention. After a tense exchange, they took some of his belongings but ultimately had him return to where they had initially stopped him and left him alive. My husband prayed prayers of thanks to God.

We were certainly grateful that my husband was delivered from the hands of those who would cause him harm. Yet many others do not experience the same outcome. The injustice we encounter in our country and in our world continues to expand and poison the relationships and systems that are intended to protect us.

Psalm 72 is described as a "prayer for guidance and support for the king." It may have originally been written for King Solomon. Its designation as a royal psalm indicates its usage at ceremonies honoring Israel's kings. But this psalm had lasting power beyond the ceremonies of the monarchy.

At its core, Psalm 72 calls for God's justice to thrive. This is the kind of justice Jesus sought to bring into the world. The discrepancy between the ideal vision of a just ruler and a just kingdom exemplified in Psalm 72 and the reality we see around us is emblematic of the ways humanity constantly fails to live up to God's vision. This psalm's lasting gift is its call for true justice.

God of justice, call us to remember your vision for the world, and empower us to be agents of your justice and peace. Amen.

Breven became a refugee when he was very young. Violence forced him to flee his home country of Burundi for the Tongogara Refugee Camp in Zimbabwe. He recalls passing through four countries and spending days without food in the jungle. His whole family had been murdered. For years, Breven was haunted by the deeply-rooted trauma. He says, "Only hope and encouragement from Christ carried me through this suffering."

Twenty-plus years later, the transformation in Breven's life is remarkable. Never in his wildest dreams did he think he would be alive, much less able to obtain a higher education degree. But today, Breven is a proud holder of a bachelor's degree in social work and is enrolled in a masters program in Human Rights and Migration. Having escaped death and overcome circumstances many of us cannot even comprehend, Breven marvels at how far God has taken him.

Being a Christian does not shield us from devastating life circumstances; on the contrary, sometimes being a Christian brings more persecution and danger, as it did for Paul. When we are on the verge of giving up on life, we must look toward a positive future ahead instead of becoming constrained by our challenges. There is hope for endurance through Jesus Christ and his promises. We can yearn for a life filled with hope and encouragement because Jesus has already promised it to us. When we look to Jesus Christ, we will endure as the scriptures teach.

Dear God, give me, those in my community, and all in the world a renewed sense of hope. Amen.

Followers of Jesus Christ ought to be the most loving and accepting people in the world. God wants the church to accept one another: It is not an option but a requirement.

Meredith had spent five years in prison and recently completed her sentence. Upon her return to church, the church members extended their arms to welcome her despite her criminal record. Meredith was amazed by the level of love and care the people at her new church offered her. She was even given some appropriate responsibilities in the church. The church leadership acted according to the will of God—they unconditionally welcomed and accepted her into God's flock.

Just as Christ accepts everyone, we are called to care and extend our love to all. The grace of God is for everyone. It is also essential for us to remember that there is a difference between acceptance and approval. Approval indicates agreement and often involves giving permission or consent based on specific criteria, whereas acceptance involves acknowledging and embracing something or someone without necessarily passing judgment or granting permission. The church did not approve of what she had done that led her to prison, but they accepted Meredith. When we are in community with one another, we hold one another accountable, yet we always offer God's extensive grace and love as we are called to do.

Christians need to love and accept one another. For Meredith, the church took heed of God's word. We must go out of our way to welcome and love one another.

Who needs to be welcomed and loved by you or your congregation? Have you closed doors to people seeking Jesus because of your judgment and unwelcoming environment?

I was taking my children to school one day when we saw an entourage of law enforcement officers. My daughter was curious about what was happening. "Mom, look at all those police officers. Someone is in trouble, right?" I smiled and told her no one was in trouble. I explained that the country's president was coming to town, and the police were doing a practice drill to prepare for when the head of state visited. These armed forces would work with local city and government leaders to ensure the city was clear of obstructions for the president.

Right before Jesus begins his public ministry, John the Baptist announces that the king is about to enter. John the Baptist is preaching in the wilderness of Judea, asking people to repent. "The kingdom of heaven has come near," he says. "Prepare the way of the Lord." This is the message for us all. We must be on alert, prepared for Christ. John is the herald, the one authorized to communicate an official message. John paves the way for the coming of the Messiah. He proclaims that the long-awaited Messiah is finally coming in the fulfillment of Isaiah's prophecy.

Each year, the season of Advent provides an extended period of time to prepare our hearts anew for the coming of Jesus. We do this by praying and sharing with others, by looking for ways to be kind, thankful, and forgiving. We repent—literally, turn around—so that we can face the right direction to see the coming of the Messiah.

Lord, you call us to repent and prepare for the coming of the Christ child. Give us the courage and the strength to prepare our hearts for the arrival of your Son. Amen.

SECOND SUNDAY OF ADVENT

In verse eight of this text, John the Baptist calls people to change their behavior in preparation for the coming of Jesus the Messiah. Believers must behave differently as they prepare for his arrival. Their actions must show that they have experienced transformation and repentance. The New Living Translation says, "Prove by the way you live that you have repented of your sins and turned to God." God looks beyond our words and religious activities to see if our conduct is aligned with what God commands.

Where the New Living Translation says "prove by the way you live," many translations say "bear fruit." This fruit is the result of the repentance we experience. Repentance is a change of heart and mind that is followed by action. It is more than just confession; it is turning to Christ entirely and bearing fruit that shows the change in our lives. Whatever we do must reflect our act of repentance.

In Jesus' day, there was a great messianic expectation that a leader would come and lead Israel out of the bondage of Rome and create an independent sovereign political state. John calls the people to repent in preparation because this kingdom of God they so eagerly await is coming soon.

Even two thousand years later, the call is the same. We eagerly anticipate God's kingdom, a kingdom that will be full of justice, peace, and righteousness. This kingdom may not look like we expect. But when we stay focused on God, we catch glimpses of it everywhere.

What do you need to turn toward God as you work to bring about God's kingdom?

Already but Not Yet

DECEMBER 8–14, 2025 • DANIELLE BUWON KIM

SCRIPTURE OVERVIEW: Isaiah anticipates a future time of total restoration—the desert will bloom, the blind will see, the lame will walk, and the people will return to Jerusalem with joy. Since ancient times, some have understood this as a description of the age of the Messiah. In Luke's Gospel, we hear the song of Mary. After Elizabeth blesses her and her unborn child, Mary praises God for God's strength, mercy, and generosity. In the epistle, James encourages his audience to be patient as they await the second coming of the Lord. In the same way, we wait for the birth of the Messiah during Advent. An uncertain John the Baptist sends a message to Jesus to ask if he is the promised Messiah. Jesus responds by affirming that he fulfills the messianic expectations written by the prophets.

QUESTIONS AND SUGGESTIONS FOR REFLECTION

- Read Isaiah 35:1-10. When has scripture strengthened you through personal or societal crises?
- Read Psalm 146:5-10. Those with power interpret scripture differently than those who are oppressed. How can you make room for perspectives other than your own as you interpret scripture?
- Read James 5:7-10. When have you had to endure frustration with patience? How have you been strengthened by these experiences?
- Read Matthew 11:2-11. What does it mean to you to be greater than John the Baptist?

The Rev. Danielle Buwon Kim serves as an associate pastor at First United Methodist Church in Coppell, TX. She is a clergy member of the North Texas Annual Conference of The United Methodist Church.

Recently here in Texas where I live, we went almost fifty days without precipitation. The foundation of my house shifted as the soil around it lost its volume from lack of water. We got some cracks around the walls of the house and watched a few trees and patches of grass die under the scorching sun. We desperately tried to water them, only to realize that the water was sliding right off of the dry land. Dry land not only lacks moisture but also its capacity to absorb water and be restored.

We find these kinds of dry places in our lives that reject any hope of restoration. The prophet saw the people of Israel invaded and captured after years of war. They witnessed heart-wrenching violence and suffering. Many people became disabled and traumatized. The land was destroyed beyond restoration.

Nevertheless, the prophet prays for the hope of restoration—that this dry land be created into a beautiful garden. Isaiah envisions a time when the people will walk with God once again in the fullness of God's glory, just like in the garden of Eden. The prophet boldly dreams of the day that all the effects of violence and woundedness will lose their power, that those with fearful hearts and anxious minds will regain strength and wholeness.

Many of us have experienced trauma and violence that are life-taking. They shake the core of our foundation beyond the capacity to be restored. We often struggle with relationships and circumstances in our lives that are so devastating that they reject all possibility of hope. Yet God works even in those places. God invites us to hope boldly in God's creative grace working in the most unlikely places.

Creator God, I invite you to the dry lands in my life. Help me to see your persistent grace at work, never giving up on creating me into your image. Amen.

Isaiah 35 is one of the most beloved chapters in the Bible, but we often miss that it was written in partnership with the chapter before it. Chapter 34 is the opposite of chapter 35. While chapter 35 blesses the land of Zion, chapter 34 curses the land of Edom, a neighboring nation with whom the Jews were in conflict. The Edomites were the descendants of Esau, the twin brother of Jacob. The Israelites were warned against anti-Edomite sentiment, as we can see in Deuteronomy 23:7, "You shall not abhor any of the Edomites, for they are your kin." But in the midst of the messiness of geopolitical struggles between these two nations, the prophet proclaims there will be a highway called "the Holy Way." In this Holy Way, there will be no threat of lions and beasts, and no one will be lost. The ransomed of God will return through this road, and it will be for God's people and not for "the unclean."

While it is traditionally read that "the unclean" meant the Edomites, we can also read that God is building a highway to bring connection and healing between these two nations in the midst of pain and division. God is determined to bring peace without any distractions (like lions or beasts). God is committed to the work of sanctification for all people. Those who do not appreciate God's work of connection and healing will not find footing on this highway.

During Advent, we celebrate God becoming human to connect with us and heal us. Where in your life is God building a "highway" to bring connection and healing? May we be captivated by God's peacemaking work everywhere we go. May we not be dismayed when we encounter those whose priorities are elsewhere.

God of peace, help me see your healing work in my life. Move me to bring reconciliation and wholeness to those around me. Amen.

The community to whom Matthew wrote was still questioning if Jesus was really the Messiah. They hoped for the Messiah to come and save them from the oppression of the Roman Empire, but they were still under Roman occupation. John the Baptist, who was preparing "the way" for the Messiah to bring the kingdom of heaven, serves in this story as the voice of many faithful people asking, "Is Jesus really the Messiah who brings the kingdom of God?"

Jesus, being a faithful Jew himself, responds to this question with scripture. The blind receiving their sight, the lame walking, and the poor having the good news brought to them are the prophetic words found in the Hebrew scriptures about the coming reign of God (see Isa. 35 or 61). He tells his disciples to go and tell what they "hear" and "see."

They indeed saw the blind receiving their sight, the lame walking, and they heard the good news. Today we see those who are suffering from trauma walking the path of healing and recovery, those who are hopeless being uplifted, and those who are at the margins finding equity and justice. In the reign of God, we witness people journeying toward fullness and wholeness in love.

The reign of God is not just a vague concept in scripture or a reality reserved for after death. It is available for us now as it is in heaven. Where do you see God journeying alongside you toward fullness of life? Where do you hear God calling you toward wholeness in love?

Gracious God, you desire that I walk in fullness of life. You labor so that I am made whole in your love. Help me to embrace the gift of the fullness of life. Mold me into the wholeness of your love. Amen.

We may read this text and wonder if John the Baptist is not as great as we think he was. After all, Jesus says that "the least in the kingdom of heaven is greater than he." While we might read this text and think *I don't want to be like John the Baptist— in prison and misunderstanding Jesus*—that would miss the point. Jesus is teaching us about the kingdom of God.

If the first part of this discourse (vv. 2-6) is about recognizing the signs of the Messiah and seeing what the kingdom of heaven looks like, the second part is about who is in the kingdom of heaven, which surprisingly has nothing to do with soft robes and royal palaces. It is rather a reality present among those who are doing the work of preparing the way for God's reign.

In verses 9-10, readers are reminded of John the Baptist, who was foretold in Isaiah and was in the wilderness preparing the way for Jesus (see Matt. 3). But shockingly, everyone who is in the kingdom of heaven is greater than John the Baptist. In the kingdom of heaven, everyday people are empowered and uplifted to do the work of the kingdom of God even greater than John the Baptist. This wasn't a way of putting down John the Baptist. After all, Jesus had said that of all who have ever been born, no one is greater than John. Instead, this was an effort to lift up the readers at the time who likely felt powerless and helpless in their witness in the world.

Where is that empty and hostile wilderness in your life in which God is calling you to build the way? For whom is God calling you to prepare the way? What does the way look like in your witness? May God uplift you like John the Baptist, preparing many to receive the boundless love of God.

God, you are a waymaker. I invite you to the empty and hostile places in my life. Prepare my heart, God. Have your way in me. Amen.

We have thus far meditated on the kingdom of heaven that builds "the way," that frees the oppressed, heals the sick, and brings good news to the poor. Many times we experience these values of the reign of God in conflict with other values in our lives. We daily witness the system in which the hungry are made more hungry and food-insecure, the oppressed are made more oppressed and marginalized, the prisoners get into more trouble while being incarcerated. How do we live out the values of God's reign here on earth already while we are not yet there? How are we called to navigate this tension?

The psalmist shares their wisdom today with us so that we can navigate this tension as we hope in God and as we find our help in God. As anti-climactic as it sounds, happy are those whose help is in God of Jacob, whose hope is in the Lord their God. Notice how the psalmist pairs "the God of Jacob" with the word *help*, and "the LORD their God" with the word *hope*. When we are in need of help, we can count on God who faithfully has shown up in the past to walk alongside us. In times of need, we can remember the help of God we received in the past and boldly ask God to help us again. We can also hope for that day when God, who is remembered as God of these monumental figures, will be called God of us, as God will have done many great things through our lives. This confidence and trust in God helps us to thrive in this in-between tension of "already" and "not yet."

May God grant us the wisdom to remember God's faithfulness in history. May God challenge us to hope boldly in God, knowing that God "who began the good work in [us] will continue to complete it until the day of Jesus Christ" (Phil. 1:6).

Reflect on a time when you experienced God's goodness. Then reflect on your deepest desire, hope, or anxiety. Thank God for the faithfulness that has carried you through, and trust that it will continue into the future.

Mary became a mother out of wedlock as a teenage girl from a small town called Galilee. She probably felt pressure from every direction, so much so that she left her community to stay for a while with her cousin, Elizabeth. I can only imagine the tension between the excitement of bearing Christ and the harsh reality that came with it. When the baby was born, Jesus was still a vulnerable baby. The tension probably did not change. Yet Mary did not lose her confidence in God. She still chose to hope in God, who had given her the gift of bearing Jesus. She still chose to find help in God, who lifts up the lowly and fills the hungry with good things. Nothing changed in her world, but in the midst of this tension, she nevertheless chose to find help and hope in God.

Just like Mary, we sometimes find ourselves in the tension between the excitement of our calling and the harsh reality in which we live out that calling. We may be energized by doing good yet face the jarring reality of unmoving hearts. We may be invigorated with visions and dreams yet be confronted with unexpected challenges. Mary chose to find help and hope in God—she chose to find help in God who had gifted her with good things; she chose to find hope in God who will nevertheless faithfully show up in her life.

As you are pursuing God's call in your life, where do you feel the tension between your call and the harsh reality of the world? Where do you hope to see God showing up as you navigate this tension in your life? May God give you the confidence that Mary had in God, so deeply rooted in God that you will find God in every corner of your journey!

Holy God, (breathe in) when I feel the jarring tension around me, (breathe out) I find confidence in your presence. Amen.

THIRD SUNDAY OF ADVENT

I grew up in South Korea with my grandparents who had a homestead and some land to garden. Each season, my grandmother transplanted little sprouts she purchased from the local nursery, praying and hoping that they would grow and bear much food for the family. During the times we went through mild to moderate droughts, she would water her garden with a garden hose and make sure that the plants got enough water to grow.

While they had developed methods of irrigation, in James' day it was still absolutely crucial to get the spring rain for the new seeds to sprout and the fall rain to ripen the crops. The farmers had to patiently wait for the rains each season, and they had no choice but to trust that rain would eventually come and nurture their crops.

The Greek word translated here as *patience* is more closely translated to mean "perseverance." It does not indicate a passive waiting but a brave perseverance through challenges. As we are called to live out God's reign here on earth as it is in heaven, partaking in the work of healing the sick and bringing good news to the poor, we live in this constant tension of *already but not yet*. We live out the reign of God that is not yet fully realized. As we are called to navigate through this in-between space, we can commit to a posture of patience and perseverance, to hope in God, and to find help in God's faithfulness.

In every season of our lives, we can expect to find God's nurturing grace, nourishing even the dry lands. May we be bravely—and actively—patient as we live through our own wilderness. May we hope in God's helping grace that goes before us, the grace that is already waiting to meet us there.

Imagine yourself in a posture of active patience. Explore your body language, emotions, and the energy around you.

Practicing Depth

DECEMBER 15–21, 2025 • MINDY MCGARRAH SHARP

SCRIPTURE OVERVIEW: This week's texts invite reflecting about depth as a practice not a product, a process not a destination. What does going deeper feel like? What does it require in a fast-paced world of split-second discernment about where and whom to engage? Isaiah goes to the king of Judah to prophesy about the boy called "Immanuel." The psalmist cries out to God for restoration. Paul's words root Jesus in the line of David. And Matthew tells of the angel's visit to Joseph. These texts seek signs in depths, yearn for deep relief from ravages of war, recall deep generational and geographical connections, and stir deep stories of messy births in a messy world.

QUESTIONS AND SUGGESTIONS FOR REFLECTION

- Read Isaiah 7:10-16. When have you asked for a sign from God? How do you recognize signs from God?
- Read Psalm 80:1-7, 17-19. When have you been consumed by your own fuming grief and rage? How has this been acknowledged? In the presence of bitter tears, how do you start to imagine and pray for a different future?
- Read Romans 1:1-7. How do you hold together deep joy and deep trauma at Advent? How many generations and in what land(s) can you trace joys and aches backward and forward in time and place?
- Read Matthew 1:18-25. Who holds and tells origin stories in your community and in your family? Does your community tell stories about births? Where do they begin? What details about the risks, vulnerabilities, and wrestling around birth are included or left out?

Dr. Mindy McGarrah Sharp teaches pastoral care and practical theology at Columbia Theological Seminary in Decatur, GA.

God has been speaking. God is still speaking. Are the people listening? Are you listening? God has been sending signs. God is still sending signs. Are the people noticing them? Are you noticing? Lingering with these few verses prompts the question, "What is a sign anyway?" In this season of Advent expectation, where do people expect to find a sign from God? Where do you expect to seek and to find?

God reminds us not to seek signs in all the wrong places. Are you looking as far into the depths of hell as imaginable? This is familiar. War continues to devastate peoples and lands. Old divide-and-conquer strategies chug along fueling dehumanization of "those people" as separate from us. Surely there are signs of salvation from amongst division's pain and loss, but we must beware the temptation to expect signs and wonders to come from these places of deep despair.

Alternately, are you looking for otherworldly signs? This is also familiar. Advent texts, hymns, and decorations depicting angels attune us to celestial inbreaking to help this world make sense of it all. Beware the temptation to expect signs and wonders beyond embodied knowledge and experience right here. Does not the Holy Spirit warm human hearts, directing attention to creation's beauty? Why do you instead seek the biggest, baddest, most blazing sign?

Ahaz sees through the temptations of seeking signs in the depths of hell and heights of heaven. Notice the depth of creation itself in everyday flesh and blood on this aching land and in this finite human community. With Advent expectation, where do you expect to find signs, and what do they signify?

God, awaken me to notice deep signs of salvation within creation itself. When my expectations seek you far away, bring my attention back into my body, into human community, into creation. Amen.

In the search for deep knowledge, you'll notice signs and wonders if you know how to look. Look closer! In this expectant season, we are called to linger in noticing, to welcome depth. Signs of world-mending healing are already being born here now. Instead of waiting for signs to bubble up from below or wonders to break in from above, we must attend to creation right around us. Before any generation begins to learn, the land is already laden with histories, heartaches, and stories to be told and heard.

I always wonder where to start and end a class. There is no true beginning, and no syllabus contains an end to learning. We begin in the middle of stories with both well-worn and yet-to-be-heard layers. We learn in the middle. Verse 15 speaks to this reality: Some of us have been eating from the land—not just scavenging, but accessing paradise-grade milk and honey, good food—before learning to differentiate between good and evil. We already participate in life's rhythms before differentiating between systemic liberation and harm. We must look and learn in the middle.

This text shows that birth in this world is already a sign. Therefore, if we look where birth is happening, we will notice lament and possibility. What does the land under our feet already know? What horrors and beauties has it already seen? What seeds are planted for tomorrow's feast? Where have plants withered in mistreated soil? We reach into the soil and find both lament and possibility. In prolonged griefs and uncertainties, new creation is possible. Each of us is a student, called to learn to pay attention right here and right now in the middle of communities and lands with long stories.

God, bring to mind losses to be grieved and births to notice. When we reach into the soil, help us learn to lament and to join in the liberating possibilities of new creation. Amen.

Today's text cries for deep, sustaining relief in a long season of loss. Such relief allows for more than one deep breath; it calls for a snack and a restorative nap even while the tumult continues. Deep, sustaining relief instills courage to be present, to abide in community, to ask for and to offer tangible help when most needed.

When there are no words and only tears, when nights of deep wrestling occlude the brilliant black starry night, people have always cried out: *Why, God? Why me? Why is this happening? How long will these bitter tears flow? Food is scarce; tears abundant. Has God abandoned creation? Will relief come? Look here, we are praying. Do something.*

Deep tears and anger signal important human responses. We must be careful when we are tempted to say to those grieving or angered, *Don't cry* or *Don't be mad.* Anger is instructive, and while rage can be all-consuming, it signals a deep need for noticing what is going on in the world. Rage is not something to be feared or quelled but is rather a warning sign we can pay attention to. We must notice bitter tears, notice anger, notice rage. We must access in our body the tear's sting, anger's burn, rage's bite.

Deep relief includes noticing, feeling, crying out, praying, and attending to human vulnerabilities. Notice God participating in this crying out. The psalmist imagines God fuming. The psalmist imagines the audacious possibility that scornful laughter among enemies can be transformed into shimmering restored faces of relief. Sometimes simply acknowledging the presence of strong emotions such as anger and desperation brings some relief.

God, remind me of your presence in the long stretches of struggle. Help me honor my tears and the tears of all creation. May the anger and rage I encounter prompt acknowledgment and action. Amen.

*G*et me through this and I'll learn. I promise. I'll never turn away *again*. Notice the pleading, calculations, and desperation. When have you scraped through, running on fumes, promising that this will be the last time it gets this far, this bad, this late? At what feels like the eleventh hour, this text makes a proposal: *Lower your hand, God, rest it in remembrance of a creation you made and love. In return for your restoration, we will never turn away again.* Yet will we?

While yearning for a final return, turning and returning form a steady rhythm throughout scriptures and our lives. When (not if) I turn away, I need assurances of God's restoration. Assurance of connection is a deep human need—being noticed, heard, believed by other people, by God. Consider times you have experienced the power of seemingly simple assurances: *I see you. I hear you. I believe you. I believe in you. I am with you.* When have you said or enacted these words? In each moment, we decide whether we will turn toward our neighbor or turn away, whether we will turn toward God or turn away. When we choose to turn toward, miraculous transformation can occur.

This psalm wrestles with the yearning for connection in a fragmented world: lands spliced from lands, people betraying people, fear turned to hate scorching the human spirit. Our innate reactions of fight, flight, or freeze are well-practiced. Can we return to one another? Where are you, God? Come back! We'll come back too! Remember God's connection to beloved creation, God's creative instinct to inspire growth and nurture care. Believe fervently that God hears and responds. *I hear you. I see you. I believe in you.* Yearn for deep connection and believe it is possible.

God, when your creation turns away, assure us of your steadfast connection. When we return, assure us of your love. In turning and returning, help us learn. Amen.

Let's review. This call to share good news far and wide is rooted in generations upon generations of prophets, supported by sacred texts and authoritative interpretations. This good news is deeply connected to Jesus, incarnate in real flesh. Paul says to the Romans, *Let's get to know one another. I'm showing up faithfully in the fullness of my calling to proclaim the good news. I'm doing the work. I'm glad you showed up. We have work to do.*

Hear a deeper introduction: *Now that we've arrived in the same time and place, will we do the work together? Can we learn to enact good news together?* Romans throws in a twist—this learning is not just for students who register for class, who can access it, who qualify with test scores, who already belong. Romans evokes generational and geographical inclusion: all the people, all the nations. This learning is for all. This education's final exam is our life practices, what Howard Thurman calls in *Jesus and the Disinherited* our "life working paper."

Life's group project is an all-hands-on-deck assignment. It's urgent—war ravages yet again; children are dying; lands are aching; people still seek healing, reparations, relief; hearts and minds need liberation. In 2023, Holy Land patriarchs declared the usual pageantry of Advent inappropriate in war time. What does "joy to the world" mean in such a context?

Thurman also addressed the twinkling lights of Christmas pageants, manger scenes, and annual parties in his poem "The Work of Christmas." The true work of Christmas, he says, begins after these traditions are completed. Now that we've shown up in the same place and time, can we greet one another well? Will we be able to do the work together?

God, awaken us to the depth of a collective call of life, love, and liberation. Embolden your co-laborers in the work to live into possibilities of new life together. Amen.

Everyone has beginning stories—stories of birth, stories of firsts, stories of momentous events that sparked new life and new directions. We can notice our beginning stories. We can notice our community's storytellers and story-keepers. Advent is a most extravagant beginning story that goes all the way back and invites us to notice something new; something deeper; something of life, love, and liberation.

This text goes back to beginnings. The story of Jesus' birth intertwines with the world's birth. How do we hold on to and tell a story like that? Thankfully, we don't do it alone. This story is collectively told again and again and again, coming from as many mouths as possible, woven into art, tucked into rituals, traditions, and practices. A story like this is alive.

But beginning stories can also get a little too familiar. Haven't we heard this story before? Haven't we been a part of telling this story before? Haven't we wondered about this story before? The Broadway musical *Hadestown* intertwines the narratives of several Greek myths to construct a story about the hope of liberation that arrives in response to love, creativity, and the possibility of new life. At the end, the narrator returns to the beginning of the story, calling out the importance of telling the story again and again.

Sound familiar? The story of our faith is cyclical, inviting us again and again into the message of redemption and salvation. As we have begun this story again, let us pay attention to what is familiar and what is new. What do you notice this time? What do you wonder this time? What is possible this time?

God, help us pause when we think we already know the whole story. Remind us that there is more to notice, more to hear, and more to tell. Help us be story-keepers and storytellers of life, love, and liberation. Amen.

FOURTH SUNDAY IN ADVENT

On this year's longest night, Matthew brings us into the conscious and unconscious wrestling with decisions. Jesus' beginning story is full of seemingly impossible situations: Mary is pregnant by the Holy Spirit, Joseph is attempting to make sense of this pregnancy in a context that would spurn if not stone Mary, and God's angel offers a name that marks this child as liberator of all creation. There is vulnerability, risk, and heart-rending wrestling. Joseph's initial plan is to leave Mary secretly, to hush it away. Before deciding, he sleeps and dreams. Once awake, his dream guides a way forward. Joseph stays. Joseph abides in the commitment and possibility of love.

Reading this text in community, Ernesto Cardinal recalls in *The Gospel in Solentiname* that the everyday artisans and laborers gathered in weekly dialogical church were struck by the depth of love and trust in it. In a world quick to shun and quick to throw the first or thousandth stone, the Solentiname community noticed that God loved and believed in Mary, Joseph loved and believed the angel, Joseph loved and believed in Mary, Mary believed in herself, and God believed in the people to welcome the birth of love and liberation into possibility. This dream can be realized.

Advent joy thrives in deep risks of loving out loud. Advent peace births possibilities for new life in places of deep vulnerabilities. Advent justice wrestles to create possibilities of love anywhere that dehumanization is used to justify destruction. Joseph wakes up to a dream's deep vision to stay in the work of love, to acknowledge the risks, vulnerabilities, and heart-wrenching wrestling. What dreams guide your waking hours? What helps you stay in love?

God, help me stay in love. Help me dream and then awaken, guided by shared dreams. Empower me to enact love. Amen.

Justice Comes

DECEMBER 22–28, 2025 • DOTTIE ESCOBEDO-FRANK

SCRIPTURE OVERVIEW: The scripture passages this week point to the need for justice and show the ways God saves us. Isaiah tells of those who bring the good news of justice and reveal the salvation that comes from God. John and the first Hebrews passage prepare us for the coming Christ child by drawing our attention to the symbols that fill the season. The psalm and the second Hebrews passage remind us of the reasons we celebrate. The Gospel of Matthew reminds us to notice the places where justice has not been found. Justice takes time, it takes work, and it takes determination. Justice only happens when we have God working alongside us showing us the way of righteousness and the road of peace. May justice come for all this season.

QUESTIONS AND SUGGESTIONS FOR REFLECTION

- Read Isaiah 52:7-10. Where have you seen good news being shared in the world? When have you brought good news?
- Read Hebrews 2:10-18. What emotions are generated in you as you approach family gatherings? What brings you joy during the Christmas season?
- Read Psalm 148. For what do you praise God? In what ways do you express your praise?
- Read Matthew 2:13-23. What similarities and differences do you see between the Holy Family's flight to Egypt and the modern-day journey of migrants around the world? How have you welcomed the children of the world in your community?

The Rev. Dr. Dottie Escobedo-Frank is the resident bishop of the California-Pacific Conference of The United Methodist Church. Dottie is the daughter of Lutheran missionaries who grew up on the border of Arizona and Mexico. She is the author and co-author of several titles, including *Restart Your Church* (Abingdon Press, 2012) and *The Sacred Secular: How God Is Using the World to Shape the Church* (Abingdon Press, 2016).

In the days of this scripture, important news was shared by runners who ran from one post to the next, sharing the happenings in one location with important people in another place. Some of the news was hard to hear: *The child is ill, Your debt is due,* or *Fighting has begun in Jerusalem.* Other news was good: *The medicine has arrived for your child, Your debt is paid in full,* or *The fighting is over and peace has come to Jerusalem.* These ultra-marathoners carried the news of the world among cities and powerful leaders. Their role was crucial and was celebrated when they came with the good news of peace and salvation.

Good news carriers are still celebrated. When a preacher reminds the world of hope, joy, and love in the middle of difficult times, their words bring a soothing balm that helps people carry on. To hear that peace on earth is happening—or is possible in the near future—brings deep joy. But good news isn't always easy to hear for everyone. When justice workers challenge what is happening in society as unjust, their news may be hard for those executing the injustice to hear. But it is good for those subject to the injustice. To hear that we need to bring justice and peace in a waring world means we have work to do.

This scripture also describes God as the one who goes before us *and* the one who is our rear-guard. When God is before us and God is behind us, we are surrounded by the one who loves, protects, and directs us.

Whatever the status of our lives and of the world, the time before Christmas is often difficult and painful for many. When the world is projecting joy and peace, we sometimes experience sorrow and stress at the dichotomy of peace to come and peace not yet attained. Yet God's presence will be with us. And that is the good news of Christ's love in our world.

God, draw near to us this day, and bring good news to our world. Amen.

Angels are part of our Christmas narrative and often sit on top of our home Nativity scenes. We do love the idea of angels as messengers who help us in our life. I began collecting angels as the main decoration for my Christmas tree when my family traditions were being formed by raising young children. We have an angel to top the tree and many others that hang on the tree. When we think of angels, we most often think of the angel choir that sang in the sky to the shepherds the night baby Jesus was born. Yet while we love to decorate our homes with their likenesses and hear stories about them, angels are more the backdrop, the background, to the Christmas story.

When we think of all the beauty in the Christmas story, we envision the shepherds and angels and innkeeper and Mary and Joseph and the donkey. But Jesus is the focus of the story. The Son came so that we could know God better and so that our salvation would be possible. In Jesus, God showed us what the rule of righteousness and goodness will look like. God showed us what God's presence can mean in our lives. God showed us love that lasts forever.

Hebrews describes the Son, known as Jesus the Christ, as greater than angels. It reminds us that all the things that were said about the Son were never said about angels. In fact, it tells us that angels too worship the Son. The Son will rule forever with justice and righteousness. The Son sits on God's right side and brings us salvation.

This year the angels sitting on top of our trees or decorating our streets can point us to the focus of the story. Their place in the story is not central. It's the Son that makes all the difference in the world.

God, make our focus be on you. Keep us from being distracted from your love this season. Amen.

CHRISTMAS EVE

One of my favorite parts of the Advent and Christmas season are the lights that shine everywhere. We decorate our streets with lights. We put lights on trees in the town square and in our homes. We put lights on our houses. Movies that are set in the Christmas season are filled with the beauty of twinkling lights among the shadows of darkness. There is something about the visual of lighting up spaces that connects with the light we desire in our souls.

John called the coming Christ child the "true light that shines on all people" (CEB). "True light" is deeper than the twinkle-lights we see in our world. The true light shines into our hidden spaces, our dirty places, our wounded spots, and illuminates them so that healing and wholeness can be ours. The true light gives us a settling in our souls that no outward brightness can match.

On Christmas Eve, Christians have a ritual of attending church services so that we can be reminded of God's light. We hear about the light surrounding the angels in the sky. We hear about a star in the sky. We imagine the light that shines on the manger, filled with hay and a baby. This baby is born to us so that God's light can illuminate our lives. We imagine that light around the Christ child as soft as a night light, as gentle as a candle flickering in the darkness.

After you return home from your church service today or tonight, sit for a moment and reflect in view of lights in your home: on your tree, in your fireplace, or somewhere meaningful. Let God's light illumine your soul. Let your heart be full and your soul be content. Hear the words God is saying to you: Christ has come to us! Jesus is born to us! The light is ours.

Dear Christ, be born in us and fill us as the light fills our room. Amen.

CHRISTMAS DAY

In this Isaiah passage, the words "God became their savior" strike a resonant chord. The sound of words that describe God as the one who saves us sound like the beautiful harmonies of music that soothe our souls. *God became their savior.*

Have you ever seen someone literally save another? I worked in the hospital for a time, and I watched doctors and nurses save people from death through medical interventions. I have been a social worker for decades and learned from the best who have saved families from the devastation of poverty, the harm of abuse, and the systems that perpetuate the same. I have been with families who daily save one another with their loving words and actions that encourage and show faith in their beloved. I have seen churches save God's beloved from living on the streets, welcome the stranger who just crossed borders of danger and despair, and send money and resources to places where disaster has devastated whole towns. I have seen pastors save lives by giving words of hope in moments of despair. We have this habit of doing our best to save others.

But when we hear that God saves us, we understand that God's gift of saving goes deep into the places that others cannot go. God saves us from the inside out, reminding us that we are cherished, beautiful, uniquely created in God's image. God saves us from the world's view and draws us to God's love that can never be removed. God saves us in love, in grace, in forgiveness, and in the depths of joy. God saves us, and because of God's saving, we can hear the harmonies of the universe, help others along their way, and sing songs of hope to the world.

This Christmas day, we remember that God became our savior! Joy to the world!

Dear God, we are eternally grateful for your saving grace and for the depth of your love. Amen.

We praise God in many ways The psalmist describes not only our praise to God but the praises of the world of nature. This scripture calls on the sun and moon, the sea creatures, the wind and rain, the mountains and trees, and all the creatures of the earth to praise God. Everything and everyone can shout and sing praise to God.

When we praise, we are lifting up the goodness of the one we praise—God. Praise is a natural response to the way we have been cared for by the God who sees us, hears our cries, and loves us for who we are. Praise rises up in us even when we don't think about it. We respond with "Thank God!" and "Praise Jesus!" and "Hallelujah!" Sometimes we don't use the religious language to praise God. We say things like, "That's amazing!" or "How did that happen?" or "So very cool!" as ways to express our praise for good things that come our way. Sometimes our very bodies praise God when we jump for joy, give spontaneous applause, or lift our arms to the heavens.

Today we can remember all the good that God has done for us. We remember that we have a community to love and check on us, and we are grateful that God gave them to us. We remember that we are set in the beauty of nature and that the natural world feeds and sustains us with breath and life. We remember that God set in us a desire to do good in the world and that purpose for living keeps us energized and hopeful. We recall moments of peace, even in the middle of storms, and thank God for that "peace of God, which surpasses all understanding" (Phil. 4:7).

Christmas Day, with all of its secular and sacred meanings, is behind us. And today we can rest a bit and breathe in the gratefulness of living and breathe out the praise of God's love. Praise the Lord, all you people! Praise the Lord, all the earth!

Dear God, we forever praise you for all you have done for us and for all the ways you have shown us your love. Amen.

The best part of the holidays to me is gathering together with friends and family. We may not agree on all things, there may be hard feelings to overcome, and we may be ready to leave when the time is over. But the best part of the time together is that we *are together*. We are known. We are beloved. The hardest thing about these holiday gatherings is when we find ourselves alone while others are celebrating: when we don't have an invitation to someone's dinner table, or we don't have enough money to travel to be with family, or when health prevents us from finding a way to gather. We need one another. We need to draw near once in a while.

In this scripture, Jesus is described as a "merciful and faithful high priest" who understands our predicament because he lived on earth as one of us. His faithfulness and mercy grew out of his time spent close-up and down-low with humanity. Truth be told, there is no better compliment in life than for someone to want to be with us, especially when that someone is God our Creator. When God chooses us, chooses to be with us, we experience the depth of belonging and belovedness that goes beyond all that we know on earth. And when God chooses to be merciful toward us and faithful to us, that chosenness is life-changing.

The days after Christmas are the quiet time of the year for my household, when the holiday gathering is done. There is a pause before the hustle and bustle of work begins again. While we pause between seasons of celebration, let us remember that God came near to us to be with us. And let that remembrance give us the confidence, security, and peace to know that all is well today and always.

Dear God, thank you for drawing near to us in the form of a baby who became fully human with us. Thank you for your mercy and faithfulness. Amen.

Throughout the ages we have heard the weeping of Rachel for her children. We have also heard the cries of Lupita, Eun-Kyung, and Dionne. Mothers have been calling out to God for their children for all of history because of the violence inflicted by political powers. Some of these struggles lead mamas to take their children and family on long journeys across many borders on dangerous roads. And often they travel without enough food, without a road map, and without assurance that the end of this troubling journey will bring stability and safety.

The scripture for today tells the story of Jesus' family migrating to Egypt to keep him safe from the king who wanted to kill him. It reminds us of all those other babies who were killed in the area of Bethlehem, leaving their mamas weeping in the night. And it shows how the journey continued when the king died and they traveled again, this time to Nazareth where they found home. The story of families fleeing death, facing danger, and looking for home was the story of Jesus' childhood. And today, it is still the story of many young children in our world.

In 2019, a Nativity was erected in southern California that depicted the Holy Family as immigrants detained after crossing the border. The display asked the question, "How would we welcome them?" As the story for so many refugees remains the same today, we must ask ourselves if we will create safe passageways for refugees around the world and close to home, or will we condemn them for fleeing danger and death, for searching for safety? Will we usher in the Christ child of Bethlehem who found safety in Egypt and home in Nazareth? Will we see the children who are fleeing to our towns as beloved little ones—God's children—seeking safety and searching for home?

God, soften our hearts for the traveling children of our world, and help us to be the welcoming arms that greet them as they find home. Amen.

Beginnings

DECEMBER 29–31, 2025 • GREG PIMLOTT

SCRIPTURE OVERVIEW: Each of this week's readings describes a beginning. Ecclesiastes describes many new beginnings, as a time for one purpose is replaced by a time for another. The psalm describes God's constant renewal of creation, in which God's relationship with creation begins anew each day. Jeremiah describes the beginning of a new season for God's people, where sorrow is replaced by joy and tears of forsakenness give way to shouts of joy. John's prologue describes the very beginning, in which all things came into being through the Word (who was with God and was God). Ephesians highlights the possibility of a new beginning for those who have been adopted into God's family through Jesus, and the spiritual inheritance that is available to us through this adoption.

QUESTIONS AND SUGGESTIONS FOR REFLECTION

- Read Psalm 147:12-20. Can you recall a time of spiritual growth in which things were not going well for you, and praising God was hard?
- Read Jeremiah 31:7-14. Have you ever praised God for something that God had not yet done? If not, can you imagine doing so?
- Read John 1:1-18. Pay special attention to verse 18. How has God been made known in your life?
- Read Ephesians 1:3-14. What does it mean to you to have been adopted by God?

The Rev. Greg Pimlott is an ordained elder in the Indiana Conference of The United Methodist Church, serving Christ United Methodist Church in Indianapolis, IN. Greg is the author of *Pastoral Pause: A Practical Guide to Renewal Leave* (Upper Room Books, 2024).

My children have been blessed throughout their lives to have people they refer to as "church grandmas." These cherished friends pay special attention to our children when they're at church and occasionally invite them to their houses so Mom and Dad can see a movie or go out to dinner. As we've moved churches, saying tearful goodbyes to some church grandmas and building connections with new ones, I've come to realize that there's nothing I can do to facilitate this special relationship for my kids at the new church we're going to. In a process that I can neither predict nor explain, our children and their new church grandmas-to-be choose one another.

In his letter to the church at Ephesus, the apostle Paul writes that God has "blessed us in Christ with every spiritual blessing in the heavenly places, just as [God] chose us in Christ before the foundation of the world." As adopted children of God, we have been showered with one good gift after another: love, faith, grace, salvation, redemption, hope. A great mystery of faith, though, is why God would do this. Why choose us at all? We can be fickle, unfaithful, ungrateful. We often turn away.

Thankfully, grace is bigger than our flaws. We are made eligible for adoption into God's family through Christ's death and resurrection. In Christ, we are redeemed. God has chosen this for us for reasons and purposes that we cannot understand or explain, and we respond by setting our hope in Christ. We have been brought into a special relationship with God through Jesus and said yes. The fact that this relationship is available to everyone doesn't make it any less special for us. Just as my children and their church grandmas choose one another, we have been chosen by God, and we have chosen God. Unlike every human relationship, though, this one will never fade away.

Thank you, God, for making us part of your family of faith through Jesus Christ. Amen.

As a young pastor starting out in ministry, it didn't take me long to realize that I could not "fix" someone's grief. I had learned this in my pastoral care classes in seminary, and I understood it intellectually. Even so, when I went to visit a grieving family after a death in the congregation, I felt like I should be able to do something. I was the pastor, after all! Armed with a Bible, a seminary education, and a caring look on my face, I thought I should be able to at least ease the pain a little bit.

Thankfully, those first few families to whom I ministered were gracious and generous. I managed to avoid uttering the worst of the "Things You Never Say to Someone Who's Grieving." They smiled and nodded when I tried to explain things about grief that they understood far more profoundly than I did. The visits went better than I had a right to expect, and yet I walked out the door feeling unsatisfied because the family was still grieving when I left.

Jeremiah's words are directed at a people who are deep in grief. They've been taken from their homeland by force. Their houses have been destroyed or co-opted; their holy places have been demolished. The prophet is wise and knows not to pretend that he can take that pain away. He doesn't offer paeans or trite phrases; instead, he offers hope in the Lord. In the midst of deep sadness, Jeremiah proclaims, "Thus says the LORD . . . I will turn their mourning into joy, I will comfort them, and give them gladness for sorrow." The promise of hope is one that only God can make: I will redeem; I will restore; I will turn sorrow into gladness and mourning into joy.

God of comfort and mercy, heal our hearts. Help us to find solace in the midst of grief. Turn our mourning into joy, and give us gladness for sorrow. Amen.

It's not uncommon at a homecoming or family reunion for someone to stand up and thank God for the opportunity to gather. "We thank you for the blessings and mercies we've experienced since we last came together." "Thank you for bringing us here safely." Thank you, in other words, for this thing you've already done for us.

Jeremiah asks something different of God's people: to give thanks for a homecoming that hasn't yet occurred. "See, I am going to bring them from the land of the north, and gather them from the farthest parts of the earth." "They shall come and sing aloud on the height of Zion, and they shall be radiant over the goodness of the LORD." The prophet doesn't say, *When God brings us home, then give praise.* Instead, he says, *Give praise now because God is going to bring us home.*

Giving thanks and praise for something God hasn't yet done is an act of faith and hope. It's a congregation gathering in a long-empty church nursery and praying, "It's been a while since anyone used this nursery, God, but there are children in our community whose families need to hear of your love. Today we're praising you for the children that have yet to use this space." It's the parents of an estranged child praying, "We know your power to heal is greater than the brokenness of our family. We thank you for the reconciling work that your Spirit is doing right now, even though we can't see it."

Jeremiah would not see the return of the exiles to Judah in his lifetime. He knew God was trustworthy, though, and so he could give thanks and praise God for a homecoming he would never see but had complete confidence would happen one day.

God of hope and promise, as we look toward the beginning of a new year, fill our hearts with gratitude for what you have done and what you have promised to do. Amen.

The Revised Common Lectionary* for 2025
Year C—Advent / Christmas Year A
(Disciplines Edition)

January 1–5
Jeremiah 31:7-14
Psalm 147:12-20
Ephesians 1:3-14
John 1:1-18

> **January 1**
> NEW YEAR'S DAY
> Ecclesiastes 3:1-13
> Psalm 8
> Revelation 21:1-6a
> Matthew 25:31-46

January 6–12
BAPTISM OF THE LORD
Isaiah 43:1-7
Psalm 29
Acts 8:14-17
Luke 3:15-17, 21-22

> **January 6**
> EPIPHANY
> Isaiah 60:1-6
> Psalm 72:1-7, 10-14
> Ephesians 3:1-12
> Matthew 2:1-12

January 13–19
Isaiah 62:1-5
Psalm 36:5-10
1 Corinthians 12:1-11
John 2:1-11

January 20–26
Nehemiah 8:1-3, 5-6, 8-10
Psalm 19
1 Corinthians 12:12-31a
Luke 4:14-21

January 27–February 2
Jeremiah 1:4-10
Psalm 71:1-6
1 Corinthians 13:1-13
Luke 4:21-30

February 3–9
Isaiah 6:1-13
Psalm 138
1 Corinthians 15:1-11
Luke 5:1-11

February 10–16
Jeremiah 17:5-10
Psalm 1
1 Corinthians 15:12-20
Luke 6:17-26

February 17–23
Genesis 45:3-11,15
Psalm 37:1-11, 39-40
1 Corinthians 15:35-38, 42-50
Luke 6:27-38

February 24–March 2
TRANSFIGURATION
Exodus 34:29-35
Psalm 99
2 Corinthians 3:12–4:2
Luke 9:28-43a

March 3–9
FIRST SUNDAY IN LENT
Deuteronomy 26:1-11
Psalm 91:1-2, 9-16
Romans 10:8b-13
Luke 4:1-13

> **March 5**
> ASH WEDNESDAY
> Joel 2:1-2, 12-17
>   or Isaiah 58:1-12
> Psalm 51:1-17
> 2 Corinthians 5:20b–6:10
> Matthew 6:1-6, 16-21

March 10–16
SECOND SUNDAY IN LENT
Genesis 15:1-12, 17-18
Psalm 27
Philippians 3:17–4:1
Luke 13:31-35

March 17–23
THIRD SUNDAY IN LENT
Isaiah 55:1-9
Psalm 63:1-8
1 Corinthians 10:1-13
Luke 13:1-9

March 24–30
FOURTH SUNDAY IN LENT
Joshua 5:9-12
Psalm 32
2 Corinthians 5:16-21
Luke 15:1-3, 11b-32

March 31–April 6
FIFTH SUNDAY IN LENT
Isaiah 43:16-21
Psalm 126
Philippians 3:4b-14
John 12:1-8

April 7–13
PALM/PASSION SUNDAY

> *Liturgy of the Palms*
> Psalm 118:1-2, 19-29
> Luke 19:28-40
>
> *Liturgy of the Passion*
> Isaiah 50:4-9a
> Psalm 31:9-16
> Philippians 2:5-11
> Luke 22:14–23:56

April 14–20
HOLY WEEK

> *Monday, April 14*
> Isaiah 42:1-9
> Psalm 36:5-11
> Hebrews 9:11-15
> John 12:1-11
>
> *Tuesday, April 15*
> Isaiah 49:1-7
> Psalm 71:1-14
> 1 Corinthians 1:18-31
> John 12:20-36
>
> *Wednesday, April 16*
> Isaiah 50:4-9a
> Psalm 70
> Hebrews 12:1-3
> John 13:21-32
>
> *Maundy Thursday, April 17*
> Exodus 12:1-14
> Psalm 116:1-2, 12-19
> 1 Corinthians 11:23-26
> John 13:1-17, 31b-35
>
> *Good Friday, April 18*
> Isaiah 52:13–53:12
> Psalm 22
> Hebrews 10:16-25
> John 18:1–19:42

Holy Saturday, April 19
Job 14:1-14
Psalm 31:1-4, 15-16
1 Peter 4:1-8
Matthew 27:57-66
 or John 19:38-42

Easter Sunday, April 20
Acts 10:34-43
Psalm 118:1-2, 14-24
1 Corinthians 15:19-26
John 20:1-18

April 21–27
Acts 5:27-32
Psalm 118:14-29
 or Psalm 150
Revelation 1:4-8
John 20:19-31

April 28–May 4
Acts 9:1-20
Psalm 30
Revelation 5:11-14
John 21:1-19

May 5–11
Acts 9:36-43
Psalm 23
Revelation 7:9-17
John 10:22-30

May 12–18
Acts 11:1-18
Psalm 148
Revelation 21:1-6
John 13:31-35

May 19–25
Acts 16:9-15
Psalm 67
Revelation 21:10, 22–22:5
John 14:23-29
 or John 5:1-9

May 26–June 1
Acts 16:16-34
Psalm 97
Revelation 22:12-14, 16-17,
 20-21
John 17:20-26

May 29
ASCENSION OF THE LORD
Acts 1:1-11
Psalm 47 or Psalm 93
Ephesians 1:15-23
Luke 24:44-53

June 2–8
PENTECOST
Acts 2:1-21
Psalm 104:24-34, 35b
Romans 8:14-17
John 14:8-17, 25-27

June 9–15
TRINITY SUNDAY
Proverbs 8:1-4, 22-31
Psalm 8
Romans 5:1-5
John 16:12-15

June 16–22
1 Kings 19:1-15a
Psalm 42
Galatians 3:23-29
Luke 8:26-39

June 23–29
2 Kings 2:1-2, 6-14
Psalm 77:1-2, 11-20
Galatians 5:1, 13-25
Luke 9:51-62

June 30–July 6
2 Kings 5:1-14
Psalm 30
Galatians 6:1-16
Luke 10:1-11, 16-20

July 7–13
Amos 7:7-17
Psalm 82
Colossians 1:1-14
Luke 10:25-37

July 14–20
Amos 8:1-12
Psalm 52
Colossians 1:15-28
Luke 10:38-42

July 21–27
Hosea 1:2-10
Psalm 85
Colossians 2:6-19
Luke 11:1-13

July 28–August 3
Hosea 11:1-11
Psalm 107:1-9, 43
Colossians 3:1-11
Luke 12:13-21

August 4–10
Isaiah 1:1, 10-20
Psalm 50:1-8, 22-23
Hebrews 11:1-3, 8-16
Luke 12:32-40

August 11–17
Isaiah 5:1-7
Psalm 80:1-2, 8-19
Hebrews 11:29–12:2
Luke 12:49-56

August 18–24
Jeremiah 1:4-10
Psalm 71:1-6
Hebrews 12:18-29
Luke 13:10-17

August 25–31
Jeremiah 2:4-13
Psalm 81:1, 10-16
Hebrews 13:1-8, 15-16
Luke 14:1, 7-14

September 1–7
Jeremiah 18:1-11
Psalm 139:1-6, 13-18
Philemon 1:1-21
Luke 14:25-33

September 8–14
Jeremiah 4:11-12, 22-28
Psalm 14
1 Timothy 1:12-17
Luke 15:1-10

September 15–21
Jeremiah 8:18–9:1
Psalm 79:1-9
1 Timothy 2:1-7
Luke 16:1-13

September 22–28
Jeremiah 32:1-3a, 6-15
Psalm 91:1-6, 14-16
1 Timothy 6:6-19
Luke 16:19-31

September 29–October 5
Lamentations 1:1-6
Lamentations 3:19-26
  or Psalm 137
2 Timothy 1:1-14
Luke 17:5-10

October 6–12
Jeremiah 29:1, 4-7
Psalm 66:1-12
2 Timothy 2:8-15
Luke 17:11-19

October 13–19
Jeremiah 31:27-34
Psalm 119:97-104
2 Timothy 3:14–4:5
Luke 18:1-8

> **October 13**
> THANKSGIVING DAY,
> CANADA
> Deuteronomy 26:1-11
> Psalm 100
> Philippians 4:4-9
> John 6:25-35

October 20–26
Joel 2:23-32
Psalm 65
2 Timothy 4:6-8, 16-18
Luke 18:9-14

October 27–November 2
Habakkuk 1:1-4; 2:1-4
Psalm 119:137-144
2 Thessalonians 1:1-4, 11-12
Luke 19:1-10

> **November 1**
> ALL SAINTS DAY
> Daniel 7:1-3, 15-18
> Psalm 149
> Ephesians 1:11-23
> Luke 6:20-31

November 3–9
Haggai 1:15b–2:9
Psalm 98
2 Thessalonians 2:1-5, 13-17
Luke 20:27-38

November 10–16
Isaiah 65:17-25
Isaiah 12
2 Thessalonians 3:6-13
Luke 21:5-19

November 17–23
REIGN OF CHRIST
Jeremiah 23:1-6
Luke 1:68-79
Colossians 1:11-20
Luke 23:33-43

November 24–30
FIRST SUNDAY OF ADVENT
Isaiah 2:1-5
Psalm 122
Romans 13:11-14
Matthew 24:36-44

> **November 27**
> THANKSGIVING DAY, USA
> Deuteronomy 26:1-11
> Psalm 100
> Philippians 4:4-9
> John 6:25-35

December 1–7
SECOND SUNDAY OF ADVENT
Isaiah 11:1-10
Psalm 72:1-7, 18-19
Romans 15:4-13
Matthew 3:1-12

December 8–14
THIRD SUNDAY OF ADVENT
Isaiah 35:1-10
Psalm 146:5-10
 or Luke 1:46b-55
James 5:7-10
Matthew 11:2-11

December 15–21
FOURTH SUNDAY OF ADVENT
Isaiah 7:10-16
Psalm 80:1-7, 17-19
Romans 1:1-7
Matthew 1:18-25

December 22–28
FIRST SUNDAY AFTER
  CHRISTMAS DAY
Isaiah 63:7-9
Psalm 148
Hebrews 2:10-18
Matthew 2:13-23

> **December 25**
> CHRISTMAS DAY
> Isaiah 52:7-10
> Psalm 98
> Hebrews 1:1-12
> John 1:1-14

December 29–31
SECOND SUNDAY AFTER
  CHRISTMAS DAY
Jeremiah 31:7-14
Psalm 147:12-20
Ephesians 1:3-14
John 1:1-18

A Guide to Daily Prayer

These prayers imply worship time with a group; feel free to adapt the plural pronouns for personal use.

O LORD, in the morning you hear my voice;
    in the morning I plead my case to you and watch.
                                 —Psalm 5:3

Gathering and Silence

Call to Praise and Prayer
God said, "Let there be light," and there was light.
And God saw that the light was good.

Psalm 63:1-5

God, you are my God; I seek you;
    my soul thirsts for you;
my flesh faints for you,
    as in a dry and weary land
    where there is no water.
So I have looked upon you in the sanctuary,
    beholding your power and glory.
Because your steadfast love is better than life,
    my lips will praise you.
So I will bless you as long as I live;
    I will lift up my hands and call on your name.
My soul is satisfied as with a rich feast,
    and my mouth praises you with joyful lips.

Prayer of Thanksgiving

We praise you with joy, loving God, for your grace is better than life itself. You have sustained us through the darkness: and you bless us with life in this new day. In the shadow of your wings we sing for joy and bless your holy name. Amen.

Scripture Reading

Silence

Prayers of the People

The Lord's Prayer (ecumenical text)

Our Father in heaven,
    hallowed be your name,
    your kingdom come,
    your will be done,
    on earth as in heaven.
Give us today our daily bread.
Forgive us our sins as we forgive
    those who sin against us.
Save us from the time of trial,
    and deliver us from evil.
For the kingdom, the power, and the glory
    are yours, now and forever. Amen.

Blessing

May the light of your mercy shine brightly on all who walk in your presence today, O Lord.

I will bless the LORD at all times;
  [God's] praise shall continually be in my mouth.
                                            —Psalm 34:1

Gathering and Silence

Call to Praise and Prayer

O Lord, my Savior, teach me your ways.
My hope is in you all day long.

Prayer of Thanksgiving

God of mercy, we acknowledge this midday pause
of refreshment as one of your many generous gifts.
Look kindly upon our work this day; may it be made
perfect in your time. May our purpose and prayers
be pleasing to you. This we ask through Christ our
Lord. Amen.

Scripture Reading

Silence

Prayers of the People

The Lord's Prayer (ecumenical text)
Our Father in heaven,
    hallowed be your name,
    your kingdom come,
    your will be done,
    on earth as in heaven.
Give us today our daily bread.

Forgive us our sins as we forgive
    those who sin against us.
Save us from the time of trial,
    and deliver us from evil.
For the kingdom, the power, and the glory
    are yours, now and forever. Amen.

Blessing

Strong is the love embracing us,
    faithful the Lord from morning to night.

For God alone my soul waits in silence;
from [God] comes my salvation.
—Psalm 62:1

Gathering and Silence

Call to Praise and Prayer

From the rising of the sun to its setting,
let the name of the Lord be praised.

Psalm 134

Come, bless the LORD, all you servants of the LORD,
who stand by night in the house of the LORD!
Lift up your hands to the holy place,
and bless the LORD.
May the LORD, maker of heaven and earth,
bless you from Zion.

Prayer of Thanksgiving

Sovereign God, you have been our help during the
day and you promise to be with us at night. Receive
this prayer as a sign of our trust in you. Save us
from all evil, keep us from all harm, and guide us in
your way. We belong to you, Lord. Protect us by the
power of your name. In Jesus Christ we pray. Amen.

Scripture Reading

Silence

Prayers of the People

The Lord's Prayer (ecumenical text)
> Our Father in heaven,
>> hallowed be your name,
>> your kingdom come,
>> your will be done,
>> on earth as in heaven.
>
> Give us today our daily bread.
> Forgive us our sins as we forgive
>> those who sin against us.
>
> Save us from the time of trial,
>> and deliver us from evil.
>
> For the kingdom, the power, and the glory
>> are yours, now and forever. Amen.

Blessing
> May your unfailing love rest upon us, O Lord,
> even as we hope in you.

This *Guide to Daily Prayer* was compiled from scripture and other resources by Rueben P. Job and then adapted by the Pathways Center for Spiritual Leadership while under the direction of Marjorie J. Thompson.